God Confronts Culture:
The Almost Complete Book on
Biblical and Christian Worldview*

Franklin E. (Ed) Payne, M.D.

Covenant Books

Augusta, GA

God Confronts Culture: The Almost Complete Book on Biblical and Christian Worldview*

© 2010
Covenant Books
P. O. Box 14488
Augusta, GA 30919

ISBN 978-0-557-32228-2

Books by Franklin E. (Ed) Payne, M.D.

Biblical/Medical Ethics: The Christian and the Practice of Medicine

Making Biblical Decisions
(Population Control, Reproductive Issues, Genetic Engineering, and
End of Life Issues)

What Every Christian Should Know About the AIDS Epidemic

*Biblical Healing for Modern Medicine: Choosing Life and Health or
Disease and Death*

*Without Faith It Is Impossible to Please God
The Almost Complete Book on Faith*

Websites published by the author

www.biblicalworldview21.org

www.biblicalphilosophy.org

www.bmei.org

Table of Contents

Introduction

*Title Information: "The Almost Complete Book on Biblical and Christian Worldview" is a somewhat grandiose statement. The author readily admits that this book is <u>nowhere near a complete</u> book on these matters. Nevertheless, he challenges any reader to find another book which contains the (1) breadth, (2) explicit nature, (3) concise summary statements, and (4) Biblically coherent and comprehensive information that is found herein.

The feature item of this book is its **Summary Principles** at the end of each chapter. These principles will present the reader with a quick overview of what a Biblical worldview might look like in that area of study and will also serve as a resource for review at a moment's notice.

All chapters have these Summary Principles, but not all chapters have discussion. This format was simply at the discretion of the author.

1. History and Providence

Events that Advanced God's Plan for History (God's Providence)

The following are selective, centering on the Reformation. They illustrate how secular events, pagan kings, and major battles are all within and because of God's plan.

Alexander the Great, 356 B.C.-323 B.C. Usually listed as one of the ten greatest military commanders in history, Alexander conquered most of the Mediterranean area and eastward into India. His conquests made Greek the common language of this large geographic area, which was also most of the "civilized" world of that time. **This common language made the spread of Christianity by Paul, the Apostles, and others far more rapid than would have been possible with many languages and dialects.** While Alexander was immoral and a bloodthirsty man of his times, nevertheless, "The king's heart is in the hand of the LORD, like the rivers of water; He turns it wherever He wishes" (Proverbs 21:1).

Pax Romana, 27 B. C. - 180 A. D. The period of relative peace throughout most of Europe, the Middle East, and Northern Africa that allowed the spread of the Gospel immediately during and after the period of the Book of Acts.

Henry VIII of England, 1491-1547. Henry VIII had "tired of his wife," Catherine, who also had failed to bear him a son that lived more that a short time after birth. He appealed to Rome several times to get his marriage annulled, but his appeal was never granted. "From this time onward, the English were steadfast in defiance of Roman authority. They were, historically, the first colony to successfully throw off Roman rule." The Bishops of England pledged their loyalty to Henry, and thus he established the Church of England.

With the power of Rome removed from the British Isles, there was a much greater freedom for the Reformation to grow. There were vacillations over the next two centuries between Roman Catholic authority (e.g., Bloody Mary) and Protestants, as well as, verbal and armed conflicts among Protestants themselves. But the British Isles had been severed from the Pope.

1

Henry's obstinacy is another example of God's ruling the thrones of kings, queens, and all state authority. While Henry VIII was an adulterer, blasphemer, and murderer, to mention just a few of his immoralities, yet God used his belligerence towards Rome to advance His cause in the British Isles, primarily Scotland.

The Battle of the Bay of Lepanto, October 7, 1571. Pope Pius V believed that the Ottoman Empire was advancing to conquer the Christian world. He called for an alliance among the Christian powers to stop this advance. If the Turks were victorious in this battle, then they could continue on to take Venice and then Italy. Ali Pasha commanded the Turks, and Don John, an illegitimate son of Charles V, but an experienced soldier, led the Christian forces.

The Bay of Lepanto is an arm of the Ionian Sea. The battle has been described as the largest naval battle since the Battle of Actium in 30 B.C. Don John's forces lost 15 ships and 9,000 men. Ali Pasha, who was beheaded during the fighting, lost 62 ships and 25,000 men, almost a total loss. There was virtually no strategy by either side, as the ships just ran together and fought, very similar to a land battle, except the soldiers were on ships.

"Only God could have saved so divided a Europe against so determined and savage, rich and heavily armed a foe. After Lepanto, the Turk remained a menace, but not an unconquerable one." (Otto Scott, *The Great Christian Revolution*, p. 110-111)

The Defeat of the Spanish Armada, July 29, 1588. The reader should note the power of the Spanish fleet demonstrated at the Bay of Lepanto. There were 131 ships against the English's 55 ships. The intent of the Armada was to bring England, who was experiencing a fragmented Reformation, back under Roman Catholicism. Phillip II of Spain was acting under a Papal Bull that had excommunicated Elizabeth I. Both the strategic use of fire ships, English maneuvering, and weather defeated the Armada, although it escaped with most of its ships intact.

This defeat allowed further growth of the Protestant Reformation in Ireland, England, and especially Scotland.

St. Bartholomew's Massacre, August 24, 1572. In France, the Reformation under the leadership of Admiral Coligny was growing against Roman Catholic resistance. Over one-third of France had become Protestants and was known as Huguenots. Through a series of deceptions, intrigue, and plotting, by Catherine de Medicis, Henry the Duke of Anjou, and the Duke of Guise, Charles IX was convinced that the Coligny and the Hugenots were a threat to himself and to France. He shouted, "Kill them all! Kill them all!" He wanted none left to reproach him. There ensued the bloodiest massacre of the Reformation and of all history. There were over 30,000 dead, including women and children. (Some accounts say 100,000 dead.)

"...the St. Bartholomew's Day massacre permanently altered Protestant thinking. The Calvinists turned away from acceptance of the 'divine right' of kings, to questioning the entire institution of monarchy." (Scott, *The Great...*, pp. 113-114.)

It is this author's opinion that this event committed France to being a second-rate nation under God's condemnation until the time that they nationally repent of this reprehensible act.

The French Fleet Sent to Destroy America, 1747. Louis XV, the French king, commissioned the Duc d'Anville, to "dismantle Louisbourg, (a strategic naval base on the southeast coast of Canada)... expel the British from Nova Scotia, ravage New England, and waste the British Indies." The British were aware of the preparations in France for this expedition and were prepared to stop it, but when the French fleet left, the British fleet was unable to get out of port because of fierce headwinds. Thus, the Americans were defenseless against 13,000 soldiers and seamen in 73 ships, who were to join with four more large warships at (present day) Halifax.

New England was helpless, but providentially it was in the midst of the Great Awakening, and a day of prayer was called. (Longfellow wrote a poem of this event.) The French fleet ran into trouble after trouble. Before they left port, a gale struck the fleet. Adverse winds or no wind hounded them all the way across the Atlantic. Food and water went bad. Sickness was rampant. Then, another storm hit, wreaking further damage. The duke died of a strange disease, and his second in command fell on his sword.

The fleet still determined to attack Annapolis Royal, but another storm did further damage, and they abandoned any further attacks, setting sail for France and home. All but two ships had been lost and at least 4,000 lives due to sickness (primarily) and accident. They never reached any destined targets nor fired a shot.

This destruction of the French fleet is one of many Acts of Providence in the history of the United States in its founding and since (see the Battle of Midway). Marshall Foster gives a rousing lecture on how the United States is the culmination of 5000 years of God's Providence, including many miracles, and that He is not through with her yet.

The Puritans

The Puritans were men whose minds had derived a peculiar character from the daily contemplation of superior beings and eternal interests. Not content in acknowledging, in general terms, an overruling providence, they habitually ascribed every event to the will of the Great Being, for whose power nothing was too vast, for whose inspection nothing was too minute. To know Him, to serve Him, to enjoy Him, was with them the great end of existence….

Hence originated their contempt for terrestrial distinctions. The difference between the greatest and meanest (lowest) of mankind seemed to vanish when compared with the boundless interval which separated the whole race from Him on whom their own eyes were constantly fixed. They recognized no title to superiority but His favour; and, confident of that favour, they despised all accomplishments and all the dignities of the world….

On the rich and the eloquent, on nobles and priests, they looked down with contempt; for they esteemed themselves rich in a more precious treasure, and eloquent in a more sublime language, nobles by the right of earlier creation, and priests by the imposition of a mightier hand…. The very meanest (lowest) of them was a being to whose fate a mysterious and terrible importance belonged, on whose slightest action the spirits of light and darkness looked with anxious interest; who had been destined, before heaven and earth were created, to enjoy a felicity which should continue when heaven and earth should have passed away.

Events which short-sighted politicians ascribed to earthly causes had been ordained on his account. For his sake, empires had risen, and flourished, and decayed. For his sake, the Almighty had proclaimed his will by the pen of the Evangelist and the harp of the common foe. He had been ransomed by the sweat of no vulgar agony, by the blood of no earthly sacrifice…. Thus the Puritan was made up of two different men; the one all self-abasement, penitence, gratitude, passion; the other proud, calm, inflexible, sagacious. He prostrated himself in the dust before his Maker, but he set his foot on the neck of his king." (Selected excerpt from Essay on Milton, by Thomas Babington Macaulay.)

History: The Great Deception or the Great Design?

History: The Great Deception

History is perhaps the most subjective of disciplines. If you were to write all your thoughts in the past 24 hours (actually more like 16 hours because of sleeping time), you would fill a considerable book. Then, as a large appendix, you could write about what you actually did. Any of the seven billion or so people on earth could do the same. And, all that for only one day of their lives! Multiply that by 60, 70 or 80 years, and likely there are not enough computers on earth to contain all the information. Then, add in all the people of history! Then, add in all their perceptions of what happened. All this history would be a staggering amount, indeed!

Now, pour that through the finest of sieves into one or several books. That is your history text. **History is the highly selective account of billions of lives, actions, and things over several thousand years of earth history.** Most likely, should the Lord tarry, I will not be mentioned by historians in the next millennium or even the next century. Neither will you, the reader. Yet, our lives have great significance, if for no other reason than the children that we bear. But even they will not likely be cited by historians! Why not? I love my children and grandchildren. Along with my wife, they are my dearest possessions on earth. Yet, historians will not care, no more than they are likely to care about you and your progeny. (I am limiting history here only as secularists see it. Certainly, our greatest worth, as Christians, is found in God's love and plan for His own. I have focused on that dimension in what follows here.)

Historians write about the great events of history, or they write about their particular interests. For example, there are historians of the world, of nations, of city-states, of small towns, and families. There are even biographies of individuals. Further, there are histories of disciplines: economics, chemistry, medicine, psychology, etc., etc. There are histories of inventions: tools, engines, ships, weapons, airplanes, toothbrushes, toilets, etc., etc.

I have belabored enough! History is what an individual or group wants it to be. It reflects their interests and values. It reflects their beliefs. It reflects their agenda. And, the subjects that they have chosen to write on reflect their worldview.

Thus, we confront the writers of history. **Historians have written from within their worldview to advance their interests, values, beliefs, and worldview.** We have the historical texts of our times with the dominant worldview of humanism. (See the Glossary.) Within this worldview, Jesus Christ becomes an insignificant itinerant preaching peasant, the Middle Ages become the Dark Ages, the Reformation is hidden behind the Renaissance, and the United States had no Biblical basis.

Providence, Predestination, and Free Will

Now, I am not about to get into the theological debate between predestination and free will. But there are some inescapable realities of history on which all Christians should agree. One is that the end is determined by the beginning. Regardless of your eschatological position, all Christians agree that Christ will return to earth -- the parousia or Second Coming. That event will happen according to God's plan. My plan is to place a period at the end of this sentence -- after I complete my plan of thoughts. Then, I have a plan to complete this paragraph, then, this chapter, then this book. Everyone who works, including the homemaker, makes a plan. It may be haphazard, but nothing is accomplished without a plan.

I live in a well-designed house that has been modified over the years. Its original design had a plan. That plan has been changed at least twice. The most complex of buildings has a plan. No skyscraper was ever built without a highly complex plan.

Now, buildings are inanimate objects. A plank or a brick will stay exactly where the builder places it. But humans will not stay put! They are not the same yesterday, today, or tomorrow. Some speakers use the illustration of herding cats. Try herding people, as tyrants have done. Well, you know the results. It cannot be done in the long run.

But God has a plan for the history of the human race. He will culminate that plan by His design in the future. So, regardless of one's eschatology, He has a plan. He has spoken; He has decreed!

And, with a plan inescapably every detail must be planned. What do you choose as your endpoint for Christ's Second Coming? The fulfillment of the Great Commission? If so, imagine the details that have to be worked out to get the Gospel to every person and tribe. Each life has to achieve certain ends: survival of illnesses and accidents, a job by the parents to put food on the table, learning how to raise children by the parents, genetics to provide intelligence for the future evangelists, and a willingness to go. Multiply those scenarios by the millions. Then, add in all those thoughts that we reviewed above that must make myriads of decisions to result in those acts. "Complex" does not even begin to describe the possibilities.

But there is more. There must be modes of travel to get evangelists where they need to go: horse-drawn carriage, steam engines, ships, and airplanes. Someone must invent these means of travel. Someone must invent and manufacture the printing press, inks, paper, boxes, and computers for these evangelists to use.

Well, you could choose other endpoints than The Great Commission, but the same almost infinite complexities would still have to be fulfilled.

Thus, to say that God has a plan inescapably means that billions of thoughts and actions must be controlled for God to arrive at His endpoint(s).

But then, He said all this more simply. "Are not two sparrows sold for a copper coin? And not one of them falls to the ground apart from your Father's will. But the very hairs of your head are all numbered. Do not fear therefore; you are of more value than many sparrows" (Matthew 10:29-31). The teaching about sparrows is obvious. How can we know all the sparrows and other birds that exist? But a subtlety about the hairs of our head may be missed. With meticulous care, one could count the hairs on a person's head, so what is the big deal? Well, we lose a number of the hairs on our head every day. By the time that you finished counting, the number would have changed! So, not only does God know at any point in time, He knows moment to moment.

After this lengthy introduction, what conclusions can we draw?

History is determined by the future. The future is logically first, but not chronologically. (This thought is not original with me but I have found several authors who have made it.) From the salvation of souls to the subduing of all nations under His feet, God has planned the end from the beginning. This plan is not His foreknowledge of events, but His planning the final stages of history, as He has determined the outcome! (For God, history does not exist. He is at once "the same yesterday, today, and forever." His knowledge never changes, so for Him, all things are now. Thus, His declaration to Moses at the burning bush, "I AM.")

Thus, **creationism is determined by God's plan for the future.** Creation had to be carried out with the most intricate design to achieve God's final plans for mankind's history.

And, **God has a plan for every individual of the human race and every thought, word, and action.** All are necessary to complete the most simple detail of His plan.

What If Jesus Had Never Been Born?

The title of this section is the same as the title of a book by D. James Kennedy and Jerry Newcombe. In their focus on evangelism and personal righteousness, Christians are prone to miss the great historical impact of Jesus Christ's life, His teaching, and regeneration of His people. Kennedy and Newcombe list the following (p. 3):

Hospitals, which essentially began during the Middle Ages.

Universities, which also began during the Middle Ages. In addition, most of the world's greatest universities were started by Christians for Christian purposes.

Literacy and education for the masses.

Capitalism and free-enterprise.

Representative government, particularly as it has been seen in the American experiment.

The separation of political powers.

Civil liberties.

The abolition of slavery, both in antiquity and more modern times.

Modern science.

The discovery of the New World by Columbus.

The elevation of women.

Benevolence and charity; the Good Samaritan ethic.

Higher standards of justice.

The elevation of the common man.

The condemnation of adultery, homosexuality, and other sexual perversions. This has helped to preserve the human race, and it has spared many from heartache.

High regard for human life.

The civilizing of many barbarian and primitive cultures.

The codifying and setting to writing of many of the world's languages.

Greater development of art and music. The inspiration for the greatest works of art.

The countless changed lives transformed from liabilities into assets to society because of the gospel. (For example, the descendants of Jonathan Edwards and a criminal of his time have been contrasted.)

The eternal salvation of countless souls!

Further, I would like to add to or expound on this list:

Human sacrifice. "Human sacrifice was a religious rite practiced in every country, by every religion until Christianity appeared" (Otto Scott, back cover). This practice included the supposed great "civilizations" of many historians, the "grandeur" of Greece and "glory" of Rome. These two "cultures" also included slavery and "torture as an instrument of the courts." (*Ibid.*)

Infanticide by abandonment and exposure were almost universal before cultures were exposed to Christianity. Consistently, "None of the great minds of the ancient world -- from Plato to Aristotle to Seneca and Quintilian, from Pythagoras and Aristophanes to Livy and Cicero, from Herodotus and Thucydides to Plutarch and Euripides -- disparaged child-killing in any way. In fact, most of them even recommended it.... They blindly tossed lives like dice." (George Grant, *Third Time Around: A History of the Pro-Life Movement from the First Century to the Present*, (Wolgemuth and Hyatt, 1991), page 12.

Limited governments created by common law and *Lex Rex*, e.g., the Magna Charta.

World exploration prompted by evangelism, e.g., Christopher Columbus in the Americas and Hernando Cortez in Mexico.

Dates in history were ordered. Time is B.C. and A.D., before Christ and *anno domini* (in the year of our Lord).

I am aware of the many controversies that surround the items in this list. Some I will discuss here and elsewhere. For others, I invite you to read Kennedy and Newcombe's book and scores of other books which give more extensive and substantive reasons that the above are facts of history.

Universal Education

One of the greatest dangers to Biblical thinking is, "What is, is what ought to be." **There is no other philosophy of life or religion in the history of mankind that supplied the force for universal education than Christianity.** God planned for His people to know His Word. The New Testament was written in the *koine* Greek, the language of the common people of the Roman world in the Middle East, not classical Greek.

And, how did Greek come to be the common language of that time? Alexander the Great! God used the ambitions of a thoroughly pagan military leader (who later claimed to be a god) to bring most of the Middle East under Greek dominance. With that dominance came the common language of the Greeks. This language provided for the Gospel to be written in the language of the common man within a large geographic location.

As Christianity began to grow in that God-provided culture medium, it provoked the common man to learn to read. To paraphrase the above proverb, it is difficult to understand that "what is, is not what has always been." Until the Reformation (see below), there was essentially no reason for most people to be able to read and write. In virtually all societies, there were castes (even if they were not called that). Most people had no money, so there was no reason for mathematics. Most people did not even own themselves, either through outright slavery or their position in society being already fixed at their birth. So, there was no reason for learning anything more than simple tasks in life.

10

Religion provided no real hope or aspirations. Entertainment could be provided by others in the way of plays or traveling bards.

I recall reading somewhere that Augustine was startled when he saw his teacher, Ambrose, sitting and reading a book. He had heard books read aloud in public, but had never thought that a book could be read for one's own edification! Of course, he went on to read -- and to write -- many books of his own. But this is an example of the reality of the lack of "book-learning and reading" in his day, even though he was of an educated class.

The Roman Catholic Church used the Latin translation of the Bible and its favored priesthood to keep the Bible out of the hands of the common people. Further, the Church believed that only the priests could properly understand the Scriptures.

And, thus the Dark Ages were dark because the Bible was kept from the common people. But God's Word intended for God's people could not be kept under a "bushel," even one as large as the Roman Catholic Church. Its seeds began sprouting with John Wycliffe, John Hus, Martin Luther, John Calvin, and other translators of the Bible. With the invention of the printing press and the translation of the Bible again into the language of the common man, a desire and impetus for universal education began and birthed the Reformation.

Christians as Martyrs and Enemies of Earthly Powers

The dominant theme of the history of mankind according to the Bible is the Revelation of Jesus Christ and the salvation of His people. All evangelicals would agree. But Christians have not been popular in many (most?) societies in history. Rather, the opposite: they have been severely persecuted with virtually every torture known to evil mankind. All evangelicals know this martyrdom. In the 3rd century, Tertullian said that "the blood of martyrs is seed" (of the church). Again, this statement is commonly accepted among Christians of all times.

But what may not be readily recognizable in an historical context is why Christians are persecuted when Christians are called "to live peaceably with all men" (Roman 12:18). Indeed, the law of love extends even to enemies.

Christians, by and large, are persecuted because they are a threat to the ruling powers! As is being discussed throughout this book, the Bible defines the stark contrast of light and darkness and goodness and evil. Darkness hates the light. Powerful people hate those that will not bow the knee to the god of

Nebuchadnezzar, the gods of Rome, the racism of Hitler, or the communism of Stalin. Beginning with the Hebrew midwives, God has instructed His people to "obey God, rather than men."

> "… the world has struck at (Christians) because it has recognized the power in them" (Rushdoony, R. J., *Salvation and Godly Rule*, page 359).

God's people are under a set of laws that sometimes differ with those of the state. (The extent of those laws I will discuss elsewhere in some detail). Again, Christians are generally called to be the best citizens that a ruler could have (Romans 13:1-7). Yet, that ruler wants absolute obedience. He knows that the Christian cannot give that total allegiance. **So, the persecution of Christians by the state is actually a premise consistent with their worldview.**

This begs a question of Christians in the West. Why are we not being persecuted? Some would say that we are, but discrimination is not persecution! I will posit this reason. The influence of the Reformation still lingers in the West, particularly in the United States. The Reformation spawned the most thoroughgoing worldview in Christianity. While its doctrinal basis has virtually disappeared, their social and legal tolerances remain.

We face an interesting divergence of scenarios. If Christians return to a more complete worldview, building on their mistakes and keeping their principles that were correct, then what will happen? Either, **they will once again force darkness to persecute them or they will reform society and the state.**

At least in the United States, it is possible that the freedoms of religion in this country can be restored. But it will not happen unless "judgment begins at the household of God" (I Peter 4:17). That is, His people confess their failure to live consistently with His commandments and statutes and then to correct that failure.

I don't know which will happen! I hope, pray, and work with diligence that our freedoms can be restored. But the more serious issue is not whether persecution will occur, but whether Christians will come to understand their failures in the Cultural Mandate. (See Glossary.) If they don't, persecution may be avoided. The state will have nothing to fear! There will be no light to their darkness.

Another possible scenario is that Christians will persecute their own. Those without the light will join with the forces of darkness to persecute their brothers and sisters. This persecution has already been played out in history between the Roman Catholic Church and Protestant churches. I fear that this is the most likely event in our times.

(One could debate whether true Christians can persecute other true Christians. "To whom much is given much is required." The apostasy of those who once believed is worse than that of pagans. God gives them over to their wrath.)

The Dark Ages of the Light of the Gospel

The Dark Ages (or the Middle Ages) are variously dated from the Fall of Rome in 476 A.D. to around 1000 A.D. or 1500 A.D. Again, such dating is concerned with one's priorities and biases in historical accounts. But just what was happening during this time relative to Christianity in Europe?

While the "civilizations" of Greece and Rome were in their flower, there were barbaric hordes all over the British Isles and Europe. The Irish, Celts, and Scots were small tribes and clans with no loyalties other than to their own little bands, and sometimes betrayal even within families. There were the warring Germanic tribes and the raiding Norsemen, who were feared by all of Europe. Slaughter, rape, pillaging, human sacrifice, enslavement, and worship of all kinds of strange gods were common everywhere.

Fast forward to the 12th-15th century. The barbarians are gone. Civilization is beginning to flourish, with its evidences of increasing liberties for the common man, great architecture of the Cathedrals, art, literature, science, music, and the chivalry shown to women. It is the eve of the Renaissance and the Reformation.

Barbarism became advanced culture and civilization in 500-1000 years, depending upon location. What happened? How did the mire of humanity presage the Enlightenment? ***Christianity!*** While Protestants have rightly condemned excesses and wrong theology, with the development of the Church came missionaries with a hunger to convert souls. **With the Christ of the Gospels came all His fruits** (listed above). And, He came with the Bible only in the hands of the priests. He came with all the imperfections and heresies of the Roman Catholic Church. But He came with sufficient light to transform the British Isles and Europe to the dawn of the greatest achievements of mankind and the liberty that would eventually be the United States.

13

Church History vs. World History

Perhaps, church history has obscured God's Providence in World History. While there are numerous books on church history, there are none of which I am aware that delineate God's Providence in world history over long periods of time. There are many that focus on American history and the removal of God and His Word from the founding of the Colonies to the writing of the Declaration of Independence and the Constitution. There are more focused books on individuals and short periods of history, especially the Reformation. But where are those similar to Western civilization history texts for high school and college classes? There is evidence that they will be forthcoming.

In July 2006, Vision Forum sponsored its History of the World Mega-Conference with 65 presentations by 12 speakers who have unique areas of study within world history. All history was covered, from Genesis 1 to the 400 year anniversary of the founding of Jamestown in 2007. It is hoped that these speakers will continue to write and publish books for Christians of all ages.

Genesis 1-11: Reverse Evolution!

Genesis 1-11 has always been controversial in the Christian community. I will deal mostly with the so-called "problems" presented by modern science in that section. Neither is this the place to discuss the unity and coherence of the Scriptures. However, in compiling a worldview of history, a brief mention of this period of history is necessary. And, the only written history of pre-Flood times is the Word of God.

John Morris estimates that there were one billion people on earth at the time of the Flood. Their civilizations would have been highly advanced, not "hunter-gatherers", as evolutionists would tell us. They were builders of cities, workers of bronze and iron, herders of cattle who dwelled in tents (not caves), and players of complex musical instruments (Genesis 4:16, 20-22). John Reed has written a fictional account of the building of the Ark, infusing the probable technologies that made the functioning of the Ark possible. (John K. Reed, *The Coming Wrath* (Evans, Georgia: Word Books, 2005).

The post-Flood world has considerable archeological evidence for advanced civilizations. As archeology over the past two hundred years has challenged and lost to Old Testament history, so evolution is falling to archeology, proving the Biblical prediction of advanced technology among peoples who were closer to the intelligence of Adam and therefore less influenced by decline in genetic intelligence. Also, their longevity allowed longer lives for them to develop their skills and knowledge.

There is archeological evidence of great ships that sailed the seas of the world, even a pre-frozen map of Antarctica. Great architectural and botanical accomplishments of Babylon, the Mayas, and Aztecs have been found. Many hieroglyphic accounts, and scientific evidence of interaction of men and dinosaurs (Job 40:15-24) have been discovered. Other items include flush toilets, complicated aqueducts, pyramids of Egypt, Gardens of Babylon, and stone monsters of Easter Island.

Evolution has man emerging from the ooze, living in caves, becoming a hunter-gatherer, then becoming agricultural, and much later technologically capable. The Bible and archeology has man living with hunting, farming, and complex technology from the beginning.

References: Chittick, *The Puzzle of Ancient Man*. Phillips and Whitcomb's lectures at Mega-history conference.

What Is Civilization?

This question must be asked in the context of a chapter on history. However, its answer is best left to a study of sociology, as it has greater application there. But one must wonder about the concept of "civilization" in which virtually every culture and nation practiced human sacrifice, sometimes by the tens of thousands (Incas and Mayas), prior to the introduction of Christianity. In Greece and Rome, wives and children were property to be used at the whim of the "husband," sometimes even in human sacrifice. Unwanted children were often exposed, that is, left to die after being abandoned in the street, wilderness, or even the city trash dump. Justice was often the whim of the King, literally having the power of life and death over everyone in his kingdom.

Although the author may not have intended that the following be a definition, it seems quite definitive. "In any given society, civilization represents, in continuous terms, the sum total of its spiritual, intellectual, ethical, and institutional values, which in varying degrees will permit those living in it to develop as completely and harmoniously as possible." [Jean DeCarreaux, *Monks and Civilization* (London: George Allen and Unwin Ltd., 1964), p. 15.]

Summary Principles

1. **God determines history**, not in foreknowledge, but plans all events in history to determine His final stages for the history of mankind. In God, there is no past, present, or future, as the great "I AM."

2. **The people and events that are recorded, as "history" are totally determined by one's philosophy of life or worldview.** Secular historians will ignore the movement of God in history: His people, His Church, and His providential plan.

3. **God has a plan for every individual of the human race, including his every thought, word, and deed**. All are necessary to complete every detail of His plan.

4. **Most of the "good" things that mankind has experienced** were caused by the regeneration and obedience of God's people through God's great plan of salvation in Jesus Christ. This "good" includes capitalism, representative government, civil liberties, abolition of the slave trade and human sacrifice, world exploration, elevation of women, elevation of the common man, the Renaissance, and Reformation. These accomplishments are "good" only when they are governed by explicit Biblical principles. And, certainly, mankind is able to pervert every one of these to ungodly purposes.

One particular of this "great good" is universal public education. There is no other philosophy of life or religion in the history of mankind that supplied the impetus for universal education.

5. **The dominant theme of the history of mankind is the Revelation of Jesus Christ and the salvation of God's people.**

6. **Christians have been and are persecuted because they are a threat to the ruling powers** when they are obedient to the King of Kings and Lord of Lords. Currently, their threat is almost harmless in the United States and in the West because of their disobedience to Him.

7. **One of the great tragedies and misunderstandings of God's Word has been the persecution of Christians by other Christians** over religious issues; for example, the burning of Protestants by Roman Catholics during and after the Reformation and The Killing Times of the Covenanters by the English in the late 18th century. Of course, theology was often just an excuse for tyrannical power and personal gain by those in power.

8. The Dark Ages (or Middle Ages) were actually the progressive age of the light of the Gospel, as most of Europe had been overrun with barbarians. Yet, this age eventually produced Scholasticism, the Renaissance, the Reformation, and all the great things that have come from those events. That is not to say these seeds were evenly distributed. Certainly, in many areas there continued to be ignorance, illiteracy, superstition, barbarianism, and tyrannical governments.

9. While church history has held some prominence among Christians, **God's Providence in world history is almost unnoticed today**, a phenomenon mostly caused by the secular writing of history in the 19th and 20th centuries. Today, some Christians are beginning to recover this providential perspective; for example, Vision Forum's Mega-History Conference.

10. While evolution would have mankind increasing in intelligence, the Creation account would have **Adam as the most intelligent man who ever lived, even after the Fall**. This high intelligence would have continued in Adam's immediate descendants, who lived for hundreds of years. Man's intelligence is actually decreasing, as the effect of the Fall continues. Archeological evidence is accumulating to prove the high intelligence of man before and after the Flood in these early years of man's existence.

11. **There is increasing archeological and scientific evidence of a "young earth,"** very close to Bishop Ussher's 6,000+ years.

12. **Chapters 1-11 of Genesis are true**. When properly understood, they have always been compatible with the best understood theories of science and archeological explorations. Until the Church proclaims this part of the Bible as true, her message of salvation will be limited in its effectiveness.

13. **Civilization needs to be re-defined with Biblical criteria.**

2. Family, Marriage, Divorce, and Sexuality

Summary Principles

In all these Summary Principles, they are not necessarily listed in priority order. In fact, priorities within families and churches are likely different. But, consideration should be given to the full application of all these principles, as a beginning exploration into each worldview area. The author is interested in feedback where error, weakness, or omission may occur.

1. Marriage and Family: The Creation Mandate. Immediately, during the week of creation on the sixth day, God commanded man "Be fruitful and multiply; fill the earth and subdue it; have dominion over the fish of the sea, over the birds of the air, and over every living thing that moves on the earth" (Genesis 1:28). Through the birth of children within the commitment of one man and one woman in marriage for life, God commanded that His Creation Mandate be fulfilled. That mandate was not abrogated by the Fall of Adam and Eve nor by the Flood, after which God re-stated it in more detail (Genesis 9:1-10). Marriage is thus a covenant with three parties: the husband, the wife, and God.

Currently, on an average, at least 2.1 children must be born to each family in order to maintain a population at its current numbers. Thus, "to be fruitful and multiply," each family should have at least three children. Since God's Kingdom work is primarily through His people, the argument could be made that Christians should have "many" children. They are a "heritage" and a great "blessing" in the Lord (Psalm 127:5). Expansion of families may occur through the adoption of children. These children should be given the full rights and responsibilities of "naturally" born siblings.

The primary intention of marriage is not procreation, but companionship and wholeness. God said, "And the LORD God said, 'It is not good that man should be alone; I will make him a helper comparable to him'" (Genesis 2:18). While the remainder of the creation was "good," even "very good," it was "not good" that neither man nor woman be alone. In addition, both need a "helper" to complete what the individual lacks in their own abilities. God intended marriage for a lifetime. Children are present for only a part of that time. They are to work to fulfill the Creation Mandate, even after their children have formed their own families.

2. Marriage and Family: The Great Commission. God's primary mode of evangelism is through the family from generation to generation. The Bible is clear that saving faith is to be passed from one generation to the next (Deuteronomy 6:1-9; Acts 2:39; Ephesians 6:4). In the Old Testament, explicit responsibilities of the covenant (land, laws, Levitical priesthood, etc.) were passed in this way. This continuity and expansion is missing from many churches in the modern era in their emphasis on the Great Commission as one of seeking individual converts and treating their own children, as being "unsaved" until they make their own profession of faith. In a real sense, this individualistic emphasis has increased the need for evangelism, as God's intended plan of the continuity of families has been minimized and neglected.

The power of this intergenerational commission and covenant has been lost. The Creation (Cultural) Mandate is fragmented and lost each time the succession of spiritual generation fails. The individualism of the 19th century evangelism and its virtual abhorrence of studied theology has crippled the ability of the Church to advance God's Kingdom, as a continuation of His original Mandate. The Church and families must reform their thinking to this intergenerational plan of God from "The Beginning." One concrete goal could be that parents strive to give their children a more Biblical foundation than they themselves had.

3. Marriage and Family: Government. God has ordained government in four spheres: the conscience of self-government, the family, the Church, and the State. Another great error of Christians in the modern era is to think of government as synonymous with the State. Again, this error has led to social discord, as the other three spheres of government have been neglected. The husband is the head of the home, the wife his help-meet, and children are to obey their parents and be nurtured in the admonition of the Lord. Wives and children may disobey their husband/father only when his directives violate clearly Biblical instructions.

4. Marriage is the norm, not singleness. Singleness can occur for a variety of reasons: lack of someone of the opposite sex to offer marriage, death of a spouse, divorce, or one's calling (Matthew 19:10-11; I Corinthians 7:7, 32-35 - - see below). Thus, it can be legitimate. However, God's overwhelming priority for His Kingdom on earth is the family.

(1) The Creation Mandate with all its directives is given to the family, for only within the family are children born legitimately (above). (2) In both the Old and New Testaments, the family is assumed in ownership of land and its

inheritance, the propagation and raising of children, and the primary unit of economy and governance. (3) Young widows are instructed to re-marry, not remain single (I Timothy 5:14). This admonition would include those Biblically divorced , as well. (4) Singleness for work in the Church and the Kingdom is such that a special gift is required (I Corinthians 7:7).

5. Marriage is for one man to one woman in unity for life. The marriage of a man and a woman forms a unique relationship within mankind. There is a complementarity and completeness of the two which exceeds what each is individual (Genesis 1:18-25). These two people, acting and interacting together as they should, begin to think, act, and feel as one person ("one flesh"). This unity must be established with priorities that separate themselves from those families from which each spouse came (Genesis 2:24). Today, there are often conflicts early within a marriage because one or more of the spouses gives priority to one or more member of the family from which he or she came.

Acts of sexual intimacy between a man and a woman may be expressed only after they are married. All other acts of sexual expression (pornography, homosexuality, bestiality, etc.) are biblically proscribed.

The modern concept of "dating" has no Biblical warrant. The only Biblical relationships between men and women are as relatives (both genetically and spiritually) and as husband and wife (assuming engagement as a prelude to marriage). "Dating" sets the stage for sexual immorality and severe emotional trauma. Any idea that "dating" is preparation for marriage is erroneous and a gross distortion of the concept of marriage.

6. God designed marriage for the life of the husband or wife (Romans 7:1-6) with only the two exceptions (following).

7. God allows divorce for sexual infidelity and desertion by an unbelieving spouse. While forgiveness with restitution is the norm for offenses, God does not mandate that the offended spouse accept back the sexually unfaithful offender (Matthew 19:9). However, the offended spouse may do so under the application of forgiveness (Luke 17:1-5).

While we should not speculate about God's intentions in His design, from a human perspective there are conditions that are unique to this situation. First, sexual immorality brings the possibility of sexually transmitted diseases that are debilitating and even fatal for the innocent spouse. Second, the ripping and tearing of the "one flesh" nature of marriage in sexual infidelity is the breaking of the most intimate of human relationships. This former union is not easily restored.

A believing spouse may allow the unbelieving spouse to leave and divorce him or her (I Corinthians 7:15). If a believing spouse decides to leave, however, that believer's church must become involved to make every Biblical effort to restore the marriage. If that believing spouse will not repent, then the church is to follow formal steps of discipline and excommunicate him or her (Mathew 18:15-20). Once the church has declared this offender an unbeliever, then the same passage (above) applies as to an unbeliever.

Nuances. Certainly, I have presented here a summary of principles. There is much Scripture, counseling, prayer, and possibly church discipline in actual situations. However, I have summarized the biblically allowable options. For a more detailed discussion of these issues, I highly recommend Jay Adams' Marriage, Divorce, and Remarriage…. (See References below.)

8. Biblical grounds for divorce. For centuries after the Reformation, covenants were made between a man and woman engaged to be married. Those covenants should be re-instituted today with sanctions against the party who breaks the contract. There should be no particular ownership of any property by either spouse while the marriage lasts. The State's only role in marriage is to enforce the sanctions of the contract, if violated by either party and the church is unable to settle disputes. The State has no role in setting conditions for any marriage before the covenant is established. Current civil law has greatly promoted the breakup of the family in our times with easy divorce, based on such nebulous concepts as "no-fault" and "incompatibility." Divorce should be final: all contact of the guilty spouse with the children should be cut off. He or she has divorced himself or herself from the family by their unrighteous and hardened behavior. This total separation is not possible today because of the state is not guided by Biblical principle. (Transported from Civil Government Summary Principles.)

Is spousal abuse grounds for divorce? One has to proceed carefully on this issue. It does seem justifiable that where a spouse's life or those of their children have been threatened and that threat has been acted upon in some tangible, physical way, the Sixth Commandment to prevent the taking of life would apply. John Frame has discussed allowing divorce on the grounds of desertion on page 31 of the reference below "MarriageDivorcePolicyPCA."

James Jordan also argues for divorce on the grounds of "serious maltreatment." (James Jordan, The Law of the Covenant: An Exposition of Exodus 21-23

(Institute for Christian Economics, 1984, page 87. This book may be found online below.)

9. Parents are responsible for the education of their children, primarily that which is spiritual. "Education" has come to be equated with formal education of primary, secondary, and university levels. However, the most important directive to parents is the spiritual education of their children (Deuteronomy 6:1-25; Ephesians 6:1-4). Tragically, the priorities for Christians are reversed today. More attention by parents is given to the education of their children towards "jobs and careers," rather than "serving the Living God." In this role of spiritual education, the man must lead.

Spiritual education is unavoidable, as "discipling" is more important than formal education. Parents are instructing their children from the time that they are born by their words and behavior, whether such is intended as education or not. Essentially, they are "discipling" as powerful authorities to their children. This "discipling" is far more influential than their speech, especially in the children's early years. Thus, the true "spiritual" commitment of the parents will be seen by their children and compared to what the parents espouse verbally. Children have an innate wisdom in the interpretation of hypocrisy, and they will tell you so!

All Christian parents should determine early in their children's lives what their goals for their education should be. How many older Christians regret "the years that the locusts have eaten?" Not too many decades ago, children achieved Biblical, theological, and classical education by their late teenage years. The breadth and depth of what children may achieve should not be underestimated, especially in Biblical and theological studies. Some Christian schools and home schoolers are beginning to recognize this potential, but it needs to be far more widespread and more fully developed than is current in most places. While the Church may or may not be directly involved in this education, its leaders should be encouraging and making opportunities for the achievement of this level of education.

Wasting time and evil education. "The years that the locusts have eaten" includes wasting time on studies that are not important to the life of a Christian. While specific subjects are far beyond our scope here, some examples may suffice. Why should Christian children study "social studies" and "abnormal" psychology which are thoroughly pagan in concept and even evil ("anti-God")? There is a place for the study of these in contrast to the Biblical worldview, but that approach is not taught in public schools and many

Christian schools. So, the focus of parents should be as much on "wrong" studies, as "right" studies.

Vocation. Parents will know their children quite well, as they observe them over their childhood and adolescence. They should apply this knowledge to help their children discover their vocation and avocations, that is, their "calling(s)" relative to God's design for their lives. The Biblical concept is that all moral occupations should be seen as working towards the fulfillment of the Kingdom of God, not as just a means of income. (See Vocation -- Link to same.)

State schools? This entire section brings serious question to the children of Christians being in state schools which today are consciously anti-Christian and anti-Biblical.

10. The husband is the head of the home. The husband is head of the home (Ephesians 5:22-24, 6:4). However, this headship bears not only authority, but the love, tenderness, and sacrifice that Jesus manifested for His Church (Ephesians 5:25-33, 6:4).

This headship is a criterion for leadership in the Church and the State. The determination of whether a man is able to lead the Church is reflected in his proven ability to lead and govern his family (I Timothy 3:4, 12), as well as his proven spirituality (Exodus 18:21). This criterion should also be a requirement for leadership in any authoritative position in society and in state government. While this application is not explicit in Scripture, it is an inescapable conclusion of Scripture with the role of the man throughout the Old Testament in the family, the government of Israel (Exodus 18:13-27), the Levitical priesthood, and the government of Israel in the Sanhedrin. Rationally, no people should want someone over them who has failed in this most important area to those who should be most dear to him.

This criterion does have a limit. There are occasions when evil children come from a Biblical home. Hardened, recalcitrant children who are older, probably even "adults" by age, were to be disinherited (see below) and even stoned (Deuteronomy 21:18-21). And, it cannot be denied that every child has a sin nature that he will follow or one that he will "deny" and follow Christ and His Word. Some children will follow that sin nature in their adult years. But, while children are in the home, the father should have control and discipline of them.

11. Marriages are not to be unequally yoked. Christians are to marry only Christians (II Corinthians 6:11-18). While this criterion applies primarily to believers, it is valuable advice to unbelievers, as well. Marriages that involve different religions are surely to involve conflict. And, a covenant of marriage is required by God for any child to be considered legitimate (Genesis 2:24).

12. Consanguinity is forbidden by God and supported by nature. God has declared that marriage of close kinship is forbidden (Leviticus 18:1-18; Mark 6:18). The genetic problems that have occurred demonstrate that consanguinity is against nature, as well. This association of law and nature clearly demonstrates that God's laws are for the good of mankind, not just restrictions on his "freedom."

13. The modern state violates its God-directed mandate to enhance and protect marriages and families, and thus, has become an enemy of God and the family.

A. The State has flagrantly violated the integrity of the home by forcibly removing children for acts of corporal discipline, spiritual instruction, circumstantial sexual abuse, and other allegations that violate the integrity granted to the family by God Himself. These intrusions violate a number of principles of Biblical justice, as well. The only justification for State intrusion into the home is the substantiated threat to the life of one or more family members and instances of sexual abuse of children that can be clearly documented.

B. The State has failed to enforce judgments against spouses who have divorced and failed to support their respective spouses and children financially. The large majority of these cases of injustice are women.

C. Tax codes fail to give adequate consideration to the costs of child-raising in its legal deductions, especially where both spouses have earned income.

D. The State has facilitated easy divorce through laws that allow it for virtually any whim or desire of one spouse.

E. Numerous laws in the name of "health," violate the integrity of the family. For example, vaccinations are mandated solely on the expectation that all children will become sexually promiscuous (hepatitis B and HPV) or intravenous drug addicts (hepatitis B). Any girl, regardless of age, may be treated by a health care worker for a sexually transmitted disease, have an abortion, or receive any form of birth control without parental knowledge or consent in any of the 50 states.

F. Current laws make alternatives to public education legally restrictive and expensive.

G. Current laws mandate studies in public education that are anti-God, anti-family, and immoral.

H. The legalization of abortion is the social justification of murder, the destruction of the life-giving essence of a mother to her unborn child, and the obliteration of God's creating activity (Psalm 139:13-16).

14. Family economics. Primarily, the husband is to provide for his family (I Timothy 5:8) and the wife is the homemaker (I Timothy 5:10, 14; Titus 2:3-5). However, the wife has great latitude in assisting in this role and being involved in many endeavors (Proverbs 31:10-31). A modern danger for both spouses is the lure of "making money" or "career advancement" to the neglect of each other and their children. Too many excuses and false justifications are used by one or both for these pursuits. Social studies actually show that most successful men are good fathers and husbands.

Children are to provide for their parents, as needed, later in their lives. Parents are to make every attempt to provide for themselves in their latter years and to provide an inheritance for their children (II Corinthians 2:14). However, such financial planning is not always successful. Their children are to guarantee that they are loved and that their needs are met until their deaths under the provisions of the Fifth Commandment and the Great Commandment "to love your neighbor as yourself."

15. Spiritual endeavors should not encroach on family responsibilities. The primary spiritual roles of husbands and wives are those for each other and their children. Ministries, including missionary activities, may never justify the abrogation or substitution of these activities over family responsibilities. The attempt to meet many "spiritual needs" of others has caused worse needs, including divorce, in the families of those who were the ministers. The busy, busy local church calendar can be such an encroachment.

16. Older, spiritually mature women are to teach younger women (Titus 2:2-4). This role is one that is not common to the Church today. There is a great deal for a young woman to learn about being a wife, mother, and homemaker. She needs help and instruction. God has commanded that older, spiritual women come alongside of them in assistance and teaching. Thus, the teaching of adult women by adult women has a Biblically defined curriculum.

The teaching of women by women does not include broad, doctrinal teaching which is the responsibility of the husband (I Corinthians 14:35).

17. Discipline of children. The first thing to say about discipline is that it has a positive side, as well as a negative side. The positive side has been covered under "education" among these principles. The negative, or corrective side, is what is usually connoted by "discipline." The Bible is clear that inflicting pain on children because of their violations of God's instructions through parents is more than warranted, as God demands it. The consequences of not applying corporal punishment is severe. "To spare the rod" is to hate one's children; "to apply the rod is to love them" (Proverbs 13:24). Certain dimensions of "foolishness" will be retained in children, if physical punishment is not applied (Proverbs 22:15). The "rod" is one means by which a child's soul is delivered from Hell (Proverbs 23:14). Corporal punishment is one mean's of implanting wisdom in a child (Proverbs 29:15).

However, in today's climate of political correctness, parents must be careful where and how they physically punish their children. Children may be legally taken from a home where such punishment is carried out. And, it should not need to be said, but physical punishment should be properly given without severely harming the child and not as the only form of corrective discipline used. Rewards, restriction, retribution, and other avenues should be used, as well.

The ultimate act of discipline is disinheritance. There may come a point in the later years of a child's life when they become incorrigible, not accepting of any form of discipline. This application is the same as that of Matthew 18:15-20. In the Old Testament, it was "putting one outside the camp," for example, Numbers 5:2-4. The greatest seriousness of this act is spiritual condemnation, not the physical separation. This act is disinheritance from the Kingdom and God and consignment to Hell, that is, spiritual separation from God and from His people forever. Today, some parents need to disinherit their children, painful though it may be. They live unproductive, profligate lives with their parents always bailing them out (literally and figuratively) and continually providing for their wants and needs. The continued support by parents is support of activities that are unproductive, immoral, and sometimes illegal. It is support of Hell on earth. It is shaking one's fist in God's face, as the provision for such a life is to support lives and actions that are anti-Christ.

18. Historical note: The Reformation established freedom of sexuality in marriage. Most of the church fathers, including Augustine, Athanasius, Tertullian, Ambrose, Aquinas, and Gregory the Great, considered sexual expression with any passion or enjoyment as "evil," "sin," "befoulment," and "adultery." Consistently, virginity and celibacy were highly honored. These attitudes became entrenched within Roman Catholic teaching, writing, and tradition. Even the Council of Trent, the Roman Catholic response to the Reformation, upheld celibacy and by implication, its attitudes towards sexuality within marriage being restricted to the conception of children.

But, then came the Puritans. The Puritans were anything but sexual prudes (as they are often confused with the Victorians who were dishonestly prudish). The men highly valued their wives and proclaimed the passion and enjoyment of sexuality within marriage. Women expected, and sometimes demanded, regular sexual activity with their husbands. Thomas Hooker wrote:

The man whose heart is endeared to the woman he loves ... dreams of her in the night, hath her in his eye and apprehension when he awakes, museth on her as he sits at the table, walks with her when he travels ... She lies in his bosom, and his heart trust in her, which forceth all to confess that the stream of his affection, like a mighty current, runs with full tide and strength.

After all, this attitude of sexual pleasure in marriage is only a reflection of what God intended and what He portrayed in Proverbs 5:18ff and The Song of Solomon!

[These thoughts and quotes for this section come from Leland Ryken, *Worldly Saints: The Puritans as They Really Were* (Zondervan Academie Books, 1986), Chapter 3.]

Resources

http://www.reformation.net/

Click on "COR Documents" in the left hand column, then scroll down to "The Christian Worldview of the Family"

http://www.monergism.com/thethreshold/articles/onsite/MarriageDivorcePolicyPCA.pdf

An excellent resource for the role of the local church in pre-marriage counseling, counseling of intact marriages, and church discipline in marriages that are in difficulty.

Adams, Jay E. *Marriage, Divorce, and Remarriage in the Bible*. Presbyterian and Reformed Publishing Company, 1980.

Jordan, James. *The Law of the Covenant: An Exposition of Exodus 21-23*. Institute for Christian Economics, 1984. Found online at www.freebooks.com.

Ray, Bruce. *Withhold Not Correction*. Presbyterian and Reformed Publishing Company, 1978.

Sutton, Ray. *Who Owns the Family: God or the State?* Dominion Press (Blueprint Series), 1986. Also, available online www.freebooks.com

3. Vocation and Career

Summary Principles of Work, Vocation, Career, Leisure, and Retirement

"Then God blessed them, and God said to them, "Be fruitful and multiply; fill the earth and subdue it; have dominion over the fish of the sea, over the birds of the air, and over every living thing that moves on the earth." Genesis 1:28

"To the woman He said:
"I will greatly multiply your sorrow and your conception;
In pain you shall bring forth children;
Your desire *shall be* for your husband,
And he shall rule over you."
Then to Adam He said, "Because you have heeded the voice of your wife, and have eaten from the tree of which I commanded you, saying, 'You shall not eat of it':
'Cursed *is* the ground for your sake;
In toil you shall eat *of* it
All the days of your life.
Both thorns and thistles it shall bring forth for you,
And you shall eat the herb of the field.
In the sweat of your face you shall eat bread
Till you return to the ground,
For out of it you were taken;
For dust you *are,*
And to dust you shall return.'" Genesis 3:16-19

"Remember the Sabbath day, to keep it holy. Six days you shall labor and do all your work, but the seventh day is the Sabbath of the LORD your God. In it you shall do no work: you, nor your son, nor your daughter, nor your male servant, nor your female servant, nor your cattle, nor your stranger who is within your gates. For in six days the LORD made the heavens and the earth, the sea, and all that is in them, and rested the seventh day. Therefore the LORD blessed the Sabbath day and hallowed it." Exodus 20:8-11

1. Man was created to work. In The Creation Mandate, man was given these tasks: (1) "the procreation of offspring, (2) the replenishing of the earth, (3) subduing the same, (4) dominion of the creatures, (5) labor, (6) the weekly Sabbath, and (7) marriage" (John Murray, *Principles of Conduct*, page 27). Man is not commanded to work because of the Fall of Adam and Eve, but "in the beginning." "Male and female, He created them," meaning that the tasks of men and women are different. But, their work was made much more difficult after the Fall because of God's curse. (See below.)

2. Man was created to have dominion. Some have used the term, "vice-gerent" or vice-regent," meaning that man rules at God's appointment in His stead. Because of unbelief, pagans cannot grasp this role. However, Christians can understand and by their regenerated state have been empowered by the Holy Spirit for this role. Unfortunately, modern Christians have mostly lost this concept of dominion. They are not to be "in the world" as mere participants of the spheres in which they live. They are to rule… to be leaders in the world, as well as, in the Church. Or, more comprehensively, **they are to rule for the Kingdom of God**. Indeed, an understanding of The Kingdom of God is necessary to grasp their role. Thomas Babington Macaulay gave a great description of this role in his vivid portrayal of the Puritans. Our articles on The Kingdom of God may be found here.

The church in American has many faults. One that is relevant here is the model of the Christian as one who makes every effort not to offend, in order to model Christ and "win" others to Him ("being winsome"). This model is not an accurate portrayal of Jesus Christ nor what the vigorous lives of Christians should be. Today, if He visited us in our churches, His manner and conversations would be so direct and without the false civility of modern times, that He would be banished, as He was banished His home town of Nazareth. Certainly, the Christian should never intentionally offend for the sake of offense itself, but a disciple of the King who is commanded to judge men, and who will judge angels (I Corinthians 6:1-11) should carry a certain authority among men both in his area of calling, social discourse, and in government of self, family, and state. The model of Macaulay and the Puritans above, is a better model for Christians than that the "winsome" Christian of today. Of course, modeling that kind of authority assumes considerable training and knowledge, and those commitments are perhaps the primary reason for such omission. A correct understanding of the "meek" in the Sermon on the Mount is consistent with this role.

3. "Six days you shall labor and do all your work." Somehow, the modern Christian has adopted the world's approach to the seven-day week. We work for five days (or less) and think that we have two days of recreation that we have "earned." (We will deal with the Sabbath below.) There are several errors in this attitude.

(A) The Fourth Commandment states that we are to work for "six days." Now, that "work" does not necessarily mean working in our employment. In the work of the Kingdom of God, one person is usually called to several tasks or "works." (We have come to call these, "good works," for this reason.) Duties in the local or universal church is one area and central to the work of the Church and the Kingdom. Ministries of mercy and outreach are others. Many modern Christians and churches are lacking in their attention to these areas, believing and letting the state provide "welfare" to those in need.

Thus, there is a two-fold "work" here: (1) to work politically to remove <u>all</u> welfare from the function of local, state, and national governments and (2) to have Christians and churches move back into this area, using Biblical guidelines in their application. Welfare, blindly applied, is not what God intends, even from His people. For example, the Apostle Paul said, "If a man will not work, neither shall he eat" (II Thessalonians 3:10). See the other worldview areas of Economics, Government, and Justice.
Of Leisure, Good Works, and Rest

(B) The concept of recreation and leisure needs to be re-considered. The Fourth Commandment says to "work" for six days and to "rest" on the seventh. Where is the concept of leisure here or elsewhere in Scripture? Where is the concept of recreation? Jesus Christ was a carpenter before His earthly "career" began. The Apostle Paul was a tent-maker in his "spare time." In fact, Paul's "tent-making" has become a modern word that we use for someone who uses some skill to make money sufficient to support their evangelism or work in the church.

I fear that "leisure" has been substituted for "rest." We find this contrast illustrated in this passage.

> Come to Me, all *you* who labor and are heavy laden, and I will give you rest. Take My yoke upon you and learn from Me, for I am gentle and lowly in heart, and you will find rest for your souls. For My yoke *is* easy and My burden is light" (Matthew 11:28-30).

Jesus invites those who "labor," yet He invites them to "work" for Him, and then they will find "rest." Is this expression a paradox? Not at all. The problem exists within those who "labor" and are "heavy-laden," not their work per se. And, this labor is not only their "work" (their job to make money), but

31

everything that they do ("work at") on a daily basis. (It also includes their burden of sin, but our focus here is work and rest.)

God has prescribed that we rest one day in seven. Yet, Jesus is instructing us here to "rest" on an ongoing, everyday basis, even as we work in all the areas of good works. "Work out your own salvation with fear and trembling, for God is at work in you to will and to do His good pleasure" (Philippians 2:12-13).

The New Testament speaks of God's people doing "good works." The Westminster Confession of Faith has a whole chapter on "Good Works." That the word, "work" or "works," is used in these areas is not accidental. **Good works are all the tasks to which God calls us, not just where we work to earn money**. And, this fullness of "work" is the problem of American Christians. We have divorced the area where we make money from the (falsely) more important concept of "good works."

Everything that we do in life should be a good work for Jesus Christ and His Kingdom. Only when we see this fullness of our calling, can we turn our attention to remunerated work and leisure.

At a minimum, we are to perform all these good works for six days and rest the seventh. On a higher level, we are to work and rest every day. As a trained nouthetic counselor and church member for 40 years, I have observed hundreds of families in evangelical, strongly Bible-taught churches. With few exceptions, Christians' lives are chaotic! They are always in a rush. The noticeable fact that most arrive within minutes of the time that Sunday worship services start is symptomatic of every day life, for on Sundays their priority ought to be worship.

Another symptom is the amount of television that Christians watch, especially relative to the amount of time that they spend in serious devotion and study of God and His Word. And, to demonstrate how broadly damaging this "out-of-control" lifestyle reaches, consider the problems that hurriedness creates in parents' relationships with children, always hurrying them to brush their teeth, get to piano or soccer practice, get to the breakfast table, etc., etc.

Until this fragmentary, out-of-order priorities is addressed, there is really not much need to discuss career and leisure because the misunderstanding of these two concepts flows out of this larger misunderstanding. Have you, reader, ever heard a serious, detailed sermon or had a Sunday School class on time management, controlled by the priorities of God's Word? In this chaos of everyday life, a "quiet or devotional time" has become the "quickie" to salve the conscience of the guilt-ridden Christian who knows that they "ought" to study God's Word. But, curiously this "quickie" only further alienates their lives from the reality of Matthew 11:28-30, quoted above. See Time Management.

The Apostle Paul tells us "to work out our salvation (that is, our sanctification) with fear and trembling." But, he not only "preaches" this, he practiced it (I Corinthians 9:24-27). He speaks of running the race, which for an athlete requires hours, days, and years of practice to be able to compete. He "disciplines" his body and brings it into "subjection" in the pursuit of his calling before God. All this discipline is directed towards an "imperishable" crown, not that which is "perishable," gained by earthly competition. How many Christians make much more effort than a five-minute "devotional" hurriedly and with other things on their mind?

So, in light of all this discourse into work and rest, where does leisure fit? I believe that those decisions are for the individual to plan under the directives of all the good works to which God has called us. Leisure is not freedom from good works. By contrast, leisure should enhance our ability to perform good works. Leisure is not mindlessly watching the television for hours every day. Perhaps, it may be occasionally watched to relax. But, then, I would suggest other ways to relax.

Let me give an example from my own life. As you might expect of a writer-thinker, my mind races from the time that I get up until I go to bed at night. When I have my devotional time, I am also thinking, learning, and exploring ideas. But, I must turn that off when I go to bed, or I will continue those racing thoughts and not sleep. So, I read a novel for 30-45 minutes as the last thing that I do before getting ready for bed. My mind is engaged by the story and the characters, mythical ones that require little, if any reflection, and my mind begins to slow from its engagement of ideas. I usually get to sleep easily and sleep well.

I am not opposed to leisure. I am not opposed to television (although most lives would be much the better if it were removed from the home or at least placed in a small, out-of-the-way corner, rather than the central place [altar?] of the home). I am not opposed to technology per se. (See Technology Is A-Moral.) **My only admonition relative to leisure is that it conform to the concepts of work and rest in the above passages and the concept of vocation below.**

Vacation. What about the modern notion of vacation? For too many people, vacation is not a time of rest and relaxation. It is an arduous, expensive expedition that is more strenuous than every day work. This "free" time can be a time for families to play together or for people to study or work in areas that they do not usually have time to devote to these pursuits. Vacations should be planned under the directives that we have discussed, not as an opportunity to just "get away" from the drudgery of everyday life. Drudgery under the Lordship of Jesus Christ and His calling to good works should not be. We are to "enjoy Him forever," and that starts now!

Vocation: The Calling and Gifting of God

4. Vocation comes from the Latin, *vocatio*, meaning "calling." It should be clear from what has been said above that God's calling includes His calling us to all "good works," not just the manner in which we make money to provide for our needs and wants. Each person's calling includes his responsibilities in the family, church, and social responsibility.

However, in our day, **vocation is virtually synonymous with career and/or employment**, that is, calling to that means by which we produce income. In fact, in high school and college groups, the question, "What is God's will for your life?," is denotative of "What would God have your career to be?" Again, "God's will" is narrowly distorted and detracts from "His will" to good works. This focus on this one aspect of "God's will" or "career" is important, but aberrant in all that God calls us to do.

For example, God's calling of many women is to their being wives and mothers, as well as activities in their church and community for which they have no monetary income. However, these roles perform the highest value of work. There is great truth in the expression, "The hand that rocks the cradle, rules the world." Also, the role of a layman who is a ruling elder is just as important at that of a pastor or teaching elder. Or, a person may, as Paul did, have an occupation that provides his monetary needs while his primary activity is evangelism or works of mercy.

Many young people are distressed, even obsessed, over "God's will" for their lives (again, meaning their career). I do not want to diminish the importance of that decision, but I believe that it is been made a mountain, when it should be more of a molehill. I am going to use the word **vocation**, now, to designate "career" and "God's will" (as narrowly defined here).

Dorothy Sayers stated, "Work is not, primarily, a thing one does to live, but the thing one lives to do. It is, or should be, the full expression of the worker's faculties, the thing in which he finds spiritual, mental, and bodily satisfaction, and the medium in which he offers himself to God." (Dorothy Sayers, "Why Work," quoted in various of her compiled works.)

(A) To re-iterate, vocation is only one part of a much larger whole of good works. By placing vocation into that larger picture, the task diminishes in size. More importantly, **the larger picture of God's directives for the whole of His calling come into focus**. A great help to understand this larger picture is a study of The Kingdom of God.

(B) The division of "sacred" and "secular" must be bridged. There seems to be far more talk of this bridge, than actually exists. When have you ever been to a missions conference and seen a booth or table on vocations other than being a missionary? When a person says that they want to "serve God full-time," when are they directed to be an architect, a scientist, carpenter, or tent-maker (in the modern sense of building houses)? **In God's economy, no one task is more important than another**. For example, how would the missionary get to the mission field without a ship or airplane? Where would the pastor in American live, if someone did not build his house? Then, there are food, utilities, and public works (including sewage, to get "down and dirty").

(C) The difference between talents and spiritual gifts should be discerned. There is a distinction between The Church and The Kingdom of God. Spiritual gifts are for the building up of the Body of Christ, The Church (Ephesians 4:7-16, I Corinthians, etc.). Talents are for benefit of all mankind. I admit that everyone might not agree with these designations, for all skills ultimately come from the Spirit of God. However, the Bible is clear that special gifts are given for the building up of The Church. So, somehow they must be distinguished from those that serve mankind in general and not The Church per se. I choose "talents" and "spiritual gifts." Others may choose some other designations.

(D) The number of variables in choosing a career is perhaps more narrow than might appear at first glance. As was once presented to me, choosing a career involves talents, spiritual gifts, and opportunities. By the time that one reaches his late teens, he is already aware of his abilities, likes, and dislikes. Choosing a career is simply matching these areas with occupations.

Truly, the man or woman who has an income-producing occupation, that he or she enjoys, is specially blessed of God. I believe that this situation

35

should occur more than it does with wise counsel and guidance of young people. **Parents should be careful not to discourage their children's desires**. Parents, even Christian parents, often try to influence children away from what a career that they want for reasons of social "status," low salary, or other reasons. While this influence is a parental responsibility they should be careful that they are **basing their directions on Biblical values**, not their own personal desires.

A Jewish and early Christian tradition, or even law, was to train all one's children in some skill or trade. Thus, in the future these children would be able to produce income for their family should their primary "career" never be achieved or should it fail. The Bible is clear that a man is responsible for the "provisions" of his family and is condemned as "worse than an infidel" (I Timothy 5:8), if he does not.

(E) People change over the course of their lives, and this change may cause a career change. Early in my life, my interests and skills were heavily skewed towards mathematics and the sciences. Because of that tendency, I became a physician. But, in a medical college where one's tenure depended upon the dictum to "publish or perish" (to publish articles in professional literature or leave academia), I was virtually forced to write. Eventually, writing became my passion, including the study that is necessarily precedes it. A unique book traces how these changes occur over one's lifetime. (See Vaillant below.) Are such changes not to be expected with the dramatic change of regeneration, when it occurs in early adulthood or later? Similarly, progressive sanctification is likely to change one's interests and abilities, as gifts or talents.

(F) The consideration of specific vocations is beyond our scope here. However, some references have been provided below.

(G) Christians need to evaluate their affluence for the advancement of The Kingdom of God. While attention to this area falls more under the area of economics, it does have a considerable bearing on vocation and leisure. **The large majority of Christians in the United States are monetarily rich by almost any measure**. The question is, then, "Are we using that wealth, under God's directives (commandments) to advance His Kingdom. I believe that Americans will have much to answer for in the Final Judgment for their use of their prosperity. The Lord Jesus Christ has given quite specific instructions about what He will be looking for in that day: clothing, food, water, housing, and care of the sick and imprisoned.

Some Christians have defended government-sponsored welfare programs as Biblical charity, but surely this position is as serious, ethically, as heresy is about the centrality of Christ in salvation! **Biblical charity is always voluntary, but government welfare requires taking money by force (at the point of a gun, literally) and re-distributing it under pagan values at a greatly diminished value, after being filtered through the costs of a huge bureaucracy!** (Again, see references on this website cited above.)

Through both vocation and leisure, Christians must begin to provide Biblical charity locally and worldwide. **Perhaps, the greatest step to achieving this goal is simply to teach what the Bible says about charity and works of mercy**.

This directive is not meant to take us back to monasticism, a denial of possessions and pursuits that pursues some higher, holy plane. And, it is not a directive to point our fingers at others in their failures. It is a belief that many American Christians are not Biblically responsible with the stewardship of their time and possessions, and a call back to that responsibility.

(H) We should not make an idol or either our work or leisure. The "Protestant work ethic" was not, and has never been, a call to being a workaholic. The Reformation in general, and the Puritans, in particular redirected believers to "vocation," work as a calling of God in all the areas that we have discussed above. Interestingly, the concept of workaholism being greatly productive is mostly a myth. Social studies show that most successful businessmen have a mostly balanced life that includes time for family, church, and social interests.

And, we should not make an idol of our leisure. Any pursuit that begins to demand a consuming focus that crowds out other good works (above) in both time and money has likely become an idol. Many Americans have a money-producing occupation that is solely to pay for another pursuit of possession or achievement. They should consider whether this activity is an idol.

(I) All this balance of vocation, good works, and leisure is an highly individualized consideration. But, before God, His Scriptures, sound teaching (of sermons, lectures, and writings), and Godly counsel, we all need periodically to re-evaluate our commitments. Being the self-centered and finite beings that we are, there is always room for improvement.

(J) All that I have said here should not be construed as a heavy load of Phariseeism. The answer of the Shorter Catechism of the Westminster Confession of Faith is that "The chief end of man is to glorify God and enjoy

Him forever." God wants all of our lives to be enjoyable under His Lordship. My only contention here is that we are all too often seeking enjoyment in many of the wrong places. The "yoke" of His commandments, when they are followed in His ways, will be found to be "easy and light." Otherwise, we will "labor" and b be "heavy laden."

John Piper has brought some balance to this situation with his "Christian hedonism." While "hedonism" perhaps denotes too much identity with excess, it does portray the serious call of God, as one with great benefits of enjoyment and happiness, rather than the dour portrayal by some pastors and teachers.

(K) The concepts of vocation, talents and gifts, and rest are central here. The idea of "work" connotes drudgery. Vocation or calling denotes purpose in activity. Talents and gifts are usually enjoyable for they are our strengths. **What could be more exciting and fulfilling than purpose in the application of our talents and gifts?** Would not we need less "recreation," as fulfilled purpose has great rewards in itself? Would we not be able to work longer and harder at what we enjoy? **And, if we ordered our lives in these pursuits to obtain needed rest, what harmony, productivity, and worship would we enjoy? And, most importantly, what would be our worship of God for ordering these things?**

5. Historical note.

> It was the Roman Catholic misconception of vocation that prepared the way for the gradual inroads of modern secularism upon the Christian view of work. In the Middle Ages and throughout the centuries, Rome limited the idea of vocation only to the priestly class. By placing the monk in a special life of isolation and rigorous self-discipline, monastic Christianity also limited the meaning of "vocation." Even today the Catholic Encyclopedia restricts the term "vocation" to priests, monks, and nuns, while the Jesuit abbreviation S.J. (Society of Jesus) suggest that one cannot fully follow Jesus outside the priesthood. In other words, Catholicism regards only the priestly class, and not the laity, as being in the service of God. (Carl F. H. Henry, *God and Culture*, "The Christian View of Work"..., page 36.)

As we have seen above, modern Protestantism has mostly lost this correction that occurred with the Reformation and the Puritans.

6. Freedom in vocation. The Christian has great freedom to choose among almost any profession or skilled work. Those forbidden are those that involve immorality in which a Christian should not be engaged for any reason. That is the beauty of "vocation." Christian young people do not have to be in a dither about "higher" callings. All the work of God's Kingdom are available to them within the parameters that are described above.

7. Retirement. Retirement is a modern concept that at the end of one's primary means of producing income, a person is free to do whatever he wants, usually what he has always wanted to do, but never had the time. It is an unbiblical notion because one never "retires" from God's Work or Good Works. However, such "retirement" can be a great opportunity for one to be more fully engaged in "good works" to advance the The Kingdom of God.

References

Articles and sermons on a scriptural basis for joy and happiness in the Christian life. http://www.desiringgod.org/

Revising the Concept of Vocation for the Industrial Age. http://www.religion-online.org/showarticle.asp?title=212

Work and creativity by one of Francis Schaeffer's disciples. http://thirdmill.org/newfiles/udo_middelman/udo_middelman.work.html

Martin Clark. *Choosing Your Career: The Christian Decision Manual.* (Phillipsburg, PA: Presbyterian and Reformed, 1981).

Carl F. H. Henry. *Aspects of Christian Social Ethics.* (Grand Rapids: Baker Book House, 1964).

Ralph T. Mattson and Arthur F. Miller, Jr. *Finding a Job You Can Love.* (Phillipsburg, PA: Presbyterian and Reformed, 1982).

Doug Sherman and William Hendricks. *Your Work Matters to God.* (Colorado Springs: NavPress, 1987.

George Vaillant. *Adaptation to Life.* (Boston: Little, Brown, and Company, 1977). A unique study of college students who were followed over a period of 30 years after their graduation from college. It demonstrates what actually happens to people, not what we think and speculate what happens to people

4. Psychology, Counseling, and Emotions

Addiction As a Besetting Sin

Addictive disorders and alcoholism cost $165 billion a year in the United States alone![1] The addict screams, "I can't help myself! I'm addicted." In response, "experts"[2] and society feel compassion with ever increasing programs for them.

However, I want to substitute "besetting sin" for "addiction." The primary problem is moral and spiritual,[3] not medical, and cannot be addressed without that perspective.

What is Addiction?

"Addiction" is a slippery term (as are most psychological labels). From my own observation, a definition of addiction should be divided at three levels. First, there are the strict and detailed definitions that careful professionals use.[4] Second, there is the careless use among professionals. Third, there is the use of the word in popular literature and less formal discourse.

The first level is the *Diagnostic and Statistical Manual of Mental Disorders (Third Edition -Revised) (DSM-III-R)*. While "addiction" is not named as a diagnosis there, Psychoactive Substance Use Disorder (PSUD) and related terms are. An introductory sentence from that section of the DSM-III-R serves as a definition of PSUD at this first level.

"This diagnostic class deals with symptoms and maladaptive behavioral changes associated with more or less regular use of psychoactive substances that affect the central nervous system. Almost invariably, people who have a PSUD will also have Intoxication or Withdrawal."[5]

The second level involves the careless use of addiction among professionals. Likely, most readers have never seen such a classification. However, it is quite real among physicians and psychologists,[6] and most other professions as well. This practice is a failure to use any formal definition in exchanges among professionals.

For example, I have yet to see any patient's chart with the diagnosis of "depression" with reference to criteria that would fit any formal definition, such as *the DSM-III-R*. Yet, millions of patients carry this label and receive

40

potent medications based upon this slipshod approach. Both the label and the medications have great potential for harm, as well as good. Further, such imprecision applies to virtually every area of medicine, not just psychiatric diagnoses. (A discussion of this "mal-practice," however, would require another paper in itself.)

An example, relative to addiction, is "sexual addiction." What is meant is a repetitive, compulsive sexual activity, such as nymphomania or the viewing of pornographic materials. If the *DSMIII-R* is any standard at all, the application of "addiction" to sexual activities is careless and certainly not "scientific."

The third level is the "popular use" of addiction and only reflects the careless use among "professionals." However, as would be expected, any connection to a precise definition is even more distant. Gambling, shoplifting, overeating, excessive TV viewing, and other habitual behaviors become "addictions."

Curiously, this careless professional and popular distortion of addiction finds its way into Christian literature. One example is found in a text on "Biblical and Christian ethics."

"An addiction is an exaggerated and pathological dependency of one human being upon another person, institution, substance, activity, or even series or pattern of interior mood states or thought patterns.... Potential addiction agents include food (compulsive overeating and other eating disorders); activity, achievement (workaholism), rigid performance standards (perfectionism), the emphasis on form rather than substance in spiritual matters (religiosity, religious legalism), or spiritual addiction; erotic fantasy and arousal (sexual addiction); money (compulsive spending, hoarding, or shopping); and interpersonal relationships (codependent relationship roles of victim, victimizer, and/or rescuer)."[7]

From such broad generalizations by this psychologist, the blurring between the careless use of addiction by professionals and its popular use is complete.

Using these liberal criteria, in the United States there are estimates of 20 million alcoholics, 80 million coalcoholics, 20 million addicted gamblers, 50 million addicted to eating too much (overweight) and 30 million to eating too little (anorexics and bulimics), 75 million addicted to tobacco, and 25 million addicted to "love and/or sex."[8] The matter of definition and treatment is no small matter!

Pleasure as a Dimension of Addiction

Curiously, any reference to pleasure in addiction is not found in the DSM-III-R or in the Christian Textbook's definition (above) either. However, I want to add that element, because it is an important dimension of addiction. For simplicity, I will use pleasure quite broadly to include a range of emotions, such as enjoyment, excitement, euphoria, elation, contentment, and satisfaction.

Pleasure may become accompanied by feelings that have more to do with comfort or security over time. Because an addict is agitated when he is separated from his addiction, the addiction becomes a relief from this agitation. In many instances, this relief (comfort or security) becomes the primary driving force of his addiction.

For example, a workaholic may initially get a great deal of pleasure from his work, but over time it becomes a burden. However, he is far more comfortable (or finds his security) in his familiar work patterns. With the drug "addict," there is no doubt that pleasure is the primary motivation for beginning that behavior. Over time, the "addiction" becomes a heavy, destructive burden. However, even here, pleasure remains a strong motivating influence, not just the compulsion and physical need for the drug(s).

Addiction as Primarily Involving Sin

There has been a great deal of debate among American evangelicals concerning whether addiction is disease or sin. Perhaps the debate could be divided into two categories according to the presence or absence of drugs. There is little or no debate that cocaine abuse or even cigarette smoking create a physical dependency. By contrast, a compulsive gambler has no physical dependency, only a mental craving.

However, in spite of this distinction, I want to keep all addicts in one category. First, many "professionals" (as documented above) do so. Second, the mental drive (as pleasure and/or comfort - see below) to an addiction far exceeds the physical drive. Thus, such compulsive behavior is better labeled "besetting sin," rather than addiction.

Besetting Sin

"Besetting sin" was common parlance in evangelical circles for several centuries until the last few decades. The concept derives from Hebrews 12:1

where this word makes its only appearance in the New Testament. "Therefore let us also, seeing we are compassed about with so great a cloud of witnesses, lay aside every weight, and the sin which doth so easily beset us, and let us run with patience the race that is set before us

Thomas Hewitt argues for besetting sin as one that "clings so closely ... to some ... who, failing to break from it, were still at the starting-post of the Christian life."[9] E.K. Simpson writes that besetting can "be used in a pejorative acceptation of a state of beleagurement, or exigencies and straits ... like ... a "squeeze.'"[10]

John Calvin Writes of Besetting Sin.

"This is the heaviest burden that impedes us. ... He (the writer of Hebrews) speaks not of outward, or, as they say, of actual sins, but of the very fountain, even concupiescence or lust, which so possesses every part of us, that we feel that we are on every side held by its snares."[11]

John Owen devotes three paragraphs to "besetting" in his Annotations to Calvin's commentary on Hebrews." [12] He concludes in this way: "The (Greek) word euperistaton means literally, 'well-standing around' ... or 'the readily surrounding sin,' that is the sin which easily surrounds us, and thereby entangles us, so as to prevent us, like long garments, to run our courses. ... If the word be taken in an active sense, then what is meant is the deceptive power of sin....

Noah Webster in his 1828 dictionary defines "beset" as "1) to surround; to inclose; to hem in; to besiege ...; 2) to press on all sides, so as to perplex; to entangle, so as to render escape difficult or impossible."[13] As an adjective, he defines "besetting" as "habitually attending."

In this way, Webster links "beset" to "addict" which is "to apply oneself habitually, to devote time and attention by customary practice more usually in a bad sense, to follow customarily, or devote, by habitually practicing that which is ill, as a man addicted to intemperance."[14]

What Difference Does a Label (Diagnosis) Make?

The cause of a problem virtually determines its solution. In medicine, the diagnosis determines the treatment. A physician does not give a heart medicine to a patient with a bacterial pneumonia who needs an antibiotic. In engineering, the cause of a bridge's collapse determines what is needed to prevent another collapse. Increased strength of materials will not give greater durability to a bridge with a foundation in soft earth.

The problem with addictions is primarily their mental component. By "mental," I mean moral or spiritual. My brief argument for this position is three-fold. First, physical dependence cannot be the primary determinant of addiction. Simply, some people addicted to the same drugs at the same dosage are able to quit while others cannot. The explanation cannot be physical, that is, purely biochemical since the biochemical situations (including genetic factors[15]) are virtually the same.

Second, addiction has been applied far beyond physical dependence on drugs, as we have seen. As described above, this extension has been almost careless.[16]

Third, the Bible clearly labels one form of addiction, drunkenness, as a sin (Proverbs 20:1; 23:29-35; Ephesians 5:18; 1 Peter 4:4). In certain passages, e.g., I Corinthians 6-9-10, drunkenness is listed among other grievous sins that can be conquered ("and such were some of you," v. 11). This passage argues strongly that God does not consider the physical dependence of one sin (drunkenness) an excuse for one s indulgence.[17] The passage argues, but much less strongly, for such passages being lists of addictions, especially in the common parlance of today.

A Definition and a Wrap-Up

In light of the above, I want to suggest a new definition for addiction. **"Addiction is a repetitive, pleasure-seeking behavior that is habitual in spite of moral or physical reasons (i.e., harm) that should rationally preclude its practice and that displaces spiritual obligations."**

Further, I want to suggest that "besetting sin" be a synonym for addiction. Jay Adams uses the term "life-dominating"[18] which is a good, descriptive synonym also. Besetting sin, however, links the modern craze to label so many behaviors as addiction with a biblical text and with past centuries. This link prevents modern psychological labels from overshadowing the reality that these repetitive patterns are sin.

First, besetting sin reveals that these sins are not new. While some particulars may be new or more prevalent (drug abuse, anorexia, etc.), their life-dominating, irresponsible patterns are not.

Second, solutions to the problems of addictions as besetting sins point to regeneration and obedience to biblical teaching rather than a psychological and/or medical approach. As a physician, I realize that physical dependence on alcohol and drugs is a real phenomenon. Further, withdrawal from some of these substances can be severe, even deadly. However, apart from the immediate withdrawal period, the mental (spiritual) craving far exceeds the physical craving.

My purpose here is not to outline a plan to manage these life-dominating problems. In changing the label of "addictions" to "besetting sins" both the counselor and physician would focus on the primary dimension of the problem. What is needed is a whole-life, comprehensive approach to the "addict's" spiritual life, as Dr. Jay Adams has directed (above). The medical and psychological models of such besetting sins are designed for failure because they do not deal with the great spiritual need in these people. Perhaps this paper will generate further discussion and implementation of a more thoroughly biblical approach.

The following thoughts came to mind after the primary article on Addiction As Besetting Sin was written. That primary article needs to be read to place the following in context.

Jay Adams addresses the "life-dominating problem" in the Christian Counselor's Manual. The person's focus in his "problem," but he has many areas to address which include responsibilities to his work, spouse, family, physical health, church, etc. (Adams names some 15-20). This broader focus is important in two ways. 1) The person has a total, and comprehensive responsibility before God. 2) Other physical and mental activities take his mind off his "problem" so that he doe not have to manage his "problem" constantly in his mind.

As we discussed this morning, words are important. I disagree with Alcoholics Anonymous that one should say, "I am an alcoholic" or "I am a drug addict." One has recognized the severity of his own problem when he is willing to seek help. That is sufficient for recovery (sanctification).

Rather, he or she should say that I am a child of the Great King, and He is my Lord and Savior. Now, I realize that may be difficult for an "addict" (I only use the word here for brevity's sake) to say, because of his true guilt and guilt feelings. But, herein is the most important issue, that person's theology. Does he understand Romans 8:1 and Psalm 103:12 to the extent that he can apply it in his own life, primarily his own mind (Philippians 4:8)? This understanding may be the most crucial item to move away from that "addiction."

To point the way to getting beyond a besetting sin (perhaps, I should use BS and PBS -- person with besetting sin!) is not to say that I do not recognize the truly life-dominating difficulty of the problem itself. But, like the surgeon, great skill is needed with words, as with a scalpel. (I never thought of that illustration before! Helpful!) Leaving some of the tumor causes great harm in the future. Perhaps, the PBS needs to be more precise with words than the theologian. For the latter, he is detached from his thinking, writing, and speaking. But, the PBS is trying to build his house... what a firm and precise foundation he needs.

I would differ with one quote in my paper from Hewitt. As we discussed this morning, some people with PBS are not at the "starting point" of the Christian life. Many are far down the road in maturity in other ways.

Well, those are some additional thoughts. PBS is a problem that the Church, including nouthetic counselors, has not adequately addressed (probably because of the serious commitment that such a program would require). And, this failure has probably allowed the continued validity of psychology and psychiatry beyond its legitimacy.

A Definition of Emotions

Emotions' are central to a modem understanding of man (anthropology). "Emotional problems" are common topics of Christian publications and conferences. Christian physicians in many specialties speak often of patients' emotional disorders. Psychologists and psychiatrists who are Christians have proliferated over the past 20 years to manage these problems. Sometimes, these problems are labeled as distinctions between the "heart" and the "head". With all this focus on emotions a correct understanding of them is a major issue of our day.[19]

Few who write and speak in this area seem open to considerations other than their own. The following may be not more than an exercise in futility. Often, I have only cited one source where I could have cited several.[20] I have discussed only briefly "heavy" areas of theology and philosophy that do not satisfy me and are not likely to satisfy anyone else. They are introduced for the completeness of my argument, as well as to demonstrate that my definition is consistent with these areas.

Nevertheless, I am not aware that anyone else has addressed emotions in quite the same way. There seem to be great ramifications for one's faith, if I am correct.

My thinking was triggered by statements from J. Gresham Machen in *Christianity and Liberalism*.

> *Pure feeling, if there be such a thing, is non-moral . . .*
> (p. 54).

> *Human affection, apparently so simple, is really just brimming with dogma. It depends upon a host of observations treasured up in the mind with regard to the character of our friends . . .. human affection is thus really dependent upon knowledge . . . . the knowledge of God is the very basis of religion*
> (p. 54, my emphasis) .

> *. . . the human mind has a wonderful faculty for the condensation of perfectly valid arguments, and what seems like an instinctive belief may turn out to be the result of many logical steps.* (p. 57).

Where should one start? Emotions are at the core of man's being. Indeed, some "experts" would make them the most central and determining of our attitudes, personality and behavior. The subject of emotions is complex. In fact, as with any subject where truth is pursued, all definitions and descriptions are necessarily determined by one's first principles or assumptions. For Christians, the necessary starting point is Scripture.

Starting Point: Biblical Anthropology

Are emotions physical or spiritual? That is, are they caused by physical substances within the body (hormones, nerves, etc.) or something in the nonmaterial dimension of man that may be called spirit, soul, heart or mind. (see below).

I shall try to skirt the periphery of dichotomy and trichotomy.[21] The central issue for emotions here is the location of the mind. Dichotomists simply divide man into body and soul or in Greek New Testament terms, soma and psyche.

Spirit, (pneuma), and heart, (kardia), also identify the same nonmaterial dimension of man.

> *A spirit is a person without a body. So, as the word soul (in one way or another) always depicts the non-material aspect of human nature in relationship to (or in unity with) the material, so the word spirit always refers to the same non-material aspect out of relationship to (or disunited from) the material* (italics in original).[22]

Thus, the dichotomist has no difficulty placing the mind within the nonmaterial dimension and knows that it may be identified by spirit, soul or heart.

The trichotomist, however, divides the non-material dimension of man into soul and spirit. Thus, man becomes body, soul and spirit. Most, if not all, trichotomists would place the mind in the soul. Biblically, this step seems logical since psyche is translated soul and, etymologically, psyche designates the mind. Most, if not all, trichotomists would place the mind, then, in the non-material dimension. [23] Thus, to proceed on the basis that both dichotomists and trichotomists believe the mind to be within the non-material component of man seems reasonable.[24] The following argument has to do with the relation of the emotions to either the physical or the non-physical. If I am allowed to use these two categories apart from the arguments of dichotomy and trichotomy, then the following can be consistent with either position.

A Definition

Authors who write about emotions rarely define what an emotion is. That omission is curious and perhaps one reason for so much confusion in this area. Dictionaries do not help much either, because they usually include words such as "feeling," "affect," and "subjective" that are too closely identified with "emotion" itself to offer a concrete understanding.

The history of the English word, "emotion," however, does have some correspondence to my argument that follows. *The Oxford Dictionary* gives the meaning of the Latin root as the adjective "of action." Its French origin means "to move out." Definitions 1, 2 and 3 are listed as obsolete. The fourth definition is "Any agitation or disturbance of mind, feeling, passion; any vehement or excited mental state." Of importance here is "disturbance of mind."[25]

My definition of an emotion, then, is the momentary (acute) and ongoing (chronic, continuous) disturbance within the mind (soul, spirit) caused by the discrepancy between perceived reality and one's desires. Emotions are momentary in that immediate circumstances trigger various emotions. For example, a person may catch his finger in a door and react with a degree of anger. He may say inaudibly, "Ouch". Or, he may react violently and jerk the door off the hinges!

An important factor in his momentary reaction is his ongoing (chronic) state of mind ("mood"). If he is "on edge," that is under a great deal of stress, then a more vigorous response is likely to occur. If he is quite happy and peaceful, then he may respond more quietly. Many other reactions are possible, depending upon one's state of mind. For example, imagine the responses of persons in these situations: the person who is severely bereaved over personal loss, the fireman rushing to rescue people in a burning house, and the young woman who has just become engaged. Also, a quick-tempered personality will react more vigorously that a staid one.

Thus, my definition begins with the totality of situations that are disturbing a person at any given point in time. Some are "momentary" (acute) and others are "ongoing" (chronic). There is much "ongoing" with any individual at a "given point in time." In fact, to some degree all past and current experiences, as well as future hopes, affect a person's acute and chronic state of mind.

We will pass over discrepancy for the present, as its explanation depends upon an understanding of desires.

An analogy may help to describe the effect of life experiences remote in our memory upon current events. Many colors and shapes may blend to form the less saturated, indistinct background in our painting of a landscape, atop which the brighter, sharper foreground figures constitute the chief theme of the picture. There need be no recollection of the specific colors which blended in the background, yet they influence the tone of the painting. So it is with past memories that, unuttered and inchoate, nevertheless influence our present perceptions and actions.

Skilled interviewers, psychological and otherwise, may be able to discern certain of the background features that are imparting disruptive feelings into current scenes. Unfortunately, nearly all such researchers (especially psychologists and psychiatrists), make the error of asserting much more than anyone could know about these past events and attribute too much power to them. The "analyzed" person is essentially viewed as a victim of her personal history. A spiritual organ known as an "unconscious mind" or the "subconscious" has been created by these professionals and elaborated so winsomely, that our whole generation believes this representation to be a fact of science rather than the fanciful creation that it is. This invented dynamic of the subconscious, a neat system of diagnosis, and allusions to the enormous power of this entity living within each person are utilized to account for our motivation and emotions at the expense of conscious, responsible processes.

The point is that, while no one is able to remember everything that he has learned or all past life experiences that have an influence upon his present feelings, no one can go beyond what is consciously accessible for explanations or remedies of the human spirit. To do so is to infringe upon what God reserves for Himself alone (I Cor. 2:11, Jer. 17:9, 10).

Desires are more complex than may be recognized at first glance. (Also, see the section on desires that follows.) Desires encompass all those things in life that we hope for, a vast array ranging from the trivial to the profound. For example, I may desire not only ice cream, but a double scoop of butter pecan from Buskin Robbins. Or, I may desire to become an overseas missionary.

A discrepancy in my desire and its fulfillment may occur with either situation. The Buskin Robbins store may be closed when I get there or I may be in a strange city and not be able to find one. With missionary service, I may not be able (for several reasons) to get the college degree for the desired area of service or some problem with my health may fall short of the requirements of the mission board.

The emotions that result can vary from the trivial to the profound, as well. When I cannot get my ice cream, I may shrug it off and settle for a Coca-Cola (Classic, of course!). Or, I may get angry and say things that I should not. When I cannot do the missionary work that I may want, I simply may look for other opportunities. Or, I may get depressed to the extent that I consider suicide. To reiterate, my emotions will depend upon my acute and chronic state of mind, as well as my personality. If my "mental life" is mostly content, then mild emotions will result. If I am under great stress or have a violent temper, then my emotions will be considerably different.

Perceived reality indicates reality as the individual sees it. "True" reality may he different, but a person reacts according to his interpretation of reality until someone or something corrects his distortion. For example, parents who wait up late at night for a teenager to come home conjure up more dire circumstances as the hour gets later. Emotions are triggered proportional to the

50

severity of those circumstances. When the teenager walks in whole and healthy, however, perceived reality changes and other emotions/actions are triggered. (Like, "Where have you been all this time?")

Emotions, then, are the disturbance caused by the comparison and contrast (discrepancy) of desires with perceived reality. The degree of disturbance depends upon one's acute and chronic state of mind (both conscious and subconscious), a reflection of all one's knowledge and life experience, as well as hopes for the future. (Other factors in the degree of disturbance will be discussed under "Practical Application").

The point is that emotions are caused by thinking. Comparison and contrast (determining discrepancy) is a rational process of the mind. It may be done momentarily or it may be influenced by many years of extensive "background painting." That is, the sum of years of specific, conscious thoughts (all that is in one's past experience) may not be deliberated upon in the experience of the moment (the "foreground"). Multiple comparisons and contrasts are going on at the same time. Thus, the sorting of all these processes at a given point in time can be complex.

I suspect that this complexity is the reason that emotions have been made into a category of its own and that "professional" research and "therapy" seem necessary. With my definition, however, what is needed for emotional control is an understanding of the discrepancies between perceived reality and desires. Then, faulty understanding can be corrected by Biblical truth (see "Practical Application").

We will now review further support for my definition and its consistency with other factors.

Do Emotions Originate Within the Physical?

Emotions seem to arise from the physical body, not just within the spirit where thinking occurs. First, we must separate those sensations that are clearly physical and those that may or may not be. To have pain from a pin-stick, to smell a rotten egg, to taste a bitter lemon, to see a blazing sunset, to hear a thunderclap, and a variety of other senses clearly come from stimulation of the skin or other sense organs. While such sensations are deep philosophical issues,[26] these sensations are commonly regarded as phenomena caused by a disturbance of the physical body. We should, however, distinguish them from the following effects.

Fatigue, fever, pre-menstrual syndrome (PMS), and other bodily states influence a person. But - are they feelings? Many times late in the evening, I have been discouraged, pessimistic, and confused over some issues) of life. The next morning (especially after a cup of coffee), I wonder what all the negativity was about. The "facts" have not changed, but my mind and my body have had a night's rest. Fever with its associated headaches and muscle aches incapacitate almost every person with it. When I have one, I only want to lie still and take whatever seems necessary to make me feel better. Premenstrual syndrome causes many women to feel irritable, tired and depressed along with other sensations. Physically, they are experiencing the dramatic changes in hormones that occur just prior to their menstrual periods.

These physical states are intertwined with the spiritual, as well. While I have a fever, there are often many responsibilities that I am able to accomplish. I don't have to be "cranky" and thoughtless of others. I can do "light" office work. I can write letters. And so on. If, however, I choose to do nothing, such work piles up and increases the burden of the work that I will have to "catch up on" when I get well. In addition, guilt may be present for my failures, causing me to feel worse and probably accomplish even less. A spiral downward then occurs.

Thus, physical states may limit some activities and responsibilities, but such states can also be an excuse to avoid our duties. In this way, a discrepancy between perceived reality and desires has been introduced, caused by a physical state.

On the one hand the separation of the spiritual and physical component may seem difficult. On the other hand, as you experience these physical states, you are mostly aware of those areas for which you should assume responsibility. You may complain and excuse yourself and others may do the same for you, but you know where you have failed.

"Sensation" is best used to describe these bodily states. True, sensation and feeling are dictionary-approved synonyms. Nevertheless the spiritual and physical components of such effects must be delineated as clearly as possible. Physical problems need the help of a physician. Spiritual problems need spiritual help (counseling, prayer, Bible study, Holy Communion, etc.). True, one may affect the other, as we have seen. Nevertheless, accurate diagnosis is always necessary to cure "disease" of the body, spirit or both.

Is There Another Dimension for the Emotions? The Heart?

I have argued above that emotions are disturbances of thinking and not physical states. Could there be another dimension where emotions arise? Biblically, this question is critical, not only for my argument, but for those who would disagree with me. The issue is responsibility. The Bible is clear that God holds all people accountable for their thoughts (Romans 12:3b; James 1:7-8), speech (James 3:512)[27] and behavior (Matthew 25: 31-46; II Corinthians 5:10). If emotions lie outside these areas, then we are not accountable to God for them. There is no greater issue than our accountability before God. That is why a definition of emotions is so important.

Frequently, Christians choose the "heart" as the seat of the emotions. Usually, when heart is chosen, it is contrasted with "head." That is, the heart is the seat of the emotions and the head is the rational mind. Many evangelists preach that salvation is a process of the heart (and thus an emotional response). They even go so far as to caution against following one's mind, rather than one's heart. Some have said that many people will miss heaven by twelve inches, the distance between their heads (minds) and their hearts ("emotions")!

Certainly, references to the heart and mind are prevalent throughout Scripture. Any distinction between the two, however, is not entirely clear.[28] Heart is used often in both the Old and the New Testament to refer to processes that clearly involve the mind, the intellect, the understanding, and the will (Genesis 6:5, 17:17; Exodus 7:3, 35:5, II Samuel 7:3, Psalm 4:4; Isaiah 6:10; Matthew 5:28, 9:4; Acts 7:23; Romans 1:21; I Corinthians 2:9). Several hundred similar verses could be listed, as well.

In some instances the heart does refer to the emotions (I Samuel 11:1; Acts 2:37, 2:46; Romans 9:2). You should note, however, that 1) such uses are far less common that those that refer to the mind and will and 2) such tees are compatible with my definition. That is, the disturbance within the person is caused by a comparison or contrast between what is desired and perceived reality.

In summary, a Biblical understanding of heart is "the non-material (nonphysical) side of man in contrast to his material side (usually with an emphasis upon the visibility of the latter and the invisibility of the former)."[29]

Again, I have abbreviated this discussion. Mere length of argument however will convince no one. For those whose minds are still open on this subject, the idea that the common evangelical distinction between heart and head may not be biblical has been introduced. These readers can further investigate other relevant Biblical texts and theological references to clarify this distinction (cited above).

Today, Christians must realize the prevalent influence of psychological theory. There is good evidence that all the emphasis on the emotions is a modem phenomenon due to such theory. Historically, philosophical and theological debates about man's mind centered upon the contribution of rational thought vs. that of the will to decision-making. That is, is the will stronger than the mind to over-ride what reason indicates is preferable, or does the mind convince the will? Emotions and "heart" came to be introduced with modern psychological theory in the 19th century.

Some Christians point to Jonathan Edwards' focus on "affections" *A Treatise Concerning Religious Affections* as an example where a great theologian discussed the role of the emotions.[30] Careful reading of his words, however, indicate that for Edwards affection was synonymous with "will". He was not referring to emotions at all, but continuing the same centuries-old debate. The same can be said of the use of "affection" by John Calvin and others.[31]

Are those who distinguish between the head and the heart consistent? It is apparent that they are not. Evangelists who preach to people's hearts, use words to communicate. Words communicate between the mind of the speaker and the mind of the hearer. Although his message is erroneous, he is still trying to influence the hearers' minds.[32] Even a decision to follow their hearts (if that were possible) would be decision first made with their minds.

The same holds for those psychologists and psychiatrists who treat people's emotions. What do they do? They talk to their patients (clients, counselees).[33] That is, they communicate from their own minds to their patients' minds with words. These "therapists" may say that they are "healing the emotions," but what they are doing is first convincing the minds of their patients and the emotions are changed secondarily.

"Mental Illness"

The real battleground lies with "mental illness." We should first realize, however, that this term is quite nebulous and useless. While I am coming to what are likely true disorders of the brain, the looseness of this term must be understood. For example, the patient with senile dementia (brain cells die or function poorly) becomes easily confused, forgetful, and inappropriate in his behavior. By contrast, the couple who goes for marriage counseling has

54

nothing wrong with their brains. Yet, they often go to psychiatrists who are trained to treat "mental illness."

This area is indeed a large one that cannot be addressed here. Nevertheless, precise distinctions within this area are almost entirely neglected by Christians from virtually all psychological and spiritual persuasions. Yet, such endeavors are crucial. If people are physically (that is, bio-chemically or structurally) diseased, then they need medical treatment. If they are not so diseased, then they need spiritual counseling. (Some may need civil or criminal prosecution.)

The question arises, "Does true organic disease of the brain cause some diagnoses that could be classified as mental (brain) illness?" Probably, some do exist. Many characteristics of schizophrenia favor an organic etiology, although a specific biochemical disorder has not been proven.[34] Likewise, a biochemical basis for all "mental illnesses" has not been proven.[35]

Whether or not such biochemical deficits do occur, however, does not necessarily affect my argument. First, schizophrenia, bipolar disorder, and other major psychiatric illnesses have definitive patterns. These are not classified as "emotional problems," the subject of our concern.

Second, these definitive problems are mostly in the small minority among problems that concern people today. The millions of patients on "mild tranquilizers" (for example, Valium TM) would hardly be classified as having major psychiatric illnesses. Neither would the millions who have phobias, are hostile or obsessive-compulsive, and have other neuroses.' So, for the large majority of "emotional problems," even mainstream professionals would not classify these problems as organic in origin.

Enough agreement seems to exist about these more common conditions of people who are sad, worried, or angry to discuss the application of my theory and who clearly do not have a physical basis for their emotional condition.

A Biblical Perspective on Desires

What, then, determines the content of one's desires as the grid for the mind to compare and contrast reality with them? We can understand and explain it up to a point, but finally it rests in God's mysterious design of each person and their life experience, both Christian and non-Christian.

Simply, why do some people have explosive anger while others burn within? Why are some extroverts and others introverts? Why are some geniuses and others of average intelligence? Of course, these phenomena involve the ongoing debate of "nature" and "nurture." That is, the influence of the physical characteristics (genes) that a person is born with and his subsequent life experience, especially within the family that raises him or her.

As Christians, however, we must go beyond nature and nurture. **First, man is endowed with a spirit.** (Trichotomists would add soul.) He is not simply bio-chemicals. While we cannot explore the relationship of physical and spiritual causation in individuals, we can at least recognize that personal traits are influenced by one's spirit, as well as one's physical body. In fact, the Bible places greater influence upon the spirit than the body (Matthew 5:29-30; 10:26; I Timothy 4:8).

Second, it is ultimately God who determines the exact nature and nurture of each person. Philosophically, there are only two choices. Either nature and nurture are accidental (random, chance) occurrences without design or they are designed with purpose. Purposeful design requires a Designer (God). The mystery of God's choices for the content of each individual must remain a mystery. The only reason that He has given us is "the counsel of His (own) will" (Ephesians 1:11). What we should clearly understand, however, is that each person is designed and not product of random nature and nurture. Individuality, as manifested in personal desires, is not random.

The most dramatic change in desires that can take place in a human life is that of conversion to Jesus Christ. The most accurate designation of this change is repentance. Literally, the Greek word from the New Testament, metanoia, means a "change of mind." This change is dramatic. The person's whole framework of life is changed. He moves from being an enemy of God (Romans 5:10) to the family of God (John 1:12). He moves from darkness into the light (Acts 26:18). He moves from death into life (Romans 6:23). This transformation is primarily, if not entirely, the "renewing of one's mind" (Romans 12:2).

With this dramatic change, his/her desires change dramatically. As one's desires change, one's feelings change. Thus, the feelings of a Christian will have a different orientation than those of the non-Christian. For example, one learns to "fear" temptation and flee it (I Timothy 2:22). One is concerned about future treasures rather than earthly things (Matthew 6:19). One learns not to be anxious about food, drink and clothes (Matthew 7:25).

Practical Application

One's understanding of emotions will determine how he is to be managed either personally, by a counselor (including psychologists and psychiatrists), and even by evangelists. If emotions are caused by physical (biochemical) abnormalities, then they should be managed with a physician's advice. If they are problems of thinking, then correct thinking will correct the "emotional problem." If the mind is the key to the emotions, the Scripture becomes most important. It is only here that true knowledge of the mind is found.

Attitude must be added to the "acute and chronic state of mind" in my definition. Attitude involves beliefs or principles that are somewhat fixed in one's minds. Again, they may be trivial or profound. I may have a fear of frogs because I believe that handling them will cause warts. I may also believe that God is truly Sovereign and good and that He has planned every detail of my life, including unexpected and unpleasant circumstances.

Contentment (peacefulness) is an accurate gauge of the extent to which each Christian actually believes God's goodness and Sovereignty. Both are necessary. I may believe God is Sovereign, but not good (at least to the foolish extent that I am willing to think that I know better than God). I may believe that He is good, but not Sovereign. The former position seems by far the most common in my experience. And, most Christians do not seem aware that their speech and behavior confirms this belief, while they think that they believe otherwise.

The classic, Biblical example is both the statement and actions of Paul in his letter to the Philippians. Writing from jail, he rejoiced (an emotion) in his being in prison because the Gospel was advanced "throughout the entire praetorian guard and to everyone else" (1:13) and others were more bold because of his imprisonment (1:14). His attitude that God was Sovereign and good was immovably fixed. Neither his acute or chronic circumstances could over-ride this attitude. He finally concludes, "I have learned to be content in whatever circumstances I am" (4:11).

Emotions are an outward expression of our true beliefs. If I am as convinced as Paul about God's control and purpose, then I will not worry, get upset or be afraid of any life experience. The extent to which 1 fail to believe this truth is the extent to which 1 will have difficulty with my emotions.[36]

There are some variables to this general truth. **First, volatility or stability of emotions is affected by one's personality.** Some people's attitudes are more easily disturbed than others. They are more spontaneous, effervescent and impulsive (to use positive connotations). Others are more staid, quiet, and calm.

Second, actual physical states can make control of attitudes easier or more difficult. When one has good health, one does not have to contend with the bombardment of the mind by negative feedback from the body. When one is racked by fever, one may be almost numb to any acute or chronic event. Third, life experiences can enhance or erode attitudes. Growing up in a stable home environment with wise, but not overly-protective parents, starts a young adult with positive and learned life experiences that promotes stability in the face of the travail that is sure to come. Growing up in a home with child abuse and divorce (or worse) hinders the development of stable attitudes. With a background of travail, new trials are compounded as they are encountered.

There may be other factors. I want to underscore, however, that these factors modify or promote an underlying attitude; they do not determine. Few have ever experienced the difficulties that Paul did (II Corinthians 11:23-33), yet he maintained the attitude that I have reviewed.

This point is the major purpose of my development of a definition of emotions. Being a Christian and living a righteous life is primarily, if not exclusively, one of learned attitude. The beautiful emotions that God offers have a cause and effect relationship to this attitude. Every person is different. For some learning is easy and for others more difficult. Some have experienced stable families and relatively stable lives while others seemed to have faced turmoil all their lives. Some are friendly and personable by personality, while others find social life difficult and taxing.

All Christians, however, will find their greatest fulfillment "in Jesus Christ" proportional to their understanding of God and His Word. While love, joy, peace, patience, kindness, goodness, and gentleness are gifts of the Holy Spirit (Galatians 5:22-23), they may also be developed and experienced more fully as He gives understanding of biblical truth. To attempt "emotional healing" by bypassing the mind is not only impossible, it is erroneous and crippling for Christians. The focus on emotions in the modern church is a serious and erroneous plague. So, also, is the medical profession's acceptance of the psychological concept of emotional "illness" where a physical cause is not present. Perhaps, my definition will cause some to think further about this subject.

58

True Guilt and Guilt Feelings: Clearing the Confusion

The Old Man and the New Man

This article was a letter written to a college student who was wondering about repetitive sins and the guilt feelings that go along with them. This letter was my explanation to her. It is a problem that all Christians must understand and manage. For that reason, we will have a fair amount of discussion on this website about feelings.

I believe that you are a real, normal Christian of Romans 7!

Everything that you said is really normal. We have the "old man," and while we are to reckon him dead, he is very much alive. The interesting thing is that if you read statements of those whom we would call the great saints of history, you will find that the older and more experienced that they get as Christians, the more that they see themselves as great sinners. Paul called himself "the greatest of sinners." Check out this article, a classic among believers at the bottom of this article.

But, let me give you some specifics that might help. You have a very active mind, which is a blessing, if you can keep it focused correctly.

1) Learn to distinguish between thinking and feeling. If you had a fever of 103 degrees, you would not feel like doing anything but staying in bed. And, you shouldn't do anything else. You body has a sickness. You can think about what you can do, but you really can't do it.

On the other hand, if you feel "bad" over sin, the feelings are triggered by your thoughts, not something physical inside you. So, you should not rest your mind or your body because there in nothing physically wrong. First, be sure that you have confessed your sin. This is not likely your problem, from what I know of you. Then, instead of dwelling on the sin, get busy with school work, bible memorization, or something else that is actively engages your mind. This is moving from your Phil. 4:6-7 to verse 8. "Think on... (right things.)

Once a sin is confessed, it is forgiven... always, always, always, Romans 8:1. So, any remorse that lingers is just a feeling -- a guilt feeling, not true guilt. We want to feel forgiven!!! But, had you rather "be forgiven," or "feel forgiven?" I feel good with a cup of coffee, first thing in the morning. The

59

hardened sinner feels good about his life. (I intend the contrast here.) Something simple can make us feel good (or bad). Something that is a fist in God's face, the sinner can feel good about. Feelings are deceptive and unreliable. They FOLLOW our thinking or our physical states. They are not to lead for the Christian.

2) The Christian life is always a put off/put on, Eph. 4:25-32. Note that we are not to just stop sinning, but to adopt the right way. We end our anger by action that same day. The thief just does not stop stealing, he gets a job and goes to work. The "put on" does not always have to be the opposite of what is put off, but it has to be something active.

Many Christians make a serious mistake when they try to just put off the sin. They say to themselves, "I am not going to do _____ (name the sin) any more." But, they don't substitute another activity. So, there is a vacuum there. You know what nature, especially our sin nature does to a vacuum. It is similar to the problem of demons (Matthew 12:43-45).

3) Remember that you can never do enough to satisfy God. Jesus Christ did that. We are to live in grace where we "work out our salvation with fear and trembling. A better verse is "come unto me all you who labor and are heavy laden, and I will give you rest." Or, the 4th commandment... we labor 6 days, and rest one. We labor... we work hard "with fear and trembling," but always there is rest.

I don't particularly like the word "tension" to describe the Christian life because it can make one "tense." I prefer work and rest. One who always works is wrong. One who always rests is wrong. Better, "work hard" and be sure that you get good rest. A daily schedule that has many hard hours of work, that ends in plenty of sleep (and not staying up late) is the right kind of day!

Modern Psychology in the Church

Without doubt, the American church is weak, if not impotent! Our culture and government continues into the moral abyss, in spite of millions of Bible-believing Christians. Perhaps, the most obvious sign of this slide is that there is no great appeal to Almighty God for forgiveness, for "judgment to begin at the household of God," and for His leading to change what needs to be changed (that is, true repentance) in order to be a godly culture and nation.

Robertson McQuilkin, former President of Columbia International University (Columbia Bible College) says:

When a new ethical (worldview) problem arises in society, such as euthanasia or homosexuality, newspaper reporters frequently consult a local professor of psychology. It would make just as much sense -- if not more -- to consult the local bartender. Psychology is descriptive and can only tell us, with greater or lesser precision, what the average person does and what may result if averages hold. It lacks any authority to speak of what human behavior ought to be. Since it lacks this authority, and since it should hold tentatively any conclusions it reaches, it is properly relativistic in its approach.

Many psychologists, however, impose relativity outside their sphere in the field of ethics (worldview) and reject all norms. For example, psychology may help us understand what produces conflict, but whether we use their information to produce conflict or to allay it will depend on our values. As a matter of historic fact, psychological insights are used by some to create conflict. And this is an ethical (worldview) problem, not a psychological one. Psychology helps people understand why they do what the do and how they may change; ethics (worldview) tells them what they ought to do." (*Introduction to Biblical Ethics*, (Tyndale, 1989) page10.

We Are (Too Often) Led by our Emotions, Not by our Thinking (The Scriptures)

The psychology of man has often been a theme of theologians for centuries. But, modern psychology has infiltrated this understanding. This much is clear. **One cannot understand oneself, others, or how God works in our lives without understanding Biblical psychology**. As John Calvin begins his Institutes, the knowledge of man begins with the knowledge of God.

Emotions. Curiously, emotions are rarely defined, but the etymology of the word is helpful. From Webster's Dictionary of 1828, emotion is "a moving of the mind or soul; hence, any agitation of mind or excitement of sensibility." Emotion is a disturbance in our soul that is heightened by its effect on the physical body.

Let me illustrate. You are at home with several children. Things have gone berserk. On child is trying to take another's toy. He is yelling, she is crying. A pot is boiling over on the stove. The dog is barking at the children. You are at you wit's end, yelling at the kids while you deal with the overflowing pot. The phone rings…

You answer, "Hello" (in a more or less calm voice). "This is Susie (your neighbor whom you dislike and to whom you would never want to admit distress), how are you?" "I'm fine…"

What have you just done? You have moved from a distressing emotional state of considerable frustration (a form of anger) to a calm answer to someone on the phone! You have instantaneously calmed yourself from a storm of emotions. Wow!

Now, what is the strongest control in this situation? Your thoughts of your appearance before you neighbor!

Now, men, this could easily be you at work. Your secretary has just bungled a task. The phone keeps ringing while you are working on an important project. Your computer just crashed! And, the boss calls. You will answer, as the housewife did, in a calm manner, as though nothing is wrong.

These scenarios illustrate that we have great control over our emotions when we have a strong motivation. We have greater control than we might think on only a brief reflection.

"I am comfortable with this decision." After a debate, sometimes vigorous, how many times have you come to a conclusion, and the leader said, "Now, are we all comfortable with this decision?"

When we are engaged in conversation with others, we often ask or are asked, "How to you feel about…?" It may be about politics, child-rearing, the price of gasoline, or any other subject of conversation.

To be sure, one definition of "to feel" is "to think." But, in our choice of words, it would be more accurate to ask, "What do you think," rather than "What do you feel." The words that we use reinforce how we think and act.

Often, we express how we are with emotions. "I feel depressed." "I feel inadequate." A child may say, "I feel stupid," when trying to learn something new. These are conclusions about oneself that are expressed as emotions.

We have come to judge decisions and our states of being by our feelings. This situation comes from modern psychologists who ask their clients, "How do you feel about…?" Their focus in on feelings. But, we must ask the question, are feelings or thoughts more important? Should we be led by our emotions or our thoughts?

Are thoughts or emotions more dominant? As you sit there, reading this epistle, I want you to be sad. Be real sad. Be in-a-funk sad. ---- Now, be happy. Be giddy, happy. ---- Now, be angry. Be angry to the extent that you are ready to hit or throw something.

Were you successful in changing your emotional states? Readily, on your own command?

Now, let's try something different. Think of the most wonderful vacation that you have ever had with your family. ---- Think of what you consider to be your greatest achievement in life. ---- Think of the saddest moment of your life.

I suspect that you were more successful in this exercise, than you were in trying to achieve a certain emotional state. Why? Did you notice that as you thought of these situations, you began to feel the emotions associated with the situations? Did you notice how much more easy it was to think certain thoughts than to cause yourself to feel a certain way?

In the latter exercise, you have illustrated Philippians 4:8, "Finally, brethren, whatever things are true, whatever things are noble, whatever things are just, whatever things are pure, whatever things are lovely, whatever things are of good report, if there is any virtue and if there is anything praiseworthy— meditate on these things." Right thinking is the way to right feelings, not the opposite.

How Emotions Re-define Theology

Are you aware that modern, humanistic psychology dominates many areas of theology in the church today?

Peace. How many times have you heard a Christian, say, "I have peace about _____" (some decision). What they are saying is that "I feel good about _____" (that decision). "I don't have any disturbing thoughts about _____" (that decision).

Do a word study on "peace" in the Bible. You will find that peace is used to describe the peace of the regenerated person where formerly enmity with God existed (Romans 5:1), peace among people (Acts 24:2), and a fruit of the Holy

Spirit (Galatians 5:22, probably related to both former meanings). It is rarely, if ever, used as a criterion of decision-making.

The use of "peace" in decision-making comes from psychology that "being comfortable" or "finding peace" is a criterion for right decisions.

Decisions by Christians should be based upon God's prescriptions. For example, "Do not let the sun do down on your anger" and "if you bring your gift to the altar, and there remember that your brother has something against you, leave your gift there before the altar, and go your way." These commands do anything but evoke "peace" in their doing (but they do bring peace between God and man when they are carried out properly).

Love. "I just don't love her (or him) any more" is a common complaint of married couples in counseling or "psychotherapy." Frequently, what they then want to hear from the counselor or therapist is, "Well, there is only one solution, divorce."

Studies of divorcees have found that only the death of a spouse carries more stress than divorce. So, modern psychology would end a marriage that 1) began with promises "in sickness and in health, for richer and for poorer… until death do us part" and 2) thereby, place the second highest stress upon individuals (not to mention children) because "love" no longer exists? And, this result does not even being to consider the morality of this counsel or honoring God by way of covenant in marriage.

We all know the two great commandments, "Love God with all our heart, soul, mind, and strength… and our neighbor, as ourselves." A pagan psychologist would say, "Love is a feeling, it cannot be commanded. Love is either there or it isn't. You can't manufacture love." Thus, the recommendation for divorce.

And, we find the same in our culture, perhaps represented best by Hollywood, as "love at first sight." "Love Story" and "Titanic" are two examples. Love just happens. Love is "chemistry" between two people. Love is some ephemeral thing that comes from somewhere, virtually beyond and outside of people's control.

When Jesus gave the second of his two great commandments, He was asked, "Who is my neighbor." His answer was illustrated by a Samaritan, whom the Jews hated. And, it was directed towards helping a wayside victim at great cost and physical risk by the one who responded. It also showed the hypocrisy of

64

people (a priest and an Levite) who are committed to being "religious" towards God, but not their fellow man when he has great needs.

Thus, love has objects, and love is helping others. **Love can be commanded, even when our emotions involve hatred and great risk to ourselves**. Psychologists know nothing of this love. But, God goes further, much further.

"Love is the fulfillment of the law" (Romans 13:10), and "For all the law is fulfilled in one word, even in this: "You shall love your neighbor as yourself." (Galatians 5:14).

Not only can love be commanded, it has specific content: all that God has written as instructions for mankind, especially for believers -- namely the law. (See Psalm 119 for synonyms of the law: statutes, precepts, testimonies, ways, etc.)

So, love is commanded by God, and has detailed instructions. (Don't confuse following the law with legalism.)

So, let's get back to our example of man-woman love and marriage. As we have seen, love can be commanded and has specific instructions. Love cannot exist at first sight, because no commitments have taken place. Now, love can begin to develop from that initial attraction. Such love would include getting to know each other, giving each other gifts, doing things together, and eventually committing to marriage.

But, even, the process of love is guided by biblical directives (law). You must avoid lustful thoughts (Matthew 5:28), lustful actions (Seventh Commandment), sobriety (Ephesians 5:18), continue individual spiritual growth (church, Bible study, prayer, etc.).

Finally, and ultimately, you actually covenant together formally, spiritually, and legally. Covenant agreed and adhered to over the period of the covenant is the highest form of love.

So, if you say, I love my church. Have you covenanted with her? With covenant, goes specific agreements: to tithe, attend, contribute your spiritual gifts, be faithful to the means of grace, etc.).

Loving children includes "building them up in the nurture and admonition of the Lord," instructing them constantly of God's ways (Deuteronomy 6), "not provoking them to anger.

Do you begin to see the serious commitment that love is? Do you see that love has specific content, that of Biblical law? Do you see the importance of the catechisms devoting almost 50 percent of their attention to law, and therefore, love? Do you see the importance of the entire Bible, as God's law, to know how to "love" in whatever context God has called us? Do you see that you must know that law to be able to follow it? Do you see that that takes considerable study, first to know what to do, and second, to follow though and do it. The Scribes were diligent students of the law, but not doers of it. "Love your neighbor, as yourself," cannot be separated from "love God with all your being." It is both knowledge and application.

May God bless us in that pursuit.

Summary Principles of the Biblical Worldview of Psychology, Counseling, and Emotions

Our **definition of psychology** is the study of an individual person's thoughts, speech, and behavior relative to himself, his neighbor, and God, as governed and defined by specific Biblical criteria. I have tried to use "secular psychology" to denote that which is practiced apart from the Bible.

"Neighbor" is anyone with whom the person may come in contact, as close as one's spouse or more distant as one's enemies in warfare, to missions around the world that provide physical help, as illustrated in the parable of the Good Samaritan (Luke 10:25-37) or that evangelize the unreached.

Counseling is the preferred term to **psychotherapy**, which is simply talking to a person, even though it may be done by a variety of methods, such as, open-ended questions, history of experiences and problems, and instructions in what to do. "Psychotherapy" may be used here to denote the practice of "psychologists," but it is still just conversation, as just described.

Groupings of various principles. Over the years, I have written considerably on this subject. Rather than collating principles from several writings into one whole, I have left them intact (with some minor editing) because they look at these issues from a slightly different perspective and content. And, they are linked to the original source for further reading.

Principles That Are New for This Book on Worldview

This first section of principles is newly developed for this website. The others that follow are from previous publications.

1. All men are regenerate ("born-again" or "born from above") or unregenerate and therefore have different resources for the direction of their lives. There are considerable differences between the regenerate and unregenerate. For example. the unregenerate have no certainty of moral instruction and may or may not have a helping spouse, family, or employer. The regenerate have their spouse, family, church, prayer, Biblical instruction, personal prayer, the prayers of others, the indwelling Holy Spirit, and the Providence of God.

2. All men, regenerate or unregenerate, are responsible to obey God's instructions and the laws of the state (to the extent that they are consistent with Biblical law). Where they fail, they are to seek reconciliation and restitution according to Biblical directions.

3. Any instruction or principle, whether theoretical or experimental, that is contrary to Biblical instruction is ethically wrong and dangerous for the good of the individual.

4. While physical problems may limit in degree an individual's responsibility before God and the state, such difficulties do not remove entirely the individual's responsibility before the law of God or man. Each person is responsible according to his or her abilities and resources (Luke 12:48)

5. Experimentation in psychology is legitimate, as long as its premises and construct are consistent with Biblical morality.

6. "All truth is God's truth" is commonly used by psychologists who are Christians to propose that psychological theory and science have the same validity as a Biblical understanding of man and his responsibility to his neighbor. This proposal is erroneous and heretical. (Link to be developed)

7. "Mental illness" should be applied only to those conditions that are almost certainly due to an organic (biochemical, structural, or traumatic) abnormality of the brain.

8. "Normal" thinking, speech, and behavior is determined by all the commandments and principles required of man in the Scriptures. "Normal" is what a person "ought" to do. All the "oughts" that are required of man are found in the Bible.

9. True guilt occurs from "any transgression of, or want of conformity unto, the law of God" (Answer to Question #14 of the Shorter Catechism of the Westminster Confession of Faith). Removal of this guilt is possible only through regeneration and confession of sins to God primarily, and to each other secondarily (Matthew 5:223-24, 18:15).

Guilt feelings have to do with recurring sins and the "feeling" that one is not forgiven, rather than believing in God's Word. Guilt feelings are only of use to lead a person to seek forgiveness from God or his neighbor, yet are a tremendous problem for the modern Christian in our feeling oriented culture. (Link to article for American Vision)

10. Psychological maturity is possible only through regeneration and obedience to Biblical instruction. "Peace" with oneself, one's neighbor, and most importantly, with God is possible only in the same ways.

11. Emotions (worry, fear, sadness, anger, happy, etc.) are produced by A) bodily states (fever, fatigue, exercise, hunger, headache, etc.) and B) thinking of past, present, or future speech and behavior. Emotions are always triggered by either A) or B). They do not develop in isolation from these two causes. Emotions, whether positive or negative, must be guided by God's instructions. In themselves, they can lead to sinful thinking, speech, and behavior.

12. Man's greatest fear is the fear of death (I Corinthians 15:25; Hebrews 2:15). See Glossary "Death."

Beliefs for Christians in Psychotherapy

If only the regenerate can receive Biblical counseling because unbelievers neither have the belief in Scripture nor the Holy Spirit to enable them to live righteously, what place do Christians have in the practice of "psychology and psychotherapy," as commonly understood in our society?

This section comes from my book, *Biblical Healing for Modern Medicine*, providing criteria for those Christians who believe that they are called or should be involved in the practice of psychology, as commonly understood in our culture. More about this book and how to order.

1. Evangelism must be the highest priority when counseling an unbeliever. Salvation is what every person needs before he will desire right behavior and be able to live it.

2. If a counselee chooses not to accept Christ, then he must be informed that he has rejected the ultimate answer to his problems and that anything else is, by comparison, worthless (Philippians 3:7-8). Counseling may continue if the counselee is still willing, since the possibility of helping him temporarily may allow the opportunity for evangelism to be pursued at a later session.

3. Counseling should never compromise an explicit or clearly implicit Biblical principle.

4. If the counselee is a Christian and Biblical counseling is available at his church, counselors must refer him there. Biblically, all counseling for Christians should have the oversight of the church.

5. A counselor should have read and essentially agree with *Competent to Counsel* **and** *The Christian Counselor's Manual* (see below) because of its analysis of the place and content of Biblical counseling.

6. A commitment to the Bible as the inerrant, infallible, and sufficient Word of God is an absolute requirement for the counselor.

7. The real work of the Holy Spirit in Biblical counseling must be acknowledged.

8. A Christian who plans to enter a counseling career should have thorough, formal, theological education rather than secular training. Counseling should then be done only under the authority of a church -- preferably as a pastor or an elder.

Experimental Results of "Psychotherapy"

This section appears from my book, *Biblical Healing for Modern Medicine*, where I cite several hundred studies reviewed by Morris Parloff. Essentially, it is a summary of the so-called "efficacy" of secular psychology. (Link here to this website)

1. No clinically significant differences among the 78 varieties of psychotherapy were found. That is, any one was as good as another, even though each theory and practice was different from the others.

2. Fifty percent of the treatment effect is lost two years after the completion of therapy. Longer-term studies have not been done.

3. The more females in the study group, the better the results.

4. Patients did better when their therapists were similar in ethnic group, age, and social and educational status.

5. Patients who were chosen or who volunteered showed greater effects than those selected at random. This method is a violation of the scientific process itself.

6. Objective criteria, work adjustment, school adjustment, personality traits, and physiological reactions were less demonstrable of therapeutic effects than subjective criteria, global adjustment, self-esteem, personal development and experiences of fear and anxiety.

7. Comparisons across professions and schools showed no characteristic differences in the effectiveness of treatment.

8. There is little relationship between length of treatment and degree of effectiveness.

9. There is little evidence that the level of experience of the psychotherapist is related to effectiveness.

10. A careful analysis of nearly 500 outcome research studies still does not provide data adequate to answer the question of what kinds of therapy are most useful for what kinds of patients and problems.

11. Placebo effects account for about half the effects which were obtained by "recognized" therapies. That is, patients improved regardless of what was done or not done.

Chapter Summary from *Biblical Healing for Modern Medicine*, Chapter 5.

These principles appeared at the end of my chapter on psychology in *Biblical Healing for Modern Medicine*.

1. Secular psychological principles have a stranglehold on the Church today.

2. Gray areas of understanding between thinking and behavior do exist, but are few compared to the extensive knowledge and domain claimed by psychotherapists.

3. Every area of thinking and behavior has been brought under the "big umbrella" of "mental illness" by secular theory and practice.

4. Psychotherapists are the priests and moralists of modern culture.

5. Christians who are psychotherapists give greater credence to secular theories and practices than to the Word of God.

6. These Christians have a superficial understanding of basic Christian doctrines at best. Thus, they teach serious error at best and heresy at worst.

7. These Christians claim to have the power that only the Holy Spirit has -- "searching the heart" and discerning the "thoughts and intentions of the heart."

8. These Christians claim that "all truth is God's truth," without proof of their philosophical claim.

9. As experimental science, psychotherapy fails by any scientific standard of authenticity.

10. Christians should first seek counseling from their pastor and then others in leadership in their own church. Beyond the church, the ones most likely to give *Biblical counsel* should be sought.

Biblical Worldview in Confrontation with Secular Psychology

These principles appeared at the end of a chapter for a book on worldview that is yet to be published. The text is posted on this website here. (Link to same)

1. The Bible is a textbook on psychology.

2. The Bible is the starting point and final authority of psychology.

3. The Bible (because of God's knowledge of man) is more accurate and thorough in its description of the psychology of man than any other source.

4. The claim of psychologists who are Christians that "all truth is God's truth," doubtfully understands the concept of truth, and their application of such "truth" can have dangerous consequences for believers and unbelievers in this life and in eternity.

5. The brain as the organic outworking of the mind can affect thinking and behavior, but this cause must be limited carefully and accurately.

6. The psychology in theory and practice of individuals is supernaturally and practically different for the believer and unbeliever.

7. The Bible never excuses sin. It must always be confessed and sought forgiveness for. In recognition of personal factors, mercy may require degrees of forbearance, but reconciliation with God, and both reconciliation and restitution with man must be directed.

8. Every man has true (Biblical) guilt both in Adam and in his own sins.

9. Feelings can be controlled by thoughts that are diligently and practically pursued (instructions included herein).

10. Guilt feelings are severely distorted and not biblically managed by many psychologists who are Christians.

11. Application of humanistic principles and practice of psychology that are contrary to Scripture cause severe harm to its recipients.

12. Modern psychologists may have some helpful techniques and knowledge to enhance Biblical counseling.

13. Jay Adams and nouthetic counselors have the most Biblical and practical worldview of any approach to counseling or "psychotherapy."

14. When needed, counsel should first be sought from one's pastor or other church leader, then the most mature Christian inside or outside the church. If medication or hospitalization is necessary, such counselor, in the order named, must continue to be involved.

72

References

All these books (except where noted) are available from www.TimelessTexts.com.

Adams, Jay E. *Christian Counselor's Manual*. Grand Rapids: Baker Book House, 1973.

Adams, Jay E. *Competent to Counsel*. Phillipsburg, NJ: Presbyterian and Reformed Publishing Company, 1970.

Adams, Jay E. *More Than Redemption: A Theology of Christian Counseling*. Phillipsburg, NJ: Presbyterian and Reformed Publishing Company, 1979.

Payne, Franklin E. *Biblical Healing for Modern Medicine*. Augusta, GA: Covenant Books, 1993. Available from Covenant Books for $10.00 postpaid at P. O. Box 14488, Augusta, GA 30919.

Scipione, George C, et al. "The Christian Worldview of Counseling and Psychology." With this link, scroll down to The 17 COR Worldview Documents, where you will find the one on psychology and counseling.

Welch, Edward T. *Addictions: A Banquet in the Grave*. Phillipsburg, NJ: Presbyterian and Reformed Publishing Company, 2001.

Welch, Edward T. *Blame It on the Brain?* Phillipsburg, NJ: Presbyterian and Reformed Publishing, 1998.

Welch, Edward T. *Counselor's Guide to the Brain and Its Disorders*. Grand Rapids: Zondervan Publishing House, 1991.

Endnotes

1. Sykes, Charles, J., *A Nation of Victims: The Decay of the American Character*, New York: St. Martin's Press, 1992, p. 13.
2. In my writings, I am increasingly putting such people as "experts, "officials," and "professionals" within quotation marks. While they have such status by academic degree, peer recognition, or rank of government office, such standing is dubious at best, because they are unable and/or unwilling to speak the moral element of problems (which is often the most important element). Almost exclusively, these people are humanists, anti-Christian, and anti-God. God says that they are "fools" (Psalm 14:1).
3. I often use "moral," "spiritual," "ethical," and "biblical" as synonyms. I am aware of the nuances of these words, but their primary meaning is often the same.
4. I am not endorsing these diagnoses as accurate or true. I am merely pointing out here that any claim that modern psychiatry is "scientific" can be countered simply by professionals' failure to use their own recognized standards!

5. *Diagnostic and Statistical Manual of Mental Disorder* (Third Edition, Revised), Washington, D.C.: American Psychiatric Association, 1987, p. 165.

6. I use the general label "psychologist" to include psychiatrists. While there are some particulars to each, their general approach to diagnosis and treatment of patients (clients) is similarly unbiblical. Using both labels, psychology and psychiatry, makes for awkward writing and reading.

7. Harrison, R .K., Ed., *Encyclopedia of Biblical and Christian Ethics* (Revised Edition), Nashville: Thomas Nelson Publishers, 1992, pp. 6-7.

8. Bobgan, Martin & Deidre, "Behavior or Disease," *Journal of Biblical Ethics in Medicine*, Vol. 4, 1990, pp. 67-69, quoting Stanley Peale, Diseasing of America: Addiction Treatment Out of Control, Lexington, MA: Stanley Heath & Company, 1989, p. 68.

9. Hewitt, Thomas, *Tyndale New Testament Commentaries: Hebrews*, Grand Rapids: Win. B. Eerdmans Publishing Company, 1960, pp. 189-190.

10. Quoted by F. F. Bruce in *The International Commentary on the New Testament: Hebrews*, Grand Rapids: Win. B. Eerdmans, 1964, pp. 349-350.

11. Calvin, John, *Commentaries on the Epistle of Paul the Apostle to the Hebrews*, translated by the Rev. John Owen, Grand Rapids, Baker Book House, 1979, pp. 394-395.

12. *Ibid.*, pp. 311-313.

13. Webster, Noah, *American Dictionary of the English Language, 1828* edition, San Francisco, Foundation for American Christian Education, 1967.

14. *Ibid.*

15. Genes that have been thought to predispose or cause addictions have little or no correlation as to whether an addict is able to quit or not.

16. There is some evidence that opiate-like endorphins and enkephlins in human brains may provide something like a drug dependence in addictive behaviors. If further research gives greater substance to this relationship, then many, possibly all, addictions could also have a physical basis. However, such findings would not negate my position here.

17. Ephesians 5:18 argues for moral/spiritual control, rather than the lack of control of a chemically induced state, drunkenness.

18. Adams, Jay E., *The Christian Counselor's Manual*, Grand Rapids, Baker Book House, 1973, pp. 206ff.

19. Feelings and emotions are synonyms. I will only use the one word, "emotions."

20. Indeed, I could have cited a voluminous literature on many of the subjects that I have dealt with herein. While such citations may give a more "scholarly" appearance, they would not give additional insights or substantiation. Anyone with a considered position can find any number of suitable publications. Further, if my brief argument cannot at least open a reader's mind to the plausibility of my position, then citing the entire world's literature is not likely to convince either.

21. Berkhof, L. *Systematic Theology*. Grand Rapids: Win. B. Eerdmans Publishing Company, 1939, pp. 191-200. Clark, Gordon. *The Biblical Doctrine of Man*. Jefferson, Maryland: The Trinity Foundation, 1984, pp. 33-44. Delitzsh, Franz. *A System of Biblical Psychology*. Reprinted from the 1899 edition in Edinburgh by T. and T. Clark. Grand Rapids: Baker Book House, 1977, pp. 196-378. Hodge, Charles.

Systematic Theology: Volume 11. Reprint. Grand Rapids: Wm. B. Eerdmans Publishing Company, 1986, pp. 42-51.

22. Adams, Jay E. *More Than Redemption*. Phillipsburg, New Jersey: 1979, p. 116

23. Some trichotomists might place the soul in both the physical and non-physical components, but I am not aware of any who do. The following argument, however, would not be substantially changed by those of this persuasion. Other positions, for example those who see the mind as an epiphenomenon of the physical, have departed from traditional and orthodox reasoning. Thus, their position is really too "far out" to merit serious consideration here or the more complex argument needed to address their position.

24. The problem between dichotomy and trichotomy relative to psychology is to whom the area of the mind (soul) belongs. Many trichotomists would direct that the body be cared for by the physician, the soul (mind) by the psychologist, and the spirit by the pastor (or other spiritual counselor). For the dichotomist this province is simple, the spirit, mind, soul and heart are one. All these designations, then, (to follow the trichotomists' reasoning) would fall to the spiritual counselor. For a psychologist to participate, he would have to have the qualifications of a spiritual counselor.

25. Again, the origin of my definition of emotion came from Machen's work, not this dictionary definition. I believe, however, that the etymology of emotion does give some support to my definition.

26. Clark, Gordon H. *A Christian View of Men and Things*. Grand Rapids: Wm. B. Eerdmans, 1952. Reprint. Grand Rapids: Baker Book House, 1981, pp. 285-325. Clark, Gordon H. *Thales to Dewey*. 1957. Reprint. Grand Rapids: Baker Book House, 1980. See Index for numerous references to "Sensation."

27. Speech is really only the audible expression of one's thoughts, so there are really only two categories: thinking and behavior.

28. Adams, *More Than Redemption*, pp. 108-118. Clark, Gordon H. *Faith and Saving Faith*, Jefferson, Maryland: The Trinity Foundation, 1983, pp. 65-79. Clark, Gordon H. *The Biblical Doctrine of Man*, pp. 78-88. Clark, Gordon H. *Religion, Reason and Revelation*. Jefferson, Maryland: The Trinity Foundation, 1986, pp. 90-94.

29. Adams, *More Than Redemption*, p. 116.

30. Clark, Gordon H. *Faith and Saving Faith*, p. 65. Clark, *The Biblical Doctrine of Man*, pp. 79-81. Stob, Henry. *Ethical Reflections: Essays on Mortal Themes*. Grand Rapids, Michigan: William B. Eerdmans Publishing Company, 1978, pp. 90-91.

31. Clark, Religion, *Reason and Revelation*, pp. 104ff.

32. Many preachers are not actually using words as instruments to influence rational thought in their hearers but solely for emotional ("disturbance") impact. They use emotional words (often devoid of logic or internally contradictory) to induce an emotional state in hearers and to induce a behavioral response (such as going to the altar) without any real change in their mind. The spawn of such preaching seeds a nation with fervent "Christians" whose faith is emotional only.

33. Psychiatrists may give drugs, but this is obviously a "bodily" treatment and not a direct treatment of the emotions.

34. The use of phenothiazines and other drugs to control the thinking and behavior of schizophrenics does not prove a biochemical deficit. Aspirin will relieve a tension headache, but this relief does not prove that this headache was caused by a

biochemical disorder. Such attributing of causality is a simple principle of logic called "asserting the consequent." While it is simple, major errors in all branches of science are based upon this fallacy. If Christian leaders and teachers knew and applied such simple principles of logic, we would likely not have such disordered thinking among modem Christians. For more discussion on this subject, see my book, Biblical/Medical Ethics, Milford, Michigan: Mott Media, 1985, pp. 155-180.

35. These "diagnoses" are another problem that we cannot address. To what degree are they spiritual problems that require obedience and repentance to correct? To what degree are these behaviors uncontrollable by those who have them? Again, such issues are rarely addressed by Christians in psychology and psychiatry, but these issues are centrally important to a Biblical framework.

36. The same can be said about behavior. The extent to which our lives are obedient to all God's instructions is the extent to which we actually believe those instructions are His commands for His glory and our good. This paper concerns emotions, so I will say no more about behavior. It should be noted, however, that what we truly believe is best measured by our emotional responses and our behavior, and not what we think or say.

5. Creation

Population Control and the Creation Mandate

Fanisi Kalusa in her wildest imagination could never have considered that she would become known world-wide.[1] In fact, her life centered around her tiny little village of Margoli, eight miles above the equator in western Kenya. She would, however, become known for her desire to have 20 children, as she was the central subject of a documentary on world population. (The money had been provided by the United Nations, the World Bank, and private donors.) Fanisi's village was located in "the middle of the most crowded farmland of the fastest growing nation in the history of the world." Her desire and her situation were perfect to portray what Robert McNamara described as the "rampant population growth (that left humanity) more certainly threatened, than it has been by any catastrophe the world has yet endured."

> The question arises whether children should always be reared or may sometimes be exposed to die.... there should also be a law, in all states where the system of social habits is opposed to unrestricted increase, to prevent the exposure of children merely in order to keep the population down. The proper thing to do is to limit the size of each family.[2]

This quote from Aristotle shows that concern about population growth is an old phenomenon. Perhaps it received its greatest momentum, however, when Thomas Malthus (1766-1834) made his "objective" studies and predictions about the sufficiency of the earth to sustain the physical needs of his projected numbers. His conclusions and those of modern population planners, however, depend upon many assumptions and distortions. To complicate matters, eugenics in this century has become linked with concern about population growth. Additional impetus came from the increasing materialism that focuses on the "good life" when children absorb large sums that could be used for personal pleasure. Unfortunately, many Christians have adopted these secular attitudes. We must, therefore, see what the Bible says about these matters.

You might ask, "How is population control related to medical ethics; isn't it properly a topic for social ethics?" Medicine is the means (birth control measures) to the end (population control). The ethics of such measures must be analyzed from two perspectives: from population control as a goal and birth control methods as medical practice. This chapter and the next are a unit, dealing with these two subjects respectively.

Fallacies of the Population Doomsdayers

First, predictions of future population numbers are extremely inaccurate. Malthus' initial projections have proved false.[3] He maintained that the population of the earth would double every twenty-five years. If his predictions were correct, the world's population would be sixty billion, nearly ten times what it actually is! Since 1973, the world's growth rate has slowed to 1.7 per cent (two per cent prior to that time) as fertility rates have dropped sharply in Asia and Latin America.[4] Colin Norman, a population expert, doubts that the world's population will ever double again, a position that contrasts sharply with that of United Nations planners.[5] Causes for his position include increased death rates from war, famine, poor farming and fishing practices, as well as increased use of birth control measures (including abortion).

Second, the potential food supply of the world is far greater than was previously realized. Colin Clark estimates that the world could sustain 35 billion people on the "over consumptive" American diet and 100 billion on an "adequate" Japanese diet.[6] Malcolm Muggeridge said that the arguments and data in Clark's books are "unanswerable and have never been seriously challenged."[7]

Third, the most serious hindrance to maximum food production are man's individual actions and national culture, particularly is determined by his religion. Historically, famines are caused by war, the prevention of cultivation, the willful destruction of crops, defective agriculture, governmental interference by regulation or taxation, and currency restrictions.[8] It should be noted that natural causes are the exception rather than the rule.

The recent famine in Ethiopia is an example. Traditionally, Ethiopian farmers had stored food for the future years of crop failure that they knew were inevitable.[9] Under the present government, however, those who continued to store food were accused of "hoarding" and executed. When others tried to transport food, they were accused of "exploitation" and their goods confiscated. Sometimes, they were imprisoned or executed. Many young, able-bodied men were forced to leave their farms. Entrepreneurial incentives were dashed by widespread looting, confiscation, and expropriation. Both individual and business bank accounts were raided. Farmers were forced into collectives

78

and associations. No plans were made to replace the former storage of food for future years or transportation to move food to those parts of the country that needed it. Even the massive giving of other countries did not get food to the people. It rotted on docks, was diverted to those in power, or was used to manipulate the populace.

The situation in other countries also shows that the major problem is inherently individual, social, political, and religious. Dr. J. S. Kanwar of the Indian Agrarian Research Institute, has concluded that modern methods of agriculture in two of the Federal States in India could produce enough food for the entire country. Then, if the entire country used such methods, one-third of the crop would exceed the country's need and could be exported. Throughout the world the typical work day varies from 45 minutes to seven hours.[10] Obviously, longer working hours would produce a great deal more. Over fishing, overgrazing, deforestation and over ploughing are additional problems that reduce productivity through the destruction of basic resources.[11] Further, the lack of productivity in the tropics has been attributed to the people who live there and is not due to the heat and humidity per se.[12]

Fourth, productivity is not necessarily limited where people are closely populated.

There is an interesting theory according to which, from an economic point of view, countries can, on a certain level, be "overpopulated," then, within the framework of a more developed economy, become under populated, and with additional industrialization again become overpopulated, and so forth (his emphasis).[13] This phenomenon may account for the fact that in the West "the birth-rate began to decrease a generation or so after the death-rate decreased without any help from contraceptives, abortion or other forms of birth-control."[14] (It is doubtful that abortion is effective as a birth control measure.[15])

The Netherlands and Japan, two of the most densely populated countries in the world have had to import workers to meet their productive capacity.[16] Tyrol, a federal state of Austria was Central Europe's "poor-house," in 1898 unable to employ and feed its population.[17] Emigration was high. Today, the lifestyle in a Tyrolean village is quite similar to that of the United States, a most remarkable reversal! Taiwan, two-thirds the size of Switzerland but with sixteen million people, has the second highest standard of living in Asia (behind Japan, another densely populated country).

Fifth, cultural upheavals have been caused by population planning because its acceptance and practice is uneven. Europeans, North Americans, Australians,

Japanese, and South Africans have been practicing birth control, but few other countries have done so to the same extent. The net result is that the "white races" and the Japanese face a declining percentage of the world's population.[18] "Genocide is now the fashion ... (of these regions) in an undeclared warfare vis-à-vis an unborn generation."[19] In the Netherlands the Catholics "overtook" the Calvinists as the 20th century began because the latter used contraception and the former did not.

It would take us far a field and require a lengthy treatise to discuss the morality of these demographic changes. It is sufficient here to note that major shifts take place when population controls are attempted.

Sixth, food production has increased more rapidly than the population on a world-wide basis.[20] This fact substantiates the above observation that the major problem lies with people and their culture, not food production per se.

It appears never to have occurred to them (the advocates of controlled population development) that the logical way out of the chronic situation in which there are more hungry people than food is not by way of reducing the population, but rather of increasing the production of the means of subsistence.[21]

Even in the United where large surpluses of food are produced almost every year, more could be produced were it not for government controls. Often, the problem of insufficient food is its delivery to the people (see Ethiopia above). Such transportation problems have to be addressed, as well.

Seventh, how can any "optimum" number for the population of a country or the world be determined? What objective standards could be used? How much land space, food, and other material goods should each person have? The ultimate question is who will make these decisions? The answer of the population planners is always the "wisdom" of an elite group, usually scientists who are quite willing to use their "expertise" from the "objective" (meaning amoral) world of science to answer these far-reaching moral questions. It is fascinating, although nonetheless dangerous, that strong advocates of pluralism are quite unwilling to determine answers to these dilemmas rather with a pluralistic approach. Such unwillingness clearly shows their authoritarian philosophy that includes coercive tyranny to achieve their ends. (Thus, we see the openness of pluralism!)

Eighth, it is not universally true that large families are "unwanted." The clear desire of many peoples to have large families has caused a prominent feminist,

80

Germaine Greer, to "change her tune." From a tour to rural villages in India she was deeply moved by a culture in which there were no "unwanted children," in which family life was strong and sex regarded as something other than an "indoor sport," in which the women's role in family and village life was important and honorable.[22]

Ninth, both the rich and the poor need their children to provide for them in their elderly years and to continue the economic development of their country.[23] Allan Carlson has calculated that the loss of 17 million children in the United States (who become producing adults) through abortion to be $1.45 trillion in national income, of which $291 billion would have been federal income tax. Consider this amount relative to the current budget deficit of $150-$200 billion dollars a year.[24] He has called this loss, "The Malthusian Deficit." His calculations include many assumptions, but the value of his work is to give some objectivity to the enormous potential "wealth" to our country from larger families.

Julian Simon has briefly summarized other arguments.[25] His answers to the question, "Why is population rhetoric so appealing?," includes: short-run vs. long-run costs, apparent consensus of expert judgment, population as a cause of pollution, judgments about people's rationality, media exposure, money, and standards of proof and rhetoric. To the question, "What are the underlying reasons for doomsday fears and rhetoric?," he answers: simple world-saving humanitarianism, taxation fears, supposed economic and political self-interest, fear of communism, dislike of business, belief in the superiority of "natural processes," religious antagonisms, racism, the belief of the more educated that they know what is best for the less educated, lack of historical perspective, and fitness of the human race.

In conclusion numbers per se are not the disease, so birth-control (especially abortion) is not the cure. The fact is that the cure is worse than the problem. There are hidden agendas, motives, and severe distortions of the facts. Allan Carlson calls us to action. Christians ... face a special imperative in ending the Malthusian charade. Its core assumption -- that man alone is vile and nature alone is holy -- represents a corruption of Christian truth.[26]

The Creation Mandate

"And God blessed them; and God said to them, "Be fruitful and multiply, and fill the earth ..." (Genesis 1:28a). This directive is one of seven given to Adam and Eve prior to their Fall: the replenishing of the earth (Genesis 1:28a), subduing of the same (Genesis 1:28a), dominion over the creatures (Genesis

1:28b), labor (Genesis 2:15), the weekly Sabbath (Genesis 2:3), and marriage (Genesis 2:24-25). They are called "creation mandates" by some theologians and "orders of creation" by others. Our focus is on the command to procreate. It is inseparable from the seventh.[27] When God limited one man to one woman and vice-versa, He limited procreation to this union. In the next section we will explore what that union means relative to the family.

Since these mandates are not taught widely today, many Christians will not be familiar with them. Likely, however, you will recognize principles that Scripture presents elsewhere. Also, you may recognize general principles that seem to issue from "Christian" responsibility, but had not yet been crystallized in your mind. Too many Christians have been "brain-washed" by the population myths and birth control advocates. The creation mandate is the basic principle by which to place these distortions in their Biblical perspective.

Some may wonder whether these mandates continue since the Fall wreaked havoc with the whole cosmos (Rom. 8:20), including its perfect moral structure. That these mandates need some modification seems necessary from Jesus' allowance for divorce (Mt. 19:1-12). First, He states the creation mandate for marriage (v. 4-6). Then, He upholds the allowance for divorce under Mosaic law," ... because of your hardness of heart" (v. 8). Again, He states the creation mandate, "but from the beginning it has not been this way" (v. 8). Finally, he re-states the Old Testament sanction for divorce when adultery has occurred. It seems that Man's sin has made divorce a practical necessity for cases of adultery. (Paul added desertion of an unbeliever as a cause for divorce later.)[28]

Since Jesus modified one creation mandate because of man's sinfulness, it would not seem inappropriate to expect some modification of the command to "be fruitful and multiply." Helmut Thielicke apparently takes this position when he says that this command is "confronted with concrete situations which resist its realization."[29] We should not, however, be too hasty. Concerning divorce we have an explicit modification made in the Bible itself by our Lord Himself. There is no such explicit modification concerning our being "fruitful." Most assuredly, Christians do not have the prerogative to modify God's commands without His own explicit instructions.

Further, we should not have to resort to the choice of "lesser evils,"[30] where the situation seems to offer only choices that are each evil. Dr. John Jefferson Davis calls this principle, "contextual absolutism."[31] It "holds that in each and every ethical situation, no matter how extreme, there is a course of action that is morally right and free of sin" (I Corinthians 10:31). That is not to say that such situations are not extremely difficult, but Dr. Davis calls us to the "cost of discipleship ... in the twentieth century American church, where believers are all too often tempted by the comforts and compromises of the surrounding culture.[32]

Thus, the creation mandate remains in effect.[33] Its repetition after the Fall and after the flood clearly underscores its continuance. It applies to both believers and unbelievers since it was given to the natural father (Adam) and mother (Eve) of the human race. Since unbelievers are not likely to respond to biblical authority, the conscious fulfillment of this creation mandate falls to believers. There are many reasons why believers should be concerned about its fulfillment. We will review some of those reasons after we develop a biblical concept of the family.

The Biblical Concept of The Family

We start with "the beginning." In Genesis 2 the purpose of marriage is clearly stated, "...it is not good for the man to be alone; I will make him a helper suitable for him!" (v.18). Then, God made Eve to complement Adam in every way, "meet" meaning "appropriate to, corresponding to or approximating at every point."[34] That is, the man would be lonely and incomplete without his wife. She is his "companion" (Proverbs 2:17) and he is her "companion" (Malachi 2:14). Further, that "... the two shall become one flesh" (Genesis 2:24) indicates the unity of this companionship since "flesh"[35] refers to individual persons (Genesis 6:17, 7:22, 8:21; Acts 2:17). Thus, "become one flesh" means that the husband and wife become one person: physically as they live together and enjoy a sexual relationship as they care for each others hurts and needs, intellectually as they share and complement each other's life. The "two persons begin to think, act, feel as one"[36] Thus, marriage is primarily a functional and physical companionship in all the endeavors of both "till death do you part." (It is an earthly unity, not an eternal unity, Luke 20:34-36).

The strength of this companionship is emphasized in its designation as a covenant (Malachi 2:14). God chose the covenant as the means by which He would establish His relationship with the nation of Israel (Genesis 17:1-14) and spiritual "Israel" (all believers, Gal. 3:29). Thus, marriage is a covenant that reflects God's plan of salvation. Even further, marriage reflects the relationship within the Trinity (I Corinthians 11:3). John Calvin commenting upon Mt. 19:5-6 states, "...whoever divorces his wife (or husband) tears himself in pieces, because such is the force of holy marriage, that the husband and wife become one man."[37]

A secondary function of this unity is the propagation and rearing of children. The Roman Catholic Church and some Protestants are wrong to teach that procreation is the primary purpose of marriage. First, children are a temporary part of marriage because they eventually leave home, whereas, marriage continues for the lifetimes of the husband and wife. In fact, the children are instructed to "leave" (separate) from their parents and "cleave" (join) themselves to their spouses (Genesis 2:24). Second, marriage is not necessary, biologically, for the propagation of the human race. The prevalence of illegitimate births and the reproductive techniques clearly cover this reality.

The sexual relationship is secondary, also. Obviously, marriage is not necessary for the act of intercourse, but marriage is the situation that God designed for its fullest and only means of expression. Sexual fulfillment flows out of the companionship of the husband and the wife. In this context of fulfillment and commitment children are conceived. It is not, however, the only dimension of the physical relationship. Couples who are unable to have sexual intercourse can still have a deeply physical relationship through their touches, embraces and other physical contact. It is the erotic focus of our society that centers on marriage as a sexual relationship. The Bible does not place the emphasis on sex even though it is not embarrassed by the pleasures and ecstasies of sex, as vividly portrayed in the Song of Solomon.

Finally, marriage is the basic unit of society and the smallest unit of government. Education, discipline, and justice, health, and economics are administered there. A man's ability to govern his family is a prerequisite for his governing the church (I Tim. 3:4-5) and by implication, any other social sphere.

In conclusion, marriage was instituted of God as a lifelong design, primarily for companionship and complementary work. It is a covenant of companionship. A man or woman is incomplete until he or she has married (unless gifted by God to serve Him without a spouse, Mt. 19:12, I Corinthians 7:7). Children and sexual fulfillment are functions of this unity, but a marriage can be fully complete without either. The marriage and the family form the basic unit of society and government; any enhancement or disruption of the family multiplies far beyond itself for this reason. All medical ethics to be biblical, must incorporate this companionship concept of the family.

Implications of the Creation Mandate and the Biblical Family

Bob's problem (he had come alone) was unusual for me as a pastoral counselor: his wife did not want children at this time. He had been married to

Jane for six years and until the last few months, both had agreed not to have children. He had been in school most of that time and she had worked to support him. Now, they were both working, their debts were paid, and he wanted children. Jane, however, seemed to enjoy buying the things for the house that she had always wanted and knew the expense of a baby would interfere with her plans. Bob was concerned that they may wait too long since Jane had two medical problems that could interfere with conception and decrease their chances of having any children at all. As I gathered more data, it was apparent that the presenting problem reflected other problems in the marriage.

Since this type of case was the first for me, I made some usual suggestions to improve their communication, partly to buy time for me to talk over their situation with other elders. They were both to come for the next counseling session. As this case turned out, I never saw them again formally. Evidently, his visit was the stimulus for Jane to re-think her position. Within a few months she was obviously pregnant and they now have two children.

Involuntary Childlessness Because of Physical Inability. As we have seen, physical inability to have children does not detract from the primary purpose of marriage so the fullness of the husband-wife relationship is not necessarily diminished. Further, even though the couple is not able to obey the creation mandate, their situation does not involve sin because personal sin is never ascribed when failure to fulfill a biblical command is completely beyond personal responsibility.

Voluntary Childlessness. A different situation is the couple who voluntarily chooses not to have children. Such is a violation of the creation mandate. Thielicke states that such a marriage should not take place.[38] A man and woman who contemplate marriage without the intention to have children, even though it may be rare, have insufficient biblical grounds for the marriage. Although they could still fulfill the primary purpose of marriage, they could possibly be in continual violation of the biblical command to procreate.

Some qualifications, however, are in order. Thielicke names several "exceptional" cases: severe illness of the mother, severe hereditary affliction, economic circumstances which will not permit the rearing of another child even with the greatest frugality, early marriages (that is, by students), housing difficulties, and job situations.[39] The most valid is that of severe illness in the mother. In this situation, the choice is actually one between the new life of a child and the life of the mother. The choice is similar to the one that is faced when a mother's life is threatened if her pregnancy is continued.[40] Other limitations on this creation mandate also apply.

Genetic Inheritance. Arbitrarily, I will divide this limitation into three categories. Into one category falls the couple whose first child unexpectedly has a genetic disorder or congenital abnormality (a problem or set of problems that occurs during the development of the baby in the mother's womb or the birth process, and is not an inherited condition.) The difficulty that such a child places on the couple financially, physically, socially and spiritually may be sufficient to limit their having additional children. This limitation is strengthened if there is a high probability that they will have another defective child. If, however, it is virtually certain that additional children will be normal, they may want to have more.

The second category involves the couple who have not yet had children, but know that they have a very high probability of having a genetically defective child. This second category as a limitation is not as strong as the first because the above couple has already acted upon the creation mandate. Usually, the stress of genetically-defective children is outweighed by unexpected benefits, as with Down's syndrome children. We do not want to say categorically, however, that this second couple should have a child. Paul Ramsey, however, believes that they should not.[41]

A third category is an older couple who is at an increased risk of genetic aberrations in their children because of their age. These rates are commonly given according to the age of the mother, although the age of the man is a factor in genetic abnormalities, as well. When the woman is 35 years of age, the chances of a "clinically significant abnormality" is 0.5 percent (5/1000 births); at 40 years 1.5 percent (1.5/1000); at 45 years 5.0 percent (50/1000); and at 49 years 13.0 percent (77/1000).[42] For the couple who does not have any children, these "odds" would not seem to warrant childlessness. These "odds" are considerably less than those inherited abnormalities that may affect 25-100 percent of the offspring. Of course, all other factors that we are discussing here would have to be considered. Having children at older ages should certainly not be undertaken lightly.

There are too many variables to cover every situation. Most genetic abnormalities are not severe. In fact everyone has several hidden genetic defects. It would seem that the expected disorder would have to be severe (multiple organ systems affected) to prevent the couple from having children. The couple would have to consider their own physical, financial and spiritual resources. They should talk with other Christians who have these children.

86

Most importantly, they should seek the counsel of their local church officers who are their God-ordained spiritual advisors.

Postponed Child-Bearing. Certain situations may require postponed childlessness.

1) A year is needed to allow for a new husband and wife to begin to learn to live together (Dt.24:5). Although this passage has to do with military and civil duties, it probably represents a general principle that allows a new husband and wife to enjoy and get to know each other without excessive demands that interfere with their relationship.

2) Immediately successive pregnancies may be difficult for some women both physically and spiritually. It would seem appropriate that some spacing between children be planned, but this decision seems to be one that each couple is entirely free to make as they consider their abilities and resources.

3) The loss of a job or other financial loss may temporarily reduce a family's means to have another child. Again, this decision is one that couple's are free to make. Many relevant factors vary considerably from family to family, so their choices here will also vary.

4) A modern limitation is the time needed to complete lengthy educational requirements, especially those that require several years in addition to the usual four years of college. For married couples this situation usually requires one spouse to work, thus effectively preventing the financial or spiritual requirements to raise children. Surely, the better choice is to marry and postpone children than to be sexually frustrated (I Corinthians 7:9b). Couples should be careful, however, that careers do not continue this situation indefinitely. They should also be aware that ten per cent of married couples have physical difficulties that may inhibit conception. To wait may decrease their chances to have any children at all.

How Many Children? How many children should a couple have? Likely, two are insufficient for most Christian couples without clearly limiting factors. The word, "multiply" (Hebrew, rabah), is used in the creation mandate. It means "to multiply, become numerous, become great ...." Basically, this word connotes numerical increase."[43] I am tempted to say that "multiply" means a greater increase than simple "addition." The impression is one of large numbers. Even so, large numbers of people may be achieved by increasing life expectancy or by large numbers of children. So practically, "multiply" does not help to determine the number of children that a couple should have. It does, however, seem to imply several.

Psalm 127 implies the same. A "warrior" is not likely to have only 1-2 arrows and say that his "quiver is full" (v. 5). Further, he would probably not go into battle or to go hunting with only one or two. Another element in the psalm is the blessedness of many children. Certainly, this description of children is far removed from them as "burdens," as the description used by many population planners.

Two conclusions seem warranted. First, Psalm 127 emphasizes the expectation and blessedness of many children. Second, the population experts have concluded that two children will not result in numerical growth. Putting these two conclusions together (with far more emphasis on the first than the second), we would say that at least three children are expected of God's people who otherwise do not face the concrete limitations that we have outlined. What is necessary is that this Psalm be contemplated personally and prayerfully by each couple as they decide what number God would expect them to have. In addition, substantive reasons call for large families.

1) Every society needs the morality of children raised in the "discipline and instruction of the Lord" (Eph. 6:4). For sure, Christian children are not always raised in that manner, but a recent increased interest in biblical principles for the home and in Christian education gives us hope for improvement. Truly, today's emphasis on birth and population control is a great opportunity for the advancement of Christianity. With larger families Christians can become a larger percentage of society, and with proper biblical training, advance the Christian worldview that has given rise to the greatness of the Western world. At a lesser level large families are necessary for Christians to defend themselves against staunch and widespread opposition to the Bible as a basis of morality and law.[44]

2) God's primary fulfillment of the Great Commission (Mt. 28:18-20) is through the family. The marital institution is sanctified by the forces of redemptive grace to such an extent that it is made one of the main channels for the accomplishment of God's saving purpose in the world.[45]

The application of the following Proverb seems appropriate to this purpose.

> In a multitude of people is a king's glory
> But in a dearth of people is a prince's ruin. Proverbs 14:28

Christians who are not familiar with Covenant Theology may not know that God's promises in the Old Testament were covenantal. That is, He made covenants with certain people and their "seed" (Genesis 9:9, 17:7, 35:12). The inclusion of the children is also clear in the New Testament (Acts 2:39). Certainly, the discipleship inherent in the Great Commission has the potential to be most thorough for the children of Christians.

3) Parents can be more easily cared for by several children if they become unable to provide for themselves. This biblical picture seems foreign because our culture has distorted the continuing relationship of the extended family, and placed the responsibility on the federal government (e.g. Social Security).

4) Advantages exist for the children as well. Children learn to share of necessity and to have fewer "things" in large families. They have to interact more frequently and with more personalities in close situations. To have spending money, they have to earn more of it for themselves. With this training, after they leave home they will have more potential resources for help in difficult circumstances. Since children have sinful natures that must be trained. I am aware of the difficulties that will occur with more children. I contend, however, that the advantages outweigh the disadvantages.

Myths against large families. The arguments against large families are largely a result of our non-Christian culture. First, there are already or soon will be too many people on the earth. This argument has been dealt with at length already. Second, raising children is prohibitively expensive today.[46] There is some truth to this argument, but it assumes a great deal. Basic necessities are food, clothing, shelter and education (the training of children to provide these things for themselves in the future). The expenses of children, however, do not increase proportional to numbers. Clothes can be handed down. Two or more children can share the same room. Food is proportionally less expensive when bought in larger quantities and the more expensive foods are not necessary for balanced nutrition. College education may be desirable, but many trades and other jobs do not require a college education. Children can also earn a large portion of (if not all) these costs themselves. Certainly, some lifestyles would have to be radically altered, but what is our standard: our culture or God's word? If children are a gift and blessing from the Sovereign Lord, does it not stand to reason that He will provide for them?

Many Chinese families demonstrate that large families can meet these challenges. Brought to this country as manual laborers, they became entrepreneurs, developing small, successful businesses primarily within family units and have provided their children with excellent educations, including college and graduate school in many instances. They are able to distinguish between "wants" and "needs," a trait that is almost foreign to our materialistic culture.

The local church is an untapped resource. The biblical order of responsibility is first for one's family (I Tim. 5:8), then for other believers (Gal. 6:10), and then for the remainder of society. The family is not an isolated unit but a part of the larger body that is the local church, primarily, and the universal church, secondarily. Certainly, a mature local church is rare.[47] The removal of our materialistic orientation and the development of vital local churches would provide those necessary resources for greater numbers of children in Christian families.

Third, we are fooling ourselves with the notion of "control" and "planning."

> The attempt to control our reproductive capacities without controlling ourselves is based on self-deception. For there are all sorts of possibilities beyond our capacity to predict, let alone regulate. The financial drain anticipated from the birth of a child may be bypassed or surmounted by an unexpected promotion, a change in jobs, or a son's decision to become a policeman instead of a Ph.D. Or the undreamed of, unexpected rewards of child-rearing may more than reconcile the parent to a flatter billfold. Or it may be as bad or worse than anticipated. But how does one know beforehand? How does one ever know?[48]

We wonder whether our technological age has blinded us to the reality of God's ultimate and final Sovereignty. He "works all things after the counsel of His will" (Eph. 1:11) and He controls the affairs of nations (Ps. 2:1-12). As Christians, He even "causes all things (that includes our sins and failures) to work together for (our) good" (Rom. 8:28). Certainly, planning is proper Christian stewardship, but we have seen that in birth control we have tended to leave out God's commands and His ultimate control. Even so, whether from teaching or the Sovereign movement of God's Spirit, it is my observation that Christians are presently having many more than the "allotted" 1-2 children.

Summary. It would be impossible to deal particularly with all the relevant decisions that couples face. I can, however, develop some general principles for use in particular instances. First, any couple who marries and chooses not to have children, even though they are physically able or do not have a severely limiting situation, violate God's creation mandate. On the one hand, contraception is never forbidden in the Bible. On the other hand, the emphasis of the Bible is the identity of God's blessing by the provision of children. Second, one or two children are probably insufficient to fulfill the biblical expectation. "The burden of proof rests, then, on the couple who wish to restrict the size of their family."[49] Third, any limitation of children should not be made without counsel from one's local church. The final decision rests on the family, however, not the church.[50] The church is then to advise, not to dictate. Fourth, the responsibility to procreate was given to the family. The state therefore has no authority to set any limits whatsoever on the size of families.[51]

Conclusions: Biblical Perspectives

The creation mandate is consistent with the principles and facts of those who oppose population control. Although clear biblical teaching does not need outside support, such consistency gives additional assurance that our interpretation is correct. Science and Scripture ultimately cannot conflict.[52] Such consistency also provides non-biblical answers for opponents who do not believe that the Bible has valid arguments.

The creation mandate is a position of faith. In spite of the evidence that the world can support 35-100 billion people, the hypothesis remains untested. We would not be honest if we did not consider that the population controllers *might* be right. Our assurance does not come from our own "planning" and calculation, but from the trustworthiness of our God.

Such trust has two applications. First, His laws and principles in general cannot be compromised because of any personal or social situation. For example, induced abortion can never be justified for any reason because it violates the 6th Commandment.[53] Individual families, however, may have limiting factors. Second, God will make provision at the appropriate time for the fulfillment of His commandments. One conclusion of our study is that population growth is quite unpredictable. Further, food production can be markedly increased by current methods and future technology is likely to cause further increase.

We frequently overlook the fact that we live in a universe were primary reality is supernatural. The Trinity and created spiritual beings preceded this universe and will continue to exist after it is gone or changed by fire. Certain conditions are predicated on God's supernaturalism. One example is the Sabbath. As Christians, we almost entirely associate the Sabbath with Sunday, our day of worship and rest, but the concept of the Sabbath also concerned rest for the fields (Lev. 25:1-22). American farmers confirm that land will produce a greater harvest in the year that follows its lying fallow. There is no naturalistic explanation for this phenomenon.[54]

Another example is the relationship of the physical world to man's sin (Rom. 8:20-22). *On this basis of natural effect by supernatural cause, is it not logical that God will provide for the fulfillment of the creation mandate?* Again, this position is one of faith, but one that has "evidence of things not seen" (Heb. 11:1). It is not a blind leap, but a conclusion based upon the character of God and His activity in the affairs of men and nature.

The "bottom line" is that man believes that he is able to plan the growth of the world's population better than God. This deception is one aspect of God's supposed "foolishness" and man's "wisdom" (I Corinthians 1:25-31). When placed in this perspective, the truly foolish thing to follow is man's wisdom.

The perspective is clearer when the population and birth control planners are placed within their own worldview. Ultimately, they are the advocates of state coercion and death (by abortion, infanticide and euthanasia) as a solution to social problems (see our Introduction). Their practical solutions represent a philosophical (religious) system that is entirely opposed to the biblical worldview. There are only two such systems.[55] As Harry Blamires has said, there is a "gigantic battle between good and evil that splits the universe."[56] The population debate is one "front" of that battle.

The family was given responsibility for the fulfillment of the creation mandate. This principle alone is sufficient to counter any argument that any government may mandate or even encourage birth control of its citizens. It is a family responsibility over which the state can claim no control. Later, we will see how this principle applies to those who carry genetic diseases and who are mentally incompetent. That population planners would advocate such state control is, however, consistent with their worldview that is not only anti-life, but anti-family (in their advocacy of heterosexual activity outside marriage and homosexuality). It is no accident that legally minor children do not need their parents permission to receive birth control prescriptions, to be treated for sexually transmitted diseases, and to have an abortion. These practices are possible only where the family and its procreative task is denigrated. It is the imposition of man's design over God's design.

Evangelicals must see population explosion as evangelistic opportunity. Today, we have more means than ever to proclaim the Good News worldwide. Directly, we have seen that God's primary means of evangelism is the family. Indirectly, we have evangelism outside the family. An increasing number of people is an increasing number of people for God's Kingdom. The greatest blessing associated with many children is for them to realize their salvation in Jesus Christ.

"Wrongful Birth"

The euphemism, "wrongful birth,"[57] illustrates the anti-life and anti-family sentiment of our day. Mostly, this change has taken place within the last twenty years. The attitude has shifted from children as blessings to children as wrongs to the degree that tort damages are sought for both healthy and "defective" children.[58] In fact, courts have ruled that wrongful birth can result for eight different reasons: "failure to fill a birth control prescription, an unsuccessful sterilization, an unsuccessful vasectomy, inaccurate pre-pregnancy counseling, inaccurate pregnancy counseling, the failure to diagnose a pregnancy, the failure to offer amniocentesis to a woman whose age makes her a "high-risk" pregnancy, and... unsuccessful abortion."

These "successful" court cases contrast with one that occurred in 1934. A man underwent a vasectomy to prevent the conception of another child after his wife had "substantial difficulty" with her first pregnancy. When his wife later conceived and had a normal, healthy child, he sued for damages from the physician who had done the vasectomy. He lost the case because a vasectomy was against public policy (how times have changed)! In 1967, a couple sued their doctors on the grounds that they were negligent to inform them of the possible harmful effects of German measles on the unborn child so that they could have had an abortion. This couple lost because the intangible, immeasurable, and complex human benefits of motherhood and fatherhood ... (weigh) against the alleged emotional and money injuries .... substantial public policy reasons prevent this Court from allowing damages for the denial of the opportunity to take an embryonic life (to have an abortion). Today, the mother has the legal right to "take an embryonic life!"

If the concept of wrongful life continues, it will take its toll on human values. 1) Increasing pressure will be exerted on women over 35 years of age, whose babies have a increased likelihood of genetic problems, to have amniocentesis for all pregnancies to evaluate the quality of the fetus and to abort those in which genetic "defects." 2) Infanticide will become the "solution" for those who are born in spite of attempt to detect and to prevent their births. 3) The effect may be severe in the child who becomes aware that his birth was "wrong." 4) Benefits for handicapped people could deteriorate. 5) Physicians could lose their legal right not to participate in or perform abortions.

6) The astronomical awards of these suits are already raising the costs of malpractice insurance for obstetricians and gynecologists so high that some are leaving their practice. To continue to deliver babies, they must raise their fees to cover this "overhead." The problem is extending to midwives, so the availability of professionals to manage pregnancy and deliver babies may become inadequate. 7) A larger dimension of the same concept is that children have the "right" to sue their parents. That is, wrongs between parents and their children may be addressed in courts of law (as if courts have all the answers). Although such action is just beginning in this country, it is already widespread in Sweden.

From a biblical perspective the concept of a wrongful birth is foreign to God's creation mandate, His blessing through children, and His design for the family. The concept of wrongful birth is another heinous side of eugenics. The corresponding breakdown of the family in which a child can sue his parents for such reasons, is barbaric.

Sexual Research and Therapy

Christians lack of response to sexual research and therapy reveals the depth to which we have been influenced by modern society. Under the guise of "desensitization" video presentations at medical and other professional meetings would be "XXX-rated" in a movie theater. The overflow crowds that attend these showings are evidence that interest is more than "academic."

The first such "research" to achieve scientific status was the Kinsey Report in 1953.[59] It is still quoted as a factual source, but rarely is it scrutinized to determine how its "facts" were obtained. Dr. S. I. McMillen is one exception.[60] He outlines the extreme bias present in Kinsey's work: 1) the ratio of single women to married women was three times greater than the general population and 2) the only participants were those women who were willing to report the intimacies of their sexual experience. Yet, from this study norms were established for sexually "fulfilled" women.

Today, the most prominent sexual researchers are the husband and wife team of William H. Masters and Virginia Johnson. Their, research is immoral since it includes the study of sexual partners who are not married to each other. Even a husband and wife who are willing to be studied under the scrutiny of others violate the intimacy that God has directed for marriage (Heb. 13:4). A morality that allows unmarried partners to engage in sexual "research" is nothing less than a perversion.

94

Before going further, you should be aware that the Bible is not prudish about sexual thoughts or behavior. The Song of Solomon is quite descriptive of intimacies between two lovers. A recent book has explored the various sexual themes of this book of the Bible in some detail.[61] In this biblical light the Puritans have been wrongly maligned for their restrictive attitude toward sexual behavior. In fact, this view ascribes to the Puritans what actually reflects the Victorian era. God does restrict sexual activity to marriage, but the design for the fullest and most joyous expression of sexual fulfillment is not restrictive!

Evidence for the association of a strong religious commitment and enjoyment of sexual intimacy comes from an unlikely source, *Redbook Magazine*.[62] In its first report *all age groups* of "strongly religious women were the most likely to describe their marital sex as `very good.'" In its second report women were "asked about religious feelings in a more complex way," but the results confirmed the first report that no other group had better sexual relationships than those who were "strongly or moderately religious." On the opposite side "the women with strong feelings against religion were the likeliest to have unhappy sexual relationships."

Two characteristics of these studies should be noted. First, "religious" people in the United States are predominately Christians in spite of our increasingly religious pluralism. Second, *Redbook Magazine*, as it promotes the modern "sexual ethic," would not likely try to refute the long-held view that strongly religious women are sexually "up-tight." Thus, the source gives greater credence to the validity of the study and credits them with honest reporting.

Unfortunately, some evangelicals have adopted an importance for sexual activity within marriage that reflects secular, rather than biblical thinking. Dr. Robert Smith's review of one such book illustrates this situation.[63] Although he makes a thorough review of the book to show many biblical and unbiblical principles, we will only examine two problems that are especially serious. First, the title of the book, *The Act of Marriage* reflects the authors' perception that sexual fulfillment is the central focus of marriage. Dr. Smith correctly states that

> The act of marriage is the binding of two people together in a
> lifelong companionship, and as a result of that bond the sexual
> relationship will be a very vital part of their life.

Second, the authors use "lovemaking," "make love," and "loving" to identify sexual activities. This selection of terms is a serious limitation of the biblical concept of love. Agape, the predominant word in the New Testament for love, is used of the relationship of God to man (John 3:16), man to God (Mt. 22:37), man to man (Mt. 22:39), and spouse to spouse (Eph. 5:25). Certainly, within marriage one expression of agape is sexual, but the breadth and depth of the word is lost when it is limited to the sexual part of marriage. Philos is used much less often that agape, but is a synonym of agape if one considers that both are used similarly in various contexts.[64] The Greek word, *eros*, that is sometimes used to denote sexual love, is not present in the New Testament.

The virtual identification of "love" with sexual behavior is a secular concept, probably Freudian in origin, that should be avoided by Christians. Anyone experienced in marriage counseling knows that sexual problems are almost always secondary to other problems. Undoubtedly, this reality reflects the biblical concept that sexual behavior is an expression of marriage, not its central feature.

The biblical standard is seriously lacking in every area of medicine and sexual research/therapy. We do not question that sexual problems within Christian marriages need to be addressed and counseled, but biblical principles and definitions must control both analysis and direction. The current knowledge that has been gained from sexual research should not be ignored, but it must be carefully scrutinized because of the immoral situations from which it was derived. At the same time further research in this area must be condemned. Sexual intimacy is reserved for marriage by the One who instituted marriage and to those believers whom He has given gifts to counsel such problems. It is a fallacy of modern thinking that we must have greater knowledge in every area than was available in the past in order to" cope." We have the same promise to us that God gave to Paul, "My grace is sufficient for you, for power is perfected in weakness" (II Corinthians 12:9a).

Summary Principles of Creation, the Fall, and the Flood (Cosmology)

In philosophy, the study of first things and origins has a host of words that include this concept: cosmology, ontology, metaphysics, ultimate reality, religion, worldview, ethic, metaphysics, epistemology, and other such terms. By contrast, a Biblical cosmology is the only true cosmology. The following are Summary Principles for its historical and scientific origins.

Philosophies of science that deny the supernatural realm, believing only in the physical universe, include such terms as naturalism, materialism, positivism, empiricism, and pragmatism. All these stand against the Biblical truth of two equally true dimensions: the natural and the supernatural (spiritual).

1. **God "Is."** The Bible assumes God's past, present, and future existence. "In the beginning (of time), God created the heavens and the earth." Before anything physical came into being, God existed. God told Moses at the burning bush, "Before Abraham was, 'I am.'" God has always been and always will be. His existence is independent of, and supernatural to, His creation. He is above and beyond time and matter.

2. **Immanent and Sustaining**. "All things are upheld by the word of His power" (Hebrews 1:3). Having created, He is omnipresent, everywhere in His creation, yet distinct from it. Being omnipotent, He is the source of all sustaining power in the universe. Being omniscient, everything in the universe, including the minds of natural and supernatural beings, is known to Him.

3. **Creation**. God created the entire physical universe ex nihilo, out of nothing, in six days along with the spiritual nature of Adam and Eve (the parents of all men and women). Any concept of evolution, including theistic evolution, is inconsistent with Biblical truth. It is also inconsistent with the best scientific understanding of the fossil record, the complexity of mature living things, the geologic column, and the commonly accepted scientific classifications of genus and species.

"Very Good." At the end of Creation, God pronounced all that He had made as "very good." Thus, everything in the universe, as He created it, is inherently moral. Man or Satan may use nature to evil purposes, but these acts are not consistent with God's original intentions.

4. **Natural and Supernatural**. There are two extant dimensions. One is nature or natural, the physical realm, that may be examined by the senses (empirically): touched, seen, felt, heard, and tasted with or without instruments. The other is supernatural, which cannot be examined by the senses. Herein exists God and the supernatural beings (angels, Satan, demons, cherubim, seraphim, etc.). Neither dimension is more "real" than the other. These supernatural beings may assume physical properties, and thus be perceived by man's senses, but they primarily exist in the non-physical dimension.

Mind. The concept of mind links these two realms. See Image of God below.

5. **Image of God in man before and after the Fall**. Man was created in the image of God. This image is primarily man's mind, which is not part of the physical, although linked to it through the brain. The Fall of Adam diminished, but did not destroy, this image. Man is able to think rationally and logically, although prone to errors.

Intelligence and communication comes from God. "In the beginning was the Word, and the Word was with God, and the Word was God" (John 1:1). "Word" is a broad and deep concept. John Calvin in his commentary on the Gospel of John translates "Word," as "The Speech." Gordon Clark discusses that hundreds of words are needed to represent adequately logos, Greek for "word." (*The Johannine Logos*, (The Trinity Foundation, 1972), page 14.

Effects of the Fall. The physical universe was affected by man's Fall in cataclysmic ways (Romans 8:19-22). Bible-believing scientists differ on exactly what these effects were. However, the Bible is specific on some changes (Genesis 3). A) Pain in childbirth for women. B) Man's struggle to produce and provide sustenance for himself and his family. C) Disease and death of living things. D) Serpents made to slither on their bellies.

Scientific studies of the effects of the Fall are complicated by changes that occurred because of the Flood. Since evolution is neither consistent with the Biblical record of creation nor with the scientific evidence, geological and biological records from archeological and sedimentary study show profound changes that cannot be explained without these extraordinary events.

6. **Effects of the Flood**. Again, Bible-believing scientists are not agreed exactly what processes were involved in the Flood or the changes in the natural world that were affected by that cataclysmic event. However, there are Biblical clues in that the "fountains of the great deeps were broken up and the windows of heaven were opened" (Genesis 7:11). It is likely that the earth's crust was changed markedly, as were many other natural processes. These effects contrast with the concept of **Uniformitarianism** (below).

Only eight people survived the Flood: Noah and his wife, their sons (Shem, Ham, and Japheth) and their wives. They are the fathers and mothers of all subsequent generations.

7. **Effects of the Last Days**. As God wraps up human history, he will destroy the present universe and create a new one (II Peter 3:10-13). Thus, the natural world will not exist forever.

8. **Uniformitarianism**. The philosophy of science that all natural process are the same yesterday, today, and in the future. **The Creation, The Fall, The Flood, and The New Creation** destroy this concept. Almost certainly, non-uniformity of natural processes, caused by events of the Flood, is the cause of mistakes being made in the dating systems of modern physics.

9. **Creation Mandate**. "Be fruitful and multiply; fill the earth and subdue it; have dominion over the fish of the sea, over the birds of the air, and over every living thing that moves on the earth" (Genesis 1:28). Man is to rule the earth and all that is in it under God's authority, as His stewards, and by His Word to give direction for this task. John Murray has named seven mandates: (1) "the procreation of offspring, (2) the replenishing of the earth, (3) subduing the same, (4) dominion of the creatures, (5) labor, (6) the weekly Sabbath, and (7) marriage" (Principles of Conduct, page 27).

Cultural Mandate. The verse above applies not only to dominion over nature, but the transformation of cultures towards the system that God has devised and written in the Scriptures.

10. **Biblical History and Modern Science**. Modern science believes that only "science" can make statements about natural events in history. A Biblical position would include Biblical history. This position gives final authority to the Biblical account because 1) God caused the events and 2) He was there to observe what happened and to have His Spirit write about these events through his chosen scribes in the original autographs. While this history is not recorded in scientific language, it is recorded as factual history, and therefore cannot be voided by natural science.

Actually, science can make no statements about creation (cosmology). Science is limited to theory and experiment. What happened in the past may be constructed, as theory, but it is just that, theory. Since the past is past, no experiments can be made upon it, so experimental science can say nothing about the past. In fact, the study of the past is an historical endeavor, not a scientific one. Thus, rules of studying and making conclusions from history apply to the study of origins, not science. Since the only Person who witnessed Creation was God Himself, only He can record the observable events. And, He has done so!

11. **Age of the Universe**. The precise age of the earth and the universe is unknown. However, their age is likely much closer to the estimate of Bishop

James Ussher of approximately 6000 years than any estimates of tens of thousands of years or more which is a capitulation to evolutionary science.

12. **Providence of God**. "God, from all eternity, did, by the most wise and holy counsel of his own will, freely, and unchangeably ordain whatsoever comes to pass: yet so, as thereby neither is God the author of sin, nor is violence offered to the will of the creatures; nor is the liberty or contingency of second causes taken away, but rather established" (Westminster Confession of Faith, III:1).

"God the great Creator of all things doth uphold, direct, dispose, and govern all creatures, actions, and things, from the greatest even to the least, by his most wise and holy providence, according to his infallible foreknowledge, and the free and immutable counsel of his own will, to the praise of the glory of his wisdom, power, justice, goodness, and mercy" (Westminster Confession of Faith, V:1). See WCF.

13. **Miracles**. "God, in his ordinary providence, makes use of means, yet is free to work without, above, and against them, at his pleasure" (Westminster Confession of Faith, V:3). Miracles are rare events after Biblical times. Before something is labeled a "miracle," it ought to examined intensively with extensive documentation. Even, then, mistaken conclusions may be made.

14. **Theory of Evolution**. Although the theory of evolution claims "evidences," close examination reveals that they are presumptions, rather than proofs. The theory was promulgated and supported by atheists as a necessary process, in the place of God, to explain the origin of all plant and animal life. Not only does it fail to account for the variety and complexity of living things, it fails to account for the origin of matter and energy.

15. **Second Law of Thermodynamics**. All of the chemical and physical processes in a closed system tend to drive that system toward maximum disorder (entropy). Evolution violates this natural law.

Endnotes

[1] Tierney, "Fanisi's Choice," 26. In an about face from previous positions that generally opposed "pro-life" positions, this magazine presented an excellent article that pointed out many fallacies of the population planners.
[2] Aristotle, *Politics*, 327.
[3] Thielicke, *Theological Ethics: Sex*, 215.

[4] Tierney, "Fanisi's Choice," 32.

[5] Norman, "Will World Population Double?"

[6] Clark, Population and Land Use. (page number not given)

[7] Muggeridge, "The Overpopulation Myth," 117.

[8] Chilton, "Planned Famine," 1.

[9] Carlson, "Famine 1985." All the information in this paragraph comes from this reference or Note 8

[10] Finkelstein, "Hard Work."

[11] Norman, "Will World."

[12] Kuehnelt-Leddihn, "Some Reflections," 77.

[13] Ibid., 74.

[14] Scorer, *Life in Our Hands*, 96.

[15] On an average 2.4 abortions must be done to prevent one live birth because the woman will be returned to the fertile state sooner than if she had completed the nine months of pregnancy. She will also not experience the relative infertility produced by breast feeding (see Chapter 2). Experience in several nations is consistent with this fact. Further, it is likely that the widespread availability of abortion reduces the effective practice of contraception because contraception is no longer the "last hope" to prevent the birth of an "accidental" pregnancy. (Potter, Additional Births," and Brackett, "Effects of Legalizing Abortion.")

[16] Kuehnelt-Leddihn, "Some Reflections, 72.

[17] Ibid., 74.

[18] Ibid., 71-72.

[19] Ibid., 78.

[20] Kazun, "The Population."

[21] Thielicke, *Theological Ethics: Sex*, 217.

[22] Young, "Literature, Literacy," 50-51.

[23] Dyck, *On Human Care*, 48.

[24] Carlson, "The Malthusian Budget," 43-46.

[25] Simon, "The Rhetoric of Population."

[26] Carlson, "Famine 1985."

[27] Murray, *Principles of Conduct*, 45-46.

[28] The importance of these verses and those that Jesus had in mind relative to the subject of divorce should not be underestimated. The rampant divorce among Christians has been further aggravated by misinterpretation of these and other relevant passages. The clearest and most thoroughly biblical treatment of this subject is found in Adams, *Marriage, Divorce, and Remarriage*.

[29] Thielicke, *Theological Ethics: Sex*, 203.

[30] Packer, "Situations and Principles," 164-5. Also, see "Voluntary Childlessness" later in this chapter.

[31] John Jefferson Davis, Evangelical Ethics: Issues Facing the Church Today, Phillipsburg, NJ: Presbyterian and Reformed Publishing Company, 1985, pp. 14-16.

[32] Ibid., p. 14.

[33] Murray, *Principles of Conduct*, 78; Thielicke, *Theological Ethics: Sex*, 202.

[34] Adams, *Marriage, Divorce, and Remarriage*, 16.

[35] "Flesh" has other meanings in other Biblical contexts.

[36] Adams, *Marriage, Divorce, and Remarriage*, 17.

[37] Calvin, *Harmony of the Gospels*, Vol.2, 380.

[38] Thielicke, *Theological Ethics: Sex*, 205-207.

[39] Ibid., 203

[40] See Notes 31 and 32

[41] Ramsey, *Fabricated Man*, 35-36, 56-59

[42] Hook, "Chromosomal Abnormality Rates."

[43] Unger, "To Multiply, Increase," *Nelson's Expository*, 254-5.

[44] Schaeffer, *The Christian Manifesto*.

[45] Murray, *Principle of Conduct*, 79.

[46] "The Cost of Raising Babies," *Perspective*, 1-12.

[47] Its function in the provision of health and healing has been developed in Payne, *Biblical/Medical Ethics*, 127-138.

[48] Wilson, "Mother Didn't Know," 31.

[49] Montgomery, "How to Decide", 10.

[50] Payne, *Biblical/Medical Ethics*, 63-64.

[51] For a description of coerced birth control, including abortion, in China, see Mosher, "Forced Abortions."

[52] Schaeffer, *No Final Conflict*.

[53] Even where the life of the mother is endangered, the goal is to save both lives if possible not to assure that the unborn baby dies (often by lethal injections), as is the current practice of induced abortion.

[54] Rushdoony, *Institutes of Biblical Law*, Vol. II, 203.

[55] Payne, *Biblical/Medical Ethics*, 11-26.

[56] Blamires, *The Christian Mind*, 70.

[57] All information in this section is from Eastland, "Who Put the Wrong."

[58] Kinsey, *Sexual Behavior*.

[59] "Wrongful life" generally refers to a lawsuit brought by a child (or his or her legal representative) born with birth defects who alleges that the physician was negligent to advise the mother of the possibility of birth defects or failed to perform the tests that would have disclosed their presence. "Wrongful birth" refers to similar conditions except that the suit is brought by the parents rather

the child. "Wrongful pregnancy" or "wrongful conception" refers to a lawsuit brought by the parents of a healthy child whose pregnancy should have been prevented by a sterilization procedure or abortion. I am lumping these terms under "wrongful birth" to avoid too much technical jargon and, more importantly, to focus on God's Sovereignty in every birth regardless of the number or severity of defects.

[60] McMillen, *None of These Diseases*. 1st Edition, 45-51.

[61] Dillow, *Solomon on Sex*.

[62] Levin, "Sexual Pleasure;" Philip and Lorna Sarrel. "The Redbook Report on Sexual Relationships," *Redbook Magazine* October 1980, pp. 73-80.

[63] Smith, Robert D., "Book Review: *The Act of Marriage*.

[64] Clark, *First John: A Commentary*, 69.

6. Natural Science and Technology

Science and Technology: A Brief Review of Basic Biblical Worldview and Ethics

The marvels of modern science are awesome to behold and to use. This very chapter is only possible by the computer and the Internet, surely two of the greatest inventions of the 20th Century. I am sure that each reader would have his own favorite. There is the simple plastic straw, which as McDonald's size, one can suck down a whole milkshake in record time! There is the microchip that makes every appliance and gadget "programmable" and adaptable (but not necessarily easier to use!).

Perhaps, at the top of the list would be manned space flights and interplanetary exploration. Space travel for people is at our doorsteps, fulfilling the dreams of young boys and astronomers who have ever gazed and wondered at "what is out there" for generations.

So, what does The Book that dates back several thousands years and written in cultures foreign to the "modern scientific mind" have to say about such science and technology? Actually, to presume that an omniscient God would not have known all that has been and will be developed is to make God smaller than He is -- for He is omniscient!

Science Cannot Determine Its Own Destiny

The first worldview principle towards science and technology is that neither can determine its own destiny, that is, what will be developed and how it will be used. Science, by its own nature of hypotheses and constructs, cannot select what will be developed or investigated. No one would argue that any industry or society has unlimited resources (time, money, equipment, and researchers). They are limited by budgets. Thus, inescapably choices of research and development have to be made. **Those decisions are not made by the science or technology department, whether in business or government.**

In business, the marketing department is likely to make those decisions, that is, what will grow the business best. In government, the budget analysts make those decisions. I am simplifying this process somewhat, but the point is that the producers and researchers develop their budgets and submit them to a "higher authority" who will determine whether they will get the funds to proceed. The scientists do not make these decisions.

These decisions come face to face with ethics: what is right or wrong in worldview (that is, Biblical righteousness). In business, virtually always the decision is made on what profit the company can make. In government, decisions are made for a variety of reasons: the greatest good for the greatest number, the greatest good for the best lobbying group, the greatest good for those deemed "worthy" (the elderly, the poor, the homeless, the crippled, the minority, etc., etc.). (The reader should note that *medical* science is included here.)

Now, any student of biblical worldview will recognize the "value" words above: "profit," "good", "greatest," and "worthy." **No area of science or technology within its own areas of expertise has any principle to govern such a decision. Choices are made on values outside the science and technologies themselves.**

Thus, the dilemma that is sometimes encountered by Christians and other moralists with the gigantism and wonder of modern science is false. Experimental and applied science can neither determine their own direction, nor even their own continued existence. Forces (values) outside of themselves will always do that for them. A pure worldview of science and technology does not exist!

Any Development of Science and Technology Is Strictly A-moral

There is no science or technology that within itself is either bad or good (moral or ethical). The science of the atom can be used to generate electricity for thousands of people or it can be used to kill and maim thousands in a horrible way. The science of smallpox can eradicate it from existence or unleash disfigurement and death. The automobile gives great freedom to people around the world, but also kills tens of thousands and injures far more. Genetic engineering has the potential to cure ravaging diseases or create an army of superman soldiers.

Perhaps, these examples will suffice to demonstrate that no technology within itself is to be feared. As the Bible tells us, "the heart is deceitfully wicked." The evil is in individuals, groups, or government who are in positions of power to use science and technology to achieve their own goals.

What Is Science?

More than a century ago, theology had been considered for centuries as the "Queen of the Sciences." (See below.) In that sense, Noah Webster's Dictionary of 1828 is helpful. Science is:

> 1. In a general sense, knowledge, or certain knowledge; the comprehension or understanding of truth or facts by the mind. "The science of God must be perfect."

> 2. In philosophy, a collection of the general principles or leading truths relating to any subject. Pure science, as the mathematics, is built on self-evident truths; but the term science is also applied to other subjects founded on generally acknowledged truths, as metaphysics; or on experiment and observation, as chemistry and natural philosophy; or even to an assemblage of the general principles of an art, as the science of agriculture; the science of navigation. Arts relate to practice, as painting and sculpture…

> 3. Art derived from precepts or built on principles…

> 4. Any art or species of knowledge...

> 5. One of the seven liberal branches of knowledge, that is, grammar, logic, rhetoric, arithmetic, geometry, astronomy and music.

> (Webster's Note - Authors have not always been careful to use the terms art and science with due discrimination and precision. Music is an art, as well as, a science. In general, an art is that which depends on practice or performance, and science that which depends on abstract or speculative principles. The theory of music is a science; the practice of it an art.)

For the location of the website where Webster's 1828 Dictionary may be found, see Reference at the end of this article.

This rather long quote is necessary, for "science" has become distorted in its meaning. (The person who is not interested in precise definition will never be competent in any area of knowledge, including his or her Christian experience.

106

I make no apology for this approach) Re-phrasing Webster's "1", we could say that "science is a systematic knowledge of any subject" (as theology was the queen of the sciences). But, "science," today, as it is generally, and even formally used, applies to such subjects as physics, chemistry, biology, medicine, and mathematics or all lumped together as "the sciences."

Herein is a serious problem of distortion. First, today's use of "science" strongly implies that any subject matter outside these disciplines is not "scientific," and therefore is a lesser form of knowledge. Second, "science" includes both the exact disciplines of physics, mathematics, and chemistry with the much-less-exact disciplines of biology and medicine. My medical training began over 40 years ago. I have seen diagnoses change markedly and new ones developed. I have witnessed significant changes in treatments, and in some cases, the exactly opposite treatment is recommended for the same disease process! Such is the nature of medical "science."

Perhaps, the worst example of this subtle inclusion of exact sciences with the life sciences is psychology. Psychology has several hundred theories of explanation and treatment. To say that psychology is a science is to generalize the word beyond any meaning at all. It would be more accurate to say that psychology is a very large group of theories with little experimental evidence. It will not compare to the precisions of physics, for example. Thus, psychology and the other life sciences receive a greatly substantive standing that is false, simply by their inclusion in the general category of "science."

So, each discipline must be evaluated as to its scientific validity on its own merits. Theology, as it was seriously practiced at the time of Noah Webster, should again be the "Queen of Sciences," for indeed, all natural revelation (including man's theories and experiments) must be evaluated in the light of God's Revelation. For a person or scholar who is a Bible-believing Christian not to make this evaluation is the most serious blunder to be made in ethics (or any worldview area).

After the above was written, I found this "classic definition" of science by Carl F. H. Henry: "any clearly defined subject matter that yields valid knowledge communicable from mind to mind and from generation to generation." Thomas Aquinas named theology as "the queen of the sciences." (God, Revelation, and Authority, Volume 1, page 202.)

Science as Function vs. Truth

Epistemology and a philosophic discussion of truth is beyond our scope here. However, it is central to the commonly accepted authority of science today. Simply, truth is reality; any subject or object in all its relations to everything else in the universe. The quick student will recognize that only God can know truth by this definition. That is one point. The second point is that because God has revealed Himself and other matters in His Word, we can know the truth that he has revealed. We can know no other truth.

(Again, I take great leaps in a philosophical discussion, but I believe that I have stated these two points accurately within philosophical and epistemological certainty. See the following reference for a greater explanation of these leaps.)

Thus, science does not produce truth. Science is either theoretical or experimental. Theory is never truth by its own definition. It is hypothetical.

Now, we are to the crux of the matter. **Experiment does not produce truth by its own design.** What does a scientist do in setting up an experiment? He sets rigid guidelines by which the experiment will be conducted. He must be precise, limit variables, and attempt to anticipate everything that might go wrong. Thus, **any results that he achieves will be limited to his experimental parameters.** The results, then, dear reader, is not truth.

Truth is all things in relation to all other things in the universe (above). Scientific results are only related to the conditions of the experiment. Note the contrast here. Truth relates to the entire universe; science is limited to its severely (relative to the universe) limited design. **Science can never be truth by its own limitations.** It is very narrowly and specifically applied to the conditions of the experiment.

Take the simple formula for a falling body in the footnote above. Its design is limited to an object falling in a vacuum. Please tell me where a vacuum exists on earth at sea level, where the formula applies. Nowhere. That limitation in reality is true of all scientific experimental results.

Now, here is the bottom line, science has great practical value, but it is not truth. The formula for a falling body and many other laws of gravity, propulsion, motion, etc. are sufficiently practical to send a manned mission to the moon and back, but none of that information is truth. Thus, **the gigantically pragmatic value of science has been grotesquely distorted to**

be truth when it is actually only experimental results within a strict paradigm.

Any reader new to this discussion will have to work at this matter. You will likely need to read other books. (See Recommended Reading). Most moderns are so ingrained in being unable to think philosophically while being indoctrinated with false reasoning that this process is indeed difficult.

So, here is the contrast. On the one side is the only truth available to mankind, The Holy Scriptures. On the other side is science, which can neither speak to its own ethics while limited to theory and an artificial construct (experimental design). It is the omniscient, "only wise God," vs. a-morality and man-made design.

Once more, we must give great credit to the **functionality** of science, but we cannot give it either a status of truth or any credence to speak to morality. Science has nothing within itself to gain status of either of these latter roles.

The Scriptures as the Cause of Modern Science

By any system of chronology, mankind lived on earth for thousands of years before the practices of modern science were developed. Why did not science appear earlier? Surely, the causes were multi-factorial, but two points should be made.

First, the large majority of the scientists who laid the foundations for modern science were Christians: Leonardo da Vinci, Johann Kepler, Francis Bacon, Blaise Pascal, Robert Boyle, Galileo, Isaac Newton, Michael Faraday, Samuel F. B. Morse, Rudolph Virchow, Louis Pasteur, Joseph Lister, and Gregor Mendel (to name only 13 of 52 listed by the late Henry Morris). Thus, there is no conflict between faith in God and the Bible and modern science. In fact, the opposite occurs. Faith in the One who "is the same today, yesterday, and forever" gives confidence to explore the wonders of His creation.

Second, the knowledge of the Bible in the hands of the common man changed a worldview that had boxed and fixed science for more than 1500 years. The Greeks saw the universe as fixed and limited the elements of fire, water, wind, and earth. The Scriptures showed a universe created by God who fixed its laws and made it predictable. The Bible energized men to create instruments (for example, the telescope, microscope, and stethoscope) to see and hear things that were never possible before.

While these developments are commonly attributed to the Renaissance, what occurred simultaneous with the Renaissance? The Reformation. As God's laws for the church and society found new meaning and application, His laws were being discovered in nature by His people (above) that were foundational to modern science.

Only the monotheistic religions (Christianity, Judaism, and Mohammedism) describe a universe created and inhabited (immanent and omniscient presence) by God according to fixed laws and holding a knowledge that is broad and deep, as a fitting testimony to its Creator.

Summary Statements

1. The values that determine what science will do, and where it will be applied, lie outside of the scientific world.

2. Science and technology within themselves are strictly a-moral. Their morality is determined in how they are applied in the lives of people.

3. In its modern use, "science" has a denotation of truth, when in actuality, it is either theory or limited to a precise experimental design. "Science," in its historical and accurate use, can be applied to any area of systematic study.

4. The Holy Scriptures, systematically applied, should once again be the "Queen of the Sciences."

5. The great functionality of science and technology belie their claim to truth (#3 above).

6. Most of the great, early scientists were Christians, and their Biblical worldview led them to great achievements in science.

Recommended Reading

Clark, Gordon. A Christian View of Men and Things. Unicoi, Tennessee: The Trinity Foundation, 1952.

Clark, Gordon. The Philosophy of Science and Belief in God. Jefferson, Maryland: The Trinity Foundation, 1987.

Davis, John Jefferson. Frontiers of Science and Faith. Downers Grove, Illinois: InterVarsity Press, 2002.

Moreland, J. P. Christianity and the Nature of Science. Grand Rapids: Baker Book House, 1989.

Rushdoony, Rousas J. The Mythology of Science. Nutley, New Jersey: Nutley Press, 1967.

Webster's 1828 Dictionary:
http://www.cbtministries.org/resources/webster1828.htm

The Epistemology of the Natural Sciences: False Objectivity and Inductive Reasoning

All knowledge comes through information from others (speaking or writing), Scriptural revelation (God writing) or through **inductive** reasoning from observations. The last method can never give us settled truth. (Or, as Francis Schaeffer said, "true truth.") Therefore, it follows, that unless one can **deductively** determine knowledge of these sciences from Scripture, one does not have a settled truth. That is the epistemological argument. Examples may help, but they only illustrate what is a sound argument in itself. (For definitions of induction and deduction in Glossary.)

Biology is **not** a settled science. Evolutionary pseudoscience is the most obvious, but not the only example. We piddle around on the beach, play in the waves, and declare that we understand the oceans. Relative to tides around the world: some locations have two tides per day, some have one tide per day, and still others have none.

Chemistry has been said to be a "closed science," in the sense that everything in it is reducible to physics, the atomic "shells," valences, etc. These account for "chemical" reactions. So, examples in physics will suffice for chemistry. Organic chemistry (the realm of living things), however, has complexities which render the theoretical reduction to physics essentially irrelevant. An astounding example is the "ribbon diagram" of a streptococcal and staphylococcal (two kinds of bacteria that infect humans) super antigen -- a rough model -- of the structure of just one immune molecule. Huge and complex! And, the body has dozens of these.

Physics is given away by its scientists who foray into cosmology -- theories of black holes, worm holes, Big Bang, string theory, multiverses, the wave/particle theory of light, etc. They are aggressive in their desire to erase any tiny remnant of a requirement for a Designer. Physicists cannot give a coherent account of gravity or time. They discourse and debate a great deal about a grand unified theory, uniting electromagnetism, gravity, and matter but such discussions are incoherent. You can watch their atom (Greek for that which cannot be split or divided) continue to get split into more and more exotic particles than quarks and the rest of their imaginary particle zoo. Some of their "explanations" make Zen Buddhism seem sensible by comparison. They take their notion of the uncertainty of the position of an electron in its peri-nuclear shell and expand that into a notion that everything is random.

These "scientists" are godless and are out to prove that there is no god by great leaps of faith in their own reasoning and flimsy theories. They present a form of 21st century witchcraft! They extrapolate beyond all sensibilities. They have measured the velocity of light in our corner of the universe for about 150 years -- results that are inconsistent and vary a great deal. They inductively conclude that our time-limited, location-limited, and methodology-limited "constants" for the velocity of light are accurate for all space and time. What hubris!

Mathematics is different. It is not a natural science at all. It is a set of decisions about how to relate anything quantitatively. It is sets of decisional rules which are made up. We like the rules because they generally "work" to correlate with our observations in nature. The Fibonacci number series, found ubiquitously in nature, is absolutely intriguing. The epistemological argument for mathematics would look like this: How do you know that two plus two equals four? Either it is revealed in Scripture (there are short books to establish this by deduction from passages here and there --Numbers for one) or one inductively notices that every time one counts and combines two with two others, one can then count four. Every time we go through this process, we inductively conclude that it is always going to be four, even for items not yet counted and combined. Philosophers like to say that such things are "intuitively true" or words to that near effect. That is just cheating to avoid saying that these things are **inductively "true."** Mathematics has its zoo as well. For example, what is the "meaning" of the square root of a negative number.

While on some practical and superficial level, some natural sciences may be considered to be "objective," at a deeper and cosmological level, scientists "faith" in a godless universe and their giant leaps of reasoning are laid bare.

* My thanks to Hilton Terrell for these insightful thoughts, first presented in an email to me.

More Thoughts on Science as Truth

The argument that the appearance of the universe being old is deceptive and that God would not deceive in this way. (1)Duh! He told us how and when He created in Genesis 1 and 2! What person is able to deceive by telling the truth, unless the listener is willing to be deceived!

(2) If the Big Bang did occur, as it is theorized, and you were there one second after it occurred, you could not tell whether it was one second old or 25 billion years old. Your decision of age would be based upon your own assumptions of the facts. The facts do not interpret themselves.

The problem of what my senses tell me. "We must 'override the apparent evidence of our senses' all the time in life... My senses tell me that the earth is flat and still and that the sun goes around the earth. My senses tell me that a friendly looking lion in the zoo wants me to pet him My sense tell me nothing about the way my computer works. Anyone who has ever observed a court case involving many witnesses knows that people's observations and senses can be very incorrect... **Moreover, our senses tell us nothing about the history of the cosmos.** Our senses react to pain and light and sound, but they have nothing to do with grand philosophical cosmogonic schemes. It is not the "apparent evidence of our senses" that Genesis 1 may "override," but rather the highly rarified philosophies of our sin-twisted reason.... It is analogous to Jesus turning water into wine in Cana. The "evidence of our senses" would say that the wine had been made the usual way over a long course of time. (Indeed the attendees senses did indicate such — Ed.) ... The same is true regarding the events of the creation of the world." (James Jordan, Creation in Six Days, Canon Press, 1999, page 117)

We should understand the difference between understanding and pragmatic value. Modern man, beginning with Thomas Edison, has marvelously learn to use electricity, but there are still considerable mysteries about how it works.

Summary Principles of Natural Science and Technology

Creation principles have not been addressed here except as they impact the natural sciences directly. Those Summary Principles of Creation are listed under their own category. However, there is considerable overlap between science and creation. In a real sense, those principles and these form a unit because they cannot really be separated. Yet, for purpose of emphasis and modern arguments they are best separated.

Discussion of these Summary Principles. The full discussion on this site of these Summary Principles has not yet been written. However, the following sources cover many, if not most of them: Science and Technology and The Nature of Science.

The following are not necessarily arranged in any priority of order.

1. **Etymology and history of the word, "science."** "Science" is being used here consistent with the modern denotation that "science" means natural sciences. However, readers should understand that historically and etymologically, "science" refers to the systematic study of any subject. For example, beginning in the Scholastic period of history, theology was the "Queen of the Sciences," which demonstrates its superior position among all the other "sciences" and natural science itself. The term "modern science," is synonymous with natural science.

Objectivity and subjectivity in the natural sciences. At first glance, mathematics, physics, chemistry, biochemistry, biology, and engineering do not appear to be affected by philosophical or religious beliefs. However, this glance is misleading. **All sciences are inductive conclusions made from observations.** By definition, induction does not arrive at truth. For induction to be truth, it would have to have observed every particular phenomena in the universe — an impossible task. So, inductive (empirical) conclusions are limited to those observations actually made: that is, the construct of the experimental design. The workings of chemistry are actually based upon physics (behavior of electrons, protons, shell valences, etc.). Physics makes such conclusions as the "Big Bang" or some sort of "grand unified theory" of the universe. Such theories defy the simplest forms of "common sense," much less qualify for serious reflection as worthy knowledge, much less "truth." For more explanation here, see "Science and Pragmatism as Truth and The Pragmatic Test of Truth" (www.biblicalworldview21.org).

Again, these natural sciences have great **function** and utilitarian value, but they come nowhere near qualifying for truth, which never changes and is always reliable anywhere and everywhere in every time period of history

Psychology, medicine, sociology, anthropology, and economics are **highly subjective**. They are behavioral sciences, having to do with the behavior of man. Biblical values impact directly on what is right and wrong in their theory and practice. Ignoring Biblical principles will greatly affect their function.

2. **Authoritative Bible**. The Bible, as God's Word to man and as truth, is always authoritative over any statements by science where both address the same issue. Properly understood, there is never any contradiction between science and Scripture. In many areas, the Bible a has far greater application in science than may be apparent from a casual consideration of the Bible itself or the attention that other Christian scholars have given it.

3. **Science is not truth**. The method of science is to discover the mechanisms (God's laws) of the universe and apply them for the good of mankind. This method does not discover truth because all its operations are theory or experiment. Theory, by definition, is not truth. Conclusions by experiment are strictly limited to the conditions of the experiment, and therefore, not universally applicable. For example, no vacuum exists in nature at sea level to make the (very useful) "law" of the speed of a falling body (over time) a universal truth. Discussion of Science as Truth

4. **Value and Ethics**. "Science cannot determine its own value... By science bombs are made and cancer may be cured. Most people think that bombs and medicine are good to have. But, there is no experiment that proves their goodness.... can any experimentation demonstrate that either the destruction of cities (and life) or the extension of life is good?" (Gordon Clark, *Philosophy of Science...*, page 95). Such values come from God's Word. Technology within itself is a-moral, that is, has no inherent morality within itself. Its morality is determined by sources outside of itself by the intent and purposes for which it is used.

The cultural and moral force of technology. Technology does bring a strong tendency to erode values. Adding numeric values to social and psychological studies gives them an appearance of objectivity that they do not have. The advancement of technology in any area is not an advancement of cultural progress (which should be defined only by Biblical values). For example, computers with greater speed and storage will be necessarily be used for the "good" of mankind. A general and immediate availability of a wide range of information (television, computers, etc.) increases one's susceptibility to a sinful response to temptation because in prior times one would not be exposed to that information. See Postman, Technopoly... for his great review of the problems of technology. However, his proposed solutions are not Biblical.

5. **Pragmatic Value or Operationalism**. To state that science does not determine truth is not to diminish its great pragmatic value. But, that greatness can be for good or evil (as in #3 above). Alfred Nobel regretted the invention of dynamite because he developed it for its great potential in construction, but armies used it to destroy human lives and property, often under the direct of dictators with evil agendas. The same science that places communication satellites in orbit can be used for "smart bombs." See The Nature of Science.

6. **Modern science and the Reformation**. While modern science cannot absolutely be said to have been caused by the Reformation, there are strong reasons to believe that it was. (1) The beginnings of modern science began in the same century as the Reformation. (2) Many, if not most, of the early scientists were Bible-believing Christians. (See Christian Scientists.) (3) Neither the Greek nor the medieval concept of nature invited the diligent examination of nature that constitutes modern science. (4) According to the Reformers, nature was a revelation to be studied, as special revelation was to be studied. As God was intelligible, they expected that nature would be, also. For more on this subject, see Christianity and the Rise of Modern Science.

7. **Nature is God's general revelation**. As God has revealed Himself in His special revelation, the Bible, He has revealed much of Himself in His general revelation of nature. As men are to study the Bible to know and understand what God has chosen to reveal of Himself, men are also to study nature in order to know the creativity of God and apply that knowledge for the welfare of mankind. As men learn to worship in special revelation, so science should also evoke man's worship of nature as the creativity of God. As "the chief end of man is to glorify God and to enjoy Him forever," the chief end of science, as one of man's occupations, would be the same.

8. **God's design of the universe and man's laws that describe this design**. God created the universe to function according to properties of matter, motion, and energy. Gravity, centrifugal force, acceleration of bodies approaching each other, the boiling point of water, inertia, and many other properties within nature are according to His design. **The only reason for these properties is that He designed them into His universe.** These properties give a precision and orderliness to the universe that makes it predictable and useful for mankind to live and work there.

As man has discovered these properties, he has formulated laws that sufficiently approximate these properties to allow him to benefit and function more fully within this orderliness. Nature functions according to God's design, not according to "laws" which are only descriptions of those properties.

116

9. **Gods Providence and His immanence in His creation**. One tenet of the Reformation was the Providence of God; that is, that He is immanently present in His Creation and determines all events "according to the counsel of His own will." Further, He is "upholding all things by the word of His power" (Hebrews 1:3). Increase Mather (1639-1723) wrote of God's activity in the thunder and lightning and terrible majesty of storms, as well as, in all the events of men and nations. Modern Christians need to recover that sense of God's unfailing and constant presence. The operations of the universe are not solely because of their inherent laws and properties, but God's present activity in them. (Increase Mather, *A History of God's Remarkable Providences in Colonial New England* (Back Home Industries, 1997, reprint of original from 1856).

10. **The universe is broken**. Both the universe and the life of all creatures have been impaired such that disease, death, extinctions, imperfections in structure, and other such calamities are the results of changes in properties and processes decreed by God upon an originally perfect universe because of the Fall of man (Genesis 3:14-19; 1 Peter 1:24-25; Hebrews 1:10-12). (Used with minor changes from the Coalition on Revival's Sphere Document on Science, #16.)

11. **Laws and properties of nature**. All laws of nature exist because God designed them that way. For example, the law of gravity exists because God designed two bodies to attract each other. There is no inherent property in these bodies to cause them to attract each other outside of God's original design. Therefore, all "ultimate" laws and properties in nature reside in God's design and ongoing Providence.

12. **Technology for warfare**. "Because at any time we may be required to resort to military defense to preserve our lives and liberty, it is acceptable and proper for a Christian to use science and technology to develop weapon systems essential to the defense of his country." (Also, from the Coalition on Revival... Science, #19)

13. **Pollution and husbandry of animals**. The Creation Mandate to "rule" and "subdue" all of God's creation does not include inevitable and unlimited pollution; cruelty to, and extinction of, animals; or irresponsible management of the earth's resources. Man must be subject to all of God's laws that govern in these areas. However, in current times, the evidences of modern science concerning these areas are being skewed to promote an agenda that is inconsistent with all God's ordinances that govern man and nature. Abuses of nature that have occurred do not mandate that they be corrected by un-Biblical

(immoral) means. All peoples, Christians in particular, ought to pursue an understanding of the best science that can be known in these areas and apply them within the constraints of all Biblical law.

14. **Global warming**. An honest review of all the information available on global warming shows that the evidence is inconclusive. To base political, social, and legislative policy on such science is dishonest at best, and tyranny, at worst. See Michael Crichton's novel, *State of Fear* (HarperCollins Publisher, 2004). For a solidly conservative, scholarly, and Biblically accurate study of this issue, see Interfaith Stewardship Alliance.

15. **God is evident in nature**. "For since the creation of the world His invisible attributes are clearly seen, being understood by the things that are made, even His eternal power and Godhead, so that they are without excuse" (Romans 1:20). The rest of the verses in this chapter of Romans demonstrate the link between man's understanding of nature and his behavior. It is the link of the natural and the supernatural, of the physical world and the world of ethics, and of the causes of health and life and disease and death. It is a link of God's immanent activity among men and in nature according to man's thinking and behavior.

16. **The civil state and science**. The role of government is to "reward good and punish evil" (Romans 13:1-5). It has no role in either the funding of science or conjoint efforts with scientists for development and research (scientific socialism) except in the development of weapons for police work and warfare.

17. **Miracles**. See Creation Summary Principles.

18. **Natural death of living organisms**. Natural science cannot account for the death of organisms that are able to propagate, but only live for a limited period of time, even when not assaulted by some outside force. The processes that propagate and sustain life fail over time for no known natural reasons. Genesis Chapter 3, accounts for the death of living creatures. All creation is under God's curse because of man's sin.

19. **More information is the solution to cultural problems**. "Our most serious problems are not technical (nor scientific), nor do they arise from a lack of information." (Postman, Technopoly: The Surrender ..., page 119). The solution is the full application of the Bible to all areas of worldview.

Endnotes

1. "Operationalism" is a word suggested by Gordon Clark (Philosophy of Science... page 93). I suggest "pragmatic value" or "functional value." "Value" shows its great utility to be used for the good of mankind. "Pragmatic" or "functional" shows its application. But, neither of the three terms allows science to approach the notion that it is "truth" or can determine what is right or what is wrong.

2. Neil Postman, Technopoly: The Surrender of Culture to Technology, (Vintage Books/Random House, 1993).

Further Reading

Clark, Gordon. *Philosophy of Science and Belief in God*. Trinity Foundation, 1964.

Davis, John Jefferson. *The Frontiers of Science and Faith*. InterVarsity Press, 2002.

Henry, Carl F. H. *Horizons of Science*. Harper and Row, 1978.

Moreland, J. P. *Christianity and the Nature of Science*. Baker Book House, 1989.

Morris, Henry. *Biblical Basis of Modern Science*. Baker Book House, 1984.

Rushdoony, R. J. *The Mythology of Science*. www.chalcedonstore.com

7. Education

Summary Worldview Principles of Education

1. **God is omniscient. That is, God knows all things**. "In (Christ) are hidden all the treasures of wisdom and knowledge" (Colossians 2:3). "In the beginning was the Word, and the Word was with God, and the Word was God" (John 1:1). Man could not think had not God created His mind. No man can ever think a thought that God has not thought of before he did. Therefore, no thought of man can ever surprise God. Most Biblical theologians have concluded that the image of God of Genesis 1:27 is man's mind.

Therefore, everything that man learns has already been known by God. No more important statement can be made about education. **Education is seeking God's thoughts in whatever area that man pursues.** The beginning of knowledge begins with the knowledge of God, else everything learned has a false nature about it, even though that knowledge in isolation from any reference to God may be greatly pragmatic. (Link)

God has revealed His mind to us in the 66 books of the Protestant Bible. Do not let the familiarity of this truth slip by too easily. The Creator of the universe, who is omniscient, who knows everything fully and completely in a way that no son of Adam ever will, has spoken to us! He has given us the only source of truth that we will know in this earthly life. Thus, the Bible is the most important book that we will ever study.

"The end of learning," wrote John Milton, "is to repair the ruin of our first parents by regaining to know God aright, and out of that knowledge to love Him, to imitate Him, to be like Him." Quoted in Clark, *A Christian Philosophy...*, vii (below). **"... A revival of godliness will always produce a revival of learning,"** (Douglas Wilson, *Antithesis*, I(4):35, "Apologetics and the Heart").

This Biblical education is far more comprehensive than many Christians might perceive initially. Biblical education includes Bible study, theology (including systematics), and everything in worldview (much of which is on this website). It is not the simple Bible teaching that many Christian schools and colleges have in their curriculum. In too many areas, such as, civil

120

government, economics, law, sociology, crime and punishment, and mercy ministries, Christians speak and behave with little difference from the non-Christians. For example, the foundation of law in the United States descended from English Common Law which was the implementation of the Law of Moses. Few Christians of any age seem to know this fact of history and law.

Some Christians have bought the notion that tradition and "classics," apart from a compete Biblical education and worldview, are adequate for primary and secondary education. "The chief end of man is to glorify God and enjoy Him forever" (the First Question of the Shorter Catechism of the Westminster Confession of Faith). Our God will "have no others before Him" (First Commandment). Thus, this notion is seriously erroneous. The moral power of God's instructions to mankind directly from His Word, or its logical deduction thereof, is infinitely greater than His word being diluted through the moral instruction of men divorced from His Special Revelation.

The highest goal of Christian schools should be to give students the best tools possible to study and learn the Bible. If the Bible is the only truth that man will ever know, then the Bible should be any student's most important object of study. Most, if not all Christian educators, struggle with what to include or exclude in the curriculum. **If study of the Bible is not their highest priority, no other education matters!** The Bible tells us truly and practically what is necessary to obey God, love our neighbor, and love God with all our "heart, soul, mind, and strength." No other study can accomplish these ends.

2. **Education is simply learning some knowledge or skill that one did not know before**. In fact, one could say that most education that occurs is not within a formal process. Skills include not only motor functions, but methods of reasoning, such as, logic, scientific inquiry, and rational thinking. See Logic, etc. below.

3. **"Education" has become synonymous with formal education: primary, elementary, college, and graduate.** There is the conditioned attitude that once a person has finished high school, college, graduate school, or _____ (fill in the blank), his or her education is completed. Sure, there may be some knowledge required for a job or other activity, but basically one's education is done. This attitude is wrong. Actually, once one finishes the "ticket" to job requirements, which is what formal education primarily is (beyond "reading, writing, and arithmetic"), then one's attitude should be that I am free at last to study what is really important (as what is discussed among these summary principles).

One example is the oversold value of college education. See below.

4. **This notion of completed education is perhaps the most deadening blow to the Church and the Kingdom of God**. There is virtually no expectation of Christians in their churches to know more than a simple understanding of the Gospel (and sometimes that is not even required). Sure, there are "Bible studies" and Sunday School, but there is no defined curriculum for the church member (Christian) to achieve. Seminaries have established curricula for ministers, and some "full time Christian workers," but "laymen" have no such course of study. No wonder that the church in the United States and other parts of the world is virtually irrelevant to social justice and can only offer "fire insurance."

Yet, never in the history of the Church have Christians had the resources that are available today! These include the Internet, books, CDs, audio tapes, distance education, etc. A Christian can get a virtual seminary education without ever leaving home!

Even so, considerable discernment is needed. In a real sense, there is too much material available. Materials with great-sounding labels can be superficial and even Biblically erroneous. Christians who want to engage in serious study should consult their elders and other mature Christians. Why waste time studying that which is not the most Biblically based? Many of us can point you to only a few books that will give a lifetime of information.

5. **Education should be a life-long and continuing process**. Every business man and professional knows that in some sense to be and stay successful, he must "keep up" or pursue continuing education. For Christians, first, there is the notion of completed education above. Second, after one has been in church for decades and begins to be part of the "elderly," then an observer can see the resignation and lassitude set in. This attitude seems to say, "I have been there, done that, and there is nothing else to learn. Anything new is for these "young whipper-snappers."

Christians should always be learning new truths of Scripture. I have observed Christians over as many as four or five decades who have really "learned nothing new." At least, they have learned nothing new of any consequence. I make this conclusion from the books that they don't carry, their lifestyles, their answers to Biblical questions, and the Sunday School classes that they attend and accept as sufficient for their "education." While every Christian is certainly not gifted to be a Biblical scholar, our God has given us a book, the study of which is inexhaustible.

I would contend that one's faith and one's worship is truncated by a limited study of the Scriptures. The fault lies primarily with those pastors and church leaders who design or oversee instruction in their churches through sermons, Sunday School, conferences, and other teaching activities. In general, Christian in these churches have not had the role models and examples set before them that is needed to direct and inspire ongoing Biblical instruction. Of course, there are those Christians who do have opportunity and do not take advantage of it.

The active and educated elderly should be one of the great resources of the Church. These elderly may be the greatest untapped resource in the modern Church. Many have retired, their children are gone, and many have financial resources. They have time and usually more than adequate finances. Yet, they languish in churches by their own sense of "retirement" and neglect by the younger people. The anti-Church crowd has their "gray panthers." **What Reformation would occur through the educated gray panthers of the modern Church?** I pray and work towards this end!

No person, regenerate or unregenerate, can achieve his full potential without continuous formal and informal education.

6. **Education is inescapably religious**. Virtually no one would consider, especially in this information age, that he or she could learn everything that there is to know. So, any area of study is chosen on the basis of value to the person. **All considerations of value are religious. All choices are religious as they either promote or detract from the Kingdom of God.**

I should re-iterate here that "religion" and philosophy along with many other words (cosmology, first principles, axioms, etc. ¾ see "Synonyms" at Epistemology) are synonyms or equivalent to "religion." James Dewey, who is considered the father of American primary and secondary education, was a pragmatist who consciously and intentionally promoted his philosophy in his educational programs. His philosophy consciously denied any existence of God, so his atheism has penetrated all levels of public education in this country. Unfortunately, it has penetrated the curricula of many Christian schools and home schoolers.

The study of epistemology, logic, metaphysics, and ethics (its derivation) is absolutely necessary to formal education with its basics being introduced and taught by the end of high school. Many Christians are lost in philosophical discussions about how Christianity fits into the way man thinks in terms of these concepts. Therefore, they are virtually useless in the world of ideas and ethics except as evangelists (more "fire insurance," converting people to a partial "gospel.") Biblical Christianity has the strongest and only coherent philosophical arguments of any religion in the world. However, Christians are commonly weaklings in true "apologetics." (Most apologetics that is called by that name is not true apologetics. See our Glossary.)

7. **College education needs to be re-evaluated thoroughly by Christian parents**. There are many dangers associated with college attendance today. (A) Children face a freedom of choices for which many may not be ready in their lack of maturity. Living away from parents and among peers influences them to make many unrighteous choices. (B) They face a barrage of philosophical attacks about their faith from professors for which few have rarely been prepared. (Of course, this lack of preparation only reflects the superficial and narrowness of teaching by Christian parents, churches, and even Christian schools.)

(C) College education is an enormous expense with questionable spiritual value. There is no doubt that a college degree gives a person an advantage in the marketplace of employment. Numerous studies have shown that fact. However, it is almost exclusive the degree itself that is the "ticket," not the education received. **There are few professions which actually use what is learned in college, unless one become a teacher himself.** (See "Training to be a teacher below.") Education has become a filter for certain attitudes and beliefs, not a agent for inculcation of truth.

(D) College students face a myriad of temptations away from parents and other adult eyes and under the peer pressure of a hedonistic lifestyle. Many lives are ruined for a few moments of supposed pleasure.

So, let's look as this scenario. Christians send their children into a strongly dominated humanistic and hedonistic culture away from their control at enormous expense (usually involving considerable debt) for an education that is largely useless (except as a "ticket" to employment). This situation, then, is a serious disconnect of Biblical values. **Even sending children to a "Bible college" is no "bargain."** Socially, many of the same pitfalls are there. In addition, few "Bible colleges" teach a full-orbed Biblical worldview, and many even teach a large degree of secularism under the pretense of being a "Bible school." See Coalition on Revival, "The Christian World View of Revitalizing Christian Colleges and Seminaries."

Dr. James Bartlett in his Biblical Concourse is putting together an alternative to college, similar to the program that home schoolers have developed around the country.

For a history of college education, which began as a requirement for church ordination, see the reference below.

8. **Training to be a teacher**. What knowledge and skills are required to be a teacher? Perhaps, an example would best get this idea across. Let's consider that someone wants to teach mathematics in high school. What knowledge and skills are necessary for them to teach (apart from the simple and narrow requirement of an B.S. - Bachelor of Science)? The answer is that this teacher would need to know their subject matter quite well, be able to teach it so that students would understand, and be able to control (discipline) the class.

So, why do teachers need the many hours of college credit in psychology, sociology, teaching methods, history, etc. to teach mathematics? Once the preparing teacher knows their subject matter to be taught, everything else can be learned in "on-the-job-training" under the tutelage of an experienced teacher. How many great teachers in particular areas for which they are gifted are never able to teach because they cannot or do not want to take all the other peripheral subjects? This situation may be a major reason that there is a shortage of teachers who truly have a talent or gift to teach children.

Teachers-to-be presently study psychology. Psychology comprises a large part of college requirements for students preparing to be teachers. At the college graduate level, there is very little difference between the courses for a Ph. D. in psychology, compared to that of an Ed.D. **Virtually all psychology is based in thoroughly humanistic and anti-God philosophies.** And, many Christian schools require their own teachers to have these same credentials! See our Worldview Area of Psychology (link).

9. **What American education is not**. In the light of what Scripture says about education and what is said in these Summary Principles, American education is not:

> To enable the student to earn a good income.

> To preserve our American system of government and political freedom (except as it involve re-learning the Biblical principles that founded this country).

To unify the world.

To teach young people a trade.

To encourage the never-ending search for the truth.

To put the student in harmony with the cosmos.

To raise the consciousness of students and train them for world revolution.

To prepare students for prospective careers.

To integrate the races.

To provide for the social adjustment of the child.

To stay ahead of the Russians (or the Japanese) in technology.

To create good citizens.

(Adapted from Clark, *A Christian Philosophy…*, page ix, below)

10. **The only unity of knowledge that can be found is where the Bible is the fully functional authority of every area.** This was the original idea of "university." Virtually all of the universities in the West were founded with the idea that the Bible gave this coherency. The idea of the Bible as the only source of truth and unifying knowledge can be found on this site at Truth, Philosophy…

The only thing about which the various educational philosophies for the last century have any unity is their opposition to Christianity. (Idea from Clark, *A Christian Philosophy…*, page ix; also see John Dewey above).

11. **Education is not only what is read or formally taught, but the speech and behavior of the teacher, as well.** Many parents recognize that children are far more influenced by what the parents say or do, rather than what they formally teach. **Such teaching and training was used by Jesus in His short earthly ministry with His disciples**. (As the Gospels record, He taught formally also in the Sermon on the Mount and the Olivet Discourse, for example.)

126

Education requires discipline in the classroom. Orderliness and quiet in the classroom are necessary to effective instruction. How this is achieved is beyond summary principles. However, many classrooms today are anything but orderly and quiet, even in Christian schools.

12. **Public education is not a "good" in itself, as highly educated people may be thieves and murderers**. There is no doubt historically that Christianity after the invention of the printing press, more than any other philosophy, promoted public education for everyone to be able to read the Bible in their common language. Yet, public education without Biblically moral instruction can cause great harm, as well. "Educated nations cause more evil than uneducated nations." (Clark, *A Christian Philosophy...* , page 10) Adolph Hitler was able to write *Mein Kampf*; Karl Marx wrote *Das Kapital*; and John Dewey wrote and lectured about public education which made a culture ripe for the sexual promiscuity and prevalent abortion that we experience today. See Prager below.

13. **For the most part, home schooling among Christians is a positive movement**. Home schooling avoids the secular humanism of the public schools. It allows a designed curriculum (within the laws of the state!) in which special subjects, such as, Greek, logic, and Christian history, can be taught. It promotes family cohesion. It reinforces the morality of Biblical values in discipleship from parents to children. And, more.

Home schooling, however, often does not have a comprehensive worldview or theological training. The great error of modern Christians is to think, first, that the gospel is simple, and that they need only a basic understanding of it. Another great error, is that the Bible can be comprehensively understood without systematics. In the New Testament, faith, law, repentance, love, justice, righteousness, etc. are not simple concepts. Much harm has been done to the Kingdom of God because of this understanding that is often wrong because it is superficial. More on this discussion can be found in the following books.

14. **Without epistemology, no other knowledge, study, or life activity has any reason to be pursued**. While every person does not necessarily have to face the question, "How do I know (for sure, with any certainty), what I know?," leaders and teachers who are Christians should. They need to know how to "fit" Biblical Christianity into the world of ideas and competing philosophies and religions.

15. **The idea of "vocation" needs to be recognized and brought to the forefront of the education of children**. "Vocation" simply means "calling." Placed into the framework of the Kingdom of God, vocation is the work to which God calls His own. Let me re-state that. **Vocation is the work to which God calls His own.**

There is too much focus in the modern Church on "full-time ministry" being the only avenue open to young people who want to devote themselves fully "to the Lords' work." For example, perhaps the greatest need among modern Christians, are philosophers. These men and women would argue overtly and covertly for the Christian faith in the world of ideas and literature. They would teach Christians in their areas of work to think and practice their professions Biblically. Then, there is the need for lawyers, who understand law as did our American founding fathers. Then, there is ... you fill in the blank! There are great needs in all areas of worldview.

Children have markedly different talents.* Early in the lives of their children, parents should begin to notice what activities their children like and are willing to spend long hours in participation. Slowly and without force, they should provide opportunities for learning and practice in these areas.

* I distinguish between gifts and talents. (Spiritual) gifts are for use in building up the Church and natural talents (which are also gifts of God) are for use outside the Church in God's common grace to all mankind. All talents and gifts should be for the Glory of God.

16. **Freedom of inquiry (academic freedom)** is necessary to increase man's understanding of God and His world and should be pursued, as opportunity, financing, interest, and ability present opportunity. However, freedom of inquiry should not include areas which violate Biblical morality. And, there should be no State funding of research activities. Again, the only true university can be found in knowledge that is founded upon the Holy Scriptures.

17. **The State has no role in public education at any level**. (A) The role of the State is quite restricted, primarily that of Romans 13:1-7. (2) Since we have already seen that "education is inescapably religious." Any function of the State is also inescapably religious. Therefore, any education that the State provides is inescapably religious and its concepts will be taught within its system. What is taught in modern schools has many examples of this religious nature.

128

Parents need to evaluate carefully whether their children should be in public schools. At first glance, private education may be too expensive and home schooling not a practical option. But, with innovative thinking, cost-cutting in family expenses, prayer, and consultation with others will virtually always find an alternative. God does not want His children educated from "the tree of knowledge of … evil." Consider this quote:

Public education is the parochial education for scientific humanism. (Joe R. Burnett, *The Humanist Magazine*, 1961.)

18. Christian schools need to re-examine their cost structure. Christian schools have often modeled themselves after public schools with their requirements for teacher "certification" and "education." They provide for the full range of sports activities. They provide for labs and other expensive equipment. And so on.

Christian schools need to re-examine their curricula. Many Christian schools are not very different from public schools except that they teach some Bible studies. **All students who graduate from Christian high schools should be able, from memory, to give several distinctives of a Biblical worldview in at least 15 different areas of knowledge**. (Worldview areas may be grouped differently by different teachers and group, but there is a central core in every list.) **If a Christian school or home school does not achieve this goal, it is not truly a Christian (Biblical) school**.

The Bible is explicit, and even stark, in its description of the two areas of mankind and knowledge that exist on planet earth: light and darkness, good (God) and evil (the world, the flesh, and Satan), and those bound for heaven vs. those who are bound for heaven. If a Christian school or home school does not reflect this stark reality, then it is not a Biblical school and not consistent with the word, "Christian."

Christian schools need to innovate. Why not have debates with secular schools about creation and evolution, the evidences for the existence of God, the Bible as the only truth available to man, the limitations of science, and the influence of Christianity on the culture of the West, to name only a few? Why not teach students to write letters to editors of local papers, magazines, and other publications on various issues? Why not bring in speakers who have developed a worldview or ethical system in their profession, as role models and for what they have developed.? And so on. Our great God has an infinite mind, why are Christians so stultified in their creativity? We should be the most creative people on earth!

On the one hand, repeated studies have shown that the size of classes has no correlation on the student's ability to learn subject matter. While this fact is not a Biblical truth, it is an empirical study that has been validated more than once. That the size of the class does not matter in this way may be used to cut the costs of Christian schools.

On the other hand, discipleship is an integral part of teaching. Perhaps, Christian schools can implement large classes for subject that are more didactic in nature, while preserving close relationships with student in other areas of study.

19. **Whether there should be prayer in public schools should not even be a question or concern for Christians!** This question is an example of how wrongly Christians think today. **The issues is whether there should be public schools at all.**

20. **You are what you read and value; you read what you value**. Yes, our God is infinitely creative and imaginative without learning. But, Christians are not. Christians are virtually irrelevant to the problems of the world because we, first, do not even recognize how our faith has answers. Second, we have no idea that we should apply the Bible to these problems. Third, if we do recognize the first and second, we have no idea how to apply the Bible to these problems. **Why are God's people so irrelevant? Because of our education: past, present, and future**. We are what we read, and we read what we value. (For more on "you are what you read, see the website below.)

One act alone could bring about the next great reformation: turn off your television sets and use that time to read the best books on Biblical theology, worldview, and history. (Add this change to the "gray panthers" above!)

21. **Children should experience physical labor, "learn to work with their hands," and be taught a trade or livelihood**. As we have briefly seen, education is not just "book learning," it is learning to live life fully in the service of God. Jewish tradition has required that a father teach his son a trade. This requirement is Biblical, as well. "Let him who stole steal no longer, but rather let him labor, working with his hands what is good, that he may have something to give him who has need" (Ephesians 4:28). "For even when we were with you, we commanded you this: If anyone will not work, neither shall he eat" (II Thessalonians 3:10). And, there are many other verses from

Proverbs and elsewhere, about being industrious and providing for one's family.

All these obligations require income, and income virtually requires a trade. Of course, teaching includes making opportunity for a son to become an apprentice or going to school or college to learn a trade. (One could make the case that even a son who inherits sufficient money to live without working should work somewhere. Money and time have the potential for profligate living. "Work out your salvation in fear and trembling" is sufficient for instruction here.)

What about a daughter? Fathers were to provide a dowry to a daughter. In today's world, a dowry might be a college education or another trade that a daughter could work, if she does not marry or becomes a widow. There are also rather explicit instructions for the Church's role in helping women (I Timothy 5:3-16).

All the details about training for children and their futures is too complex to discuss here. Our concern here is education of children. Biblically, parents are responsible to provide the spiritual and pragmatic education that will allow their independence at the proper time to leave home and form their own families.

A last word about working with hands. These verses (I Corinthians 4:12; I Thessalonians 4:11) seem to imply that physical labor is "good for the soul." I am not sure that physical labor can be made an absolute requirement under parental responsibility, but certain lessons are taught experientially from work that is menial and unskilled that cannot be taught otherwise. Today's world includes cutting the grass and other odd jobs around the house and yard that are beyond the practicality of always being able to hire someone to do them.

22. **While "all truth is God's truth," this phrase is frequently used to elevate theoretical and experimental knowledge (that is not truth) on the level of Biblical truth, especially by Christians who are psychologists, scientists, and other professionals**. Thus, it is essential that students learn what truth is and what is not before they finish high school. See my discussion on this website, "All truth is God's truth."

23. **Most churches are neither teaching Biblical basics nor the full Gospel**. The full Gospel includes individual (A) salvation (past, present, and future), (B) discipline (preaching, teaching, sacraments, and investigation of overt sin¾ process of Matthew 18:15-19), and (C) a Biblically complete worldview and

ethics. Most churches leave out the fullness of what salvation is, the process of dealing with overt sin, and worldview and ethics. Thus, they are teaching and preaching only about one-half of the Gospel.

Biblical basics include the specifics of Hebrews 6:1-2: "Therefore, leaving the discussion of the elementary *principles* of Christ, let us go on to perfection, not laying again the foundation of repentance from dead works and of faith toward God, of the doctrine of baptisms, of laying on of hands, of resurrection of the dead, and of eternal judgment." I wonder how many churchmen today can give a clear explanation of those "elementary principles."

24. **Perhaps, the role of preaching should be re-examined**. Not every person who attends worship services at church also attends Sunday School or other educational programs of the church. On this basis, ministers should re-evaluate the content of their messages so that it presents the "elementary principles" of Hebrews 6 and the full Gospel defined above. With two sermons morning evening on Sunday and years of attendance by members, this broader coverage should not be difficult. Also, congregants should be encouraged to take notes on sermons and discussion in Sunday School and other places could reinforce this more comprehensive teaching.

25. **Methodology: facts, definitions, logic, rationality, and axioms**. Over the past several decades, there has been an educational theory that facts and memorization are tedious and limit creative thinking. Actually, the opposite is true. The more options and knowledge that a student has, the more options he has from which to choose and to build from one or more ideas into a new idea.

The following are so brief as to make scholars cringe, yet they need to be introduced here because they are a large part of what is wrong with the education of Christians today. These matters are developed more fully on other areas of this website.

Definitions. I think that one of the most amazing aspects of human existence is that social interaction takes place as efficiently as it does without the explicit references to definitions. This common discourse, however, disguises the necessity of definitions for more important matters. Few Christians today, and I suspect many pastors, as well, could give exact definitions of law, love, faith, hope, regeneration, revelation, etc. Thus, Christianity flounders because of the lack of study of what these words really mean. Early in their studies, children should be taught the meanings and derivations of words and the necessity of their accuracy in important matters.

132

Axioms. There are many synonyms for axioms which include first principles, presuppositions, postulates, basics, and assumptions. Students need to know that these concepts are not reasoned (different from being reasonable), but accepted on faith. This process is taught in some of the sciences, such as, geometry, calculus, and physics, but it is true in every area of knowledge. **Knowledge is based upon faith (in these first principles), but students usually hear that knowledge is different than faith**. This teaching has separated Christianity into the upper and lower stories about which Francis Schaeffer wrote. Such error has been severely destructive to both Christians in their personal lives, their ability to affect their culture, and argue coherently for Biblical Christianity.

Logic. Logic is the only method of reasoning that can derive truth from other truths. For example, "Trinity" does not appear in the Bible, but it can be logically derived from statements of Scripture. Then, **this word that does not appear in the Bible** becomes a test of orthodoxy, that is, a test of whether one is truly a Christian or not! (I am aware that logical reasoning from false presuppositions produces false conclusions, so that logical truth is dependent upon these starting principles.

Fact or facts. As Francis Schaeffer said, there are no "brute facts," that is, facts that are true in themselves. Facts are always tied to first principles, so facts are always product of faith. See **Axioms** above.

No doubt I have left out some other basics. But, these should be sufficient to identify some of the major deficiencies in modern education.

References

Books

Clark, Gordon C. A Christian Philosophy of Education. The Trinity Foundation, revised, 1988.

Machen, Gresham. Education, Christianity, and the State. The Trinity Foundation, 1987.

Rushdoony, Rousas J. The Messianic Character of American Education. www.chalcedonstore.com

Rushdoony, Rousas J. The Philosophy of the Christian Curriculum. www.chalcedonstore.com

Online Resources

http://www.biblicalconcourse.com/

College level courses patterned after home schooling.

http://www.frontline.org.za/articles/you_are_what_you_read.htm

"You Are What You Read" - online article

http://reformed-theology.org/ice/newslet/reconstruction/cr97.01.htm

History of college education, beginning with the Church, and its secularization

http://www.townhall.com/Columnists/DennisPrager/2007/11/06/dear_senator_dodd_education_is_not_the_answer_to_every_problem

Dennis Prager on morality and education

8. Medicine

Modern Medicine under the Authority of Scripture

In 1977, Robertson McQuilkin wrote that "the functional control of Scripture over any discipline will vary in direct proportion to the overlap of that discipline with the substance of Biblical revelation." [1] Concerning psychology, he wrote that "the potential area of conflict is much greater than in the case of medicine or agriculture." From that statement and others, I doubt that he would place medicine at the second level (see below) of control as he did psychology. However, medicine should be placed under that second level because of the role that *health and medicine* have been given in modern America.

Dr. McQuilkin's Levels of Functional Control

Dr. McQuilkin suggested this paradigm.

- "Highest level of functional control: Subject matter completely overlaps with revelation, so that control will mean the ideas should be derived from Scripture exclusively.
- "Second level: Overlap with revelation is great though not complete, so that subject matter should be derived from Scripture but extended by empirical research and experimentation.
- "Third level: Overlap with revelation is slight, so that subject matter should be derived from natural sources but remain under the judgment of Scripture for its interpretation and application.
- "Fourth level: There is no direct overlap with revelation, so that subject matter may be derived wholly from natural sources but should be compatible with Scriptural truth.
- "Fifth level: Subject matter may be unrelated to Scripture."[2]

In the highest category, Dr. McQuilkin included theology and Christian philosophy. In the second level, he included the behavioral sciences (psychology, sociology, and anthropology). In the third level were history and the arts. The fourth level included the physical sciences. At the fifth level were typing and other purely technical skills, "unrelated to Scriptural truth except in the person of the practitioner." Even in the third to the fifth levels, Dr. McQuilkin maintained that subject matter must be compatible with Scripture where they overlap and that Scriptural truths should govern the work and person of the practitioner, whatever his field of endeavor. Thus, the Christian and his vocation are never totally removed from God's authority and revealed truth.

My intent is not to debate Dr. McQuilkin's categories. Indeed, his paper was not intended to establish and debate iron-clad categories or hard definitions. His concern was about pagan ideas that were controlling too many Christians in the behavioral sciences to the detriment of individual Christians and their culture. My concern is that pagan ideas control too much of modern medicine to the detriment of the health of individuals and society.

There is a huge difference in medicine today, which I shall call "modern medicine," with that practiced only one generation ago. The purpose of medicine is to heal, care for, and comfort the diseased and injured.[3] However, modern medicine both intentionally and unintentionally promotes the opposite: disease and death. Intentionally, medicine aborts more than 1 million unborn babies each year, has greased the slippery slope toward euthanasia, and endorses homosexuality. Unintentionally, modern medicine has fostered an epidemic of sexually transmitted diseases; children who are poorly educated, socially disruptive, and sometimes criminally inclined; and a cost that exceeds individuals' and society's ability to pay.

Medicine has grown from an almost insignificant portion of a family's budget and social cost to a $1 trillion industry that consumes 14 percent of the United States' Gross Domestic Product. For this high cost, it has actually increased morbidity and mortality--because it has failed to be under the functional control of Scripture. Yes, it may be too much to expect "society" to embrace Biblical revelation, even for its own health. However, it is reasonable to expect Christians committed to the authority of Scripture to discern the errors of modern medicine and promote a different understanding from that of the World (Romans 12:1-2).

The Experience and Science of Medicine

There is no doubt that modern medicine "has subject matter (that should be) extended by empirical research and experimentation" (second level), and even "subject matter unrelated to Scripture" (fifth level). These endeavors occupy the bulk of what modern medicine does. Positron emitters virtually take pictures of the brain. Tiny scopes can be inserted into almost any body part with startlingly clear images. Surgeries are performed with lasers and at microscopic levels with short recovery periods. People crushed in automobile

136

accidents are kept alive and often returned to a normal life. Indeed, the capabilities of modern medicine seem to border on the miraculous.

Thus, *there is a technology and science of medicine.* I would not only be foolish to say otherwise, I would be extending the functional control of Scripture beyond its bounds. Some Christians have made this error. Reginald Cherry, M.D., states that "Within the Bible's holy writ are all the principles needed by each of us to find the healing of body, soul, and spirit."[4] His chapters include "Bible cures" for heart disease, diabetes, ovarian cancer, stomach cancer, etc. Interestingly, Roy Maynard, who reviewed Dr. Cherry's book, observes that he is "not careful with language." For example, his "Bible cure" for breast cancer includes surgery, chemotherapy, and nutrition. These are obviously not Biblically directed treatments, but those of modern medicine.

Again, there is a technology and science of medicine outside of Scripture. Here, modern medicine has Biblical legitimacy. Its research and applications bring comfort, and sometimes cure, to many patients with various diseases. I want to state this clearly and unequivocally because it will occupy only a small place in my efforts here.

Why do I say "small" place? Because this legitimate area of medicine in the large scheme of health, disease, and injury occupies only a small place. In cost and public attention, this area is gigantic, spending most of the $1 trillion each year. But, its effects on the overall health of individual patients and society are small.

First, modern medicine has received a credibility that it does not deserve. Modern medicine claims to have eliminated the infectious disease killers of the past, such as measles, tuberculosis, whooping cough, and diphtheria. Yet, charted declines of these diseases indicate that they were mostly eliminated *before* there were effective vaccines or treatments.[5] These disappearances were due to better sanitation, housing, and personal maturity,[6] not public health or medical measures. Yet, modern medicine is credited with conquering such infectious diseases to cause the marked increase in life expectancy of about 25 years that has occurred since 1900.

Second, the efficacy of modern medicine is vastly overrated. By efficacy, I mean the ability of medicine to impact the morbidity and mortality of individuals. Of the patients seen in a generalist's office, 80-90 percent have problems which are self-limited. That is, they will get better without treatment or can be treated as well with non-prescription drugs. Or, as we physicians say among ourselves, "Patients will get better in spite of what we as physicians do to them"!

A plethora of coronary care units has had little, if any, impact on the survival of patients with heart disease, far and away the leading cause of death. In fact, the causes of the 40 percent decline in coronary artery disease mortality since 1960 are unclear, but are almost certainly not due to medical intervention. Changes in lifestyle give a mixed message. While some people have cut their saturated fat intake, our population in general has become more obese and sedentary. More likely, this decline is due to the observed phenomenon of a natural ebb and flow of diseases over time.

With a few exceptions in childhood cancers, the war on cancer has been lost. For 30 years, billions have been spent on research for better treatments and early detection, but this great effort has, at best, produced a slight gain when all cancers as taken as a whole. Almost all of this gain has occurred with childhood blood diseases. Among all age groups, cancer remains the second leading cause of death.

Strokes (cerebrovascular diseases) continue to be the third leading cause of death, but nothing has ever really been found to treat this severely crippling disease, including recent attempts to bring stroke patients in very early and rapidly treat them.

Third, the science of medicine is difficult and usually is not the basis for what physicians do. The "gold standard" of medical research is the double-blind, randomly controlled study. However, such studies probably account for less than five percent of what physicians actually do every day. Their actions are not necessarily invalidated by this lack, but it certainly undermines the notion that modern medicine is "scientific" and research based. When these controlled studies are actually performed, "orthodox" treatments may be found to be beneficial, have no net improvement in a patient's condition, or actually be found to be *harmful*. Further, patients rarely take medication according to directions, which decreases the likelihood of benefit.

Fourth, medical treatments are sometimes harmful. There are medication errors in hospitals, complications of surgery and anesthesia, complications of investigative procedures, and untoward effects of drugs--to name a few. Indeed, it seems that the increasing complexity of medicine and newer, stronger drugs has increased these harmful effects. This "iatrogenic" harm must be considered in any overall evaluation of modern medicine.

I could go on, but my purpose is not to invalidate medicine. My purpose with this brief review is to remove modern medicine from its god-like pedestal apart from the immorality that exists outside the functional control of Scripture.

Were medicine as effective as we pretend, giving us a good return on our 14 percent investment, then one might understand its worship. But, medicine, even modern medicine, is a seriously flawed science.

Immorality: Modern Medicine Outside the Functional Control of Scripture

What are the evidences for modern medicine's being outside the control of Scripture, and what are the effects of this position?

Abortion. The worst offense is abortion, with its destruction of 1.5 million unborn lives each year. The American Medical Association, the American Association of Obstetricians and Gynecologists (AACOG), and the nurses division of AACOG once legally defended abortion as "sound medical practice." The Bible is clear that individual human life begins at conception (Genesis 4:1, Psalm 51:5, Luke 1:31) and that it is a special work of God's design (Psalm 139:13-15). God even plans the creation of individuals and their life's work before they are born (Psalm 139:16-18, Jeremiah 1:5).*

Modern medicine has had to juggle its own science to justify abortion. Conception was re-defined to mean implantation of the embryo in the uterus. The rationale to define when the embryo and fetus become "human" or a "person" would be laughable were it not so morbid. Simply and "scientifically," individual human life begins with the unique cellular complement that is formed by the union of a sperm and an egg.

Under this same failure to defend fully human life, medical organizations and governmental agencies have failed to take a stand against infanticide, so-called assisted suicide, and euthanasia. We are on the brink of another holocaust.

Marriage. Modern medicine has failed to uphold and endorse sexual relationships within marriage. This failure has a widespread fallout in ways that may not be readily apparent. First, sexually transmitted diseases are epidemic. Not only are syphilis and gonorrhea prevalent, but there are literally new epidemics of sexually transmitted diseases, such as hepatitis B, cervical cancer, herpes type II, and HIV/AIDS. Nearly one in four Americans has or has had one or more sexually transmitted disease.

Second, this failure to endorse marriage has destroyed the secure environment of homes for children. There are hundreds of studies that show that children of single and divorced parents have a far more difficult time than children of two-parent homes. They perform more poorly in school, are more likely to drop out of school, and are more commonly involved in crime.

Third, even apart from sexually transmitted diseases, unmarried adults (never married, divorced, and widowed) have more disease and difficulties than the married. In 1977, James Lynch, M.D., wrote *The Broken Heart: The Medical Consequences of Loneliness.*[7] In that book, Dr. Lynch cites a plethora of statistics in which married people have less mortality from virtually every kind of disease, including heart disease, hypertension, stroke, cancer, diabetes, and kidney disease. They have fewer deaths from automobile accidents, homicide, suicide, and even accidental falls.

Homosexuality. While failing to endorse traditional (Biblical) marriage, modern medicine *has endorsed* homosexuality. The homosexual lobby bullied the American Psychiatric Association in the early 1970s until 1973 when its board removed homosexuality as a pathological diagnosis and made it an "alternative lifestyle" (that is, a legitimate sexual relationship).[8] This endorsement has progressed to the extent that one psychiatrist has threatened that "clinicians" who continue to call homosexuality a "disorder" and attempt to change homosexuals to heterosexuals "may soon find themselves confronted with malpractice litigation."[9] Thus, the medical profession has called evil "good" and good "evil."

The homosexual lifestyle is unhealthy and deadly. Even apart from AIDS, the life expectancy of homosexuals is only 42 years.[10] No doubt this shortened life is caused by the fact that homosexuals have a far greater frequency of sexually transmitted diseases than heterosexuals, have other diseases that are endemic to their group, and have a higher incidence of crime and other socially destructive behavior.[11]

Parental authority. Modern medicine has failed to stand for the parental authority necessary to the health and welfare of families. **Single or married women of any age** can be treated for sexually transmitted diseases, receive birth control of any kind, and even **have an abortion without parental or spouse's consent** anywhere in the United States! It is even argued that teenagers and individual spouses should be able to present any problem to a physician without their "fearing" that their parents or spouse will be told. The American Academy of Pediatrics has taken an official stand against spanking, God's own design for disciplining children (Proverbs 19:18, 22:15, 23:13).

Godless psychiatry. Since Sigmund Freud, psychiatry and its practitioners have usually viewed Christian beliefs as pathological and destructive to the individual and families. Indeed, one could argue that psychiatrists (and psychologists) have become the priests of modern medicine (and society). Certainly, psychiatry has facilitated, if not endorsed and caused, many of the other problems discussed here.

Let me be clear. **There is a place for medical treatment of problems that are caused by organic brain diseases.** However, far too many besetting sins have been excused as "diseases" or beyond the control of the "patient."[12] These include alcoholism, gambling, sexual promiscuity, theft, and both legal and illegal drug abuse. Indeed, "addiction" has become a shibboleth to excuse almost any harmful habitual behavior (although most who use the word "addiction" never bother to define it).

Psychiatry has entered the world of individual, marriage, and family counseling for everyday problems, a realm that is definitively moral rather than medical. Also, psychiatry (and psychology) have penetrated the Church of Jesus Christ to the extent that pastoral counseling is commonly taught by these "professionals" in many seminaries. This movement into the moral and spiritual arenas of society is evidence of the prevalent authority that has been granted to psychiatry (and psychology).

Modern Medicine Under the Biblical Authority of Scripture

The place of modern medicine under the authority of Scripture is no less than that determined by Dr. McQuilkin, that is, "in direct proportion to the overlap of that discipline with Biblical revelation." I contend that that overlap is far greater than that envisioned by most Christians and never even grasped by non-Christians.

The overlap lies at the heart of the Biblical message, salvation. The Greek roots, *sozo* and *diasozo* are translated "save" or "salvation," most commonly referring to salvation from personal sins in this life and hell in the afterlife. However, they are also translated for salvation of the physical self (Matthew 8:25, 14:30) and healing of the body, as the woman with the flow of blood (Matthew 9:21), blind Bartimaeus (Mark 10:52), the lepers (Luke 17:19), and the man lame from his mother's womb (Acts 4:9).

Iomai may refer to both physical and spiritual healing. For example, there is the healing of paralysis (Matthew 8:8), leprosy (Luke 17:15), a severed ear

(Luke 22:51), fever (John 4:47), and dysentery (Acts 28:8). The noun form, *iatros*, designates physician. Relative to spiritual healing (i.e., salvation) are Matthew 13:15, Luke 4:18, Hebrews 12:13, and I Peter 2:24.

Hugies (hygiene or health) is similar. References to physical healing from this root include that of a withered hand (Matthew 12:13), bleeding (Mark 5:34), and lameness (Acts 4:10). Texts that designate spiritual healing are Luke 5:31 and 15:27. Indeed, several contexts may be recognized to use derivatives of *sozo, iomai*, and *hugies* interchangeably.

This clear association of healing, health, and salvation of both body and soul (spirit) leads to my first principle of functional authority of Scripture over medicine. *No fullness of health is possible without belief in Jesus Christ as Savior and Lord.* As medicine mends broken bodies, the Gospel mends broken spirits. The word "fullness" is used rather than complete health, because neither complete health of the body nor of the soul can be experienced in this life.

I am not advocating that every physician devote most or all of his time and energy to evangelism. I am advocating that the health of the soul be recognized as an absolute prerequisite to fullness of health for every person. The frequency with which Christians in medicine, particularly psychiatrists and psychologists, ignore this foundational principle is appalling.

The second principle of functional authority for modern medicine is that **human responsibility, not disease, is the cause of problems to which the Bible speaks clearly**. The following are not "diseases" but sins: alcoholism (drunkenness, Proverbs 20:1, 31:4-6, Ephesians 5:18), homosexuality (Leviticus 18:22, 20:13; Romans 1:26-32; I Corinthians 6:9-11, I Timothy 1:10), lying (Exodus 20:16, Ephesians 4:25), theft (Exodus 20:15, Ephesians 4:28) and heterosexual immorality (Exodus 20:14).

Addictions are better understood as "besetting sins."[13] That is not to say that there is not a physical craving, even a physical biochemical proclivity (which is certainly not proven) toward some addictions, such as drugs and alcohol. However, that proclivity is not primary. Many alcoholics and drug addicts have broken the stranglehold of their problems, thereby proving that alcoholism is not entirely physical. If the physical element were primary, none could ever quit. Even the substitution of another chemical in the place of the harmful drug would remain an addiction.

A larger area to which this principle speaks is that of psychiatrists dealing with "everyday" problems of family disruption, career decisions, and personal disputes. Such problems are the province of Scripture. "'Be angry, and do not sin,' do not let the sun go down on your wrath, nor give place to the devil" (Ephesians 4:26). "Therefore do not worry about tomorrow, for tomorrow will worry about its own things. Sufficient for the day is its own trouble" (Matthew 6:34). "Husbands, love your wives, just as Christ loved the church and gave Himself up for it" (Ephesians 5:25). And so on. Virtually every problem faced in life has a Scriptural solution, either directly or derived.

A third principle for Scriptural control is *the sanctity and structure of the family*. The father is the loving head (Ephesians 5:23-33), the wife is his help-meet (Genesis 2:18, Ephesians 5:22), and both are responsible for their children (Ephesians 6:1-4). How can children be brought up in the "nurture and admonition of the Lord" if there is a place (the physician's office, school-based clinics, abortuaries, etc.) where they can receive treatment and advice on some of life's most crucial issues? Husband and wife are "one flesh," with nothing happening to one that the other should not know about (Genesis 2:23-24, Ephesians 5:22-33).

A fourth principle is *the sanctity of sexual expression within marriage*. One can escape all sexually transmitted diseases, the most serious epidemics of modern times, by following this admonition. Is this principle, then, not a health message? Interestingly, if fullness of sexual expression is a concern, studies have shown that married men and women have better sex lives than the unmarried. Also, *religious* men *and* women who are married have better sex lives than the married who are not religious![14]

There are other principles that could be derived, but these four address major intrusions of modern medicine into Scriptural authority. Medical science's own studies show the health that is possible by following these prescriptions and proscriptions. Would we not expect that only healthy instructions would come from the Maker of mankind Himself?

The Surgeon General's Office Is a Bully Pulpit

When C. Everett Koop was Surgeon General, he said that the Surgeon General's office is not a bully pulpit. That is, it is a place from which to dispense health, not morality. Many without and within the Church have agreed with him.

Not so! Allowing 1.5 million babies to be born each year instead of being aborted, avoiding all sexually transmitted diseases, prolonging health and life in marriage, raising children to be better achievers and more healthy, and solving problems before they lead to destruction and death are indeed messages of health.

The World Health Organization has stated that "health is a complete physical, mental, and social well-being and not merely the absence of disease or infirmity." While this definition is overly broad, it does link bodily health to social and spiritual concepts. "Well-being" concerns what is "good," and good is necessarily determined by right and wrong. The Bible is the only true Source about right and wrong.

The functional control of modern medicine by Scripture has more to offer toward the prevention of morbidity and mortality and health promotion than all of modern medicine's skills and knowledge. The Bible is indeed about health. The science of medicine and sociology have hundreds of studies that demonstrate the healthy admonitions of the Bible. There is indeed an empirical realm of knowledge and expertise for medicine that is its primary function. However, modern medicine has overstepped this primary function with resulting disease and death in the millions.

Is the functional control of modern medicine by Scripture important? It is-- only if the *hubris* of modern medicine is willing to bow its knee to Godly wisdom. It is--only if the American people truly desire maximal health and longevity over their own sins. Neither seems to be forthcoming any time soon.

* Note: In supplying Bible texts that support my contentions, I have made no effort to be thorough. I have found that those who would differ are neither persuaded by one text or every relevant text in the Bible. For the same, I have made no effort to document a plethora of medical-scientific resources that support my positions.

Regimen Forgotten: Prescription for Health

In a chorus from his poem, "The Rock," T. S. Eliot wrote:

> "Endless invention, endless experiment, brings knowledge of motion, but not of stillness; knowledge of speech, but not of silence; knowledge of words, and ignorance of the Word. All our knowledge brings us nearer to our ignorance, all our ignorance

brings us nearer to death, but nearness to death no nearer to God. Where is the Life we have lost in the living? Where is the wisdom we have lost in knowledge? Where is the knowledge we have lost in information?

In teaching medical students and others, I have noted a limitation of thought in what should be done about a diagnosis in a patient. In the Western World, physicians practice almost exclusively in three ways: we cut (surgery), we burn (radiation, electrocautery, and cryosurgery), and we poison (pharmaceuticals). All other treatments are considered "adjunctive." Research focuses on these three areas, since research is expensive and financial incentives are concentrated in these three activities. **The older notion of a "regimen" has virtually disappeared**. Some doctors do not even know how to spell it, adding a military "t" at the end of the word. Others stick "pharmacological" in front of regimen as the only regimen they know. We have reaped from this narrow conception a harvest of polypharmacy (treatment with many drugs) which staggers the imagination at 15 to 20 daily drugs per person in some cases -- a now uncommon phenomenon. These three activities are also popular since each of them has the doctor as the active agent, while the patient is usually passive. "Hold still while I freeze this wart." "Wait a minute while I write these medication prescriptions."

We now require computers to help us remember all the available drugs, their side effects, their doses, their costs, and interactions with other medicines. We have masses of data at our fingertips. Increasingly, our patients are also accessing the same data files. Yet, with all of our getting, we have not improved our understanding proportionate! Rather, we have **avoided** understanding. These three mainstay approaches, along with some of the "adjunctive" ones, make us think that the issue before us is a disease. **We have forgotten that the issue is the patient**.

The patient is a unity of body and spirit. It is foolish to try to cleave neatly the one from the other, though in the very short-term analysis, it seems advantageous to do so. We lack wisdom -- Biblical wisdom. We act as though a great deal of data will suffice without much wisdom. We imagine that heaps of data will self-organize itself into knowledge, a process that we Christians call evolution, and our application of it in medicine has as much validity as it does to origins of man. (Ponder that correlation, brother and sister!)

There was a time when Western medicine, possessed of only a few really helpful options for cutting, burning, and poisoning, **offered something else – a treatment regimen**. It is quite an ancient practice. The patient was actively involved. Under consideration were such matters as the patient's character, disposition, intelligence, station in life, and habits. The physician would recommend a fairly comprehensive course of action for the patient. Not being handed anything pharmaceutical, the patient apprehended that following the **regimen** was his responsibility. A **regimen** could be crafted of a wide array of practices. We retain a few of these today – diet and exercise mostly. Trying this ancient practice through the years, clumsily and without the support of a medical or general culture for it, I have found it well-received with some benefit. **A physician really skilled in the matter might make it actually shine even in our culture**. I suspect that some "alternative medicine" practitioners commonly address at least some of these issues.

- Here are some ingredients which may be pulled from the shelf to construct a regimen beyond or instead of cut, burn, poison:

- Prayer, especially for others. It should not focus on the patient's own illness.

- Doing something useful for someone else, especially if it can be done anonymously.

- A regular bedtime and a regular time to get out of bed. It staggers my mind the numbers of Christians who live chaotic lives in terms of a schedule. By so doing, they have lost the war before they even get into battle!

- A time of quiet reflection on Scripture, regularly, preferably daily.

- Memorizing Scripture.

- Reducing some of the nonessential noise of daily life. The radio and television remain off most of the time. Any programs that are watched are selected carefully and spiritually.

- Worshipping with the saints on Sunday and at various other times, if not too impaired to do so by illness.

- Partaking of communion, the more regular the better.

- Reading a piece of good literature.

146

- Singing and listening to quality and/or spiritual music.

- Teaching a child something – a catechism section, how to weave a basket, how to make bread, enjoying the freshness that children bring to life.

- Learning something new – a language, a dance step, a craft -- you can teach an old dog new tricks -- because people are not dogs!

- Caring for and training a pet.

- Keeping the Lord's Day in worship, reading God's Word, and acts of mercy.

- Having a regular plan for each day and each week, with due allowance for providential interruptions. Most of us schedule 30 hours into 24. Again, we have lost the war, before we get into battle.

- Due care in self-grooming. However bad you feel, you must bathe, comb, dress. I am still amazed at what a good shower will do for aches and pains, as well as one's feelings.

- Writing a letter to someone who has not been heard from in awhile. Writing to someone whom you think never gets any mail.

- Throwing out unused possessions -- as we clutter our houses, we clutter our minds and our lives, and vice-versa.

- Keeping a daily journal for presentation at the next visit to the physician to report on your adherence to this regimen.

- Bringing to memory a past relationship which needs mending and seeking to mend it.

Somewhere in such things is likely to be found "the Life we have lost in the living." Somewhere in such things, real preventive medicine may reside. For those whose illness is intractable, there may be in these practices a nearness to death which is nearer to God. There may even be recovery of that wisdom we have lost in our knowledge and data of modern medicine.

Present-day medical training and practice are covertly, and sometimes overtly, hostile to such a conception of medical practice. The private corporation which has charge of granting accreditation of all specialty training, the Accreditation Council for Graduate Medical Education, imagines that it has captured the essence of what all physicians should know in six general categories. Though it does not forbid it, I have yet to see any development of these categories which practically implements the notion of **regimen**. The diagnostic categories which comprise modern medicine permit consideration only of the material aspects of the issues that we face. At most, there is only a *pro forma* bow to the individual and spirit who is a patient, since these data are not suitably quantifiable. The financial arrangements in medicine powerfully limit practices of stillness, reflection, and broad, or "soft" interventions of a **regimen**. Payment for services rendered by physicians is connected to books of codes which discriminate in favor of "endless invention" and "knowledge of motion." Role models for young physicians are lacking of practical inclusion of a **regimen**. Diagnostic and therapeutic pathways in hospitals and elsewhere are blind to these options.

Many medical ethical guidelines instruct physicians and nurses that we should take no notice of any defects we note in the character of our patients, which advice is absurd. How can one treat another human being after stripping away who he is at his most important level? How can comprehensive healing neglect the very attitudes and habits of thought which may lie at the root of the problem and at the door of opportunity for relief? Bringing up habits and character is a dangerous enterprise for a healer to undertake. I have approached it timidly, lest I offend my patient. I do not believe it can be quickly rubbed onto a patient like an ointment or plunged in like a needle. Yet, introduction of **regimen** in the right spirit, with the patient willing to be a co-laborer, is usually well received. At worst is the literal or figurative rolled-eyes. **More often, there is an immediate torrent of connections on which the patient has already been considering**.

The woman in Scripture who was crippled by a chronic issue of blood represents a large constituency still among us. She had used all of her money and yet was not healed, but rather made worse by physicians. If there is to be a recovery of regimen, soldiers in the contest for it probably exist among those Christian patients who have been ridden down by the commonplace, narrow biomedical model of cut, burn, and poison. Recovery will likely arise outside of the guild of medicine. Gifted teachers in the Church, active elders, or some collaboration between pastors and physicians might be one place to start, for those who see merit in regimen. It would make a great application in a sermon on texts having to do with ethical Christian living.

Worldview in Medicine: Choosing Life and Health or Disease and Death

Reader, suppose someone were to ask you this question, "What would you do with your life to promote the greatest health for the greatest number of people?" Before reading further, please pause and reflect on this question. It would be a good exercise even to write down 2-3 answers.

Here is the Biblical answer, "To achieve the greatest health for the greatest number of people, one should become a Biblical preacher or a evangelical missionary!" Was that answer among what you wrote down?

This answer introduces you to the Biblical worldview of medicine, no matter what country of the world in which you live. **Any Biblical worldview always starts with the Biblical view of man, anywhere, at any time in history**. The first man and woman (Adam and Eve) were created in a perfect state. Had they not sinned, they would have lived eternally with complete health. Because of their Fall, disease and death were introduced. "The LORD God commanded the man, saying, 'From any tree of the garden you may eat freely; but from the tree of the knowledge of good and evil you shall not eat, for in the day that you eat from it you will surely die' " (Genesis 2:16-17).

David Livingstone, the great missionary to Africa, had this Biblical understanding when he gave up the practice of medicine to concentrate on evangelism, discipling, and church planting. His time was best spent in evangelization and preaching, rather than in medical care that, at best, would give only temporary relief.

The practice of medicine is inherently religious. (See Medicine Under Scripture.) If it is practiced on the fundamentals that man is basically good and makes choices consistent with that understanding and that he is only a collection of molecules, every answer to any problem is biochemical or surgical.

Or, by contrast, medicine can be practiced by the believing Christian with the Biblical view that man has a soul, responsible to God for his thinking and behavior.

What is normal? What is health?

The World Health Organization (WHO) states that "health is a state of complete physical, mental and social well-being and not merely the absence of disease or infirmity." Biblically, **health by this definition, exists only in the Garden of Eden (pre-Fall) and in heaven for believers**. No matter what advances in medical and scientific technology, because of the Fall, disease is going to be prevalent and death will always occur (until Christ returns). So, the WHO definition, while it may be a noble goal, will never be achieved on planet earth.

What, then, would be a Biblical definition of health? I propose this definition: health is that physical and mental state of a person in which he or she is born-again, obedient to God's commandments , and makes maximal use of the best medical science that can be discerned within a Biblical understanding. Let's explore this definition in detail for it is basis to a biblical worldview in medicine.

1) **A person**. Health is always an individual matter, relative to one person only. It ranges from a body like an Olympic athlete and a mind like Einstein to the severely retarded and physically incapacitated child or adult with a severe genetic disorder. Thus, exercise, diet, intellectual development, medications, physical therapies, and other modalities maximize one individual's capabilities according to one's inherent physical and mental abilities. Those who are basically "healthy" of body and mind require, perhaps, only basic diet and exercise. Those with severe genetic disorders may require a wide range of frequent physical and medical interventions.

2) **Born-again or regeneration**. This chapter is not the place to present the different Christian beliefs about what being "born-again" means. I refer here simply to the fact that the Bible divides all mankind into two groups, the saved and the unsaved (for example, Matthew 25:32-33). How can a man or woman who is rebellious towards God (Romans 5:10) be considered healthy in mind, if not in body? How can an unbeliever be motivated to make his body a temple of the Holy Spirit (I Corinthians 6:19-20)? (See Regeneration.)

3) **Obedience to God's commandments**. "If you love me, you will keep my commandments" (John 14:15)." Commandments" mean all of God's instructions to His people, not just the Ten Commandments or those that are called commandments. If you read Psalm 119, you will see the many different nouns that are synonyms for "commandment."

150

Moses instructed the Hebrews, as they were to enter Canaan and after they had received the entire book of the law (from Genesis to Deuteronomy), "See, I have set before you today life and prosperity, and death and adversity," (Deuteronomy 30:15. Also read verses 11-20). My paraphrase of that choice for a Biblical worldview in medicine is "Choose life and health or disease and death." (See also, Exodus 15:26.)

One example of Moses' choice is HIV/AIDS and all sexually transmitted diseases (STDs). Spouses who are chaste before marriage and sexually faithful after marriage never have to worry about contracting HIV/AIDS or any of the other worldwide epidemic of STDs. Thus, a major fear among the earth's populations is erased by simply following God's directives!

4) **Makes maximal use of the best medical science that can be discerned within a Biblical understanding**. There are some subtleties here of which the reader should be aware. "Best medical science" means a **Biblical** and **statistical** discernment that is careful and thorough. An example of Biblical discernment is that the law in every state in the United States allows any physician to treat any age girl for birth control, pregnancy, or sexually transmitted diseases without parental consent or knowledge. Such law is unbiblical, striking at the health that is the unity of the family.

An example of statistical discernment is screening for prostate cancer which does not alter morbidity (experience of disease) or mortality (increasing life expectancy). Even the U.S. government's own position in its "Report of the U. S. Preventive Services Task Force does not recommend screening for prostate cancer.

There are numerous examples of other conflicts between the Bible and modern medical "science," a few of which we will explore here. There are **hundreds** of examples of statistically irrelevant practices that are commonly accepted by health care workers. **Biblical discernment includes scientific, as well as, biblical understanding because God is Sovereign over both the spiritual and physical universe**. Most opinions spoken and written by Christians fail the Biblical standard at many points. Scientific analysis is almost non-existent. (Note: I have been involved in Biblical medical ethics for almost 30 years, publishing several books, a journal, and two newsletters. Most of that material has been moved to this website where you are reading this article. For these articles see the articles under Journal of Biblical Ethics in Medicine and Biblical Reflections on Modern Medicine.)

Governments and Health

Government has a great deal of influence on the health of its people. We have already addressed the issue of treating girls without parental permission and a policy on prostate cancer. The official promotion of condoms, non-intercourse sex practices, and other non-statistical recommendations, rather than sexual fidelity before and after marriage, as answers to the HIV/AIDS epidemic is another heinous example. Countries that pass laws to allow same-sex marriages will also be severely hurting the health of their peoples, striking at the health that true families provide and increasing sexual promiscuity. Public health measures, or the lack of them, may affect the health of hundreds of thousands of people. So, a Biblical worldview in medicine is necessary for governments, as well as, individuals. We will see this necessity in this next section.

Abortion

"Now (Adam) had relations with his wife Eve, and she conceived and gave birth to Cain" (Genesis 4:1). Very simply, this verse defines when human live begins: with the sexual union of a man and woman that leads to conception. Human life begets human life. The issue is no more complicated than that.

For those who might want more Biblical support, I could cite the following.

- John the Baptist leaped in his mother's womb at the presence of Jesus (Luke 1:41). John has sufficient consciousness, that is, personhood, to react to His Lord's presence. Now, the exact age of John in the womb of Elizabeth in not precisely known, but drawing the line anywhere during gestation from conception to birth can only be defined by some arbitrary standard that denies the continuity of human life from parents to their children.
- David had a sin nature at conception (Psalm 51:5). Only a person can have a sin nature. David (and, therefore, any descendant of other humans) are persons from conception.
- In Psalm 139:13, the unborn child is being "knit" together by God Himself. Does he "knit" at certain times before birth and not others? If so, how do we discern when He does not work that we may consider the unborn child non-human in order to abort it?
- In Jeremiah 1:5, we are told that God ordained and sanctified Jeremiah before he was born! Thus, persons begin in the plan of God, starting at conception, when the person is first formed a unit of being.

Citing other verses will not convince the person who is unwilling to accept the authority of God's Word which clearly states that the individual person begins at conception, and that it constitutes murder to intentionally kill that person any time later in life (6th Commandment).

Euthanasia

For the most part (at least superficially), Western civilization is a pretty picture. Tall, strong lines of skyscrapers and huge ships, libraries and universities, hospitals and physicians' offices, asphalt and concrete roads, computers that stagger the imagination in their capabilities, and dozens of other marvels. But, if you go into any nursing home and look at the bodies of the people there and observe the functioning of their minds, you will see the devastating effects of the Fall of Adam and Eve. For all our "advances and technology," we cannot prevent much of the ravages of disease and the dying process.

These devastating effects cause a great deal of human suffering by the persons themselves and their families. On an emotional level, one can understand the drive to find a "solution" to end this suffering. (It is also costly and a great inconvenience.) No one wants this tragedy for himself, herself, or a member of one's family. But, **God speaks from Mount Sinai, "Thou shalt not kill!"** He does not need to say more.

What is most needed in these difficult situations is the presence of tenderness and longsuffering, the "until death do us part" commitment of spouses, the "honoring of father and mothers," the reconciliation of conflicts (before the opportunity is gone forever), the creativity of care and comfort, and the greater heights that men and women are sometimes called to scale in their love or one another. Unfortunately, Christians are too often no better than non-Christians in these circumstances. Surely, we should strive to fulfill the criteria by which the world may judge our testimonies (John 17:20-25).

You see, dear reader, the reality of Moses' choice that he gave his people, "choose the way of life or death" is the same choice today. **The unbeliever (call him humanist, atheist, agnostic, communist, socialist, spiritualist, or whatever) answers difficult problems with the solution of death: death to the unborn child and death to the aging and diseased ridden person.** God's answer is life, as difficult as it may be under the effects of the Fall.

A Word about Psychology and Psychiatry

The human individual is a unity of both body and mind. Thus, we cannot avoid considering the sciences of the mind (psychology) in a chapter on medicine.

Virtually all professionals in this field trace modern psychology and psychiatry to Sigmund Freud. This man was an atheist who tried to find a solution for the problem of guilt. Voila! We are face to face with the Bible again! **There is no solution for guilt other than the forgiveness provided in Jesus Christ and to be born-again**.

Some writers who are Christians pose the question, "Is the Bible really a textbook on psychology?" (The only difference between psychiatry and psychology is that psychiatrists are M.D.s and may prescribe medications. **Both** use the same "psychotherapies.") You should answer, "It most certainly is!" What is psychology about? Thinking and behavior. What is the Bible about? Thinking and behavior.

Now, there are a couple of differences. The Bible is truth; psychology is science (see the Chapter on Science and Technology), based upon an evolutionary concept of man. The Bible is God's Word; psychology is man's word (as theory and experimental knowledge).

One other comment should suffice for a very brief overview here. **There are diseases of the brain**. Some are obvious, like brain injury: accidents with head injury, strokes, Parkinson's disease, cerebral palsy, Alzheimer's, brain tumors, etc. Some are likely due to brain disease: schizophrenia and bipolar disorder. Some are very questionably caused by brain disease (at least in most cases): depression, attention deficit hyperactive disorder, and panic disorders. The borders in many of these areas between disease and behavioral choices is yet to be worked out definitively. Yet, today, a far greater number of these have been labeled "mental disorders" than are truly organic. In all cases, the Bible must be applied to behavior in all areas where choices can be made.

Drug Use and Abuse

We started this chapter with medicine being practiced on the basis that man is a body (biochemicals) only or he is both body and soul (the Biblical view). So, let me ask you this question, "Both legally and illegally, what do most societies believe the answer to their problems is?" The answer is, "Drugs." People go to physicians to get drugs. (They care little for spiritual answers based upon mine and many others' experiences.) If they can't get the drugs that they want there, they get them "on the street" (illegally).

You see, a man's view of himself will determine his approach to medical care for himself and his family, whether he is the patient or the physician. **Medical practice is the reflection of a culture**, as is every other area of endeavor.

A Brief Review

1. Physical health (health of the body) is mostly dependent upon one's spiritual health: regeneration and obedience to God's commandments for living.

2. Physical health is mostly an individual phenomenon, as each person has different abilities and physical composition.

3. Only a discerning Christian can practice medicine that is fully Biblical, and therefore, most healthy.

4. Since God calls for truth, the Christian in health care should be discerning of what is and is not efficacious medical care according to the best understanding of medical science.

5. The government of any nation has responsibility for public health. It does not have responsibility for one's individual health.

6. Abortion is the wrongful death of unborn children, any time after conception. Even though abortion may be legal in many nations, it is wrong morally, and God condemns its practice.

7. Euthanasia is any act that intends the death of a person for reasons of "suffering." Acts of health care workers that inadvertently cause the death of a person, either from withdrawal or institution, and that is intended to relieve suffering only, may not be euthanasia.

8. Psychology and psychiatry are mostly governed by a godless morality and a defective science.

9. Medications (drugs), either legally or illegally, will never solve people's moral and spiritual problems.

Questions to Consider

1. List at least five ways that an understanding of physical (bodily) health from a Biblical anthropology (understanding of man) is different from that of a non-Christian.

2. What are the two criteria for men and women that will prevent their ever becoming infected with any sexually transmitted diseases?

3. What errors has the government of your country made relative to health care? What have they done right?

4. Is all medical practice that results in the death of a patient consistent with euthanasia? Why not?

5. Define "healthy." Define what is "normal"

Summary Principles of Medicine

1. **Man is a unity of body and spirit**. Biblically, wholistic medicine must involve both body and spirit. Perfect health was experienced by Adam and Eve prior to their sin and will be experienced by believers in Heaven. Since man remains under the curse in a sinful world, perfect health is not possible on earth. Health and healing may be maximized by an understanding and application of Biblical and medical knowledge, although Biblical knowledge has primary importance. The most important factor in health is one's spiritual condition. Maximal health is not possible for the unbeliever, because his spirit remains "sick," that is, unregenerate and opposed to all standards of righteousness.

2. **God's will for the believer and his family is a higher priority than physical health**. God's will for some Christians (for example, missionaries and martyrs) may not be optimal physical health. Their sacrifice may even result in their deaths.

3. **The practice of medicine and Biblical principles**. Non-Christian physicians cannot practice wholistic (Biblical) medicine. The practice of medicine may not violate Biblical principles to promote physical health (for example, the use of vaccines to prevent cervical cancer caused by the Human Papilloma Virus (HPV). The health practices of the Old Testament should be seriously considered for their application today. Sometimes, traditional

medical care must be refused. Sometimes, it must be accepted. Sometimes, the right decision is unclear, and much time should be spent in prayer, searching the Scriptures, and in seeking Godly counsel. Christian physicians must look for spiritual causes of disease in their patients, especially in Christians. Its presence in medical offices is common.

4. **The relationship between sin and sickness (physical disease)**. The most common medical problems in the United States are directly caused or aggravated by sinful practices. All sickness and injury is caused either by personal sin, the sins of others, the sin of Adam and Eve, or God's sovereign plan. Sin always causes more problems than man is able to solve, even with his most sophisticated, modern technology.

5. **Health is primarily the responsibility of the individual and family and not that of the medical profession**. The Bible gives no explicit instruction for a believer to seek the services of a physician. Modern medicine should not be rejected entirely, but used with understanding and discernment. Ideally, Christians should choose only Christians for their primary care physicians. Many dilemmas occur in medical ethics simply because the patient's physician is not a discerning Christian. The responsibility to choose such a physician falls to the patient and his family. The Christian is not limited to traditional practices of medicine, if he is careful with the alternatives and does not overrate their efficacy. (See The Christian and Alternative Medicine below.)

6. **The role of the Church in health and medical care**. Ordained elders have a specific role in the illnesses of those in their "flock" to discern what possible role sin might play in those illnesses. They also have a duty to pray for them.

7. **Medicine and the Bible**. All recorded healings in the Bible are miraculous. The Bible never mentions healing by a physician. Satan can cause disease and "miraculous" healing of that which he has caused. Modern "scientific" medicine does not have the worldview to prevent its use of occult and other religious practices.

8. **The practice of medicine and Biblical counseling**. No Christian physician ought to select a practice site where Biblical (nouthetic) counseling is not available for his patients. If already in practice, he should seek to make it available through someone in his community, bringing someone in, or be trained to do it himself.

9. **The false efficacy of modern medicine**. The major hurdle to a more rational approach to modern medicine is the recognition that its efficacy is

unclear and that it often causes more harm than good. Examples of this lack of efficacy are legion. The efficacy of modern medicine rests primarily upon socioeconomic conditions and changes in disease patterns that had little or nothing to do with the actual practice of medicine. That "quacks" can often practice as licensed practitioners illustrates the lack of distinctives of modern medicine.

10. **The Christian and alternative medicine**. The movement among Christians toward alternative therapies is both good and bad. Most needed is some systematic approach to determine efficacy. Most Christians greatly overestimate the value of alternative approaches. They should not ignore the biochemical and physiology that has been learned by modern science.

11. **The goals of medicine**. The first goal of medicine is to diagnose. The second goal of medicine is to manage the patient in several ways: to heal (when possible), to relieve suffering, to prognosticate, to rehabilitate, to prevent illness and injury, and to perform research. The third goal of medicine is to subscribe to some objective system of values and ethics. The fourth goal of medicine is not to preserve life at all costs, that is, to prevent death. All goals of medicine may be included as the relief of suffering.

11. **The cost of medical care is one of the major issues of the 1990s**. Present costs of medical care are a result of excessive and inflationary spending by the federal government.

12. **Major hurdles that prevent Christians from exercising Biblical discernment in medical care**. (A) There is the great lack of efficacy for modern medicine in contrast to the huge expenditures. (B) Government provision of medical care is a seriously flawed concept of charity that is believed by many Christians. © The "right" to medical care, conceived in the late 20th century. (D) Principles of traditional insurance cannot be applied to health and medical care because of their lack of precise definition. (E) Health is inseparable from morality. The costs of medical care without moral limitations are limitless.

13. **A Biblical alternative to medical insurance**. Samaritan Ministries is one example of a Biblical approach to payment for medical care. See Internet reference below.

14. **Caring vs. medical care**. A distinction must be made between caring and medical care. Caring is possible without full benefits of medical care, yet may be far more efficacious than medical care.

158

15. **Psychology and psychiatry**. These two disciplines are central to the concept and practice of modern medicine. However, those principles are established under that area of worldview.

16. **Dying, death, and euthanasia**. Death is inherently a spiritual concept, being caused by the sin of Adam and Eve. There are four "kinds" of death in the Bible: physical death, regeneration (death to the "old man"), spiritual death before regeneration, and the second death (eternal punishment). The avoidance of suffering is not a Biblical criterion upon which to seek or cause death. The Golden Rule is a reasonable guideline whether to continue or discontinue life support in severely ill patients and allows for the flexibility necessary to govern these complex situations. Physical life should not be elevated above other Biblical principles. For example, economics is a major factor in "end-of-life" issues. Who pays for the high costs of catastrophic and terminal illness often determines what medical practices may be implemented? Patients should never be neglected, nor their suffering minimized, even though medical treatment may be limited. (See **Caring vs. medical care** above.)

17. **Organ transplantation and "brain death."** The formal UDDA (Uniform Determination of Death Act) definition of brain death fails practically and Biblically. The Biblical concept of death precludes the transplantation of heart, lungs, pancreas, stomach, and other unpaired essential organs. Most major organ transplantations would be precluded on the basis of cost alone in a truly "free" market.

18. **"Near-death experiences" is a patently false concept**. People who are truly dead do not come back to life (Hebrews 9:27). The images and experiences in near-death situations can as easily be explained by the profound pathophysiological changes that take place at the time.

19. **End of life issues for individuals and families**. Living wills are a wrong transference of family authority to the State. Durable powers of attorney and wills for inheritance are necessary legal documents, regardless of age or health status in today's medical-legal climate. Life and medical insurance are necessary to avoid financial hardships on families. A family's choice of a physician may be the most important decision that they make concerning end-of-life issues. Families are losing control over medical decisions for their members with the increasing intrusion of the State into health care. Families must give particular attention to reconciliation and any other "loose ends" with a dying member. Pastoral oversight is a necessity in these situations. For more

detail and an official church document on end of life issues, see Heroic Measures Committee of the PCA.

20. **Abortion**. Modern "civilization" practices a form of child-sacrifice by its widespread practice of abortion. The whole of society shares in guilt and condemnation before God for the practice of abortion. There are 1.3 million abortions each year in the United States. Over 9,000 of these are after the age of viability! (Early 1990s statistics) Prior to the legalization of abortion, there were only 10 percent the number of current abortions. See Abortion and the Ancient Practice of Child Sacrifice.

The Bible is clear that individual human life begins at conception. (A) Conception is linked to the subsequent named individual. (B) God is active in the development of the unborn, God speaks of the unborn as persons, and the unborn can be filled with the Holy Spirit.

Orthodox Protestant theologians have long believed that the soul is present at conception. Being anti-abortion is a non-negotiable ethic for the Christian. Abortion represents the destruction of the family, as much as the destruction of a life. The legalization of abortion increases the fragmentation of the family and cause serious physical and psychological problems for the mother. Abortion is a watershed issue for the sanctity of all human life. Wherever it becomes legal, other forms of killing become "legitimate," even legalized. Abortion is a possible precedent for the persecution of Christians, as it was for Jews in Nazi Germany, as "unwanted human life." The economic loss to a society from abortion is severe.

21. **Childlessness and Artificial Conception**. Man's attempts to circumvent God's ordained pattern of procreation through families did not begin with the modern era. Sin always causes more problems than man is able to solve, even with his most sophisticated technology. The number of infertile couples has tripled in the past two decades with personal sins accounting for this increase. These causes include sexually transmitted diseases, postponed childbirth, scientism, and the consequences of abortion, which kills 1.5 million babies per year that could be available for adoption.

The major Biblical principle for reproductive issues is the unity of the husband and wife. This unity prohibits the use of sperm or eggs that come from donors. Sperm for artificial insemination (donor) are obtained by masturbation, commonly using pornography. Artificial insemination may use the husband's sperm, but this method is rare. In vitro fertilization typically requires the fertilization of several eggs. All these should be transferred to the mother for potential implantation in her womb. None should be frozen because of the potential risks to the nascent life. No Biblical justification is possible for surrogate mothers.

Compassion and principle concerning childless marriages. Considerable compassion should be shown to the infertile couple, but Biblical principles must not be abrogated by their strong emotional desire for children. In vitro fertilization cannot be prohibited by Biblical principle, but the procedure has many problems that make its moral foundation uncertain. No Biblical justification is possible for artificial wombs, except possibly for purposes of therapy of the developing baby, but not as a substitute for the development of the fetus and unborn child that takes place in the womb.

The kinsman-redeemer and the levirate are Biblical provisions for the continuation of a family and its inheritance. Neither is applicable to modern reproductive methods.

22. **World overpopulation and birth control**. God's command "to be fruitful and multiply and fill the earth" is still in effect.

Birth and population control, eugenics, abortion, genocide, and mandatory sterilization reflect the same humanistic philosophy that seeks total control of the environment and of people. Christians must develop a positive attitude and vocabulary that reflects God's blessings through their children. Under "normal" circumstances, three children seems to be a minimum for Christian families, that is, the number needed to exceed the death rate and thereby "multiply" the human population on earth. Limiting factors include poverty, genetic deformities, and temporary postponement.

Birth control pills interfere with normal physiology and may be an immoral method for this reason. All other forms of birth control are less effective, but are more clearly moral and are adequate for spacing pregnancies. The condemnation of all abortifacients is consistent with the Biblical pro-life position. The prescription of any method of birth control to an unmarried woman except for specific medical reasons that do not have to do with birth control is to be severely condemned and is incompatible with a Biblical position. Sterilization may be a choice for some Christians after they have seriously considered after three or more children or for solid reasons of genetic abnormalities.

23. **Miraculous healing**. A focus on miraculous healing sometimes ignores the more important role of a lifestyle that is physically and spiritually healthy.

God's usual pattern is to work through common means or the wonderful healing powers of the body itself, not through miracles. Christians should understand the difference in the two concepts. Miraculous healing has specific Biblical characteristics. It is instantaneous and complete, but not normally God's means of dealing with people. The purpose of miraculous healings was to authenticate God's activity among men, a purpose that is not needed today (except in some remote regions) because of the Scriptures and regeneration. It was manifested only by Prophets, Apostles, and Jesus Christ in His incarnation.

The gifts of healings have not been proven to be present in modern times and have doubtfully been present since completion of the Canon (that is, all 66 books of the Protestant Bible). Subjective interpretations of illness complicate the claim for miraculous healing. These include psychosomatic illness, understanding by patients, and the placebo effect. Certainly, almost all claims of miraculous healing are false for these subjective reasons. The Bible presents irrefutable evidences for miraculous healing. Thus, modern Christians ought to have such evidence or not make the claim, else they falsify God's witness in the world.

The sick ought to call for the elders of the church in cases of serious illness. The elders ought to inquire about the possible relationship of sin to the patient's illness. The application of James 5:14-16 does not always result in healing. Healing that is dependent upon the sick person's having "enough" faith is not a Biblical concept and a cruel burden to place upon him.

24. **The State and the practice of medicine**. The State does not have the Biblical right to govern the practice of medicine. Consistent with this principle, the State should not be involved in the licensing of physicians. The licensing of physicians and other professionals has not "protected" the public and has actually promoted disease and death. Under the present system, medical care is strictly limited to those standards that are acceptable to the State (for example, abortion, birth control to unmarried women, and medical care to children without their parents permission.) Pre-payment systems (HMOs, PPOs, etc.) have their own inherent problems, placing a barrier between the patient and the physician with the State looking over their shoulder. Health is promoted most effectively by a society that is moral and governed by Biblical ethics and law. Under a Biblical system, medical schools would be rare. Physicians would be trained primarily in apprenticeships. The State has a legitimate role to provide medical care for diseases and injuries acquired in the "line of duty" by policemen, firemen, and other civil servants. The State has a legitimate role in sanitation and refuse disposal and in the control of infectious diseases, but it

162

should not be careful to overstep its bounds here (as it is prone to do, everywhere). Without current State control, more responsibility for personal health must be assumed by individuals, families, and churches.

25. **Medicine and the Church**. The church must develop Biblical plans for meeting medical costs and not follow the world's standards that are now failing. (For example, see http://www.samaritanministries.com/.) Basic medical care (colds, "prevention," minor aches and pains, etc. to the exclusion of major medical problems, such as, cancer, heart attacks, etc.) are uninsurable maladies. The church must re-establish itself as the counseling resource for Christians and not continue to allow medical redefinition of sin as disease. All local churches ought to have an official plan for the practice of Matthew 18:15-20 and James 5:13-16. Pastors and other church leaders should develop a close working relationship with one or more physicians, especially with those who are open to Biblical teaching, the application of Biblical principles in medical situations, and who understand the failed efficacy of modern medicine. The church is the backup resource for its families, including the provision of medical care. Preaching and teaching should include the care of the body as the Temple of the Holy Spirit. Mission boards have largely adopted the "medical model" for its missionaries, in both medicine and psychiatry. A fully implemented program of church discipline would prevent many medical, as well as spiritual, problems. The church ought to consider carefully its role in chronic care institutions and medical clinics.

26. **Medicine and the Family**. The greatest effect on health or ill health occurs in the home. Many Christians need to apply basic Biblical principles to make their homes more honoring to God and healthy to themselves. In the next several years, a transition from institutional care to the home can be expected, as institutions become overcrowded and unsafe places. This change will mostly be a positive one, as the home can be a place for special treatment of family members. It has several advantages that can have a favorable impact on treatment and recovery. Practical books on health care for families need to be written. Christian physicians need to re-evaluate their approach to medicine in light of the Bible and coming changes in our health-care system. The church will need to develop systems of support for families burdened by in-home care.

Endnotes

[1] J. Robertson McQuilkin, "The Behavioral Sciences Under the Authority of Scripture," 1/20 *The Journal of the Evangelical Theological Society* (March 1977), 31-43.

2 *Ibid*, 32.

3 The purpose of medicine is more complicated that this simple statement, but it will suffice for this paper. A more detailed analysis may be found in my book: Franklin E. Payne, *Biblical Healing for Modern Medicine*, (Augusta, GA: Covenant Books, 1993).

4 Roy Maynard, "Taking the Bible Cure" (book review), 13/32 *World* (August 22, 1998), 22. Reginald Cherry, *The Bible Cure* (Creation House, 1998).

5 Leonard A. Sagan, *The Health of Nations: True Causes of Sickness and Well-being* (New York: Basic Books, 1987), 67-70.

6 *Ibid.*, pp. 187-188. "Personal maturity" is my phrase not Sagan's. His "psychological characteristics of the healthy person" included being "confident of (his) ability to make competent decisions," "having a high regard for themselves," having "a high value (for) health and survival," being "future-oriented," "forming strong and persistent affectionate bonds (in) social networks" (especially marriage), "relishing companionship," and "pursuing knowledge of themselves and the world around them."

7 James Lynch, *The Broken Heart: The Medical Consequences of Loneliness* (New York: Basic Books, 1977).

8 The removal of homosexuality as a pathological diagnosis was correct (Biblical). Making homosexuality legitimate was incorrect (unbiblical).

9 Stanley E. Harris, "Aversion Therapy for Homosexuality" (letter), 259/22 *The Journal of the American Medical Association* (June 10, 1988), 3271.

10 Paul Cameron, William L. Playfair, and Stephen Wellum, "The Longevity of Homosexuals: Before and After the AIDS Epidemic," 29/3 *Omega* (1994), 249-272.

11 Paul Cameron, Kirk Cameron, and Kay Proctor, "Effect of Homosexuality Upon Public Health and Social Order," 64 *Psychological Reports* (1989), 1167-1179.

12 Franklin E. Payne, "Addiction as Besetting Sin," 7/4 *Journal of Biblical Ethics in Medicine* (Fall 1993), 96-99.

13 *Ibid.*

14 Robert J. Levin, "The Redbook Report: A Study of Female Sexuality," *Redbook* (special report, 1975); Philip and Lorna Sarrel, "The Redbook Report on Sexual Relationships," *Redbook* (October 1980), 73-80; "The Janus Report," *Redbook* (March 1993), 69-71, 114, report based upon Samuel S. Janus and Cynthia L. Janus, *The Janus Report on Sexual Behavior* (New York: John Wiley and Sons, 1993).

9. Civil Government, Law, and Politics

The Right to Medical Care Within a Biblical Worldview: The Declaration of Independence and United States Constitution

Ed's Note: The following was a presentation delivered in Pittsburgh at the conference on Health Care in Crisis: A Biblical Response, May 2, 1992 by Dr. Herb Titus, former Dean of the College of Law and Government at Regent University. He is now an attorney, specializing in constitutional litigation and strategy, and President of Forecast Foundation, an educational ministry dedicated to restoring America to her Biblical foundations. The presentation was transcribed, edited by the journal staff, and finally reviewed by Dr. Titus.

Any discussion of rights must begin with definitions. What is meant by "right" today is often different from what was meant by America's founders.

In Webster's Third International Dictionary, there are at least three categories of "right'-not a definition with several nuances, but three categories of definition. These categories of "right" cover much of the page. Rather than review the whole, here is the essence.

1) "Disposed to do what is just or good; being in accordance with what is right, good, or proper; agreeable to a standard or principle; fit." This definition applies when a teacher tells a student who answers correctly, "You are right! It is not what is generally meant when one speaks of "the right to medical care.

2) "Something to which someone has a just claim; something to which someone is entitled; a legally enforceable claim.' This category- is what most people mean when they refer to not just the right to medical care, but to the right to have medical care without paying for it (at least not paying the full cost).

3) In light of this definition of right, the third category is quite interesting: "In accord with a standard of justice and duty"!

165

The second category connotes that one can define his own entitlements-those entities to which he has a right. The third definition, however, denotes that one's right depends upon its accordance with a standard outside one's own claim-an externally defined standard of justice and duty.

The difficulty in the United States today is that there is no general acknowledgement of a source outside of man himself to define what is just and what is right. In law schools, generally, there is no acknowledgement that God has spoken and that He provides the standard of justice and rightness. Individual professors may believe God's Word is the standard, but there rarely is an institutional statement to that effect. Thus, lawyers and judges today generally do not believe in any objective standard of any kind that defines justice and right. Man seems able within himself to establish his own standard.

This posture contrasts with law governing the physical world. In physics, teachers acknowledge the Law of Gravity as something that man has not contrived. The Law of Gravity is just there. We have to discover it, define it, and conform our conduct to it. It is doubtful that any American physicist would say, "The Law of Gravity binds you only if you want to be bound by it.'

No teacher would concede that the person who did not believe in gravity could safely jump off the top of a budding and avoid injury or death. However, few in law school today would concede that laws govern sexual behavior, for example, are binding on man whether he wants to believe them or not. There is a huge, reason-defying assumption that man can reconfigure or reshape the law that governs human behavior to conform to whatever are his basic desires.

So, this conflict between the second definition of "right," that is, something to which you are entitled by your own definition of entitlement, is very different from the third definition of an external standard by which is determined what is right and wrong.

Without God, the third definition is not possible. Chief Justice Marshall wrote, "We are a government of laws and not of men." If there is no God, this declaration is either a cruel or a foolish statement. How can there be a government of laws and not of men, if men are the inventors of law? If God exists, however, the statement is true and presents us with laws to which we must conform.

Illustrations of the second definition of "right," as evoked by people across the country, are legion. Name any entitlement. In Washington, D.C., our legislators think that budget items cannot be changed because they are

166

"givens,' e.g., Social Security, Medicare, and Medicaid. People have a "right" to this whole array of entitlements, so they cannot be touched. Budget reductions must come from somewhere else.

By this second definition of "right," people believe that they have a right to other people's money to live, to eat, to drink, to be fed, to be clothed, to be housed, and of course -to be provided with medical care. This right extends further to require the employer to provide medical care. In legal terms, this process is called "taking" as opposed to "giving"

"Taking" requires individuals to pay a disproportionate share of the cost of civil government. That's the reason that the Constitution forbids taking property without just compensation of the owner. A good example would be the munitions industry. During wartime, if they were not reimbursed, they would pay a disproportionate share of the war effort. Under the Constitution, munitions manufacturers would not be required to pay more than the ordinary taxpayer does. Their goods (property) could not be seized without just compensation. Today, people claim that they have a right to force their employer to provide a certain minimum, as well as the right of taxpayers to provide similarly.

This modern definition conforms to the second definition, which is actually a self-contained definition of entitlement. But, that was not our forefathers' understanding of rights. The Declaration of independence says, "We consider these truths to be self-evident, that all men are created equal and endowed by their Creator with certain inalienable rights, and among these are life, liberty, and the pursuit of happiness. That to secure these rights, governments are instituted among men.' They chose that language very carefully.

Rights are God-created, not man-invented. Man's purpose in any civil society is to secure what God has given to all mankind-not to redefine or restructure them. Unfortunately, the civil rights movement connotes that rights are defined by the civil government, instead of recognizing that rights are defined and given by God and secured by the civil government. Thus, it is incumbent upon us to discover those "certain inalienable rights" of "life, liberty, and the pursuit of happiness" in the Declaration of Independence.

Return to the Scriptures

The definition of "right" itself must be given by God, or else we make the same mistake as the secularists, starting with ourselves. In Revelation 22:14, your right to the Tree of Life depends upon your obedience to God. Consistent with this truth, the Virginia Constitution says that the definition and free exercise of religion is the duty that we owe our Creator. The Greek word is exousia, which is often translated "authority." Indeed, in Matthew 28:18 Jesus claims "all authority.' But, how did He get that authority - that right ?

Philippians 2:8 tells us that He was obedient and humbled Himself to the point of death on the cross. So, *Christ was given the right and the power to rule Heaven because of His obedience to God!*

So, our *duty* to God is what defines our right. The source of our rights is God Himself, the definer of those rights is God, and obedience is the key to possession of those rights. For example, the key to the "right to liberty" is obedience. Christians often make a mistake here. They say, "Yes, I believe in free will. Adam and Eve exercised free will." Actually, they did not. They exercised their will, but it was not free. Their "free will" put them in bondage.

When discussions turn to free will, we ought instead to look to Christ's example in the wilderness. At every point where He was tempted, He obeyed God, the Word of God, the plan of God, and the will of God. That is true liberty!

As Christians, we must think differently from the world (Romans 12:2) about rights-and liberty. Otherwise, we fall into a fantasy of our own to imagine what a right is. Whatever the right is---a right to health care, to some sexual practice, to any claim-we must look to the Biblical definition of "right."

Back to the Declaration of Independence

With this foundation, the Declaration of Independence gives us the framework to analyze any rights question or issue. Relative to medical care, the three categories of "life, liberty, and the pursuit of happiness" are key. The right to medical care relates to length of life, quality of life, and every other aspect of life. Think about this connection-one that is crucial to the abortion debate. If *there is a right to medical care, what is the argument on behalf of the unborn child but a right* to life?

God has given us life, not death. Death is not a right. We don't have a right to die. (Note the application! Editor) We have a right to live. It is a duty owed to God. We are acknowledging that God is the giver of life, the taker of life, the author of life, the finisher of life, the alpha of life, and the omega of life. Man's duty (and right) is to live unto God for the period that God has ordained him to live. A physician responding to the call of God serves God by protecting and improving that life, not by terminating it.

Thus, the right to medical care is lifegiving and life-sustaining. In the Beginning, God breathed the breath of life into Adam's nostrils (Genesis 2:7). God did not stop with Adam. He told job that the breath of God has made him (Job 33:4). Throughout the generations. God is breathing life into every human being. The Psalmist asks God to show him the number of his days. By contrast today, someone goes to the physician to ask how many days that he has to live. Who knows better: God or the physician? Only by the Holy Spirit does the physician know.

Moses asked God, "Teach us to number our days" (Psalm 90:12). Our very life exists only in our relationship with our Heavenly Father: the beginning of life, the end of life, and everything in between. Thus, medical care must be designed to promote and protect that life. A claim on any other basis is illegitimate.

One of my favorite Scriptures on abortion is Ecclesiastes 11:5. It says that if you do not know the path of the wind or how the body is formed in the womb, then you cannot understand the work of God, the Maker of all things. It is sheer arrogance for man to think that he can discover when life begins. The only way that he can know when life begins is if God reveals it to him. It is only because of God's revelation in the Scripture that we have any idea when life begins. Psalm 139:13-16 reminds us powerfully of this incredible revelation! We dare not attribute to ourselves anything other than what God has revealed to us on that matter!

Still, defective children and pregnancy by incest are often claimed as exceptions to this protection of unborn life. "These are emotionally charged issues, after all." Well, God speaks to them as well. John 9:1-3 recounts the man born blind. Jesus' disciples asked, "Who sinned, this man or his parents?" Jesus answered, "Neither this man nor his parents sinned, but that the works of God should be revealed in him."

Many people today believe that a defective child will live a terrible life, but we are all born defective! We are all born with a fallen nature. That spiritual defect is far more serious than any physical defect! With any abortion "exceptions" for defective children, we transform God's standard to fit our own perception of quality of life. As to suffering and pain, God commands us to endure it patiently. If we do so, He is pleased (I Peter 2:20-25)- But to the human mind, no one should suffer.

Then, there is the matter of pregnancy by incest. Surely, some say, "That child should not be born." Yet, in Jesus' genealogy (Matthew 1), there is an incestuous link in one generation. Judah impregnated Tamar, his daughter-in-law who had disguised herself as a prostitute (Genesis 38:14-30). Twins were born: Perez and Zerah. Perez is included in Jesus' genealogy. God has a purpose and plan for every life! No matter what man sees, God sees far beyond him.

Without some sense of the nature of life, we will not have a correct understanding of the right to life and the right to medical care. God has defined the framework, not so-called "experts" or politicians. There is a clear duty of the civil magistrate with regard to the protection of life. The civil ruler wields the sword against the evil doer (Romans 13:4). That's the ruler's primary responsibility! He rewards good and punishes evil.

The primary purpose of the civil order is to protect innocent life that bears the image of God (Genesis 9:6). Prior to God's Covenant with Noah (Genesis 9:117), no human authority had any right to impose any penalty upon any sin. However, God states that "whoever sheds man's blood, by man his blood shall be shed." Underlying the right to life is this Noahic Covenant. If the civil government does not enforce this covenant, then it loses its right to rule.

According to Scripture, Israel lost its place as a nation because it did not protect the innocent blood of the children. The law of the land operated to vomit out the people, just as God warned in Leviticus 18. God built this protective principle into the land itself. When Cain killed Abel, it was the blood of Abel that cried out of the ground. That was the testimony that God heard and by which He convicted Cain. The law that protects human life does not depend upon a state legislature passing a statute.

People say that the U.S. Supreme Court legalized abortion. That is impossible. The Court cannot legalize what God has made illegal. Man cannot -make straight what God has made crooked, as the writer of Ecclesiastes has stated. Man may rebel and not enforce God's law, but he cannot change God's laws.

The right to medical care must begin with God's definitions and His principles governing life, not some sociological or economic assessment with regard to some nebulous quality of life.

170

The Principle of Liberty

The liberty principle in the context of the right to medical care concerns the relationship between the family, the physician, and the state. God created the family; He also created the authority of the family (Genesis 1:26-28). The first duty given to the family is to be fruitful and multiply. That right extends to the nurture of the children conceived within that union.

In Genesis 2, God said that it was not good for man to be alone, so He made him a helpmeet. From Adam's "knowing" Eve, she conceived, and children were born. In fact, her name, "Eve," meant "the mother of all living" (Genesis 3:20). But, it is not just the mother who is responsible. Fathers have a duty to bring their children up in the nurture and admonition of the Lord (Ephesians 6:4).

Reflecting back to Cain's killing Abel, Cain deserved to die because he killed his brother. But God said that any man who destroyed Cain, God would avenge sevenfold. At that time, the only human institution that had any authority was the family, and the father had no duty (and thus no right) to impose death upon an erring child. His duty was to bring his children up in the nurture and admonition of the Lord.

When all nations were to descend from the families of Noah, then civil authority was created and the death penalty was instituted. Only the civil magistrate, not the father in a family, was given the authority of the death penalty. The father's mission was still the nurture of the child.

This principle is absolutely crucial to understanding the relationship of the physician, the family, and the state. "Honor your father and your mother that it may go well with you and that you may enjoy long life on the earth" (the first commandment with a promise). God does not say, "Honor your physician..." or "Honor the civil magistrate..." Why? Because it is the father and the mother who have the duty to nurture the child and raise him up in the Lord. If the child does so, then he will live long on the earth and things will go well with him.

A personal story will illustrate. Once, when we had our child in a Christian school, the principal insisted upon our giving him a physician's statement that our child should not participate in physical education activities. Our child had been sick, and we just did not think that he should participate. We did not think that we had a duty to furnish the principal with such a statement because *our duty was to determine whether this child should be engaged in physical activities*, as part of our duty to nurture and raise him up in the admonition of the Lord.

We had a real conflict. We were perfectly willing to provide a physician's statement if there was some question as to whether or not we were doing what was right. The physician's primary duty was to help us determine the proper course for the child's well-being. *The option of medical care rests primarily with the family*. One option may be intercessory prayer without medical attention. We have certainly made that choice on some occasions, and we likely made some mistakes. But as likely, we made mistakes in taking our children to the physician when we should have only prayed for them.

The liberty claim is that medical choice is first of all a family choice, because of the duty of nurture and admonition. The duty of the child is to honor the father and the mother, *with the promise of health and long life*. (Note the "medical" benefit here -Ed.)

Medicine, then, is a helping and serving profession. It stands along side and helps the family with counseling, education, basic medical care, diagnostic testing, prevention, and prescription of medications, etc.

The medical profession also plays a key role as the mediator between the family and the state. The medical profession provides to the state the expertise that the state needs to protect life within the family from some who might pervert their duty to their children. The state has a duty to protect children from decisions by parents that would harm or destroy the children.

I am troubled by child abuse statutes because they are ill-defined. It is not that child abuse does not exist, but that these laws are confusing. The old-fashioned statutes that defined battery, assault, and murder were preferable. Now, definitions of child abuse are open-ended and encroach more upon the duty of the parent than to protect the child from true abuse by his parents. The state does have a role in protecting children where actions of battery, assault, and murder are concerned.

The state also has a role in the area of communicable diseases. Since people engage in activities that expose others to serious diseases, the authority to quarantine would be one possible action. I am amazed how we treat AIDS in America. The one with AIDS is protected more than the one who is threatened with AIDS.'

The Pursuit of Happiness

At the heart of the pursuit of happiness is the family. Not only did God command the family to multiply and replenish the earth, but to subdue it and exercise authority over it. When God saw that Adam needed a helpmeet, God did not create the United States Congress! Today, congressmen would have you believe that they are the helpmeet to the man to help him provide for his family. No, God created Eve. *God did not even create the church to help Adam*! He created Eve. It was a family free-enterprise system.

In our *laissez-faire*, capitalistic thinking, we have the notion that free enterprise is an individual affair. Thus, we have the individual vs. the state when God created the family to exercise this right.

A physician, then, is to help the family exercise dominion over the family's property, creative opportunities, and how they will spend their money. It is *not the role of the state to decide how families will spend their money*. Therefore, the state should not decide whether the family should spend its money for one kind of medical care vs. another (e.g., allopathic vs. alternative medicine).

For the state to take away money from one family in order to support medical decisions by another family is contrary to that dominion authority, because the duty of the state is to foster and protect the family. *Indeed, the state is substituting for the family because it does not think the family can make right choices.*

Again, Romans 13:4 does not say that the civil magistrate is to do good, but he is to reward good and punish evil. In effect, today's government says to the family, "You don't do good, so we will do good for you. We know better than you whether you ought to pay a certain wage or work a certain number of hours."

One of the most difficult tasks that we had with our children was getting them into the workplace. We had to have a juvenile judge's permission to let our children work before the age of 14. What did that judge know about my children? Nothing! Yet, I had to have his permission for my child to work for someone else.

Today, kids usually don't do any work, other than domestic, until the age of 18, unless a parent is self-employed. Or, they are employed illegally (which most employers will not do because of severe governmental sanctions). The state has usurped the authority of the family instead of fostering and protecting that authority.

Happiness, Welfare, and the Poor

Welfare, as the responsibility of the government, violates the law of love which governs our duty to the poor. You find this law in the Old and the New Testaments. "Pure and undefiled religion ...is...to visit orphans and widows in their trouble" (James 1:27). James does not say that this duty is that of the civil magistrate. His declaration is a summary of all the duties that God sets forth in rather specific terms in the Old Testament.

Two principles concerning love are absolutely critical. 1) Love must be voluntary. The nature of a tax-supported welfare system is involuntary. One has no choice whether to pay or not to pay his taxes.

"For God so loved the world that He sent His only begotten Son." God did not force His Son to come. He came voluntarily-the ultimate act of God's love.

2) Love must be unconditional. Christ did not say, "Let's see, God. I will sacrifice myself on the condition that You will guarantee me at least one soul." No, He would have gone to earth even if there were no souls to save. He went unconditionally. "While we were yet sinners, Christ died for us" (Romans 5:8). In Medicaid, Medicare, or any other tax-supported medical system, there are conditions. Therefore, any system that is supported by tax money would violate the law of love.

In the Old Testament, God required duties to the poor. The farmer had to leave his field open for gleaning. Interest was not to be charged for loans to the poor. People were required to reach out to the poor who needed something that another had in abundance. *But, in no instance did God require a humanly enforced sanction if a person neglected that duty. It was, and is, a duty owed exclusively to God,* because it is enforceable by reason and conviction and not by force and violence.

These principles of life, liberty, and the pursuit of happiness must be honored in the discussion of the right to medical care. If they are not, then "rights" is not the issue, because the claim is inconsistent with the standards that God has given us to determine what is and is not just.

1. Herbert W. Titus, "Winning the War Against AIDS: Our Nation's Response" vs. a Biblical Response, in Franklin E. Payne, What Every Christian Should

Know About the AIDS Epidemic, (Augusta, Georgia, Covenant Books, 1991), pp. 168 180.

Question-and-Answer Session

Question: Is there a conflict between the role of a Christian physician as a priest to serve God and his duty to the state?

Answer: The jurisdictional authorities are separate, but there is an interrelationship between the several jurisdictions. For example, if the church is not interrelating with the state, then the church is not doing its job. That is why God says to pray for those who rule over us (I Timothy 2). The same is required of the physician. He does not choose being a physician as a profession because of licensure standards set by that state. Nonetheless, to neglect his civic duty as a physician is to neglect the duty of a physician that God has ordained him to be. So, there is an interrelationship, but not a jurisdictional encroachment.

Question: What is the role of the state to allow Christian Science parents to "only" pray for the medical needs of their children and neglect care by physicians?

Answer: It's a question of intention.

That is, what is the intent of the parents? In some cases, their claim may be so bizarre that it could be questioned whether the parents' intent is justified. Indeed, prayer is oftentimes what God leads us into with regard to the health of our children. We have to be very careful how the state interferes with that responsibility.

However, if a parent decides to put his child on an altar to slit his throat, claiming that he will be raised from the dead, then there is no doubt that the parent is breaching his duty to honor the life of his child.

Free exercise of religion is not limited to Christians, but only a true Christian would be absolutely in harmony with a truly lawful civil society. Many people in the name of religion are out of step with the law of God and, therefore, out of step with the civil society that God has ordained. Because we are finite and fallen, we will sometimes be mistaken about the limits on the powers of civil rulers. We make an accommodation in a gray area to avoid making mistakes on one side of the line or the other.

Actual decisions depend upon determination of relevant law that governs and the factual assessment of what has happened. There are always difficult cases of application. Those difficulties do not mean that the principle is wrong, but that the application of the principle is difficult. That's where the struggle comes.

Question: What is to prevent a liberal from interpreting the "right to life" in the Declaration of Independence as including a right to medical care that the poor cannot afford

Answer: The only response is to challenge what is meant in his definitions of life, liberty, and the pursuit of happiness, and how the government is to secure those rights. Some people do take the Declaration and conclude something quite different than what I have said in this talk. One's conclusion depends upon one's worldview. We have been fighting conflicting world views throughout the ages because different people have different presuppositions.

We have to reclaim Madison, Jefferson, and others for our side. Then, we must ask our opponents whom they have on their side to prove that they have the more persuasive reading of the language than we have. It is difficult task. We must know our history and must have done our investigative homework to prevail.

Question: How do you answer the claim that the Declaration and Constitution have to be interpreted relative to the greater knowledge that we have today rather than the knowledge of yesteryear?

Answer: We must ask, "What is the nature of the Constitution?" Briefly, the Constitution was based upon the Biblical concept of covenant. What makes the Constitution a constitution is four perpetuity principles along with three contract principles that are unchanging. If a constitution changes with changing times, it is not a constitution, because it no longer binds each generation to certain enduring principles. Even in my law classes, several sessions are required to show the connection historically and the principles Biblically.

One perpetuity principle is that it is binding on future generations. We see that in the New Testament when Christ made a new covenant, that bound and benefited not only the generation of his day, but all future generations as well. The Preamble of the Constitution "secures the blessings of liberty for ourselves and our posterity." From this continuity, one professor has stated that the

Constitution could not possibly be construed to authorize abortion because that act takes away a blessing of liberty from one's posterity.

The nature of the Constitution is inescapably a battle of worldviews; that is, a theological argument, because all law ultimately rests upon the premise of who is the ultimate author of law- God or man.

A Biblical Perspective on the Problem of Illegal Aliens

In the following discussion, the reader will note that the problem of illegal aliens has been created by the State (federal and state government) and cultural policies that already exist. Note the overlap of many worldview areas: economy, sin, matters of the heart, law and social justice, licensing, charity, education, etc. **The problem of illegal aliens is not just a problem all its own**. It is mostly, if not entirely, created by all the unbiblical polices and practices that are common in the United States.

The following is only a preliminary, virtually an "off the cuff," presentation of the issues. But, the reader will note that all of these issues have been addressed throughout this website. And, few people are addressing this problem on a Biblical basis.

1. **State welfare in its myriad, if not medusa-like, forms must be progressively stopped**. There is no Biblical warrant for State welfare. (See welfare.). **The major issue of absorbing illegal aliens into the American economic system has been their cost to the welfare system**. This system includes state-sponsored schools, medical care (especially emergency rooms, emergent hospital admissions, and Medicaid), the myriad of "entitlements" (aid to children, pregnant women, single-parent families, workman's compensation, etc., etc.), and many other programs.

Churches need to be increasingly involved with true welfare. For the most part, the church has turned it responsibility for charity over to the state. Numerous deleterious effects have occurred because of this neglect. (A) Churches have lost status in the community. (B) Churches have lost purpose and work for their members. It is the problem that Francis Schaeffer called "personal peace and affluence." A "personal relationship with Christ" (poorly understood) and recruiting others under this rubric (disguised as evangelism) has become the virtual endpoint of Christian experience.

(C) Charity (welfare), properly administered, includes a strong component of morality and evangelism. Charity includes moral instruction of family responsibilities, such as, marital fidelity, moral instruction of children, and responsible work for all but the crippled. Evangelism provides the only real hope for change in regeneration. So, not only is immediate help provided, but the accompanying moral instruction moves those helped towards independency and being socially responsible. State welfare only creates dependency, and worse, an entitlement attitude that often boils into rage and resentment. Charity by the Church and welfare by the State contrast starkly. One builds up, the other destroys individuals, families, and eventually, ordered society.

2. **Do away with the minimum wage**. A minimum wage pushes these workers into unemployment and into all the "welfare" schemes above. This movement is a double drain on the economy, as workers for "low end" jobs are not available, increasing costs of the goods and services in these areas. These potential workers then move from being workers and producers to drains on the welfare system, and even into crime because their "idle hands being the Devil's workshop.

3. **Redefine U.S. citizenship to exclude babies born of illegal immigrants**. The concept that babies born in the U.S. are automatically citizens of the United States is a noble and right one **for parents who are citizens**. But, granting citizenship to children of criminals ("illegal immigrants") is easily arguable as beyond the intention of this statute.

4. **Stop foisting the enforcement of illegal immigration onto employers**. It is the State's job to handle all things that are illegal.

5. **Require some penalty for second offenders who sneak into the U.S**. They could be kept in work camps until they had paid for the cost of their capture and incarceration, working at some minimum wage. Or, they could make fencing for the border!

6. **Require English for all civil proceedings**. Certainly, one can make the case that the bilingual movement of the last few years has been caused by the sheer numbers of illegal immigration. Making Spanish available to all facets of society is a capitulation to an illegal activity. Thus, **these illegal immigrants are winning** -- they have the power to turn us into a bilingual society.

Worse, it is a capitulation to one primary basis of unity for Americans. For any culture to exist, it must have some basic kinds of unity that provide grounds for basic communication and morals. **The eventual fate of multiculturalism is anarchy and/or the rise of some tyrannical power that seizes the weakness brought on by fragmentation of cultural groups.** Bilingualism is one major pillar of unity that has been demolished.

Who rules here? Who should be given prior consideration? Illegal aliens or law-abiding citizens? The answer should be obvious to anyone who has any sense of law and order and of a just society.

7. **Deny voting rights until the second or third generation of citizenship.** That is, newly naturalized citizens would not have all the rights of citizenship, but their children or grandchildren could. Learning a culture and being absorbed into it takes time. (Of course, we are rapidly losing any cultural unity of any kind. See discussion at the end of this article)

We were once a largely Anglo-German-Christian culture. Thanks to massive changes in immigration law under John Kennedy, we are becoming a polyglot with inadequate cultural glue to hold us together. We are not going to make millions of Mexicans into productive, time-valuing, and self-governing citizens overnight. **Illegal aliens are going to make us into a syncretistic Roman Catholic-pagan, graft-ridden culture.**

The only real glue that will hold all nations and cultures together is Biblical Christianity, best manifested in the Reformation and the common laws of England that became the Constitution and early laws of this country. Everything else is a tower of Babel.

An historical example occurred in South Africa. The Calvinists of Natal and Orange Free State allowed the Zulus and others to enter (the land was largely vacant as the Dutch entered it) in order to have cheap labor for their ranches and mines. They were soon outnumbered eight to one and lost their nation to them within our lifetime. Had the Boers allowed much more gradual immigration and evangelized them as they settled, then they would have retained ownership of their country. The reader should note that **economic greed was the incentive that eventually destroyed their state.** Do you see any application to the problem of illegal immigrants in the United States?

(Actually, the Boers let the British come in to work the mines, which gave Britain an excuse to invade and defeat them, and then Britain encouraged the Zulus, Mashonas, and others to immigrate.)

8. Legalize the possession and use of narcotics. Without the financial incentive, their use would decline, but not disappear. The border patrol now estimates that well over 90 percent of all drugs smuggled into the U.S. are undetected. Narcotic abuse is a matter of the spirit and heart. Narcotic smuggling is in commensural relationship with illegal immigration. Of course, State programs to treat "addiction" would have to be abandoned, as well.

9. Gradually return the nation to a gold and silver standard. This move would deny the State's ability to stimulate the economy artificially and decrease the lure of Mexicans into over stimulated areas. This principle is one of the most basic to economics.

10. Slowly reduce all government support of education at all levels. Many students are enticed to stay in educational tracks beyond any need of the economy for their degree of training. Perhaps, more would consider becoming competent chefs, masons, carpenters, electricians, tailors, and other valuable and necessary occupations that do not require college degrees, especially at the post-graduate level. These mid-level vocations would displace some less qualified people into more menial jobs, leaving less room for immigrants.

11. Stop industrial subsidies of industrial farms. For example, tax dollars allow the semi-desert central valley of California to grow rice, lettuce, and other water-intensive crops, using expensive federal water distribution programs. Smaller farms would be able to use local resources, if they did not have to compete with these federally subsidized farms.

12. Stop all government welfare, health care (except life-threatening emergencies), maternity care, education, and any other benefits for illegal immigrants. This system is doubly disastrous. First, there is the unbiblical concept of State welfare in itself, a common theme of a truly Biblical worldview. Second, what serpentine manner of reasoning can justify welfare for criminals?

We should not refuse immigration! The above steps would encourage people who want to come and become a part of the fabric of the nation. Currently, we have people who come and share in our (fake) prosperity and then use their income to fund all manner of nefarious activities, including Al Qaeda.

But, will we even continue to be a nation? The prior question is, "What is a nation?" Most nations did not even exist prior to the mid-nineteenth century

180

when the nationalist fervor began in Europe, in Russia, and in the United States with Abraham Lincoln. Nationalism cannot tolerate the diversity of cultures. Thus, the political correctness of modern times. Diversity, for all its arrogance of inclusion, is ultimately an adoption of sameness: big and centralized government, homosexuality, sexual promiscuity, hedonism, individualism (within allowed tolerances), that is, all principles of Biblical Christianity. **True diversity is ultimately anarchy**. That situation is upon what the United States is teetering.

Biblical ethics and law that emphasized the family, the Puritan work ethic, free capitalism, and one language (that happened to be English) is what built and has held this country together. With the destruction of law, the family, and an anti-God attitude, what held the U.S. together is rapidly dissolving. What will be left will either be a tyrannical state, a merging of Mexico, Canada, and the U.S. into one such state, or several groups of states that form on the basis of common language and culture, for example, a group of Mexican states in the Southwest, a black group in the South, and a Midwestern conservative state.

The primary hope of the United States, as we have known it, is a Reformation among the Christians of this country that know sound theology, solid and comprehensive Biblical ethics (worldview) and law, and a community of love and mercy to those within and without the Church. That is the goal of this website and other worldview ministries.

Summary Principles of Civil Law, Government, and Politics

State or civil government. I will use these terms interchangeably, capitalizing State to recognize its legitimacy as a God-ordained authority. In certain contexts, "state" will be used to designate a state of the United States, but mostly it will be used to designate civil government at all levels: local, state, and federal.

Definition of politics. From the Greek, *polis* or state. "The science of government; that part of ethics which consists in the regulation and government of a nation or state, for the preservation of its safety, peace and prosperity; comprehending the defense of its existence and rights against foreign control or conquest, the augmentation of its strength and resources, and the protection of its citizens in their rights, with the preservation and improvement of their morals. Politics, as a science or an art, is a subject of vast extent and importance." (Webster's 1828 Dictionary)

Necessary background understanding. The reader will better understand the following with the background of law, love, grace, mercy, justice, and equity. (Click here.) Civil law is a derivative and particular application of God's law. Thus, God's law is central to salvation **and** to the peace of a society on earth. To miss this connection is to miss both the fullness of Christ's sacrifice to fulfill the law and the great freedom for civil society that is made possible by the application of God's law in government.

1. **Law is inescapably derived from ethics**. "Ethics deals with the voluntary conduct of individual man insofar as it is judged to be good or bad in reference to a single, inclusive, and determinative principle of moral value grounded in and validated by ultimate reality." (Henry Stob, Ethical Reflections, page 24. Civil government and law is unavoidably grounded in ethics, some basis by which right and wrong is determined. And ethics is grounded in "ultimate reality", by definition. Ultimate reality is religious, even though secularists (and even Christians), may try to avoid or obscure the issue. As a religious subject, then, government and law must necessarily be defined and prescribed by God Himself speaking through His Scriptures. Also, this worldview area should be understood with the background of Social Justice. (See those Summary Principles.)

2. **Law involves force, implied or exercised**. While all law is based in ethics, behind civil law is a power that intends to enforce it, while ethics is "voluntary" (above). That is, the rule of law under the civil government carries the "power of the sword." Thus, civil law is "involuntary," that is, "enforced." The large part of this enforcement is functionally voluntary (for the Christian, this obedience is a duty under God), as a police force is not stationed in every home or with every individual. But, the "power of the sword" behind the law should not be minimized. And, herein lies the great error of many Christians that State welfare is "charity." The difference is free, voluntary decision vs. the threat on one's life and property, if not obeyed! See **the not-so-great welfare state**... below.

3. **The Bible is a book on civil law**. While the Bible is centrally about salvation, by definition, as God's ordained code of morality, it is a book for the basis of civil law. An expression that has been bandied about among Bible-believing Christians is that "the Bible is true in all areas to which it speaks." Relative to law, this belief statement reasons that a theocracy existed under Old Testament Israel, but the New Testament gives little in the way of a pattern for civil government. This reasoning is seriously false.

In any area where human behavior is concerned, the Bible must be central for the Christian. This limitation of the Bible has not only made it irrelevant to essential areas of life, but has greatly contributed to Christianity being irrelevant in the market place of ideas and to Christianity practically being placed in a ghetto! **The Bible is The Book on Civil Law, as the only source of ethics for God's people, as it is The Book on Psychology**.

All Christians must begin active, vigorous studies and debates about the Biblical application of law to the civil state today. It is accepted that direct application of many Biblical laws, especially case laws, to modern times is difficult. However, **with the Bible as The Book on law**, it is mandatory that modern applications be made.

Historical note: Throughout history, civil government and religion have been intertwined. With law grounded in ethics, and ethics grounded in religion ("ultimate reality"), this union is inescapable. However, Biblical Christianity separates the power of the sword in the State from the Church. The States to be influenced by individual Christians in public debate and through their various positions of authority in civil government and in society. The Church through its teaching and preaching is to keep its members informed on moral and spiritual matters that arise in matters of State policy. At times, the Church may even need to take formal positions against State policy that is flagrant against Biblical social justice.

4. **Biblical law is the most basic and important area for mankind to know and understand**. Biblical law is representative of God's character, that is, His righteousness. God's law is perfect and holy. Biblical law is the standard of responsibility that God requires of man. Failure to live up to this standard caused man's misery and ruin in the Fall. Salvation is made possible by Jesus Christ's fulfillment of the law in His perfect life and substitutionary atonement for man's failure. Biblical law is the only means by which man may live freely and cooperatively with his fellow man at all levels of social interaction. See Law and Love.

5. **"What is" is the greatest stumbling block to "what ought to be" for modern Christians in America**. Since the United States was begun, her great foundation in Biblical law has been gradually eroded in civil government and law. Now, it is so greatly distorted by "what is" that the typical American Christian has virtually no grasp of "what ought to be." We have moved from the "inalienable rights of life, liberty, and the pursuit of happiness" to legalized abortion, ever encroaching restrictions on freedom, and no real understanding of what "happiness" is.

Failure of preaching and teaching and to understand grace and love. The greatest fault in this erosion is Biblical preaching and teaching that has failed to preach the "whole counsel of God," that is, Biblical law. The paradox of this failure is that the "gospel of grace" which has been individualized and restricted to mostly an emotional experience, is greatly elevated in significance by an understanding that God's law is a measure of His righteousness and love. Our inalienable rights, the Bill of Rights, and all the intentions of the Declaration of Independence will not be realized in our time until Christians begin to understand the importance of God's law in His Providence and Common Grace for mankind. (See Welfare later in this document.)

6. **Self-government**. Webster's Dictionary of 1828 states as its first definition of "government," that of "(an individual's) control, restraint. Men are apt to neglect the government of their temper and passions." In modern times, "government" is linked with "civil government." However, no society that is not primarily ordered by men who govern themselves (morally) and who govern their families similarly, either can come into existence or exist for very long once established.

The loss of this foundational view of self-government is a major stumbling block to Western society today. As long as the concept of "government" exists outside of men in the form of civil government, their responsibility of government of self under God will not be prominent and will prevent the formation of a truly moral civil government.

7. **The Christian's duty to understand and apply the Bible in government and law**. Christians who serve in civil government or work with the interpretation and application of law in any way have failed in their duty under the Lordship of Jesus Christ and to those whom they serve, if they do not have a basic and reasonably complete understanding of Biblical law and how it applies to their position of responsibility. Every Christian in every State bears two offices at all times: elector and juror. He does have these opportunities to influence the law and the civil government.

8. **God's directives, brief but comprehensive**. "Let every soul be subject to the governing authorities. For there is no authority except from God, and the authorities that exist are appointed by God. Therefore whoever resists the authority resists the ordinance of God, and those who resist will bring judgment on themselves. For rulers are not a terror to good works, but to evil. Do you want to be unafraid of the authority? Do what is good, and you will have praise from the same. For he is God's minister to you for good. But if you do evil, be afraid; for he does not bear the sword in vain; for he is God's

minister, an avenger to execute wrath on him who practices evil. Therefore you must be subject, not only because of wrath but also for conscience' sake. For because of this you also pay taxes, for they are God's ministers attending continually to this very thing. Render therefore to all their due: taxes to whom taxes are due, customs to whom customs, fear to whom fear, honor to whom honor" (Romans 13:1-7)

These statements summarize a comprehensive program for both the civil government and its citizens. These are the skeleton and the remainder of the pertinent Scriptures are the flesh of the whole system. As a Hermeneutic, the reader should note that these verses in the Bible follow Chapter 12, in which is found government by the church and an individual's government of himself.

9. **No conflict.**   Rightly understood within a complete Biblical worldview, there is no conflict in what is right for individuals, families, churches, social groups, and state governments at all levels. This statement is earth-shattering in its import, as State policy is often designed with some special interest group in mind.

10. **"All authorities that exist are appointed by God."**   While there has never been a perfect civil government on earth, nevertheless they are all appointed by God in His Sovereignty. "Whoever resists (this) authority resists the ordinance of God" (above). Differing with, and going against State policy, is tantamount to resisting God Himself, and such action will bring not only punishment from the state, but judgment from God Himself. Citizens are not only to obey their rulers, but "hold them in esteem and honor." (John Calvin, Commentary on Romans 13:7)

Historical note.   The American colonists understood this concept, derived by John Calvin, so that the Declaration of Independence established a "lesser magistrate" of the American colonies that could Biblically resist the tyranny of England. Thus, a "lesser magistrate" may challenge a greater one, but the process of duly forming this entity proscribes revolution, vigilantism, and violent resistance by anyone or any group who have not form this "lesser" entity.

There are two exceptions to this commandment of State obedience. (A) **"We ought to obey God rather than men"** (Acts 5:29). Where the commandments of God to His people clearly conflict with the laws of the civil government, then God's commandments are to be obeyed in spite of punishment that is threatened by the state. Peter's commitment to evangelism in one example. The disobedience of the Hebrew midwives to the Egyptian authorities is another example. The lying to the authorities by Rahab is another.

(B) **The right of individuals to protect themselves**. Sometimes, there is not time or opportunity to form a lesser magistrate. Alexander Solzhenitsyn has regretted that the Russian people did not resist the night raids of the KGB. He ponders what might have happened if each family had wounded or killed one or more soldiers, each time these raids took place. Over time, this resistance might have weakened the regime or caused them to reconsider their actions. What does one do when soldiers come to rape one's wife or daughter? Clear violations of God-given rights to life in immediate circumstances may call for violent resistance in self-defense. In essence, this resistance is an extension of (A) above, but different in the violence of the situation. Also, one should ponder the results of such resistance. When resisted, the State may inflict greater damage on the person or family than they would have otherwise.

11. **Morality can be legislated**. The epithet, "You cannot legislate morality," is false on two levels. (1) Morality is the only source of law, as concluded above. (2) Civil laws strongly direct overt behavior. Speed limits slow most motorists down. Many people do not steal because of the possibility of getting caught. Abortion was severely limited before it was legalized. Tax breaks on home ownership greatly influence that industry (not necessarily for the "good"). Civil law, as Biblically directed, then, is one of the greatest aspects of the common grace of God.

That **civil law does not necessarily cause moral behavior** at all levels is true. It will not cause a husband to give tender affection to his wife. It will not make every person generous toward charitable works. It will not cause children to honor their parents. However, the effect of civil law on overt behavior, and the tendency of overt behavior to affect one's attitude and thinking, should not be underestimated. Civil law will not make a "bad" person good, but by threat of punishment, and sometimes reward, it may influence that "bad" person not to commit acts of evil and occasionally even to do "good."

12. **Law and its sanctions are a deterrence to crime**. Christians should not accept the premise that punishment is not a deterrence to crime. First, it is clear from empirical evidence that punishment is a deterrence. Speeding for the large majority of motorists does not occur. Speeding on a military base (where punishment is severe) is almost unknown! But, beyond empiricism, God says that punishment is a deterrence. "When the sentence for a crime is not quickly carried out, the hearts of the people are filled with schemes to do wrong" (Ecclesiastes 8:11; see Deuteronomy 19:20 and Romans 13:1-7 - above). Where God speaks, empirical evidence is not necessary, but the latter should correspond to God's truth when properly performed.

Law, of necessity, must be a deterrent to crime. No police force has ever, nor will it ever, catch every perpetrator of a crime. A police force cannot be everywhere all the time. Thus, the fear of punishment is necessary to a "civil" society, to keep would be evil-doers in check where law enforcement cannot.

13. **Does the Bible endorse one form of government?** While the Bible does not explicitly endorse one form of government, Biblical characteristics of law argue for a representative form of government. Then, it would be necessary to have an executive arm to enforce law that was thus legislated, and a judiciary would be necessary to interpret that law.

Biblical Characteristics of Government and Law

A. Rule by men of character. Jethro advised Moses to appoint "able men, such as fear God, men of truth, hating covetousness" (Exodus 18:21). King David was "a man after God's own heart" (I Samuel 16:7). Men (elders and deacons) who are to rule the church must meet certain moral requirements (I Timothy 3; Titus 1). These are men who have learned to govern themselves and their families, before being allowed to govern others. God does not allow immoral, or men with disorderly lives, to govern.

B. Local rule, primarily. Jethro advised Moses in the selection of men to rule small groups outward to larger groups (Exodus 18:21). Central rule, especially by one man, was not of God's choosing (I Samuel 8). Rule by churches is by local representatives (I Timothy 3; Titus 1). Only for special situations was regional rule necessary (Acts 15).

C. Leadership by men, primarily "heads of households." Throughout the Scriptures, God's method of rule is through men, not women. Men are to have proved themselves with the government of themselves and their own families and in being able to provide for them (success in employment or business).

D. Leadership by property owners. As heads of households, these men would have owned property. Property in Israel was so important that it was transferred from one generation to the next.

E. Representative government. (A corollary of [A].) The rule of law, lex rex, mandates that those who govern seek to serve under God's law, not under *vox populi*, the vote of the people or under their own ideas. While they may be elected by the people, their allegiance is not to them, but to God. In fact, the more that such representatives ally themselves with their constituents, the more that those who rule are likely to be influenced negatively and sinfully by the desires of their electorate. "You shall not follow a multitude (majority) to do evil" (Exodus 23:2). In addition, the population in its manifold daily duties does not have the time to devote to the intricacies that are involved in governing.

F. Plurality for wisdom. For sufficient wisdom to exist in one man to rule fully and adequately would be unusual, if not impossible. Thus, operating under Biblical statute and principle, a plurality of godly men is necessary for godly rule.

G. Limited law. The Bible establishes a "pyramid" of legality. From the two great commandments of Jesus Christ, to the Ten Commandments, to all the commandments and laws of the Bible, and finally to the case laws of the Old Testament, a pattern of laws is established that is unified and limited.

H. A judiciary is necessary. Laws cannot be written for every conceivable circumstance. Indeed, in general, the fewer the laws that should be written the better for those governed. Thus, a judiciary is necessary to interpret and apply law to specific situations. However, this judiciary must interpret the law, not define law which is the responsibility of the legislature.

Historical note. The leaders of the American colonists who wrote the Declaration of Independence and the Constitution understood these principles (in the main) and established the United States system of government on them. Prior to these documents was the **Reformation** which focused on the Scriptures as the Very Word of God Written, and within that, the recognition of laws to govern man as an individual, family, society, and nation.

14. Laws should be limited so that they can be understood and obeyed by those who are governed by those laws. God wrote the law upon man's heart. He wrote the Bible which contains all the laws that He intended for mankind in one Book. In the same way, positive law should be limited to that which (in the main) can be understood by the common man who is then able to live within its parameters and understand his offense when he breaks it. A reasonably intelligent person should be able to argue his own case before a judge in most matters of civil action. All mankind will stand before the Great Judgment Throne in the Last Day and will clearly understand his transgressions before a Holy God. If God in His infinite wisdom can make laws intelligible to man, man is no less required to make laws that can be learned and known by those subjected to them.

James Jordan (*The Law of the Covenant*, page 63) writes:

> Increasingly in our modern world, law has become a complicated, esoteric matter which can be understood only by lawyers. This is a trend away from Hebrew-Christian law, which is simple and public. In the ancient world, both cultic and judicial laws were often hidden from the people, but in Israel the law was to be read to everyone, every seven years (Deuteronomy 31:10-13). Moreover, since the law is addressed to everybody, not just to rulers and priests (indeed, Israel was a "nation of priests"), "everyone is held personally responsible for the observance of the law. This leads in turn, to the concept of individual and joint responsibility. No longer is it the sole concern of the leader of the community (e.g., the King of Mesopotamia) to maintain justice and to protect the rights of his community. This responsibility is shared by every member of the society..." (Jordan is citing Umberto Cassuto, A Commentary on the Book of Exodus, [The Magnes Press, 1967], page 264)

Positive law should be minimal. Based upon the above, positive law should be minimal and legislated only where it is imperative for social order. We live in a day of laws upon laws. For example, there are laws against child abuse, racial crimes, "hate" crimes, and many others. All these easily fall under already existing statutes against bodily harm, murder, theft, and other such laws. Therefore, such particular laws distort and even change the justice system from its purpose of justice and equity to that which is not its purpose, social engineering.

15. Rights. Rights are given by God. The obligation of the State is to protect those rights for her people. If a State were to have the authority to grant rights, then it would also have the authority to take them away. No State has that authority for it would exceed God's authority.

Right to life. Perhaps, all God-given rights can be summed up in the "right to life." Human life cannot be lived in it fullness without the protection of the State from harm and violence from perpetrators of evil. Every person must have the have freedom to live righteously, according to God's laws. **Ownership of property** is established by the Eighth Commandment and necessary to making physical provision for oneself and his family and necessary to the preservation and propagation of life. In order to go about all the tasks that God has assigned to man, he must have **freedom (liberty)** to pursue these tasks, not having to worry unreasonably about threats to his life and property. For the propagation of life, civil laws must be designed to enhance family life and severely punish those who violate its integrity. And, thus is **happiness** made possible.

Historical note: property and happiness. About the time that the Declaration of Independence was written, the common phrase about "rights" was "life, liberty, and property." For some reason, "happiness" was inserted into the Declaration, instead of property. Its intent and consistency with Biblical law is better understood as "life, liberty, and property."

Caveat. The right to life and the right to freedom may be forfeited. "Whoever sheds man's blood, by man his blood shall be shed; for in the image of God, He made man" (Genesis 9:6). The Bible is clear that there are capital crimes. What those are is beyond our purpose here. Suffice it to say that pre-meditated murder is one. Thus, the right to life is forfeited. For lesser crimes, such as theft, the right to one's own property will be forfeited to the extent that restitution is required. Obviously, in both these instances some degree of "freedom" is lost because of irresponsible behavior or criminal activity. See Crime and Punishment.

Wrong understanding of rights. Because rights have been divorced from God, the government believes that it has the authority to issue rights. Thus, we have in America today a right to medical care, cradle to grave security, pornography, family leave, and many others. Perhaps, the distortion and heinous error of rights is most clearly seen in the defense of unlimited abortion under a woman's "right to privacy," issued by the Supreme Court of the United States. This action was a violation of the responsibility of the judiciary (above) only to interpret law.

16. **All governments are theocracies by definition of ethics and law.** A theocracy is a government which is ruled by God (theos, God; kratos a rule, regime, strength). Israel was a theocracy until the anointing of kings, beginning with Saul. However, philosophically this definition is too narrow. As we have established, all law comes from ethics (concepts of right and wrong), and all ethics comes from one's concept of ultimate reality. As has been discussed many times on this website, ultimate reality is one's most fundamental philosophy of life. It is religious, whether one actually believes in a supernatural being or not. Whatever is one's ultimate reality is that person's god, for he bases all his decisions on that reality. And, given the power to do so, he would govern all men under laws that were developed under his god (belief system). Thus, all law is ethics, and all ethics is derived from a god. Thus, all system of laws and government are god-derived, a theocracy, an inescapable concept. (I am thankful to Gary DeMar of American Vision for this concept.)

Theonomy and reconstruction. In modern evangelical circles, theonomy and reconstruction are virtually anathema even to be mentioned or discussed. But, I contend that few other Bible-believing Christians are wrestling with the difficult issues of civil government, law, and social justice. That theonomists and reconstructionists have their rough edges and overbearing authoritarianism is accepted. But, their intent to govern every area of life under Scripture should be unquestionable to Bible believers. Who else has their comprehensive scope? For reasonable reviews of theonomy and reconstruction, see Reconstruction and Theonomy.

17. **God's pattern: covenant or constitutional law**. The whole of God's dealings with men is about covenant. Covenants that have been named, include the Adamic, Noahic, Abrahamic, Mosaic, and Christocentric. While the theological nuances and "problems" with these cannot be dealt with here, nevertheless God established contracts (constitutions) with mankind. Some theorists have called government a "social contract." A contract, by definition, has obligations (forgotten in America today), rights, and penalties ascribed to both parties.

18. **God sanctions capital punishment based upon human observation**. An argument is often made against capital punishment that an error in due process may have been made and an innocent man would be killed. The Christian, however, cannot take this position. God has ordained that (1) capital punishment be exercised by civil government (Genesis 9:6; Romans 13:4) on the basis of (2) two or three witnesses (Deuteronomy 19:15-19). Jesus

191

instructed that a person could be excommunicated on the same basis, a matter far more serious than capital punishment.

> "(The magistrate) is an executioner of God's wrath; and this he shows himself to be by having the sword, which the Lord has delivered into his hand. This is a remarkable passage for the purpose of proving the right of the sword; for if the Lord, by arming the magistrate, has also committed to him the use of the sword, whenever he visits the guilty with death, by executing God's vengeance, he obeys his commands. Contend then do they with God who think it unlawful to shed the blood of wicked men." (Commentary by John Calvin on Romans 13:4)

Capital punishment from the perspective of eternity. If the executed person is a believer in Jesus Christ, he is bound for heaven. If he is bound for Hell, we just have done society a great favor, for he was indeed evil, even if not guilty of his crime. On the one hand, secularists are consistent that if life on earth is the only life, then indeed they should be fearful of putting an innocent man to death. On the other hand, they have no reason to choose any right or wrong, so they cannot even speak to the matter of capital punishment.

19. **Natural law theory**. For centuries, many scholars have advocated "natural law." It has its appeal in that it is somewhat divorced from "religious" concepts and that it is "universal." Many conservative Bible scholars were among these advocates. **However, natural law is too vague and arbitrary to be implemented as specific civil law**. For example, nature is "red in tooth and claw," as well as showing tender affection for its own "family." Even murder, in some societies, has certain justifications, even being praiseworthy. The bottom line of natural law theory is a rule of majority or tyranny. That is, either several "governors" vote for what they believe is natural law or one person arbitrarily implements his interpretation. Natural law does not escape the "ultimate realities" of decision-making, which is law that is derived from within man himself.

The great expositor of law, William Blackstone, did not make the natural law error.

> "Yet undoubtedly the revealed law is of infinitely more authenticity than that moral system, which is framed by ethical writers, and denominated the natural law. Because one is the law of nature, expressly declared so to be by God himself; the

other is only what, by the assistance of human reason, we imagine to be that law. If we could be as certain of the latter as we are of the former, both would have an equal authority; but, till then, they can never be put in any competition together." (William Blackstone, Section II, of the Introduction to Commentaries on the Laws of England.)

20. **The not-so-great welfare state**. The great illustration of how far the American government has gone astray from its foundations in Biblical law is the cost of federal, state, and local governments today. Welfare (including all its auxiliaries, such as Medicare, Medicaid, Aid to Dependent Children, Social Security, etc., etc.) is far and away the largest cost to these governments. So, most of the taxes that an American pays is for unbiblical reasons. And, added to this fact, is that all these programs have made the situations that they intended to help, in fact, worse. Then, the trillions of dollars being spent today on these programs is both foolish (unbiblical) and ineffective! Truly, this cost, both physically and spiritually, illustrates the depravity of man's thinking in its full development! Violation of Biblical law is costly beyond measure in both dollars and injustice to the whole of society!

State welfare is not Biblical mercy and charity. There is nothing right about state welfare. It steals from one group to give to others. It imposes a huge administrative cost. (I have seen estimates from 75-90 percent.) It promotes laziness among its recipients. It gives without regard to responsibility and true need, based upon some arbitrary category of persons. It dehumanizes its recipients, making them into helpless victims. It promotes class warfare, giving "rights" to recipients, as well as establishing groups of "haves" and "have nots." It trains recipient children in "the ways that they should (not) go." It promotes illegitimate marriages and weakens the role of husbands. And, more.

21. **Remember, Christians, your social responsibility**. While I am making Biblical application to the civil government and its law, you, Christian, must remember the other area or worldview, Social Justice. Christians and their churches have the responsibility for "welfare" (acts of mercy under the direction of love and the law). If that responsibility seems too massive, the reason is that it is not Biblically understood. The principles of social justice are not those of State welfare. I have named many of these in that Worldview Area. I will cite one here, "If anyone will not work, neither shall he eat" (II Thessalonians 3:10). That principle is neither unloving nor inconsistent with mercy. Its implementation will demonstrate the believers' comprehensive understanding of Biblical concepts.

22. **Separation of church and state**. God has assigned bodily restraint and punishment to the State alone, "the power of the sword." God has assigned spiritual authority and judgment to the church alone, "the power of the keys" ("good" standing within the physical church). The issues of the Reformation illustrate the abuses of the Roman Catholic Church and the remedies provided by Biblical scholarship of the Reformers, in particular John Calvin and John Knox. The States not to interfere with the authority of the Church in any way. The Church influences the State through its preaching and teaching on moral issues, directed at both believers and unbelievers. This influence, however, is always spiritual. The Church never has any Biblical authority to coerce the State in any way other than the spoken word of its ordained men and individual Christians, as they exercise their political responsibilities as citizens and government officials (as they are duly appointed or elected). Those in positions of civil authority, whether Christian or non-Christian, have a duty under the authority of God to implement Biblical morality and laws in the most complete manner possible.

The Church is far more powerful than the state. While the State has the power of the sword and has executed millions of Christians throughout history, the Church has far more potential power than the state. **This power has not yet been fully exercised because the Church has failed in its role to teach its members the whole counsel of God (that is, a Biblical worldview) with only a few exceptions in history**. The power of the Church is the power of the Holy Spirit working through Biblical truth in regenerated Christians. Examples in history are Christianity becoming the official religion of the Roman Empire (with such imperfection that it rapidly disintegrated), Geneva under Calvin (limited to a city only), Scotland during the Reformation (for a short period of time), and most fully realized in the founding of the United States with the Declaration of Independence and the Constitution. The Church will never be able to exert this power again until it once again teaches the whole counsel of God which—does not yet appear to be happening with any regularity or frequency, as of this writing (2007).

"The time has come for judgment to begin at the house of God (1 Peter 4:17). Individual Christians and churches must ask forgiveness of God for their failure in the above responsibility. The political mess that is present everywhere in the world is due to this failure. Christians cannot point to the news media, liberal politicians, or anti-God scientists for the present political condition on earth today (with the possible few exceptions of military *coup d'etats*)

23. **The Kingdom of God**. The Kingdom of God is the Spirit of God at work in the world to accomplish His righteous purposes. This work may include both believers and non-believers and churches and secular institutions. It works most powerfully under overt Biblical principles of justice, administered by believers. Evangelism is a part of the advancement of the Kingdom, but fails in the purposes of the Kingdom, if it does not teach and implement comprehensive principles of Biblical justice to all worldview areas. The Kingdom of God has no identification with civil government, but the influence and advancement of the Kingdom is a God-given duty to Christians in government with an overt understanding that they are to apply these principles of justice as they have authority and opportunity. The Kingdom of God is not limited to the Church, but the Church is the major power towards the advancement of the Kingdom through its preaching, teaching, and work. While the Kingdom of God will never be fully implemented on earth, Christians are to work towards that end, as directed by the King of Kings. See Kingdom of God.

24. **Christians and churches are to pray for their governments**. "Therefore I exhort first of all that supplications, prayers, intercessions, and giving of thanks be made for all men, for kings and all who are in authority, that we may lead a quiet and peaceable life in all godliness and reverence. For this is good and acceptable in the sight of God our Savior..." (I Timothy 2:1-3).

25. **The American system of punishment is largely unbiblical**. The Bible requires retribution in varying amounts where theft or fraud has been perpetrated. American "justice" does not. Imprisonment, as punishment, is unbiblical and prevents the reconciliation of the offender to his victims, the spiritual "healing" of both parties that comes with that process, and its model that could possibly lead to spiritual reconciliation to God. See Crime and Punishment.

26. **The civil government is to provide for a police force**. The police force should be adequate to catch, prosecute, and punish criminals. This police power should be limited to those laws that are consistent with Biblical justice.

27. **The civil government is to provide for a military sufficient for national defense and use in just wars**. Whether this army is best implemented in a standing military or a citizen military, is open to debate. For sure, citizens have a responsibility to serve in the military and provide this effort towards their own defense. Whether this military should be by draft or by volunteerism is also debatable. I have not decided on these two issues myself.

An all-volunteer military limits the possibility of military adventurism, but does today's military complexity require a professional military? In an all-volunteer military, will it have sufficient strength in numbers and expertise to be as strong as it needs to be? What should the penalty be for men who will not volunteer to protect their families and their neighbors?

The civil government is to make certain provisions for the individuals and families who are involved in police and military action. This provision is limited to injury and disease from actions that are directly a consequence of their official duties. This provision includes an adequate income, insurance (life, medical, and disability) to provide for themselves and their families. The State is not responsible for the health care or any other provision for these families beyond the consequences of their duty.

28. **The civil government has a role in public health matters**. This role must consider the best science available and must be carefully balanced against the rights of individuals and families. Clearly, today civil governments have greatly overstepped this role in mandating immunizations (especially those efforts to prevent harm from sexual immorality), OSHA regulations, workers' compensation, a myriad of "safety" prescriptions (seat belts, wheelchair access, zoning, etc.), Americans with Disabilities Act, and many others. In these laws, the civil State is functionally asserting its ownership of industry and business.

29. **Marriage and divorce**. For centuries after the Reformation, covenants were made between a man and woman engaged to be married. Those covenants should be re-instituted today with sanctions against the party who breaks the contract. There should be no particular ownership while the marriage is intact. The State's only role in marriage is to enforce the sanctions of the contract, if violated by either party and the church is unable to settle the dispute spiritually. The State has no role in setting conditions for any marriage before the covenant is established. Current civil law has greatly promoted the breakup of the family in our times with easy divorce, based on such nebulous concepts as "no-fault" and "incompatibility. Divorce should be final: all contact of the guilty spouse with the children should be cut off. He or she has divorced himself or herself from the family by their unrighteous and hardened behavior.

30. **United Nations, national sovereignty, and obedience to God**. Membership by the United States in the United Nations (UN) is illegal by the laws of the United States, for example placing our military under the command of foreign officers who are not subject to the United States Constitution. God

requires subjection to the laws of the state. (See above.) The UN requires subjection to its laws, many of which conflict with the laws of the United States. As the President, all other government officials, and the military swear to uphold and defend the Constitution, any other allegiance demands violation of their oaths of office.

31. **The civil government of a people and its laws reflect the moral culture of that people**. In general, the government of a people is no more righteous or evil than the people and culture that it governs. A people's heart is made known by the moral codes by which it lives, and these find their way into law. Of course, there are exceptions, such as foreign invasion or military coups where power is imposed rapidly from within or without. But, over time, the heart (moral values) of a people will determine its government and its laws.

32. **Civil government is a servant of the people**. "Magistrates ... are not to rule for their own interest, but for the public good; nor are they endued with unbridled power, but what is restricted to the well being of their subjects; in short, they are responsible to God and to men in the exercise of their power. For as they are deputed by God and do his business, they must give an account to him: and then the ministration which God has committed to them has a regard to the subjects, they are therefore debtors also to them." (John Calvin on Romans 13:4)

33. **Historical Note on the State as plaintiff and prosecutor**. "From the fall of Rome (circa 500 B.C.) to after 1200, the courts of Europe were in varying degrees governed by Biblical law. True, much barbarian legal practice remained, and true, the law was far from being fully faithful to Scripture. At one point, however, the courts were very different. A criminal prosecution required a plaintiff. Without an accuser, there was no case and no judgment. The accusation had to be grounded in God's law, and the plaintiff had to be an aggrieved or damaged person. The accusation and charge was in the name of God and His law." With Frederick II, "the State now became the plaintiff on its own initiative, and high treason became a major offense... It was this step by Frederick II which "introduced the principles of totalitarian government into the Christian Commonwealth, contrary to its basic conceptions.'" (Systematic Theology, Rousas J. Rushdoony, pages 701-702) This historical note shows the extreme distortion of modern law where virtually all crimes are "crimes against the state."

34. **Equity and the common laws of England**. Equity is defined as body of legal doctrines and rules developed to enlarge, supplement, or override a narrow, rigid system of law, as in the history of English common law which

had a settled and formal body of legal and procedural rules and doctrine to protect rights and enforce duties that had been fixed by substantive law. Equity provided remedies in situations in which precedent or statutory law might not apply or be fair. Thus, "common law" is not "common" in the sense that it is established by "common" society, but is actually the application of Biblical law to situations that are "common" to everyday life.

35. **Equality under the law**. As far as is possible within the parameters of social justice and other applications of Biblical law, all men should have equal opportunity both to be found innocent or guilty of crimes of which they are accused. The proof of guilt resides in the accuser.

36. **Power corrupts and absolute power corrupts absolutely**. While no dictator ever really has absolute power, many have come close to it in their own nation. The dangers of State power cannot be underestimated. While "the power of the sword" is ordained of God, this power is handled by fallible, selfish (sinful) men and women. As power increases in a person or persons, the damage that can be inflicted increases proportionately. Thus, any government must have a means of checks and balances, as does the United States, showing the brilliance of the Founding Fathers. The people must also have checks and balances in their possession of firearms; the gold standard for currency; freedoms of speech, religion, and right to assemble, freedom from unjust seizures, among many others. **Those who do not fear government power, even in the United States, have neither studied history, grasped the depravity of mankind, nor realized the power of the Constitution, The Bill of Rights, and certain other Amendments to protect American citizens**.

37. **Licensure and laws of partiality that create welfare recipients**. While licensure is sold to "protect the public" from unscrupulous practitioners, it *de facto* is a State-created monopoly. By definition, licensure sets standards of practice to which these "professionals" have to adhere, or else they do not get a license. For more, see Licensure of Medicine.

"Modern laws are increasingly partial. Special laws are passed to favor or protect business, unions, farmers, blacks, women, etc. Thus, our laws have become a means of welfare, with each group seeking legal favors over against other groups. The result is a warfare society." (James Jordan, *The Law of the Covenant*, page 167.

38. **The civil government has no role in the education of children, public or private**. The responsibility of the education of children has been given to parents (Deuteronomy 6:1-25, Ephesians 6:4). Thus, any education is

198

inherently religious. Any education by the State will have, as its agenda, the progression and growth of itself, as it currently exists. That agenda is also inherently religious and is an abomination to the role of education that God has given to parents.

For Further Reading: Other Sources

Bandow, Doug. *Beyond Good Intentions: A Biblical View of Politics.* Crossway Books, 1988. Great review book, but contains some inconsistencies of principle and application.

Calvin, John. *Commentary on Romans 13:1-7.*

DeMar, Gary. *Ruler of the Nations: Biblical Principles of Government.* Dominion Press, 1987. Also, found online at www.freebooks.com.

Henry, Carl F. H. *Aspects of Christian Social Ethics.* Baker Book House, 1964.

Jordan, James. *The Law of the Covenant: An Exposition of Exodus 21-12.* Institute for Christian Economics. Also, found online at www.freebooks.com.

www.lonang.org. Website whose URL comes from the Laws of Nature and Of Nature's God. Blackstone's Commentaries may be found there, as well as many other historical documents.

www.lexrex.com A website dedicated to the principles of lex rex and the foundational principles of the United States.

North, Gary. Healer of the Nations: Biblical Principles for International Relations. Dominion Press. Also, found online at www.freebooks.com . Primarily on international law.

North, Gary. *Tools of Dominion: The Case Laws of Exodus.* Institute for Christian Economics, 1990. Also found online at www.freebooks.com

The Laws of Nature and of Nature's God @ www.lonang.com A website devoted to law and the history of law.

Witherspoon Lectures on Law, Government, and Culture.

10. Sociology and Social Justice

The Ecological Indian: Myth and History

Book Review: *The Ecological Indian: Myth and History*, by Shepard Krech III, published by W.W. Norton and Company, 1999, 318 pages, $27.95 (used copies now widely available from such places as Amazon.com).

It has been described as possibly the most famous commercial that has ever been produced. In 1971, "The Crying Indian" portrayed Iron Eyes Cody, clearly an American Indian, with a tear running down his cheek and the caption, "Pollution: it's a crying shame." This image is the politically correct version of the American Indian: always and perfectly living out the best practices of ecological balance before the White Europeans came and destroyed the pristine "Eden" that was the North American flora and fauna.

This book lives up to its sub-title, *Myth and History*. In an unusually fair and balanced manner, Krech presents the known facts. America was not an Eden when the "white man" came, and the Indians were often destructive to the ecology of America, even as they tended to its protection and enhancement in many ways.

Perhaps, what struck me most about this book is the difficulty of the concept of history. Krech tries to portray all the "facts" about the history of the Indians and the flora and fauna of America. (He gives almost exclusive attention to the "fauna," but does discuss some of the flora, as well.) "Experts" do not agree. "Experts" are as (or more so) influenced by their own biases, as historical "facts." In fact (pardon the pun), the "facts" are not that easy about which to make conclusions. Certainly, without question, Krech presents a plethora of facts from virtually every point of view, such that some conclusions are just not possible.

Two characteristics of Krech's book are unusual today. First, he discusses many of the Indian practices as being based upon their beliefs or religions (cosmology, first principles, etc.). For example, "Do not throw beaver or bear bones to the dogs, but place them in water or hang them in trees; for the beaver and bear will use these bones again when they are reincarnated" (page 202). If these and other taboos (which varied widely and even were complete opposites in some tribes) were followed, then the beaver and others animals would make themselves available to be hunted and killed. Sometimes, by following these taboos, certain Indians "believed they could not kill too many" animals of a kind (page 204). So, the Indian religions sometimes supported ecological practices and sometimes not.

The philosophical (religious) forces of history are often omitted today in any historical discussions today to protect the image of the "noble savage." For example, the prevalence and extent of human sacrifice and torture are expunged from any serious discussions of the Incas, Aztecs, and other native populations. Krech tells of religious practices that did help wildlife and then discusses those that were destructive of the same.

Second, Krech deals fairly with Christianity. While these mentions are brief and infrequent, in his "Epilogue," he states that "some look toward an alternative 'ecological' Christianity that would reconcile this religion with environmental care" (page 227). Indeed, Biblical Christianity should include the practice of the Creation Mandate to "husband" the flora and fauna of the earth, while not adopting the myths and false science of the extreme environmentalists and global warming crowd. Also, see Interfaith Stewardship Alliance.

The importance of this book is the destruction of the myth of the ecological Indian. While there is no doubt that Indians had many practices consistent with that image, they had many practices that were destructive. While fire was used to clear underbrush, to send signals, to allow certain plants and animals to flourish or re-populate a region, and to trap game animals, it often raged out of control and became a severely destructive force that devoured large regions and populations. Animals were maimed with the loss of their eyes, fur, and burns, from which they eventually died or were killed by predators, days or weeks later.

Buffalo were stampeded off cliffs¾ the numbers killed often greatly exceeding those that were needed for meat and other body parts. Again, animals were maimed, often suffering for weeks or longer before dying of their injuries, starvation, dehydration, or being killed by other animals.

All these practices preceded the "white man" by hundreds of years. **Then, the Europeans came,** changing the flora and fauna of the United States more than any other event. **But, the Indians were complicit and culpable in virtually all destruction of animal life.** Indians killed animals in numbers that ran into the millions for their skins, meat, and other body parts. The buffalo almost went extinct from original numbers that could not be counted with accuracy. Deer and beaver populations were decimated and virtually disappeared from certain regions of the country. (Krech has whole chapters on the buffalo, beaver, and deer.)

Now, many "experts" would argue that blame for this destruction still lies with the "white man," since the Indian was only feeding their need and greed. However, this argument will not stand scrutiny. **The test of a man's or culture's integrity is the strength of his or its beliefs in the face of challenge and temptation**. Had the Indian the fortitude that is blindly credited to him by political correctness, he would not have been complicit in the destruction of animal life. But, he often slaughtered thousands of animals simply for items to trade, some of which were needed (knives, guns, etc.). However, sometimes he destroyed simply for rum and other liquors that were gone in a moment of carousing.

In the final analysis, neither the American Indian nor the Europeans were any worse that any other peoples or culture. Since Adam and Eve, man has always been involved in inhumanities to man and the destruction of the earth and its plants and animals. The story of North America is just another chapter in that history.

Krech has destroyed the myth of "the ecological Indian," but he has done it in a way that people on all sides of the issue would have to concede that he has been fair¾ not perfectly, as no one is able to accomplish that end. Anyone who thinks otherwise of this book shows a partiality and bias that supersedes any practical level of being reasonable.

Summary Principles of Social Justice

There is a great deal of overlap between the areas of social justice and civil government (legislation, judicial, executive, and political). To a great extent, civil government determines whether social justice can be implemented because it has earthly power to determine what is and is not done in society. Ideally, the government allows freedom to pursue all Biblically legitimate activities. However, there are currently many legal restrictions to this pursuit And, state welfare (man's wrongly devised system to help all the "poor") has taken over much of what has been the individual's and church's responsibility. "Welfare" now receives the largest portion of federal and state expenditure. As such, welfare is about power and control by persons with the power of the sword, not about Biblical, social justice. Before much of what follows can be done, legislation would have to be passed gradually to eliminate all government oversight and funding of "welfare."

1. **Definition of social justice**. The Biblical definition of social justice is the comprehensive application of Biblical law, love, mercy, justice, and equity to all levels of government: self, family, voluntary groups, churches, and state (local, state, and national). **Social justice cannot be considered without explicit attention to these Biblical areas**. Love without law has no direction, and law without love punishes without mercy. The Biblical background for what follows here is critical to its understanding: Summary Principles and Discussion of Law, Love, Mercy, etc.

Sociology is a humanistic term for social justice that has no guidelines and is only implemented according to the power of the giving organization, whether civil government or private. Sociology has no governing principles to determine what should be done or whether what is done is right or wrong.

2. **Definition of civilization**. No nation is truly civilized which is not, in some measure, being directed by Biblical justice. In fact, no nation or culture can continue to exist without consciously or unconsciously being governed with some consistency by the rule of Biblical justice. Definitions of civilization, then, must include this concept of social justice.

3. **Christians and churches have a duty to seek social justice**. The Creation and Cultural Mandates, The Great Commission, and The Ten Commandments all include the call of Christians, their families, and churches to the task of social justice in all its various forms. The proclamation of "The Gospel" is incomplete without the full application of all these mandates. The primary group, to whom Biblical justice should be directed, are the "powerless": the widow, the orphan, and the fatherless, but Biblical justice includes everyone in a society. Who is or is not included in these Biblical directives need to be determined by the modern church. The failure of Christians and churches to address all social evils in their times of history is their failure to be salt and light worthy of being trampled underfoot (Matthew 5:13-14).

4. **No conflict**. Rightly understood within a complete Biblical worldview, there is no conflict in what is right for individuals, families, churches, social groups, and state governments at all levels. That is not to say that the resolution of any conflict in these areas will be simple, but God's law by the unity of Himself can never conflict with His designed institutions.

5. **The role of civil government (the state)**. The role of the state is "to reward good and punish evil" (Romans 13:1-5). This role includes military and police action to catch, place on trial, and punish perpetrators of crimes among individuals and treason against the state (except when mandated by a "lesser magistrate" against an evil regime). The state is to maintain a military capable of national defense and employ it for self-defense and in just wars. The state has a role in public health that should be careful not to intrude on private lives and property without clear warrant that the health of its citizens are in danger from an epidemic or toxic substances.

The civil government can legislate (affect) moral behavior. While the civil government, by legislation, cannot cause its people to behave morally, its laws do greatly affect their behavior. For example, laws that set speed limits restrain drivers who fear the penalties of "getting caught." More importantly, laws that limit divorce to Biblical standards and have severe penalties for non-support of the family by the offending spouse have a great influence on keeping families intact. Moreover, all laws are legislated morals that come from some philosophy, worldview, or religion. For more on laws and morality, see Summary Principles of Civil Government to be written next. Link.

6. **Freedom**. In "rewarding good and punishing evil," the state is responsible to create a free society in which anyone may pursue gainful employment or be self-employed to the extent of his or her abilities and opportunities. Within this freedom, all measures of social justice can be pursued.

7. **Welfare**. The state has no role in what is commonly called "welfare" of all kinds, including the provision of medical care. This role has been assigned by God to individuals, families, churches, and voluntary social organizations.

The cost of the violation of Biblical principles. Intrusion of the state into God's design of welfare will always fail and be costly in lives and expense. The trillions of dollars spent in the United States in the "war on poverty" has not improved the lot of any class of people (except the bureaucrats who administer it). It has been destructive to economic growth and has violated the property rights of taxpayers.

8. **The poor defined**. The Bible defines the "poor" in three ways. (1) Those who are "poor in spirit" (Matthew 5:3) whether they have earthly needs or great prosperity. (2) Those who are destitute of earthly needs and possessions, yet **who are willing to work and better themselves**, "those who are bowed down... the righteous" (Psalm 146:5-9) Also, see Job 5:11-16; Psalm 10:17-18, Psalm 103:6, Psalm 109:30-31, Psalm 140:12. These could be called the

"deserving poor." They are to receive charity and help towards responsible provision of themselves and their families. (3) Those who are destitute of earthly needs and possessions **who are not willing to work and better themselves**. They "waste opportunities (Proverbs 6:9-11), bring poverty on themselves (Proverbs 10:4), are victims of self-inflicted bondage (Proverbs 12:24), and are unable to accomplish anything in life (Proverbs 15:19)." While these should be given every opportunity and assistance to change, "subsidizing sluggards is the same as subsidizing evil. It is subsidizing dependence... slavery." (Quotes and ideas are from George Grant, In the Shadow of Plenty, [Thomas Nelson, Inc., 1986), pages 52-55.) For more on the "unwilling to work" poor, see Dalrymple under Endnotes.

The great failure of Christians and the church: individual and family responsibility to receive physical goods and service. One great failure of modern Christians and the Church is to require responsible behavior of the recipients of its welfare. The Apostle Paul said, "If anyone will not work, neither shall he eat" (II Thessalonians 3:10). This little phrase has powerful and far-reaching implications. In our day, Carl F. H. Henry said, "We urgently need a comprehensive social ethic whose Scriptural content protects justice from subtle compromises with benevolence" (Aspects of ..., page 155)

First, recipients must be determined whether they are able to work or not. Certainly, those who are completely disabled may receive charity, even though they are not able to work. However, the large majority of people are able to perform some kind of work. What work they do requires creativity on the part of the givers. For those who do not work, and therefore do not eat, obviously, they will die. But, then again, perhaps their hunger will drive them to work! But, the central message of Paul's statement is that non-workers are not to be provided physical help without limit.

"Harsh, cruel," you say. Here the Bible-believing Christian errs in a major way: **if God said it, we are to obey!** You cannot argue that this example is "unloving." **There is never any conflict between God's law and His requirement of love**. This subject has been covered on this site in considerable and necessary detail here. The violation of this unity of law and love has been costly beyond measure in dollars and lives.

9. **Love vs. state welfare**. Some Christians have defended government welfare as "charity." That concept is a violent distortion of God's directions of love. Love, by anyone's definition, is uncoerced except as a duty of conscience within individuals and groups owed to God Himself. Taxes that are used for welfare (whether for food, shelter, clothing, medical care, "aid to dependent

children," etc.) are taken by armed force, "the power of the sword." By no stretch of any consistent reasoning or Biblical hermeneutic can "welfare" by civil government be considered "charity."

10. **Equity and legislative law in establishing state justice**. Certainly, social justice requires the development and application of Biblical law and its equity at all levels of state government. See Civil Government, Law, and Politics.

Judges and justice. The principles of justice that apply to wrongs that can be committed among individuals, families, and groups is virtually unlimited. Therefore, judges are needed to settle these disputes and discern matters of pertinent law. In general, and perhaps in all particulars, these disputes are not crimes against the state. The state should only be involved where the two or more parties are unable to work out restitution or a fair settlement. The Church (inclusive of all) must be diligent to settle problems among its members without government help. (I Corinthians 6:1-7). Settlements should be restitution of loss, and in some cases where severity or repetition of wrongs occurs, restitution may exceed several-fold the loss incurred.

Physical harm or death. Where severe physical harm occurs, the civil state must be involved to adjudicate cases. Those principles will be developed under state Civil Government.

11. **Availability of materials, resources, and resourcefulness**. The concept of limited resources in many discussions about social justice is a misnomer. God said, "Be fruitful and multiply and fill the earth." By reasonable measures, the earth can support far more people than now exist on planet earth. New "resources" are discovered continually, and man has great ingenuity to make present resources last longer, create new technologies that require different resources, and use technology to discover and produces new resources. Problems of "limited resources" are often those created by civil government through tariffs, subsidy payments, restriction on (moral) research and development, and other measures that impede the free market and freedom of men to discover and create new technology and resources.

12. **Ownership of property**. The Eighth Commandment, "You shall not steal," establishes ownership of property. More on this subject will be found in Summary Principles of Economics.

13. **The family: education and evangelism**. The most important aspect of social justice is education of children from infancy to adulthood, under the authority of the family primarily, and under the Church secondarily. God's

primary method of evangelism is from one generation of Christian families to the next. The husband and father is the most important person in this process. Historically, Christians allowed John Dewey, Horace Mann, and others to promote the idea of the formal education of children being the responsibility of the state. Many of the problems that the family faces today are the consequences of that mistake. See Summary Principles of Education, to be developed later on this website.

The family is the basic unit of society. The family is the most basic unit and foundation for any society. The stability and morality of society is directly correlated with the soundness of the family unit and its protection by the civil government. The father is the head of the family with his wife and children under his authority, protection, and provision. Most of the problems of modern day America can be attributed to wrong ideas and practices concerning the family. Most of the huge federal and state budgets are an attempt to "help" individuals and families damaged by these wrong ideas and practices.

The Biblical family is the only family approved of God. The Biblical family consists of a man and a woman married to each other for life (except for the Biblical reasons for divorce: sexual infidelity and desertion) and any children that the marriage brings. The family is intergenerational, with responsibilities of children to parents and parents to children.

14. **A culture determines its social justice**. The prevailing worldview (thought-system, ethic, ethics, philosophy, religion, etc.) of a culture determines both the laws that it makes at every level of civil government and the morals that it practices among its people. Since its foundation, **the United States** has been steadily moving away from the Biblical principles upon which state laws, The Declaration of Independence, and the Constitution, as well as, the morality of its people at the time were based. The only methods by which this decline can be overcome is by **evangelism** that produces regeneration, Biblical education, and obedience.

15. **The greatest social reform in world history has been regeneration by the Holy Spirit and obedience to Jesus Christ**. Most of the "good" (as Biblically defined) that mankind has experienced was caused by the regeneration and obedience of God's people through God's great plan of salvation in Jesus Christ. This "good" includes capitalism, civil liberties, abolition of the slave trade, abolition of human sacrifice, world exploration, elevation of women, the Renaissance, and Reformation, and representative government that is limited in its laws and promotes freedom. For all these to be "good," they must be Biblical consistent. That mankind is able to pervert every

one of these "goods" to ungodly purposes is just more evidence of his depravity.

Universal education. One particular of this "great good" is the opportunity for everyone to have a basic education or more. There is no other philosophy of life or religion in the history of mankind that has supplied a similar impetus for universal education. The underlying premise is that everyone should learn to read in order to learn God's Word.

16. **Rights**. Rights are discussed under Civil Government. However, it needs to be said here that rights are defined by Biblical standards, not by civil legislation. Those interested in social justice should not define rights in terms of human need, but rights as God has defined them. While civil government has the responsibility to protect God-given rights, it does not define them. Most "rights" now defined by social activists and enacted by legislation and adjudication are not Biblical rights.

17. **Christians' priorities in social actions**. Christians' priorities in social responsibility are first to themselves and their own family (I Thessalonians 4:11-12; I Timothy 5:8), then to those of the "household of faith" (Galatians 6:10), and then to all others (Luke 10:25-37).

18. **What is to be provided in social responsibility**. Assistance to others includes only those basics that are necessary to the sustenance of life: food, shelter, and clothing. There is no obligation to bring all households up to some arbitrary economic standard or equality of wages (except as employers have moral duties to their own employees - see Larger Catechism, Q/A 123-133). In today's world, however, basics may be slightly broader than in the past, for example, access to, or provision of, certain utilities (water, sewage, electricity, etc.) and limited medical care.

19. **Christians have great opportunities for social change**. Christians have a great opportunity to effect social change through instruction of their children in the "nurture and admonition of the Lord." This instruction must include systematic theology and worldview (ethical) concepts. Their next greatest opportunity is to understand their own vocations in the light of Biblical ethics. Beyond, that they may have specific opportunities through ministries implemented by themselves, their families, their churches, or voluntary organizations.

20. **Genetic and environmental causes of immorality and crime**. Those true (Biblical) injustices that exist in society are due to man's inherently sinful

nature and his failure to understand and apply Biblical standards of justice. God created the physical universe and declared it "good." Therefore, the immoralities and crimes within society are not physically, but spiritually caused. The physical environment of poverty and exposure to frequent immoral and criminal activity in one's neighborhood may incline a person towards those evils, but this environment does not inevitably force one into that lifestyle and does not absolve him or her of individual responsibility.

In the same manner, a "respectable" and socially upscale neighborhood may not inculcate any greater moral (Biblical) values than the "poor" neighborhood. The problem is not the physical universe, but the spiritual condition and immoral education that he learns.

21. **The Bible knows nothing of racism**. The only criterion for the full benefits of church membership and the blessings that God gives especially to His children is belief in Jesus Christ is regeneration, evidenced by belief in Jesus Christ as fully God and the only Savior from man's sins. Any racial bias, including the marriage of one race with another, is Biblically wrong and inimical to the oneness of true Christian unity everywhere.

22. **Commandments 5-10**. Commandments 5-9 are the greatest summary of all social responsibilities that men and women have to each other in all their relationships.   Commandment 10 is where sins of these other five commandments begin. These commandments are fully explained by all the other Biblical commandments and principles. Jesus summarized them under "loving one's neighbor as himself." One comprehensive explanation of Commandments 5-10 are Questions and Answers 122-148 of The Larger Catechism of the Westminster Confession of Faith.

23. **Abortion**. The greatest social evil of modern times is abortion, now legalized by the civil government at the international, federal, state, and local levels. Failure to agree that abortion is Biblically immoral is to bring one's testimony of salvation into question. Christians and churches should be supportive of, or involved in, activities change the laws that promote this great evil and the social institutions that directly minister to prevent abortions and support difficult pregnancies.

Historical connection with capital punishment. The legalization of abortion did not happen in a vacuum. A giant step towards this legalization was the downgrade of capital offenses to "life imprisonment." This downgrade is actually a degradation of the value of human life, " Whoever sheds man's blood, by man his blood shall be shed; for in the image of God He made man"

(Genesis 9:6). Capital punishment is the most severe retribution that can be enacted by man on earth, because murder blots out forever, in history, God's image in the person murdered. That is, **murder strikes at the highest value of human life, its being made in the image of God**!

Endnotes

Theodore Dalrymple is a physician who has spent his life working in London with the "down and out." While he is not a Christian, his insights are provocative. His entertaining and engaging style is a side benefit to his writings. For example, one of his books is *Life at the Bottom: The Worldview That Makes the Underclass* (Ivan R. Dee, 2001).

George Grant, *In the Shadow of Plenty*, [Thomas Nelson, Inc., 1986). Entire text may be found online here. You will need to click on "Authors" in left hand column and find the title under the author's name.

Carl F. H. Henry, *Aspects of Christian Social Ethics* (Baker Book House, 1964).

11. Anthropology and Salvation

Heart and Head, Affections and Feelings, Edwards and Machen

I have made that trip of 18 inches from the head to the heart and I am sure of my salvation. Now God has confirmed it to me and never again will I wonder about the state of my salvation, for I'm saved, saved, saved! Amen and may you be able to say the same thing with that blessed assurance I have.

Most likely, all readers have heard this distinction between "head" and "heart." Indeed, you may have made this illustration yourself in one application or another.

Dear readers, those of us who espouse a full Biblical worldview, must begin to discern the invasion of unbiblical thinking into our evangelism, personal growth, and theology. This invasion comes from both a pietistic influence of the 19th century and modern psychology.

Curiously, some Christians use Jonathan Edwards to bolster their position about head and heart without carefully reading what he actually wrote. I would posit that there is an historical-critical method needed for reading of past Christian writers, as well as, for Scripture.

Let us explore the nuances of head and heart, feelings and affections, and what Jonathan Edwards actually said.

Feelings in Body and Soul

To begin we should understand what are "feelings," (a synonym for "emotions"). Feelings are a slippery subject, and possibly one reason for the confusion that abounds.

Feelings are, perhaps, best understood by their various names: sad, mad, afraid, worried, anxious, fearful, distressed, angry, happy, dejected, despaired, gloomy, down, blue, furious, glad, surprised, outraged, steamed, troubled, and longing. These may loosely be grouped as glad, mad, sad, and afraid ("afrad" to continue the rhyme).

The etymology of emotion provides some understanding. The Latin root has the idea of "action." The French root describes "to move out." The word "disturbance" is used in one definition. So, for a beginning definition of feeling and emotions, I propose "a disturbance of the person."

Now, where does this "disturbance" take place? It occurs in both the material (body) and immaterial (soul, spirit) components of a person.

(I am trying to avoid the dichotomy-trichotomy issue here. For either camp, there can still be only material and immaterial. Even the "soul and spirit" of the trichotomist are both immaterial, that is, non-physical. That limitation seems adequate for our considerations here.)

For example, you are driving along in your car, relatively at peace with the world (see below), when another driver cuts in on you, barely missing contact, and speeds on! All of a sudden, your heart (body) is racing, you grip the wheel tighter, and your muscles tense. Similarly, your mind begins to race. "Wow, I just missed getting hurt! Whew! I'm glad that he missed me! You ____ so and so, I hope that you wreck somewhere!"

All that in less than a second! Fear, relief, gladness, anger. Strong emotions and feelings, "disturbances," occurring in both body and mind (soul).

Another example occurs from the physical side. You awake with a fever of 102 degrees. You "feel" bad. You don't want to get up. You don't want to think, just get back in bed and forget the responsibilities of the day. Body and mind are affected. We are a unity.

For a more lengthy discussion on feelings and emotions, see "A Definition of Emotions".

The Biblical Heart

The word "heart" is used more than 1000 times in the Old and New Testaments. It is one designation of the non-material side of man, along with soul, spirit, mind, conscience, and will. It is unusual, if not rare, for "heart" to be used to describe emotion, but two examples are I Samuel 1:8 and 2:1. Far and away the common use of "heart" concerns the thoughts of man. "As (a man) thinks in his heart, so is he" (Proverbs 23:7). "Do not think in your heart"

212

(Deuteronomy 9:4). "Nor does his heart think so" (Isaiah 10:6). "Why do you think evil in your thoughts" (Matthew 9:4). "If anyone among you thinks he is religious, and does not bridle his tongue but deceives his own heart" (James 1:26). Thus, the heart is inseparable from the mind and the understanding. The heart gives values to the things that the mind understands.

At this point, the reader should do his own research. Simply, use a concordance and look up verses on "heart," Old or New Testament, and study the context and meaning of the use of the word. He or she will confirm what follows here. (You can also use the Bible Gateway word/phrase Search at the end of this article.

"Heart in the Bible is the inner life that one lives before God and himself, a life that is unknown to others because it is hidden from them... the most fully developed, most far-reaching and most dynamic concept of the non-material man." [1] One is tempted to say that "heart" is the "real you" -- the real person. But, that is not the case. Each person has many thoughts, both good and especially evil, that never "overflow" into the physical world. These thoughts are never acted upon by the will. The "real you," or better, the "total you," **includes** the restraining forces (conscience and will, for example) that prevent these thoughts of the heart from overflowing into speech and actions.

Yet, the overflow of the heart does reveal ourselves in ways that sometimes surprise us and others. In these ways, we find more of the reality of who we really are, often to our consternation, but testifying to the accuracy and depth of a truly Biblical psychology in which only God can fully "search the heart" (Jeremiah 17:9-10).

The importance of a right understanding of "heart" can be more fully understood in the First Great Commandment, "you shall love the LORD your God with all your heart, with all your soul, with all your mind, and with all your strength" (Mark 12:30). The reader should note that the emphasis here is on the non-material side of man (heart, soul, mind). Strength could be physical or spiritual, but is more likely both. This commandment is not some mystical, powering up of emotions but a concrete command to have **knowledge** of God in all His attributes, His names, His history, His redemption, His Second Advent, and more, much more. Then, we are to have a thoroughgoing **knowledge** of His statutes, directives, laws, and commandments in order "to love our neighbors as ourselves."

Our salvation is dependent upon a right understanding of "heart." "If you confess with your mouth the Lord Jesus and believe in your **heart** that God has raised Him from the dead, you will be saved. For with the **heart** one believes unto righteousness, and with the mouth confession is made unto salvation" (Romans 10:9-10). The mind and the heart are inseparable in these verses. In the heart is where regeneration takes place.

The following was added after the original essay. However, I believe that is fits well with the flow of this article and adds much to it.

The Distinction between the Heart and the Mind (Head). "The heart, regenerate or apostate, gives the mind its basic "set," but it does not, in this life, completely control the mind. The unregenerate heart, because of common grace, does not come to full expression in the unbeliever's mind. The regenerate heart, because of sin, does not come to full expression in the Christian's mind.

"There is an unqualified and absolute antithesis between the regenerate and unregenerate heart. There is not an absolute antithesis between the Christian and non-Christian "mind." He who in his heart is a Christian, in principle Christ's, may have a mind that embraces egregious error and breathes a reprehensible spirit. He who is in his heart a non-Christian, in principle Satan's, may have a mind that embraces much of truth and breathes a temperate spirit. In the case of both the Christian and the non-Christian, the mind, though for different reasons, can be false to the heart." (Henry Stob, Theological Reflections, Eerdmans, 1981, page 236)

Jonathan Edwards (1703-1758) and His Affections

> The affections are no other than the more vigorous and sensible exercises of the inclination and will of the soul…. God has endued the soul with two principle faculties: The one, that by which it discerns and judges of things, which is called the understanding. The other, that by which the soul is some way inclined with respect to the things it views or considers: or it is the faculty by which the soul beholds things… either as liking, disliking… approving or rejecting. This faculty is called … inclination, will… mind… often called the heart. (Emphases are mine).[2]

Edwards is equating heart and affections, as the inclination of the will, one of two "faculties" of the soul in the "mind." What is important here is that the "inclination" of the soul includes knowledge ("liking, disliking" etc.). So, affection is a deeper, ongoing attitude than the fleeting emotions that we

214

reviewed above. Webster's 1828 Dictionary of a similar time period confirms the same thoughts with his definitions of "emotion," "passion," "affection," and "heart."[3]

It is a mistake, then, to equate Edwards' affection with "emotions," especially with all the psychological and pietistic baggage with which they are attached today.[4]

A Wedding and a Caution

Such discussion of these subjects is difficult to manage in this short article. The reader needs to search out numerous passages in the Bible to see how "heart" is used in context. He should go to Webster's 1828 dictionary and look up the words named above. He must wrestle with what are and are not emotions. So, with those directions, let me suggest a wedding between emotions and affections.

Emotions are more temporary, superficial, with a paucity of associated thoughts. Affections are more abiding, deeper, with thought-through conviction. Consider some of the affections of the Bible: love, joy, peace, patience, kindness, gentleness, self-control, faithfulness, hope, and peace. Each involves considerable Biblical understanding and are an abiding, deep presence in believers. To be sure there is some overlap, but the distinction should help to clarify these issues.

J. Gresham Machen gives succinct insight.

> Human affection, apparently so simple, is really just brimming with dogma. It depends upon a host of observations treasured up in the mind . . .. human affection is thus really dependent upon knowledge.[5]

And, finally a perspective from Gordon Clark about "heart" in Scripture.

> In eighty percent or more of (Bible verses)... the context shows... that the intellect or man's mind is intended. Maybe ten percent mean volition. Another ten percent signify the emotions. Hence the actual usage very nearly identifies the heart with the intellect.

Conclusions

Apart from those feelings that originate entirely within the body (fever, disease and infection of organs and disease or injury), both feelings and affections are "brimming" with knowledge. Our goal under the Two Great Commandments is to be studied in the knowledge of God and the knowledge of man from the Bible, so that we can have right understanding in our hearts. Then, its overflow (Matthew 12:34) in word and action will be righteous: honoring to God and promoting the good of our "neighbors."

The separation of head (as mind and knowledge) is a Biblically false identification. It is one of the more serious issues for Biblically minded Christians today. The concept of "heart" has been too much determined by secular psychology and pietism, as a hangover of the 19th century.

Christians who would be world-changers through evangelism and world-view must be students of Biblical definitions, as well as Biblical theology and ethics. A right understanding of emotions, affection, and heart is one of the foundations that is necessary to that end.

Summary Principles: Anthropology and the Religions of Man

1. **Anthropology is the study of man, but the study of man begins with the study of God (His Revelation)**. "Anthro-" is man, and "-ology" is the study of. Therefore, anthropology is the study of man.

The first thing to note is that this study potentially encompasses everything that man does. Indeed, I have found areas under "anthropology" to include sociology, economics, social science, psychology, political science, education, history, geography, medicine, sociology, and Latin American studies (and by implication, the study of any or the races or cultures of man). This inclusion, then, is virtually a pursuit of an entire worldview. As such, it is unavoidable that cosmology is at its foundation. Indeed, anthropology is the study of the conflicts of the only two cosmologies that exist: Biblical Christianity and humanism by that name and all the religions that mankind has been able to construct (with Satan's help) over the centuries.

As cosmology, some of the first principles of Biblical Christianity can be named. (1) "In the beginning God created the heavens the earth." God existed prior to man. If He existed before the universe was, then all power is derived

216

from Him. (2) God created man. Therefore, the Creator is superior to man in knowledge and power. A creator is always superior to what he creates.

These simple first principles of cosmology require the most profound decision that any man or group of men can make: who and what is God. Then, as Creator, what does He require of them? **Thus, the God of the Bible stands against every other cosmology that man can ever devise or imagine**. One need go no further than the first chapter of Genesis for these conclusions.

A Christian may challenge, "Jesus Christ is The Issue for mankind, not the creation of man." My brothers and sisters, this challenge is truncated. **The issue of Jesus Christ has no meaning apart from Genesis** 1. I will grant that often the burden and conflicts of one's sin brings a person to salvation in Jesus Christ. However, all coherent philosophies (all religions, including Christianity are philosophies) must have a basis in a cosmology, because all systems must have an origin. Perhaps, nowhere is this conflict seen more clearly than in the debate about Christian missionaries. (See below.)

The Christian should note that even apart from the issue of sin (Genesis 3), Genesis 1:1 places God against all other belief systems. From that origin, then, the specifics of creation, the Fall, Jesus Christ, and all other Biblical truth follow.

The religions of the world are too complex to define here, much less to discuss. However, as I have stated, there are at the most basic root, only two religions. **The more that one knows the particulars of Biblical Christianity, especially those worked out in the historic creeds (e.g., Apostles,' Nicene, Athanasian, etc.)¾ as these were worked out against the prevailing heresies of the time¾ the better one is able to see the errors and heresies in all other religions**.

The case can be made that anthropology and its accompanying social sciences are actually products of the influence of evolution, as they are attempts to "know" and solve the problems of mankind from a non-Biblical perspective. As long as Christianity dominated the West, the problems of mankind were defined and discussed relative to the Biblical understanding of Creation, The Fall, salvation in Jesus Christ, etc. However, Evolution gave the Enlightenment the "scientific" basis upon which to construct a worldview without God. These social sciences are in the main products of that change in philosophy. As we will see, there are Biblical principles for a construct of social sciences.

2. The first and continual challenge is always about God's veracity, and many, if not the majority of Christians today, had rather listen to the Angel of Light than study and deduce answers from God's Word! The Serpent said to Eve, "Did God actually say…" (ESV). The greatest issue that men and women face has not changed since that question. The question is simply, "What has God said?" vs. "What has anyone else (including fallen angels) said?"

I know that I am perhaps being too persistent here. However, Christians often make many issues too complex. Choose any question about truth or ethics, and there is ever and always only one question, **"What has God said, and what has anyone else said."** If II Timothy 3:16-17, II Peter 1:3, and the unity of Scripture are true, then **every question that man can pose has its first principles in God's Revelation**.

In too many instances, the cry of the Reformation, *sola Scriptura*, has not even been applied, "*Sola Scriptura* for what?" In the most conservative of Christian circles, Biblical answers are ignored, even aggressively attacked. While the **theonomists and reconstructionists** may not have every answer right and do not even agree among themselves, **theonomists are at least trying to address every problem from a Biblical perspective**. Too many, if not most, "evangelicals" give answers that are as damaging to the Kingdom of God, the Church, and mankind in general, as any influence of Satan and his minions since the serpent first spoke to Eve! (For sound evaluations of theonomy and reconstructionism, see Biblical Worldview Areas under Reconstruction and Theonomy: Reviews.)

I am fully aware of the strong indictment that I have made here. I will give **two gigantic examples: poverty and medical care**. Since Lyndon Johnson, the U.S. government has conducted a War on Poverty that has spent the largest sum of money for any cause in the history of the world, perhaps $50 trillion or more. What has resulted from this expenditure¾ a worsening of the problem! That is always the result of answers founded in humanism (non-Biblical Christianity)¾ huge costs with no chance of success or the problem made worse. Relative to **medicine** in the United States, $2 trillion is spent yearly (as of 2007) for a net negative effect* on the health of the American people. And, that negative effect excludes abortion which modern medicine vigorously defends as "sound medical practice!" For more explanation of this paradox, see: Medical Efficacy, Average Life Expectancy, and *Health of Nations* (book) by Leonard Sagan.

Now, for our particular concern here, **where are the evangelical voices analyzing and decrying this enormous expenditure that degrades men and women, as creatures made in the image of God?** Sure, there are a few who address the subjects, but largely this issue is ignored by Christians selfishly focused on their "personal peace and affluence" that Francis Schaeffer addressed and decried 40 years ago. Where are the powerful denunciations of this cruelty from the pulpits of our land? Where are any such cries of cruelty, even in "still small voices," consistently and widely? As an historical reminder, **the pulpits of American rang more loudly than the Freedom Bell against the injustice of our English oppressors for issues that pale in comparison to modern concerns!**

Yet, among **the theonomists and reconstructionists**, this issue and many others are always front and center of their discussions. They indeed need to be heard and analyzed more closely.

3. **The issue of evangelism**. "OK, Ed, you have been severe on Christians about social issues, what about evangelism and missions. Is not the salvation of souls more important than problems of economics?" I am glad that you asked that question.

God has never divorced the issue of evangelism from all His other commands. I have argued elsewhere on this website that The Creation Mandate, The Great Commission (The Gospel), The Kingdom of God, and the mission of The Church are one and the same. (See The Kingdom of God.) Within the Great Commission itself, God says, "teach them to observe all things that I have commanded you." So, I simply make the claim that "all things" includes not only the message of forgiveness in Jesus Christ, but the entirety of Scripture which includes commandments about social justice, as well. That is, The Gospel is the entirety of a Biblical worldview.

1-3 Summary. Anthropology is both simple and complex. Anthropology is simple in that there are only two competing ideologies on planet earth: Biblical Christianity and all others. The complexity comes from the integration of the Bible alone as a coherent system of truth and ethics (righteousness) and its practical application to all worldview areas. **The primary problem of Biblical anthropology today is not its complexity, but its being ignored by those who claim *sola Scriptura***. These theologians are quite familiar to complexity in theology and are quite well equipped to handle it. The problem here is that they truncate the fullness of The Great Commission.

Possible practical application to evangelism and missions. Missionaries have found that some cultures do not have the problem with guilt and awareness of sin that we experience in the West. (That is not to say that every culture does not have its "taboos." See Henry…, "Anthropology," in **References**.) But, all men should be concerned with their origins, ethics, and future (especially after their own deaths). Perhaps, there could be a richness in evangelism as much in the translation of Genesis and later the Gospels that supercedes the current focus on the Gospels alone.

4. **The most dominant belief system (religion) in the West is that of scientism**. Scientism is the philosophy that only through the natural sciences may truth or knowledge be obtained. Therefore, all the solutions to mankind's problems are to be found in the "sciences." (For a Biblical use of the word "science," see What Is Science?

It is no accident that all the "-ologies" listed under **Number 1** above have been called "social sciences." Until the Renaissance and its cosmology in Darwinism, answers to the problems of mankind were sought in religion. Now, make no mistake, **scientism is a religion**. But, scientism is rarely discussed as a religion. While humanists rail at the supposed "evils of Christianity," **the evils of scientism and its effects stagger the imagination**.

I have already presented the evil of the War on Poverty and the deception that masquerades as modern medicine. Others evils of scientism are widespread and legal abortion, Medicare and Medicaid, state-sponsored and dictated education, imprisonment as rehabilitation and payment of debt to society, euthanasia in the Netherlands, HIV/AIDS and an epidemic of sexually transmitted, etc., etc. In fact, modern science, masquerading as a non-religion, is one of the leading causes of suffering and death in the history of mankind. This result has been far more devastating than the witch-doctors of Third World countries at whom these modernists laugh.

And, amazingly this monolithic religion of science has no clothes. That is, science can say nothing about morality, nor even determine its own experiments and application. See the Worldview Area of Science and Technology and its Summary Principles.

The modern church is thoroughly indoctrinated with scientism. Secular psychology dominates the most conservative Bible colleges and seminaries throughout the world.

220

Various forms of evolution, "old earth" theories, and distortions of Genesis 1-11 are prevalent in these institutions and churches, as well. The god of medicine (the health and attempted preservation of the body) is worshipped and receives more than a tithe of American income (16 percent). And, so on.

If my conclusion is correct, then the modern "evangelical" church continually violates the First Commandment, "not to have any other gods before God Himself." A god is a god whether it is a wooden idol before which one bows down or an "enlightened" ideology of modern science. As I have said often, no wonder the American church is unable to affect its culture. It blends (syncretizes) Christ with the idol of modern science.

If the modern Church is thoroughly infiltrated with scientism, what hope is there for non-Christians to discover the best (Biblical) solutions for humanity? "Let judgment begin at the household of God."

5. **The physical world (matter) is not inherently evil**. This heresy is best countered by the Nicene, Athanasian, and Chalcedon creeds, and later the Westminster Confession of Faith, in Christ's taking upon Himself in His Incarnation, a fully human body. As completely sinless and holy, He could not have been incarnate in something that was inherently evil.

Man is composed of both a material body and an immaterial soul.* Again, the body is not inherently evil, but through the sin nature apart from regeneration, the most central being of man, is heart, is only oriented towards selfishness and evil (its depth and breadth of application limited only by God's common grace).

Man was created in the image of God (Genesis 1:26-27) which is man's ability to think and reason. See my thoughts on The Image of God.

(*I have not the length here to discuss the immaterial components of man. However, simply, my position is that the spirit, soul , heart, and mind are all part of the immaterial component. This is the bipartite view.)

6. **Everything material in the universe, along with the fallen angels, is radically different from the original creation**. Only God and the righteous angels are unchanged in history. The "normal" state of existence for the universe and for mankind was the period of time before The Fall of Adam and Eve. But, their Fall, along with the Flood, greatly affected the material universe, as well as men and women. See Summary Principles of Creation, etc..

The radical change is most demonstrable in men and women. All are "dead in trespasses and sin" (Ephesians 2:1). "All come short of the glory of God" (Romans 3:23). "All our righteousness is as filthy rags" (Isaiah 64:6). "There is none righteous, no not one" (Romans 3:10).

The answer to this "fallen nature" is regeneration of the Holy Spirit (John 3:3) and belief in Jesus Christ as "the only name under heaven by which men must be saved" (Acts 4:12). Since these worldview areas are addressed to Christians, I present only the basics of what is wrong with the human race and what the Answer to this problem (The Fall and man's sinful nature). But, the radical nature of these distinctives in understanding the human race and its pretended answers in its various philosophies and religions must not be underestimated.

7. **Man's value and his treatment by other men is solely determined by the cosmology of those who have authoritative power**. If man is an animal and "dogs (or any animal) are people too," then why should man not be treated with the same ethics as animals? Why should man not be euthanized when his usefulness and chronic diseases of aging become costly? Why should unborn babies not be aborted? Why should people not be managed as herds of cattle? Why should any individual have rights over those of the group? Why should populations not be controlled in any way that "works," regardless of what it does to choices within families?

Within American society, it may be that the religion of evolution in its ethics and application has gained more consistency than that of Biblical Christianity. The remnants of a fading Biblical ethic, a weakening Constitutional basis of law, and a few voices of Biblically knowledgeable Christians is all that separates us from the horrors of Nazi Germany, Stalin's communist Russia, and the other totalitarian regimes of history.

8. **On a Biblical basis and "according to the good pleasure of His will, the most basic division of mankind consists of the regenerate and the unregenerate**. The Scripture uses various names for these groups: sheep and goats, wheat and tares, those of light and darkness, those of the Spirit and the world, etc. This distinction is so simple as not to require further comment. **Yet, its application is virtually ignored by the regenerate in their applied ethics and "social justice."**

No man or woman can be "fully human" (to the extent that such is possible in his or her earthly existence) until they are regenerated and

practicing consistent obedience to God's commandments. Perhaps, this error is most pronounced by Christians who are psychologists and psychiatrists. Rarely, do they concern themselves with the "heart status" of their "clients." Yet, the difference in the regenerate and the unregenerate should be the most profound difference to be found among men and women. (I say "should be," because most Christians have not been educated fully to develop their regenerate status.) See Summary Principles of Psychology, etc..

9. **"So God created man in His own image; in the image of God He created him; male and female He created them" (Genesis 1:27)**. No more really needs to be said. The modern notion that boys and girls, men and women are essentially the same except for their sexual organs (and some choose to change those!) is foolish and absurd. The Scriptures are replete with the roles of men and women for which they are naturally designed, even though they may struggle with these roles because of the Fall.

10. **The concept of predestination is logically inescapable**. While both Christians and non-Christians rail against the idea of God's total predestination of the lives of all men, including the elect and the non-elect, some concept of predestination is inescapable. Whether one chooses the dominant influence of nature (one's genetic and spiritual composition) or nurture (parents, education, etc.) or a combination of the two, no person is ever given a choice of these total influences. **All decisions that are made at any point in the course of one's life, are predicated on nature and nurture over which the individual had no "choice," OR are predicated on God's predestination of all things. There are no other choices except supernatural intervention by other gods**.

Perhaps because of *hubris*, notable philosophers and many laymen (in contrast to these learned philosophers) have tried to defend the notion that any concept of fairness (whether Christian or otherwise) requires man to have **free will**. But, as we have just presented, such a position is indefensible logically.

The beautiful nature of Biblical Christianity is that it is always consistent with the structure that God has given to man's mind. Predestination is inescapable. Only in Christianity is man given a Personal kind of predestination. All other forms of predestination are impersonal, fatalistic, and blindly cruel. One wonders at the impact of evangelism, if Christians were to witness on this basis, instead of the simplistic devices now used.

11. **Atheistic models of anthropology have proven false**. (A) The Noble Savage in a pristine, sin-free paradise has been found by voyagers to the New World (and archeologists since) to practice human sacrifice in the most horrible ways with tens of thousands of victims. (B) The idea of man progressing from a simple language of grunts and single syllable words is false. The most backward tribes on the earth have been found to highly complex languages, more complex than those of modern man in some areas. (3) The architectural construction of the pyramids, statues of Easter Island, the stones of Stonehenge, and other "wonders" of the world give a profound genius to "primitive" peoples.

If one works from the Genesis model, mankind is actually degressing, not regressing in intelligence. While much of this model is still being worked out in archeological finds (many are already impressive), there are even evidences within recent centuries. Without computers and with quill pens, Augustine, Calvin, Luther, and others did scholarly work in both depth, breadth, and volume that virtually no modern scholars can match. Their education by their late teens exceeded the graduate level of many students today. **The Biblical model fits again!**

12. **Soteriology or doctrines concerning salvation**. It is not my purpose here or on this website to present systematic theology except as it relates to principles of worldview and to areas that I believe have been neglected by conservative theologians either in doctrine or application. Thus, I leave the doctrines of salvation to the theologians of your persuasion.

However, **Creation (Genesis 1-2), The Fall (Genesis 3), our Biblical ancestors and history (Genesis 4-5), Noah and the Flood (Genesis 6-9), and the immediate post-Flood history and Tower of Babel (Genesis 10-11) are first principles of a truly Biblical anthropology**. Throughout this website, these are both discussed in their application to particular areas of worldview and assumed where they are not explicitly discussed.

Those readers who have spent much time on this site know that I come from the Reformed and Presbyterian persuasion where the Gospel is best summarized in the Westminster Confession with its Larger and Shorter Catechisms. Logically, these documents are the most consistent and coherent with a Biblical worldview. I truly believe that the application of sound principles of hermeneutics within the parameters of formal logic would bring all the regenerate into a greater agreement.

13. **The chief end of man**. The primary reason that man was created was and is "to love the Lord our God with all our heart, soul, mind, and strength and to love our neighbors as ourselves." Or, in the words of the answer to the first question of the Shorter Catechism, "The chief end of man is to glorify God and enjoy Him forever."

Anthropology and Religion References

Books

Adams, Jay E. "The Doctrine of Man," *A Theology of Christian Counseling: More than Redemption*. Zondervan, pages 94-138. Discussion on the bipartite-tripartite issue.

Anderson, J. N. D. *Christianity and Comparative Religion*. InterVarsity Press, 1973.

Clark, Gordon H. *Predestination*. Presbyterian and Reformed Publishing Company, 1969.

Hodge, Charles. "Anthropology" in *Systematic Theology*, Volume 2, Part II. Eerdmans, Reprint 1986.

Priest, Robert J. "Cultural Anthropology, Sin, and the Missionary." In *God and Culture: Essays in Honor of Carl F. H. Henry*, Eerdmans, 1993.

Online Resources

http://www.biblicalworldview21.org/bmei/jbem/volume1/num4/the_image_of_god_and_the_practice_of_medicine.html

On the image of God by the author of this www.biblicalworldview21.org website

http://www.biblicalworldview21.org/Worldview_Areas/COR_Link_Social_Action.asp

Coalition on Revival Sphere Document on Social Action

http://www.desiringgod.org/ResourceLibrary/AskPastorJohn/ByTopic/105/141 8_What_does_John_Piper_mean_when_he_says_that_he_is_a_sevenpoint_Ca lvinist/

John Piper's short defense of "This is the best of all possible worlds"

_____

Endnotes

[1] Jay Adams, *More Than Redemption*, (Philipsburg, NJ: Presbyterian and Reformed Publishing Company, 1979), p. 115).
[2] Jonathan Edwards, "Religious Affections."
[3] Webster's 1828 Dictionary
[4] For a more complete discussion of feelings and emotions, see "A Definition of Emotions".
[5] J. Gresham Machen, *Christianity and Liberalism*, (Grand Rapids: Wm. B. Eerdmans Publishing Company, Reprint 1981), p. 55.

12. Economics and Business

Debunking the Politically Correct History of the "Robber Barons"

The following is most of the Foreword, written by Forrest McDonald, in *The Myth of the Robber Barons: A New Look at the Rise of Big Business in America*, by Burton W. Folsom, Jr. (Young America's Foundation, 1991). While neither the Foreword nor the book is explicitly Biblical, it 1) corrects an historiography that is false, 2) shows the power of capitalism to benefit everyone in a free society (not just the "big businessman), and 3) illustrates Biblical principles of limited government and free enterprise. (For a longer discussion of this issue, see internet reference at the bottom of the page.

> Folsom shows that the "Robber Baron" school of historians of American business enterprise was partly right and partly wrong…. There are two kinds of business developers… "political entrepreneurs" and "market entrepreneurs." The former were … comparable to medieval robber barons, for they sought and obtained wealth through the coercive power of the state, which is to say that they were subsidized by government and were sometimes granted monopoly status by government. **Invariably, their products and services were inferior to and more expensive than the goods and services provided by market entrepreneurs, who sought and obtained wealth by producing more and better for less cost to the consumer**. The market entrepreneurs, however, have been repeatedly -- one is tempted to say systematically -- ignored by historians….
>
> Folsom's study has profound implications for American historiography beyond the immediate subject to which it is addressed. It is commonly held that the Whig Party of Clay and Webster and its successor Republican Party of Abraham Lincoln and William McKinley were the "pro-business" parties, and that the Jacksonian Democrats were anti-business…. (Actually) the Whigs and Republicans engaged in a great deal of pro-business rhetoric and in talk of economic

development, but the policies they advocated, such as subsidies, grants, of special privileges, protective tariffs, and the like, actually worked to retard development and to stifle innovation. The Jacksonian Democrats engaged in a great deal of anti business rhetoric, but the results of their policies were to remove or reduce governmental interference into private economic activity, and thus to free market entrepreneurs to go about their creative work. The entire nation grew wealthy as a consequence.

Folsom's work... has a powerful relevance to current political discourse.... In the last decade or two, many corporate businessmen have joined with leftist ideologues to clamor for a "partnership" between government and business that would involve central planning, protective, tariffs, and a host of restrictions upon foreign competitors.... Political promotion of economic development is inherently futile, for it invariably rewards incompetence; if competence is rewarded, incompetence will therefore be the product; and when incompetence is the product, politicians will insist that increased planning and increased regulation if the appropriate remedy.

Adam Smith warned us more than two centuries ago. "The statesman, who should attempt to direct people in what manner they ought to employ their capital, would not only load himself with a most unnecessary attention, but assume an authority which could safely be trusted, not only to no single person, but to no council or senate whatever, and which would nowhere be so dangerous as in the hands of a man who had folly and presumption enough to fancy himself fit to exercise it."

For further reading on this same issue, see http://www.mises.org/story/2317.

A Return to Hard Currency in Post-World War II Germany and France under DeGaulle

"Now (a return to the gold standard) has been attempted in modern times by several people; for example, it was attempted by Ludwig Ehrhard and Konrad Adenauer in Germany after World War II with astonishing success. Germany went from a highly inflated currency, which was the old Reichsmark of the Hitler period (by 1947, it had slipped in value until it was worth about 1/600 of a dollar) to a very hard currency, the new Deutsche Mark, **contrary to the advice given by the American and British economists who had been sent over to help the Germans**. This was done to a certain extent at the instigation of the Genevan economist, Wilhelm Roepke, who was German by birth. It proved, as you know, a tremendous success, leading to what was called the *Wirtchafts-wunder*, the economic miracle of German post-war recovery.

Any description of what happened in the days of the economic reform in Germany in 1948 is extremely fascinating. Even on the day before the reform, secrecy was well kept. Overnight the old currency was abolished; everyone was given forty marks in the new currency to start with, and overnight the stores, which had been empty because no one was willing to sell the things which eh actually had in stock for the old currency at any price, suddenly became full again. People found that there were goods which could be sold, as long as it was know that they would get something in return

General DeGaulle, in the early days following his return to power in 1958, also made an attempt to re-establish a hard currency in France. Although French currency is not entirely hard, at the moment (1978), it is harder than American currency and certainly the subsequent economic recovery of France, which DeGaulle initiated, is due in large measure to the fact that he established a sounder currency." (Emphases are mine.)

Harold O. J. Brown, "Before the Crash -- A Biblical Basis for Economics," Christian Studies Center, 1978, pages 14-15.

Summary Principles of Economics

Worldview areas intertwine. The following are arranged in no particular order except some definitions and basics in the first few sections. At some points, the reader is directed to other Worldview Areas. As you go through the various Areas, there is overlap and dependency of each area to every other area. A review of economics is not possible without particular attention to

Social Justice and **Civil Government** because these three areas involve so many of the same issues. And, virtually every other area influences to one degree or another.

1. **The Bible is a textbook on economics**. The Bible, especially with a systematic organization of the subject, is a textbook on economics. As we have seen with psychology, social justice, and civil government, any activity that involves relationships and interactions among people, the Bible is the governing textbook.

That the Bible has not been seen as such a textbook in these areas, perhaps, stems from two reasons. (1) The Bible is not written systematically. If a person takes any subject (especially any of those named here), and goes through the Bible citing every verse and noting the context, the result is amazingly detailed and compressive! Economics may have more applicable verses than any other worldview area. (2) Christians have not been taught the comprehensiveness of the Bible on the many subjects to which it speaks. This second is a derivative of (1), but it also results from some 200 years of pietism in which the Bible has become narrowly focused on personal salvation only with a smattering of personal morality considered.

2. **Definition of wealth (prosperity)**. Wealth, as it will be used in these principles, is defined as having the money (resources) to provide for all of an individual's or family's "needs," and some discretionary money for at least a few "wants." Any definition of wealth is somewhat arbitrary because wealth is more subjective than objective. What is wealth for one person, may be far short of what another considers to be wealth.

3. **The incredible lure (lust) of money**. ""No one can serve two masters; for either he will hate the one and love the other, or else he will be loyal to the one and despise the other. You cannot serve God and mammon" (Matthew 6:24). "For the love of money is a root of all kinds of evil, for which some have strayed from the faith in their greediness, and pierced themselves through with many sorrows" (I Timothy 6:10). These and many other verses of the Bible indicate that money and what it can buy (things and power) is one of the major temptations to which man is subject. Two things may be commonly overlooked here.

The "love" of money and the "poor." (1) It is the "love" of money, not money itself that is the problem. Neither a large amount of money, nor the accumulation of "things," are intrinsically evil, even though they are a great temptation to sin. (2) Many "poor" or those without wealth are as prone as the

230

"rich" to this temptation and sin. It is widely recognized that the "poor" are the primary buyers of lottery tickets and other means of gambling, evidence that they will sacrifice that of which they have little in order to get "rich." And, they can envy and want material possessions as strongly as any "rich" person, even though they will likely never have the possibility of owing such items.

4. **The cycle of prosperity and righteousness**. There is a cycle that seems to be almost inevitable. The righteousness of a people brings prosperity (see all that follows here). Then, as soon as prosperity is achieved, degradation of morals (unrighteousness) follows until the sin of a people settles them back into poverty. The challenge of American Christians today is to become such good stewards of their wealth as to disrupt this cycle.

The United States today: good and evil, principalities and powers. The United States is a nation of great and powerful contrasts. It has the greatest resources, and it's the most "giving" nation on earth. When disasters occur, the United States is there with the most and best equipment and resources. Her people give three percent of their income to "charitable" organizations. She sends more missionaries than any other nation. Yet, she continues to increase the powers of government and is becoming a nation of perverse and heinous immorality which has become "politically correct." The conflict is great! However, "salt" is a preservative that may be greatly diluted and still be detectable by taste.

5. **Scarcity**. Scarcity is defined simply as needs and wants exceeding the resources available to meet them at the price that people want them. This term is another one that is relative. Mostly, it is time dependent, as increased production, discovery of more raw materials, changing wants and needs, and other factors may reduce or even eliminate the scarcity. Scarcity often leads to ingenuity and increased efforts to remedy scarcity. In today's world, persistent scarcity usually occurs due to some statist intervention of tariffs, restriction on production, limitation of transport, condemnation of a faulty product, etc.

Population of the earth. In the account of creation, God said, "Be fruitful and multiply; fill the earth…" (Genesis 1:28). By reasonable measures, the earth can support far more people than now exist on the planet. New "resources" are discovered continually, and man has great ingenuity to make present resources last longer, create new technologies that require different resources, and use technology to discover and produce new resources. The greatest limitation on adequate food, shelter, and clothing is State controls, tariffs, redistribution, and other measures that interfere with the free market, individual ingenuity, available resources, and other means of production to provide these needs. See Overpopulation and the Creation Mandate.

Drought is not the primary cause of famine. When one thinks of famine, one envisions dry, dusty barren fields due to lack of rain. However, in the world's history and in modern times, drought is not the primary cause of famine -- man is. Crops are destroyed by invading armies through physical destruction, disruption of farming, and theft of produce. The State sets regulations on what farmers can and cannot grow and when they can grow their crops. In many nations, storage of food for future consumption in times of hardship is called "hoarding" and punishable by law. Famine occurs through farmer's failure to replenish the soil. In places like India, the predominant religion, Hinduism, proscribes the practice of eating cows that could provide meat for many children who desperately need protein. Modern agricultural methods could actually provide enough grain for India's entire population and one-third more could even be exported! (Link) Thus, famine should be thought of as a much greater problem of man's devastation of his environment and whatever religion that he believes than a lack of rain. Without such devastation, the earth is capable of feeding many times the current population of the earth.

Natural disasters. The United States now has laws that punish those who charge "above market" prices for goods in the midst of a crisis, such as a hurricane. But, what this law does is stifle the incentive for entrepreneurs to respond quickly to the disaster. It actually prolongs recovery and rebuilding in the long run. Our natural tendency is to abhor those "pirates" who would take "advantage" of those harmed by a natural disaster. However, they have sacrificed themselves to get to the site quickly and with the goods needed. And, no one in the disaster is forced to buy!

6. **The tithe**. The tithe of one's increase in wealth over a period of time is owed to God (Malachi 3:8-12), whether a person is a Christian or not. God has promised prosperity to those who tithe (same text). The tithe is directed to the church for its worship and work to advance the Kingdom of God.

7. **Acquisition of wealth and the blessing of God**. Generally, hard work and frugal living produces wealth (for example, Proverbs 8:21; 14:24 . But, finally, wealth is a blessing of God (Proverbs 10:22). There is a correlation between one's being righteous and being wealthy (Proverbs 15:6, 22:4), and one's sins and waste of resources (Proverbs 21:10, 29:3). I once did a detailed study of the verses in Proverbs that have to do with the accumulation of wealth. The principle thus stated was obvious in that book of the Bible. See the second definition of the "poor" above.

8. Material value is an entirely subjective concept. "One man's trash is another man's treasure," says one proverb. "Beauty is in the eye of the beholder" is another. Millions of dollars have been paid for "modern art" by some buyers while others would throw it in the trash. Within societies, however, there are consistencies of value. For example, gold and gem stones are almost always considered "valuable." However, there are times of crisis in which these valuables would be traded for a minimal amount of goods for survival. God placed value on gold and silver for His temple design, but He is also a Person. Perhaps, food, shelter, and clothing are the most valuable items for any person, since they are necessary for the sustenance of life. But, even with these, there are subjective choices (for example, gambling) that one values above even these basics.

9. Work established during Creation. "Fill the earth and subdue it; have dominion over the fish of the sea, over the birds of the air, and over every living thing that moves on the earth" (Genesis 1:28). "Then the LORD God took the man and put him in the garden of Eden to tend and keep it" (Genesis 2:15).

The curse of the Fall on work. Part of the curse of Adam's sin is the difficulty of work. Prior to the Fall, work would have come naturally and more productively. While we cannot be sure what these differences might be, there is no doubt that man's difficulty with production in a fallen world is greater than it would have been.

The blessing of the Fall on work: (A) The difficulty of producing anything under the curse also has the blessing that men must work together to provide for themselves and their families. Where there is any concentration of population, it is usually more beneficial for one man to concentrate on what is able to produce well and efficiently, selling those items to others, and using the money to buy food and other items that he needs. Thus, both he other benefit from each other.

> **(B) Division of labor**. God has created, even under the Curse, such a diversity of interests and talents among men, that every need and many wants can be fulfilled through their productive and cooperative efforts. This division is one of the great blessings of his Common Grace.
>
> **(C) Scarcity**. The fact that there is never enough of anything for all people at one time at the prices that they want to pay

means provides incentives for this division of labor to work towards the provision of goods and services at prices that others will pay.

10. **Vocation**. (From Latin, vocationem, "spiritual calling.") With the Reformation came the Biblical understanding that everything "under the sun" is under God's Providence. While there is a sense in which "secular" is applicable to ideas that are not Biblical, strictly speaking no work in which man is engaged is "secular." Every activity of man should be consciously brought under Biblical scrutiny and its direction. Within this purview, all activities of man, especially his primary occupation should be consciously recognized and pursued as being administered under God's hand. The particular focus of this activity should be that this work is directed by the applicable Biblical principles.

Christian's neglect of learning and applying Biblical principles in their work. One of the great tragedies of Christians today is their failure to understand Biblical principles that govern their profession or area of work. For example, I spent over 20 years working in medical ethics from a Biblical perspective, in spite of the fact that the word "physician" is only mentioned seven times in the Bible. While Christians achieve college level educations in the liberal arts and sciences, they function through life on a First Grade level of Bible and theological understanding. Thus, they have no clue how to reform their work under God's mandate to do so.

11. **The private ownership of property is a clear mandate of the Bible**. Primary to this mandate is the Eighth Commandment, "You shall not steal." For theft to occur, prior ownership must have been established. Many laws of the Old Testament protected property from seizure or damage from others. Property belonged to the family and was passed from one generation to the next. This property also was protected by various laws in how it was to be passed within families and who had specific claims on it. Blessings and cursings accompanied these laws. Many of Jesus' parables were implicit or explicit on the ownership of property, for example, the one that ends with "Is it not lawful for me to do what I wish with my own things?" (Matthew 20:15).

Fact of history. While empirical evidence is not necessary to prove the truth of Scripture, such evidence does illustrate its truth. **All community-owned experiments of history have failed miserably or have been local and temporary**.

Acts 4:32-5:11 - The early Christian church, communism, and Ananias and Sapphira. This passage is not an example for all churches. (1) One principle of hermeneutics is that historical passages must be interpreted by the didactic. Or, what is recorded as history is not necessarily to be considered to be doctrine (principled teaching). (2) Giving of one's goods was **voluntary**. Ananias and Sapphira were judged, not because they held back some of the proceeds of their sale, but that they "lied ... to God" (5:4). (3) This period of time was unique in the history of the church. Nowhere else is communal property remotely suggested. Likely, the members of the Jerusalem church were anticipating the destruction of Jerusalem that Jesus had forecast and selling their possessions to prevent their assets being destroyed. (4) Communal property would negate the Eighth Commandment that ownership of property was not the norm. By necessity, some property might have to be communal, for example, roads, rivers, and seas. However, most communal properties are abused and not preserved or developed over time (for example, the Boston Commons of early Massachusetts).

12. **The role of the State in economics**. The primary role of the State in economics is to insure that the free actions of men may take place without fear for their lives or their property being stolen.

The State is to have no role that disrupts the free exchange of goods and services around the world except as may be required to disrupt or destroy the trade of declared enemies in a just war. Tariffs, property tax, subsidized costs of production or research, payment for non-production, minimum wage standards, price controls, etc. are not the Biblical duties of the government. All these favor one person or industry over another, interfering with market forces that determine prices that are acceptable to the buyer and seller.

Licensure. Licensure of services, for example of physicians and realtors, provides a state-sponsored monopoly of these professions, distorting the free trade of goods and services.

Shortages, inflated prices. Interference by the State in the above ways will eventually cause shortages and inflated prices of those goods and service thus regulated.

Communism, Nazism, communism, etc. That the State has no role in regulating an economy or the free exercise of trade, simply, but powerfully, eliminates these state-involved philosophies.

13. **Employers, employees, and trade unions**. Trade unions distort the relationship of the employer and employee. An employer hires a person for a specific job at a wage/salary that is agreeable to them both. Each evaluates their ongoing relationship over time. The employer evaluates the performance of the employee, whether it matches the wage/salary that he is paying the person. The employee evaluates the wage/salary that he receives and his working conditions. Weighing their respective interests, the relationship continues or is dissolved at some point. Each is free to evaluate and negotiate with the other.

A trade union interferes with this freedom on both sides. A trade union sometimes assumes that all workers produce the same output which is patently false by any measure. A trade union severely restricts the options of a person who is not in the union through "closed shops" and wage controls. A trade union severely handicaps all employers who must monitor the cost of production so that he makes a sufficient profit to stay in business. In essence, the trade union becomes a barrier for a business to be successful and against the creation of more jobs. The more that a business is successful, the more employees that it can hire and pay them their negotiated wage.

14. **The family, child labor laws, and the State**. The family is an institution ordained by God which is to be governed without any outside interference from the State except where there is good evidence that severe bodily harm or murder has occurred. This restriction seems harsh and antiquated in modern times, but the family must have that God-ordained freedom to perform its responsibilities under God's commandments. For example, children have different talents and mature in different degrees. Who can best tell when they are ready to be employed, the family or the state? Obviously, the family is best able to make that discernment because they have observed the child from birth to the present. The State can only assume that all children are the same, a patently false notion.

Historical note. Without doubt, in the past and present, children have been severely abused in the work place. However, for the State to interfere is for the State to provide "foster care," placement agencies, restrictions on businesses, police powers over the family, and violation of the integrity of the home, to name a few. Whenever the State steps outside of its God-prescribed roles, it creates a myriad of agencies and bureaucracies that try to emulate what the family unit is capable of doing with only a mother and a father. That families abuse their children is accepted. But, far greater abuses of children will occur with and by State interference. For example, the State now investigates spanking of children (a God-instructed responsibility) and will remove children from the homes of Christians on this basis alone.

15. **Value**. No goods or services have intrinsic value. For example, a man might pay an ounce of gold to buy one loaf of bread in a time of crisis. That same ounce of gold would buy dozens of loafs of bread in times of stability. Relative to services, a man may be willing to pay only an ounce of silver to be ferried over a quiet stream. Yet, if he is in danger of losing his life due to flooding, he may pay a bagful of silver or even his lifetime of savings.

Value is an entirely subjective concept. Value lies within the heart of a person or group of persons. For example, gold is valuable because of its beauty and certain natural properties. Even so, certain people will kill to get more of it while others do not care whether they ever have any.

It is this subjectivity of value that makes any sort of regulation of the market place impossible. No man can determine what another is willing to pay or sacrifice for a particular item. Any outside influence interferes with the negotiation of the value that the seller places on his item and that buyer is willing to pay. The buyer does not have to buy and the seller does not have to sell until they reach an agreement. Any outside interference gives an unjust advantage to one over the other.

"A person **imputes** value to an article or a good because he forms an opinion about the potential desirability or usefulness. This is true whether we speak about the food we eat, the wood that we burn, the paintings that we enjoy, or the women that we love." (Rose, *Economics: The American...*, page 159)

While value does reside across groups to a large extent, for example, most people value gold, and the market place determines a fairly standard price for an ounce of gold. However, as stated above, individuals within those groups will value gold more or less than that determined price. So, not even the market place can determine the subjective value that a person places on gold or any other object.

16. **Money**. Money is simply a designated and denominated medium of exchange, ideally tied to a bimetallic standard.

17. **The gold standard**. Since money is simply a medium of exchange, there must be come way to determined its value. And, since value is inherently subjective, in a worldwide market the monetary base must be something that all people value and the supply of which does not change rapidly. If the supply

of the medium of exchange were to change rapidly, then the value of families' possessions in monetary price would change with the supply. Of all the possible items that fit this criteria, gold or silver are surely the best. To increase the supply of either of them, a considerable effort of mining and purification is necessary. There is not going to be a sudden increase in production of these items. And, there is a built in safeguard in the cost of production. If the supply did suddenly increase, the value of the gold or silver loses value. As it loses value, there is less incentive to continue mining and processing (expensive procedures), so production falls off and the market again begins to level out.

The American dollar. The Mint Act of 1792 established the dollar and tied it to designated weights of gold and silver. Except for the period that began with the Civil War until 1878 and with minor changes in the weights of precious metal, the bimetallic standard was continued. In 1900, the link to silver was abandoned. In 1933, gold coins were withdrawn from circulation and the unit weight of gold tied to the dollar was markedly reduced. In 1975, all linkage of the dollar to gold was abandoned, allowing the dollar to "float" on international markets. Click here for more a more detailed history.

Why have a gold standard? Part of the reason for a gold standard is reasoned above. The biggest reason for the gold standard is to prevent governments from just printing money for whatever reason that they conjure. When governments print money, they steal from those who hold that unit of currency because it will buy less than before the supply was increased (inflated). Another reason is to allow citizens to retain monetary power that the government cannot easily change. Artificially created money also entices people toward unwise investments by stimulating an unsustainable set of wants.

Inflation. The problem of inflation is the problem of a monetary standard divorced from the gold standard or a government policy that continually decrease the amount of gold that a unit of currency represents. Apart from a government being able to simply print money, all other methods that could cause inflation are slow and ponderous. We have seen how difficult is the production of gold and silver, and even that its cost of production is a natural safe-guard against inflation. If the demand of an item results in its inflation, that higher price attracts suppliers who want to profit on that item. This increased production, then, brings the price down. While market forces cannot always prevent supply or monetary crises, such forces will correct the situation in the shortest period of time that is required to produce the products and move them to the place of need.

18. **Love and social justice**. Principles of economics necessarily include principles of love and social justice. Christians as individuals, families, and churches are called of God to minister to the poor (defined below). First, there is evangelism to the "poor in spirit," regardless of economic status. Second, we are to minister to the economically poor." This administration is not automatic, as it requires discerning who are those who are the "deserving poor" and "undeserving poor." These actions fill in the gaps of those who temporarily or permanently are unable to provide for themselves economically. Social justice is more complex than just giving handouts. The Summary Principles of Social Justice and the discussion there are necessary to understand the concept of love and social justice within the parameters of economics.

Definition of poor (poverty). The Bible defines the "poor" in three ways. (1) Those who are "poor in spirit" (Matthew 5:3) whether they have earthly needs or great prosperity. (2) Those who are destitute of earthly needs and possessions, yet who are willing to work and better themselves, "those who are bowed down... the righteous" (Psalm 146:5-9) Also, see Job 5:11-16; Psalm 10:17-8, Psalm 103:6, Psalm 109:30-31, 140:12. These could be called the "deserving poor." They are to receive charity and help towards responsible provision of themselves and their families. (3) Those who are destitute of earthly needs and possessions who are not willing to work and better themselves. They "waste opportunities (Proverbs 6:9-10), bring poverty on themselves (Proverbs 10:4), are victims of self-inflicted bondage (Proverbs 12:24), and are unable to accomplish anything in life (Proverbs 15:19." While these should be given every opportunity and assistance to change, "subsidizing sluggards is the same as subsidizing evil. It is subsidizing dependence... slavery." (Quotes and ideas are from George Grant, In the Shadow of Plenty, [Thomas Nelson, Inc., 1986), pages 52-55.) For more on the "unwilling to work" poor, see Dalrymple under Endnotes. (Transferred from Summary Principles of Social Justice.)

19. **The family is the primary unit of economics**. In the Old Testament, property (land) belonged to the family and was passed from generation to generation. Fathers are to provide other forms of inheritance for their children (Proverbs 13:22). A father who fails to provide for his family is "worse than an unbeliever" (I Timothy 5:8). Thus, family economics is both present and future, intended to be **intergenerational**.

This centrality of the family is not to disparage the roles of single men and women in an economy, especially those who are called to singleness (I Corinthians 7:6-8). However, an individual is not a functioning unit, as the family in which there is a head, a wife and children. There are mutual roles within the family of education, training, and provision. Even as one generation lives their lives as God's stewards on earth, they are making provision for the next. A major weakness of Christians and churches on their culture has been the loss of belief from one generation to the next. This loss is not part of God's preceptive design.

20. **The Eighth Commandment.** The Eighth Commandment has a broad and general application towards both the duties and sins that it encompasses. This application is clearly seen in the Larger Catechism of the Westminster Confession of Faith which summaries a large number of other Biblical principles.

> *Q. 141. What are the duties required in the eighth commandment?*
>
> A. The duties required in the eighth commandment are, truth, faithfulness, and justice in contracts and commerce between man and man; rendering to every one his due; restitution of goods unlawfully detained from the right owners thereof; giving and lending freely, according to our abilities, and the necessities of others; moderation of our judgments, wills, and affections concerning worldly goods; a provident care and study to get, keep, use, and dispose these things which are necessary and convenient for the sustentation of our nature, and suitable to our condition; a lawful calling, and diligence in it; frugality; avoiding unnecessary lawsuits, and suretiship, or other like engagements; and an endeavor, by all just and lawful means, to procure, preserve, and further the wealth and outward estate of others, as well as our own.

> *Q. 142. What are the sins forbidden in the eighth commandment?*
>
> A. The sins forbidden in the eighth commandment, besides the neglect of the duties required, are, theft, robbery, man-stealing, and receiving anything that is stolen; fraudulent dealing, false weights and measures, removing landmarks, injustice and unfaithfulness in contracts between man and man, or in matters of trust; oppression, extortion, usury, bribery, vexatious lawsuits, unjust enclosures and depredation; engrossing commodities to enhance the price; unlawful callings, and all other unjust or sinful ways of taking or withholding from our neighbor what belongs to him, or of

enriching ourselves; covetousness; inordinate prizing and affecting worldly goods; distrustful and distracting cares and studies in getting, keeping, and using them; envying at the prosperity of others; as likewise idleness, prodigality, wasteful gaming; and all other ways whereby we do unduly prejudice our own outward estate, and defrauding ourselves of the due use and comfort of that estate which God hath given us.

21. **The Fifth Commandment: superiors, inferiors, and equals**. The Larger Catechism of the Westminster Confession of Faith has some interesting discussion of the economic relations of what it calls "superiors, inferiors, and equals." The answer to Question 124, "Who are meant *by father* and *mother* in the *fifth commandment?*," is "By *father* and *mother*, in the fifth commandment, are meant, not only natural parents, but all superiors in age and gifts; and especially such as, by God's ordinance, are over us in place of authority, whether in family, church, or commonwealth." Then, the Q/A's go on to elaborate. For example, "It is required of superiors, according to that power they receive from God, and that relation wherein they stand, to love, pray for, and bless their inferiors; to instruct, counsel, and admonish them; countenancing, commending, and rewarding such as do well; and discountenancing, reproving, and chastising such as do ill; protecting, and providing for them all things necessary for soul and body ..." (Answer to Question 129). The reader is invited to review these Q/A's, as they give moral instruction to all that is beyond just the "letter of the law" in economic transactions and everyday interactions among all peoples of a culture. See the Larger Catechism, Q/A's 123-133.

22. **Capitalism**. Capitalism is a natural tendency of mankind. In one of God's most amazing providences, man's self-interest and selfishness works for both his own good and that of society relative to economics. To increase his own possessions, he must produce goods or services that others want and for which they are willing to give up a portion of their own wealth to acquire what he produces. And, he must have a good product at a price that others are willing to pay or he will lose business to his competition. Capitalism is a win-win (producer-consumer) situation.

American enterprise. The American War of Independence was war over economics, "taxation without representation." This war illustrates how closely free trade is linked to other freedoms. From that experience, limited government, especially concerning free trade, caused the United States to become the most prosperous and powerful nation on earth. Now, as we destroy virtually every God-ordained foundation of our country, we are losing not only our world power status, but our economic freedoms, as well. That we have continued to prosper until now testifies to the power of the free market, even with the restrictions now placed upon it. But, this power will not last forever, as these foundations are eroded.

Perhaps, the place where this self-interest and "common good" are most clearly seen is the "black market" of regimes in which a State has restricted trade through tariffs, fascism, favored industries, etc. At the risk of severe punishment, and even death, entrepreneurs will produce or acquire items or services that others want. Entrepreneurs strive to produce and provide what others want in the most difficult of circumstances.

23. **Government intervention**. In every culture or nation, government at every level has tried to restrict trade in various ways (as just mentioned). Such intervention has always harmed everyone over time by limiting the expansion of production and trade. Even those who benefit in the short term will lose in the long term because when the laws of God are violated before they will eventually cause the destruction of the violators. People will leave a country, establish "black markets," revolt, assassinate, destroy, and in many other ways seek to correct violations of their freedom. Unfortunately, those coming to power rarely have better solutions than those that they overthrow. God's laws are as certain to destroy, as they are to build up, when they are ignored or flagrantly violated. God's laws only bring prosperity and the good fortune of all who abide by them.

A modern example in the United States. Through thousands of minute laws, the American government has tried to increase its revenue by taxation. For decades, studies have shown that the income to the federal government, as a percentage of Gross Domestic Product, has not significantly changed over the last several decades. The creativity and ingenuity of mankind (in this case, Americans) will always far exceed the legislative powers of a State.

24. **Abuses of capitalism**. Capitalism has been much maligned, even by conservative and Christians. What is often portrayed is the vision of the "robber baron," charging exorbitant prices for the "common man" and the poor. However, this image is mostly a myth. As we have seen immediately above, entrepreneurs (even when restrained in many ways) have a creativity and ingenuity to get around these restrictions. The same is true for so-called monopolies. Industrious men will establish alternatives. Then, there is the price of the product. A "robber baron" or monopolist cannot just charge whatever he wants because the consumer will make his own evaluation of the price that he is willing to pay. Market forces with any degree of freedom just regresses to

242

the needs and wants of buyers and the prices that they are willing to pay. See the Myth of the Robber Barons.

Many monopolies are created by the State today, for example, the Federal Reserve System and regulation of utilities and insurance. These are problematic and are proscribed by previous principles that do not allow the State to be involved in economic enterprises.

25. How much profit is too much? The answer is determined solely by the seller and buyer. The seller can make as much profit as the buyer is willing to pay for the product. The Bible is quite clear from cover to cover that God encourages, even demands, profit in man's economic undertakings. The parable of the talents is a great example. Large profit is a lure of entrepreneurs to "get in on the action," so market forces "even out" the situation over time. In a free economy, the buyer is never forced to pay for what he does not want to pay.

Risk of the entrepreneur. Those who are critical of capitalism value the risk that the entrepreneur takes. "The latest statistics from the Small Business Administration (SBA) show that 'two-thirds of new employer establishments survive at least two years, and 44 percent survive at least four years.'" The entrepreneur places his present and future (a loan) capital at risk, as well as the welfare of his family. And, there are considerable costs to any business. Thus, profit is necessary, if for no other reason than the bills (costs of business) have to be paid. Also, the prospect of "bettering" oneself and his family provides an incentive for entrepreneurs. **Profit is the motive to take risk**. Without it, there would be no economy!

Lessons of history. Price controls of the early 1970s in the United States during a period of "high" inflation led to shortages and a recession. Price controls anywhere and everywhere have always produced such scarcity. The great experiment of Communist Russia led only to bare shelves and failed crops. The sale of grain to Russia by shiploads from the United States is well known. God's laws of economy cannot be thwarted in the long run!

26. Usury and interest. There has been and is much misunderstanding about the difference between charging interest and usury. "Usury in the Bible means any increase in the amount of repayment above the principle, *but only in the case of charitable loans*." Old Testament lenders were not to charge interest to a Hebrew brother. (North, Inherit the Earth, page 88-89). But, in common use since the Middle Ages, "usury" has been defined as "exorbitant interest rates," those above common or legally proscribed limits. However, the Hebrews were

243

to "lend to many nations" (Deuteronomy 28:12). That they were not to charge interest would have been an unreasonable expectation. Their capital would be at risk of non-payment, so interest pays for that risk.

Someone in need and interest. Herein, we have discussed that Biblical Principles of Social Justice give balance to market forces. Here, too, "For an individual to be merciless to someone in need when he does have the extra assets available to help that person is, in effect, to deny that he too is a debtor to God and is also in desperate need for God to intervene and repay his own debt" (North, *Inherit the Earth*, page 89). Again, social justice includes careful judgment on the part of the helper, not just an automatic hand out. Social justice is not helping everyone who comes along, but helping in a careful, Biblical way.

27. **Loans and borrowing**. "The borrower is servant to the lender" (Proverbs 22:7). The Bible permits loans at interest, but it adds cautions and conditions. Gentiles could be charged interest (Deuteronomy 22:20). A loan generally should not be taken out for more than seven years, as it was to be cancelled at that time (Deuteronomy 15:1-2). Collateral should be used to guarantee loans,, but not without consideration of excessive harm to the borrower (Exodus 22:26). We saw above that the very poor and brothers should not be charged interest which would be "usury" (Exodus 22:25; Leviticus 25:35-38). Perhaps, many of these laws are not to be taken literally, but certainly the principles that they represent should be implemented, even in modern times (the equity of the law).

Loans should always require collateral. Borrowing without collateral increases the money supply of a culture, thereby inflating the denominated cost of all items. **Inflation is theft**, as the same amount of money will no longer purchase what it would before inflation occurred. The result is the same as though that percentage of inflation had been stolen by a thief who broke into and stole from every household affected.

28. **"Fiat" money is an even worse form of theft**. When a bank loans money beyond its resources on deposit, "fiat" money has been created, that is, money that does not really exist. Such practice causes great potential disruption for economies, as has been seen in "bank runs" in recent history. Further, that increase in the money supply is inflationary, virtually stealing from anyone who holds assets of any kind.

29. **The Sabbath**. "Remember the Sabbath day, to keep it holy. Six days you shall labor and do all your work, but the seventh day is the Sabbath of the

LORD your God. In it you shall do no work: you, nor your son, nor your daughter, nor your male servant, nor your female servant, nor your cattle, nor your stranger who is within your gates. For in six days the LORD made the heavens and the earth, the sea, and all that is in them, and rested the seventh day. Therefore the LORD blessed the Sabbath day and hallowed it" (Exodus 20:8-11).

There is far too much in this Commandment to unpack here. However, the person who would understand and apply Biblical economics must seriously consider its fullness. Sometimes overlooked is "Six days you shall labor and do all your work." Almost universally throughout the world today, a work day week is five days or less. The implications of a six day work week should be contemplated. Work" may be understood more broadly than one's employment (see Vocation herein). For the Christian, "work" should be considered any activity that advances the Kingdom of God. In fact, the Christian's primary work may be to that end, rather than his employment (as the Apostle Paul made tents).

Far and away, the intent of the Sabbath is "rest," worship, and contemplation of God and His Word. For our purposes here, we will focus on "rest,:" which is the primary focus of the Commandment itself. **Any activity which prevents "rest" on the Sabbath is a violation of this commandment**.

Now, the Westminster Confession of Faith (XXI:8) and other teachings allow for "works of necessity and mercy." Jesus briefly discusses this issue in Matthew 12:1-14. My argument in this regard is two-fold. **(1) The emphasis is on "rest."** In today's fast paced society, most individuals and families do not get enough rest. The Sabbath, now Sunday, is that opportunity. Many "works of necessity" are just excuses to "catch up" on both employment-related and personal tasks. Even physicians who care for patients often cover-up work that is not truly a "necessity" with this excuse.

(2) The idea of "rest" should be extended to an every day application. My impression is that Christians are governed as much by the "tyranny of the urgent," as non-Christians. That is, their lives are one frantic attempt to meet a schedule of activities that is difficult, if not impossible to fulfill. A pattern of both vigorous work and rest should be characteristic of a Christian's life. (See Matthew 11:28-29.) A practical gauge of whether there is rest is the hour or so before bedtime in the home. Do adults and children begin to wind down calmly and deliberately or is there a frantic rush to get last minute things done and jump into bed? (See Time Management.)

There is one caveat. Life is quite unpredictable, and none of us is perfect, so many days and nights may be unavoidably frantic. However, in the main, the latter part of all evenings are a gauge for the fulfillment of work and rest in an individual or family's life.

Resources

www.freebooks.com Go to bottom of home page, click "Page Two." At the top of the page, click "Main Area." Look in the left margin column for "Books by… subject." Scroll down to Economics. I suggest for basics, these books by Gary North:

> *An Introduction to Christian Economics*
> *Honest Money*
> *Inherit the Earth*

By George Grant:

> *Bringing in the Sheaves*
> *In the Shadow of Plenty*

Books by Tom Rose, purchased new:
http://www.biblicaleconomics.com/body_books.html.

Tom Rose used books at www.amazon.com.

13. Law, Love, Grace, Mercy, Justice, and Equity

An Encounter Concerning the Practical Application of Love and Law with a Learned Professor

I recently visited a friend at one of the Reformed Theological Seminary campuses. He invited me to sit in on his Bible class, held in the evening. It "happened" that the professor was discussing the latter chapters of Exodus, including Exodus 21-23, which are detailed applications of the Mosaic Law. Briefly, he mentioned the theonomists, Christians who believe in a more particular and detailed application of the Old Testament Law, than most "evangelicals." (For some reasonable reviews of theonomy, see these links.

He was mostly fair-minded with their position, but he condemned the position of some theonomists who call for the death penalty of homosexuals. He did not, then, go on to state his own beliefs about the ethics or laws that should apply to homosexuals.

So, during break, I talked with him. I said, "If you don't think homosexuals should be put to death, what should be our ethics or laws to govern their behavior?" "Oh," he said, "I think that we should try to evangelize them. I would not shun them. In fact, I would be willing to have them in my home." He spoke in the winsome way of a loving evangelical. **But, he made a major mistake**.

"OK," I said. "What will you do, if while he is in you home, if he tries to molest your son? What will you do, if he is in the park and approaches your son? What are your recourses, then?" I could see a light go on in this "learned" professor's head, as though, "I had never thought of that."

Whatever you think of them, **the theonomists are about the business of practically applying Biblical truth**. It is not sufficient to just criticize them, you must offer an alternative. **This professor, as many Christians, have not thought through the issue of homosexuality**. Yes, we want to evangelize them, if possible. Yes, we want to befriend them and show them love. But, no, we do not want them either to approach our children, and we want to minimize their opportunities to approach our children.

247

So, the "broadly evangelical" may draw a line differently from the theonomist. **But, you either stick your head in the sand and ignore the issue, or you draw a line somewhere that the homosexual does not cross on penalty of law.** God requires government to restrain evil (Romans 13:3). But, **we cannot have this patronizing nonsense of limiting our actions only to loving them into the Kingdom!**

The Law (Known and Practiced) Before Sinai

* The following is re-printed from *The Law of the Covenant*, by James Jordan (Institute for Christian Economics, 1984). It may be found on the web at Freebooks. Emphases are mine.

> Paul tells us that the law was in operation before Sinai, when he says "for until the law sin was in the world; but sin is not imputed when there is no law. Nevertheless death reigned from Adam to Moses" (Romans 5:13, 14a). Before the law "came ," the law was already in operation, for it was already dealing death to sinners. (Similarly, before the New Covenant "came, " it was already in operation, for it was already granting resurrection life to repentant men.) At Sinai, the law was given a definitive publication, but it was already operating in the world, and was already known to men.[1]

> Indeed, Paul says "just as through one man sin entered into the world, and death through sin, and so death spread to all men, because all sinned" (Romans 5:12). In other words, the same law which came at Sinai was operating in the Garden. This is the connection between the Old (Adamic) Covenant and the Old (Sinaitic) Covenant.'[2]

> **It is often thought that at Sinai God set up something new, a new administration of law, which had not been in force previously.** We have seen from Paul that this was not the case, for the law was in operation in the Garden, and in the period between the Fall and Sinai. We can also turn to passages in Genesis and in Exodus before Sinai and see that people knew the law before it was written down by Moses.

248

First of all, we have demonstrated that the laws of slavery were known and functioned in the life of Jacob and in the interaction between Moses and Pharaoh. *Second*, the law of evidence concerning torn beasts (Exodus 22:13) is referred to by Jacob in Genesis 31:39. *Third*, Exodus 21:1 and 24:3 call these laws *mishpatim*, and Abraham is said to know the *mishpatim* in Genesis 18:19. Also, in Genesis 26:5, Abraham is said to have "kept My charge, My commandments, My statutes, and My laws ." This is surely more than the Ten Commandments !

Fourth, Deuteronomy 22:28-29 does not order capital punishment n the case where a young man forcibly seduces a young girl, but commands him to marry her. This law was clearly being followed to the letter in Genesis 34, which concerns the relations between Shechem and Dinah. Because Simeon and Levi broke the not-yet-written law, Jacob condemned their actions (Genesis 49:5 -7).[3]

Fifth, the laws of sacrifice were known, including the distinctions among various kinds of sacrifices (Ex. 20:24, which comes before Leviticus 1-7). *Sixth*, Noah knew the difference between clean and unclean animals (Gen. 7:2), yet the rules for these distinctions were not given in written form until Leviticus 11. *Seventh*, even though we do not read of God's commanding the people to have a tent of meeting until He ordered the building of the Tabernacle, from Exodus 33:7-11 it is clear that there already was one. It was the place of religious meeting and worship, and God talked with Moses there, before the Tabernacle was built.

Eighth and last, although other examples can be found, the law of the Levirate, requiring a brother to raise up seed for his childless dead brother (Deuteronomy 25:5, 6), was clearly known and operative in the history of Tamar (Gen. 38).

Of course, unbelieving scholars use passages such as these to argue that somebody rewrote the "original myths" of Genesis to make them conform to the "later Mosaic legislation." The fact is, rather, that God had been telling his people all along what He wanted them to do. The law was given many times before Sinai; but it was definitively written down by Moses, in connection with the preeminent redemptive event of the Old Covenant period (Deuteronomy 4:2).[4]

Law and Love Are Founded in God's Truth and Holiness (Righteousness), But Love Must Be Directed by God's Law

Christian (Biblical) doctrine is a harmonious unity whose main axis is the nature of God. For this reason, a correct understanding of the whole range of Christian (Biblical) faith and duty turns on a proper comprehension of divine attributes. How the theologian defines and relates God's sovereignty, righteousness, and love actually predetermines his exposition of basic positions in many areas -- in social ethics no less than in soteriology (salvation) and eschatology (future events). **Even the smallest deviation from the Biblical view of divine justice and divine benevolence eventually implies far-reaching consequences for the entire realm of Christian life and truth**.

It is important, therefore, to note the historic evangelical emphasis that righteousness (law) and benevolence (grace mercy, and love) are equally ultimate in the unity of the divine nature. **In accord with Biblical theology, evangelical Christianity affirms that justice is an immutable, divine quality not reducible to a mere mode of divine benevolence on the fallacious theory that love is the exclusive center and core of God's being**.

"Dissolving of justice into love cancels any separate function for justice in the moral order of the world, shifts the motive force of ethical theory (worldview) to benevolence instead, and misinterprets love as a universal rather than a particular manifestation of the divine nature... (this) **love blurs and erases the fundamental distinction between justice and benevolence in the politico-economic realm**. (Carl F. H. Henry, *Aspects of Christian Social Ethics*, pages146-147 -- Ed's emphasis and insertion of corresponding words.)

"If God's laws were not wise and holy, God would not enjoin them; and if they are so, **we deny infinite wisdom and holiness in God by not complying with them**." (Stephen Charnock, *The Existence and Attributes of God*, page 95 -- Ed's emphasis.)

250

Love, law, and justice, mercy, and grace, comprise the most central message of the Bible. However, their use among Christians is often misplaced. Quite common is the verse, "God is love." Less common, if not rare, is "God is law." Yet, which is more important? Which is prior?

Of course, "God is law," may be stated as, "God is righteous" or "God is Holy." But, as we will see, God's law is a manifestation of His righteousness and holiness. Even, prior to those attributes, He must be truth. For, if God cannot be trusted in what He says, what He says does not matter. If we have to ferret out His truth on our own, the Bible is of no help to us. We are still on our own with or without the Scriptures. But, the central message of this website, The Christian and Biblical Worldview for the 21st Century is that the Bible is infallible, inerrant, and bears the full weight of God's voice and authority, as truth.

But, what is God law? First, all Christians would agree that God is righteous. But, to be "right" or "righteous," requires a standard by which to judge what is right or wrong. **God is that standard**. But, God is not present here on earth for us to question Him or to have Him write down his standards. But, then, why should he? He has already done so in the **66 books of the Protestant Bible**.

One source cites 613 commandments in the Old Testament![5] Virtually all of the commandments of the New Testament are represented in those commandments except perhaps the fullest expression of the commandment to love (John 13:34, 15:12, 17:20-23; I Corinthians 13; etc.).

Ah, I hear it coming, "We (Christians) are not under law, but under grace!" That is not really the issue here (although we will address it later). **We are concerned with God's standard, His character, and what He requires of us. That requirement is the detail of the 613 commandments and the new commandment of love.**

God is infinitely Holy, and to have fellowship with man, he must be "holy as I am holy." Man cannot begin to achieve that standard. It is infinitely above him. In fact, C. S. Lewis said that a recording of moral statements that any individual makes over his lifetime would convict him without applying any outside moral standard.

You see, if you do not understand the exact and detailed standard of God's law, you cannot fully appreciate the greatness of the sacrifice of God's Son for sinners. The Shorter Catechism defines sin as "any want of conformity unto or transgression of any law of God."

So, Christians start at the wrong place in starting with God's love. God's love enters because God is truth, and He has a standard, His law. "For God so loved the world…" (John 3:16). What was the situation that called for this love? What was wrong that the world needed God's love? What is wrong is that man (first, Adam, and then ourselves) has broken God's law and is unable to pay the price that God requires.

So, God's law is prior to God's love in salvation. For that reason, law is the most important understanding of God's character after His being Truth. Many, many Christians have this reversed. **God's love has no content apart from God's law. The fullness and greatness of Christ's sacrifice is empty and meaningless without understanding God's law being fulfilled in Christ for His people.**

What is Biblical Law?

Biblical law is probably the most complex subject in the Bible. Robertson McQuilkin cites his father's book in which "law" is used at least twelve different ways in the Bible.[6] Dr. McQuilkin goes on to name six of these uses.

> 1) **The Moral Law.** "Law as the expressed will of God that people be like Him morally (ethically).… There are, no doubt, other elements in man's likeness to God, but a morally right character is primary (consistent with my thoughts above).… Mankind has ever neglected this aspect of God's image and worked to attain likeness to god in His attributes of knowledge and power.
>
> "This most important use of the word *law* is often called the 'moral law,' God's expressed will concerning what constitutes likeness to God.… the work of the law written in the hearts of those who do not have the written law (Romans 2:14-15).… 'Through the law comes knowledge of sin' (Romans 3:20… or all the commandments of God which deal with human

behavior" (Romans 4:15, 7:2,5; I Corinthians 7:19; Galatians 3:13; I Timothy 1:8; Hebrews 8:10ff (to name a few).

2) **The Mosaic Legal System** … "the entire network of regulations given by God to Israel for the era beginning with Moses and ending with Jesus Christ, who came to fulfill the law …" (John 1:17, Romans 5:13, Galatians 3:23, for example).

3) **Obedience to the Law**. "Sometimes the term law is used figuratively to refer to a person's obedient response to the law …" (Romans 3:20 - "works of the law"; Galatians 2:21).

4) "**Law as the Old Testament**… The Hebrew Bible was commonly divided into three sections, commonly called the Law, the Prophets, and the Writings (sometimes called the Psalms)…. Christ spoke of … the law of Moses, the prophets, and the psalms" (Luke 24:44).

5) "**Law as Specific Laws**… Sometimes, the term law refers to specific commandments, such as the Ten Commandments (Romans 2:20ff…). "We have a law (John 19:7) is another example of a specific law in mind. When Paul speaks of fulfilling the law of Christ in Galatians 6:2, and when James speaks of the royal law (James 2:8), the reference is to the specific law of love."

6) "**Law as an Operating Principle**… Sometimes, the New Testament uses the term law to mean a principle much as we would say 'the law of gravity.' 'The law of my mind' and 'the law of sin (Romans 7:23, 25), 'the law of the Spirit of life' (Romans 8:2), and 'the principle of faith' (Romans 3:27) are all examples of the term law being used as a synonym for 'principle.'"

Robert McQuilkin goes on to name six other uses of "law" in his book, but this will suffice for our study here.

(**Teaching momen**t: Now is a good time to reinforce the need for hermeneutics or principles by which Scripture should be interpreted. One of the most important is that the same word can have different definitions. "Law" probably has more than any other! The remarkable thing about this hermeneutic is that it is true for the understanding of any writing or book, not just the Bible. For more on hermeneutics.)

(**2nd Teaching moment**. As a practical exercise, list how many synonyms of "law" are present in the Bible. Psalm 119 is a good place to start where testimonies, His ways, precepts, statutes, commandments, righteous and judgments appear under the first section! There are many others throughout the Bible.)

In this paper and on this website, **"law" will be used to designate all laws (and their synonyms named above) of the Old and New Testaments except those that were explicitly ceremonial and those applicable only Israel as a nation within those geographical boundaries prescribed by God.** (See Webster's 1828 dictionary for his 26 definitions of "law," below.)

"Love" must be seen in the context of this "law." Even to begin to understand the breadth and depth of John 3:16, "For God so loved the world, that He gave His only begotten Son..." absolutely must be framed by the background of God's law or righteousness.

Robertson goes on to say:

> This is exciting. It means that the foundation of our moral standard is not man, his wisdom, his fallen nature, his desires, his values, his traditions, nor his culture... Since God Himself is our standard, our standard is not relative, changing with each age or society. God's law is absolute, perfect, unchanging, and eternal.
>
> (And) This standard is personal, living, and visible rather than a dead code... It derives from His own nature.

Love Considered with Law as Background

Robertson McQuilkin. Let us start with the views of some others to demonstrate the intimate relationship of love with law. Since we have been spending time with Dr. Robertson McQuilkin, we will start with him (pages 28-29).

Perhaps, the most extensive descriptions of love are the commands of Scripture.... The commands of Scripture reveal God's will for those to whom they are addressed and that his ultimate will is that we be like him in moral character. Since "God is love," it should come as no surprise that the entire Old Testament revelation of God's will for man hangs on the law of love (Matthew 22:37-40). After stating The Golden Rule, Jesus concluded, "For this is [the essence of] the law and the prophets (Matthew 7:12). Paul repeats the thought: "For the whole law is fulfilled in one word, 'You shall love your neighbor as yourself' (Galatians 5:14). Again, he says that this law of love sums up the Ten Commandments.

This basic fact about the relationship of love to the commandments of Scripture means that every command applicable to Christians is a description of how love will behave. **In other words, the instructions for life in Scripture give substance and definition to the basic law of love**. (McQuilkin's emphasis).

G. I. Williamson. Perhaps, the most widely read commentary on The Westminster Confession of Faith was written by G. I. Williamson. Concerning Chapter 18 of the Confession, he divides the Ten Commandments into two sections:

The Love of God -- Man's Duty to God (1-4)

The Love of Man -- Man's Duty to Man (5-10)

Thus, the Two Great Commandments of Jesus Christ (Matthew 22:33-38) are made more explicit by the Ten Commandments.

Henry Stob. Henry Stob taught at Calvin Theological Seminary in Philosophical and Moral Theology. He was founder and editor of *The Reformed Journal*. He has one of the best books on Biblical ethics that I have in my library. It is an unknown gem. And, for our purposes here, he has the best material that I have read on the interrelatedness of law and love. (Later, we will cite him on justice, as well.) In this book, he has a chapter on "Love and Law: The New and the Old Morality." In general, the old morality is that of Old Testament law (a morality of rules of right conduct and of obedience). The new morality has to do with ends (as the Greeks first posited).

> The new morality is a morality of love. But, it does not therefore repudiate law.... The new morality speaks, accordingly, of a veritable law: the law of love.... But this means that love is law... Love absorbs law and virtually removes it from sight.... The old ethic is an ethic of law. But it does not repudiate love.... A unity of law and love is effected which is a virtual identification of the two. Law absorbs love and virtually removes it from sight.
>
> Law, in order to rightly to function as a guide, must be informed by the sensitivities of love, just as love, in order to do the same, must be structured by law.
>
> Law and love are not to be smelted together beyond recognition, so that one is at liberty to construct, at a whim, either a pure teleology or a pure deontology. What is needed is not simple identity, but holy marriage and mutual embracement. What is needed is a loving obedience and an obedient love.

Herein is essence and end of the law-love debate. Love is blind and must have the direction of law. Law must have the sensitivity, and Stob adds later, the sacrifice and extension of love that far exceeds law.

To put everything together, one final characteristic of God is needed: justice.

Love, Mercy, and Grace

Some theologians discuss the interrelatedness of law and grace, while others discuss law and love. Still others discuss law and gospel. That difference in approach has caused me to reflect and research a great deal on these Biblical terms. In addition, mercy seems closely related, as well.

In reviewing these terms, there is a great deal of overlap.

In salvation: "For God so **loved** the world that He gave His own begotten Son that whoever believes in Him should not perish, but have everlasting life" (John 3:16), yet "By **grace** are you saved through

256

faith, and that not of yourselves, it is a gift of god" (Ephesians 2:8-9). "He has mercy on whom He wills" (Romans 9:18).

Attribute of God: "God is **love**" (I John 4:8), but Jesus Christ was "full of **grace** and truth" (John 1:14). The Apostle Paul introduce his Epistles with "Grace, **mercy**, and peace." "You are not under law, but under **grace**" (Romans 6:14). "**Love** is the fulfillment of the law" (Romans 13:10). "God who is rich in **mercy**" (Ephesians 2:4).

From these few hours of review and reflection, "grace" and "love" seem to be virtual synonyms, as they apply to God's favor towards His own. However, His "common grace" applies to all mankind. He never expresses "love" for all mankind.

While mercy seems to carry the full weight of God's saving activity and a particular attribute of Himself, it does have some nuances that separate it from love. Mercy denotes being applied to someone who is miserable and pitiable. Love and grace can be given to people in all situations, whether they are miserable or relatively comfortable. And, of course, mercy within the Godhead is not applicable at all.

And, these distinctions are the best that I can do after consulting about a dozen books and dictionaries, many Bible verses, even reviewing some of the New Testament Greek words. If some readers have some specific ideas on these words, or have a great source that discusses all three, please email me.

But, for our purposes here. **Any distinctions in love and grace do not matter**. We are considering the intimate connection between law and love. Since one of my references contrasts law and grace, in my discussion, **I will consider grace and love as synonyms**.

Justice, Love, and Law Meet at the Cross and in Worldview!

> Justice is concerned with the distribution of goods and evils to each in accordance with what is *due* to each. Justice has to do with due allocation: goods to whom goods are due; evils to whom evils are due. The formula is: To each what is coming to him… Justice is concerned with moral symmetry.

Justice is best defined as "giving every one his due," the term "due" being a wide and neutral term serving to cover all forms of justice. (Stob, page 124.)

Justice, then, would require that God should punish all men because "all have fallen short of the glory (righteousness, law) of God (Romans 3:23). God's love saves all those who "believe on His name." **Thus, God's love supercedes His justice to save some**. For Christians, this understanding should temper their call for justice in all situations.

But, there is another side to God's love, and that brings us back to God's law.

> **If you want to know what to do (that is, to love), you have only one place to go -- to law**… Love is by nature "empty"; it is constitutionally unable to give guidance… This law¾ fixed, constant, and unbending¾ ignores variable situations and circumstances, stifles every imaginative and creative form of compassion, and leaves no room for adaptation and adjustment.

> Law in order rightly to function as guide, must be informed by the sensitivities of love, just as love … must be structured by law…. What is needed is not simple identity (of each) but holy marriage and mutual embracement. What is needed is a loving obedience and an obedient love. (Stob, page 145)

And, from John Murray:

> The norms and canons which define the biblical ethic (worldview) are simply the reading of love's dictates, the crystallizations and formulations of the necessary outflow of love to God and to our fellowmen…. The Biblical ethic (worldview) (is) the sum-total of the ways in which the renewed consciousness (regeneration) reacts to the demands of the diversified concrete situations in which it is placed. (Murray, page 21-22)[7]

These wise men are only telling us what God has already told us in His Word.

If you love me, keep my commandments (all the commandments of the Old and New Testaments). John 14:15

If you keep My commandments, you will abide in My love, just as I have kept My Father's commandments and abide in His love. John 15:10

He who loves another has fulfilled the law. Romans 13:8

For the commandments, "You shall not commit adultery," "You shall not murder," "You shall not steal," "You shall not bear false witness," "You shall not covet," and if there is any other commandment, are all summed up in this saying, namely, "You shall love your neighbor as yourself." Romans 13:9

Love is the fulfillment of the law. Romans 13:10

For all the law is fulfilled in one word, even in this: "You shall love your neighbor as yourself. Galatians 5:14

If you really fulfill the royal law according to the Scripture, "You shall love your neighbor as yourself," you do well. James 2:8

The concept of God's law in relation to God's love in salvation is the most important concept in the Bible (after God is Truth and His Word is truth). The definition of sin cannot be known without knowing God's law, as representative of God's righteousness. "Sin is any want of conformity or transgression of the law of God." (See above.) What is the perfection that God requires for salvation, the perfect keeping of the law? All 613 commandments (above) or the equity (below) thereof.

Some have said that there are two purposes of the law. 1) The law demonstrates our inability to keep God's standards of righteousness, and therefore, leads us to Christ who perfectly fulfilled the law and applies His righteousness to those who believe on His name. 2) The law gives direction to the love after we have been born-again.

The Situation Determines Which Biblical Principles and Law Apply

To mention "situation" in the context of discussion among Christians is to cause a vigorous, almost knee-jerk, response among evangelicals. Since Joseph Fletcher's Situation Ethics, the word "situation" has become anathema to us. And, that has happened for good reason. (Read carefully.) Fletcher and other non-evangelicals say that the situation determines the ethics, or the right or wrong behavior to follow. The Bible says that the situation determines the commandments or the principles that we are to follow.

With Fletcher, there are no absolutes or fixed principles, only those determined by the moment. **With God, His commandments and principles has already been established. The situation determines which ones apply.**

Let us consider an example relative to justice. With a criminal caught in theft, the modern situation (of public opinion and court justice) is to punish the criminal by imprisonment only.

But, biblical justice has five purposes in justice: 1) restoration to the one from whom goods were stolen, sometimes several-fold of what was stolen (!), 2) punishment, not by imprisonment, 3) deterrence, 4) rehabilitation, and 5) satisfaction of the criminal's own concept of justice.

Another example is the modern concept of adultery, commonly called divorce due to "incompatibility." That is, if one finds himself or herself in a marriage where one spouse finds that they do not "love" the other, the situation (and modern state laws) allows them to divorce and remarry. Historically, modern divorce laws can easily be traced to the liberal "ethical" ideas of Fletcher and others.

But, biblical justice requires that divorce be granted only for adultery or for desertion of an unbeliever from a believer.[8] And, Biblical justice requires that churches deal with situations of divorce within their congregations.[9] These are commandments and principles that one will never find among situational ethicists (that is, pagan, non-Biblical worldview).

I have heard and read of pastors and other Christians who have tried to "justify" their adulteries with pagan concepts of "love." But, this is a illustrative example of "love" that is unbiblical contrasted with Biblical love. Please re-read, if you do not remember what Murray and Stob said on the guiding directive of "law" for love. **Biblical law is the only limit on "love" being anything that one wants it to be!**

Biblical Justice in Different Situations

Let us suppose that Mr. Smith has stolen a car, valued at $25,000 from Mr. Jones, both members of the same congregation. Mr. Smith has been caught by the police with clear evidence that he is guilty. How would this sin/crime be handled at different levels?

(Caveat: What follows is within the principles of Biblical justice. I am not saying that they are either comprehensive or the best principles to be applied. I am only illustrating how justice varies with different authorities, and the great practicality of these principles.)

Biblical justice between Christians. Mr. Jones must make restitution of the car to Mr. Jones and any expenses that he incurred from the absence of the automobile. Mr. Smith must also ask forgiveness from Mr. Jones, and Mr. Jones must forgive him (even if Mr. Smith is a repeat offender -- Matthew 18:22).

Biblical justice in the Church. The church leaders (elders or deacons, depending upon the form of church government) must investigate the situation and determine what oversight that they must give (Matthew 18:15-20).

And, if Mr. Jones does not forgive Mr. Smith, Mr. Jones may become the offending party! The church leaders must give oversight to both.

Biblical justice in the courtroom. The state (used for all levels of government, not just the states of America) has the authority of God to "punish evil" (Romans 13:1-4). Automobile theft is a crime and punishable by state law.

But, in an ideally Biblical society, does the state have to be involved? Does the local church have to be involved. No!

If Mr. Smith and Mr. Jones work out a Biblically satisfying arrangement, the situation can end there! The church does not have to be involved: the verses cited above clearly state that if either party is not satisfied, then one or both takes it to the church. Now, if Mr. Smith is a repeat offender, it may be wise for Mr. Jones to take it to the church.

And, the state does not have to be involved, if Mr. Smith and Mr. Jones can work out an equitable (Biblical) arrangement.

Practical application: if individuals were allowed to settle interpersonal crimes, this would greatly reduce the caseloads of the states! However, in today's litigious and pagan society, I would grant that this application may not work. But, in a Biblical conscientious society, I contend that it would.

Capital punishment. In cases of the loss of human life (not due to "natural" causes), God has mandated that the state investigate, for only the state has the power of capital punishment (Romans 13:4). Of course, the individual has the God-given right to kill in self-defense, a situation where the state should declare the killer innocent.

These issues of Biblical justice ever so brief, but I have expanded them a more fully at the following URL with a reference there to a more comprehensive discussion of justice by Vern Poythress. (Crime and Punishment)

Social Justice

Perhaps, what comes to mind most frequently when someone mentions the word, "justice," is social justice. "Giving everyone their due," then, becomes the removal of all things that appear to be "unfair" in society: racial inequality, salaries for men vs. women, equal employment opportunities, sexual harassment in the work place, "right" to medical care, providing income to those below the "poverty" line, "fair" wages for blue collar workers, access for those with disabilities, etc. The list is virtually endless. We are a society which is overly concerned with "social justice."

Yet, what have been achieved with this focus? After at least $50 trillion, poverty is unchanged. Little progress has been made against gender inequality of salaries. Medical care is demonstrably producing

262

more harm that good. Mothers abort one in three of their children. The elderly literally rot away in nursing homes. Euthanasia looms on the horizon in America, while it is a reality in The Netherlands. Pornography is a growing industry. Social security is bankrupt. The federal budget is ballooning out of control. And, on and on.

With a society so focused on justice, what is wrong? **I would posit that the fundamental problem is the concept of justice. We want a society that gives the "good" to everyone regardless of responsibility**. Children cannot be failed in school because "it might hurt their feelings." Everyone must have the latest and best medical care, regardless of their ability to pay or their responsibility for their own injuries and illnesses. Everyone must have the same pay scale, regardless of the market value of their services. Everyone must have social security income, regardless of their need. "Art" cannot be defined, because it must have its freedom of expression. **And, it is the state's responsibility to make sure that all these things happen by legislative or judicial fiat**.

Now, I recognize the global nature of the three prior paragraphs. But, they are sufficiently in the "ballpark" for our application here.

Let me take my position, one step further, **we need the Biblical concept of justice**. The three "inalienable rights" of the American Declaration of Independence are "life, liberty, and the pursuit of happiness." But, the signers of the Declaration posited these concepts **on the Biblical concept of justice, the laws of nature and of nature's God**. Writings and speeches from those times clearly demonstrate that rights and responsibilities were linked.

Perhaps, the best illustration comes from the undisputed father of American and English jurisprudence, William Blackstone. In Section 2 of his Introduction to his commentaries on law, he begins.

> Law, in it's most general and comprehensive sense, signifies a rule of action; and is applied indiscriminately to all kinds of action, **whether animate, or inanimate, rational or irrational**. Thus, we say the laws of motion, of gravitation, of optics, of mechanics, as well as the laws of nature **and of nations**. And, it is that rule of action which is prescribed by some superior, and which the inferior is bound to obey... the

supreme being formed the universe, and created matter out of nothing. (Ed's emphasis)

Blackstone moves in a few paragraphs of continuing discussion on the theme that, as the universe and all forms of life are governed by the laws of nature, man is also subject to laws, the obedience of which will lead to individual happiness and an ordered society.

The most major mistake that is made by those who might contend for "natural law" or "the law of nature's God" is to miss its need for the specificity of the Scriptures.[10] Blackstone does not make this error.

> This (man's corrupt reason and ignorant, erroneous understanding) has given manifold occasion for the benign interposition of divine providence; which, in compassion to the frailty, the imperfection, and the blindness of human reason, has been pleased, at sundry times and in diverse manners, to discover and enforce its laws by an immediate and direct revelation. The doctrines thus delivered we call the revealed or divine law, and they are to be found only in the holy scriptures. These precepts, when revealed, are found upon comparison to be really a part of the original law of nature, as they tend in all their consequences to man's felicity. But **we are not from thence to conclude that the knowledge of these truths was attainable by reason,** in its present corrupted state; since we find that, **until they were revealed,** they were hid from the wisdom of ages. As then the moral precepts of this law are indeed of the same original with those of the law of nature, so their Intrinsic obligation is of equal strength and perpetuity. Yet undoubtedly **the revealed law is of infinitely more authenticity than that moral system,** which is framed by ethical writers, and denominated the natural law. Because one is the law of nature, **expressly declared so to be by God himself**; the other is only what, by the assistance of human reason, we imagine to be that law. If we could be as certain of the latter as we are of the former, both would have an equal authority; but, till then, they can never be put in any competition together.
>
> **Upon these two foundations, the law of nature and the law of revelation, depend all human laws; that is to say, no**

human laws should be suffered to contradict these. (Ed's emphasis)

My knowledge of the history of natural law theory is almost nil. I do not know upon what premises such theory was based. I do not know who posited these theories and in what ages. Nor, do I know to what extent such theory has been developed. Perhaps, such law was founded upon certain Scriptures (for example, Romans 1:26, 27; I Corinthians 11:14). But, one Biblical hermeneutic is that explicit statements interpret all those statements that are less clear. Scripture is "explicit" revelation and nature is "general" revelation, if you will. (Link to specific principle in Hermeneutics.)

But, this I know and proclaim with every fiber of my rational and regenerated understanding, paraphrasing Blackstone himself: **the explicit statements of divine ethics and law always, always trump natural law derived in any other manner where any difference is found**.

This derivation of law with the Scriptures, as the explicit determining factor of law, is the great neglect of Bible-believing Christians. (Non-Bible-believers do not care about the Scriptures, so they are irrelevant here.) They have not been able to be both pro-life and pro-capital punishment, as Scripture is. They have not been able to show mercy to homosexuals, while upholding laws against homosexuality. They have believed that the provision of welfare by the state is Biblical charity. They have helped to enact state law for disabilities. They have not been able to support "just" wars. They have misunderstood the separation of church and state. They have just accepted the current penal system imprisonment as the only form of punishment. They have not understood the concept of civil liberty, as it grew out of the Reformation. And, and hundreds of other wrong or omitted conceptions of Biblical law.

Trying to Bring All This Together

There is a beautiful unity to love, law, mercy, justice, grace, righteousness, and holiness within this Biblical framework that is centered on God Himself.[11] These words and their corresponding concepts are like the facets of a diamond of perfect construction. The concept of man's salvation, corresponds to the concept of law and justice in society and in the state. We have these concepts rooted in

God Himself, as He is described in Scripture, for He cannot be described accurately in any other way. We have a system that promotes the summon bonum of individuals, families, churches, and nations, while never compromising the rights of anyone. O, Christian, grasp the fullness of your heritage!

There is a saying that "The Devil is in the particulars." But, in this case, Christ is in the particulars!

The letter of the law is brutal. It would make no provision for applying capital punishment to both the pre-meditated murderer and the motorist who lost concentration for a moment and killed a pedestrian. Love and mercy would allow both to go free, realizing that all men are fallible and subject to their nature and nurture.

But, Biblical justice is the answer. Distinctions are made between pre-mediated murder and accidental manslaughter. A man could flee to a "city of refuge," where he would be tried, and if found to be innocent of pre-meditated murder, then he could live there until the high priest died. There is a distinction between a woman who cries out in rape and the one who does not. And, hundreds of other factors in laws governing other crimes.

"Oh, how I love thy law," the Psalmist cried. The law? Yes, the law. The law is foundational to love, mercy, justice, and all other Biblical concepts.

Christian, do you cry, "Oh, how I love thy law?" Do you love the whole law, the whole law of the Old and New Testaments? Do you know the whole law? Do you know the law? If not, what is your intention today to study and learn the law?

Biblical law defines the Biblical worldview and Biblical ethics.

Mercy and Equity

From a study of casuistry, one comes to realize that it is impossible to write sufficient details in ethics or law to cover every possible human situation. This complexity requires judgment, judges, mercy, and equity. If the law were sufficient to cover all crimes, then no judges would be needed. Any person could just look up the particular crime in a book and prescribe the penalty. But, there is the situation to be considered. Was the murder premeditated or in the heat of passion? Was this murder an isolated event, or did the person have a pattern of similar offenses? What are some principles?

1) **Justice must be fulfilled**. For guilty man to be saved, God's law had to be satisfied. God focused the full wrath of His perfect justice on His own Son. In a sense, the law was twice fulfilled. Christ, the Son, fulfilled the law of God perfectly. God, the Father, fulfilled the law perfectly in punishing His Son in the perfect fulfillment of the law. **Only after this double fulfillment of the law is love, mercy, and grace demonstrated and applied to some**.

Mercy cannot be shown without the background of God's law, for how else can mercy be known as mercy? For what sin or crime is mercy being shown? So, the details of God's law written in God's Word shows mercy in its prescription of sanctions for different situations.

But, let's be careful here and not make the modern error of compassion (pretended mercy and love) over justice. What is the worst sin or crime under God's judgment? Pre-meditated murder? Stealing from the church offering? Robbing widows and orphans? Drunken driving?

No, a hardened heart evidenced by unrepentance. Pre-meditated murder shows deliberate intention over time. Repetitive crimes show a pattern that has no regret. Vicious crimes show evidence of a disregard for the value of human life.

Now, **there is a difference between sorrow at getting caught and repentance**. The Bible describes this in II Corinthians 7:8-12. We do not have the time to go into these distinctions, but this incorrigibility is of central importance to Biblical justice. **The goals in justice are always restitution, reconciliation, and repentance (a changed mind and behavior)**. However, the evidences of a hardened heart in the absence of any concept of the value of property or animal and human life and repetitive crimes demonstrate the difficulty, if not impossibility, of these three goals.

So, even within the particulars of Old Testament law, justice and even mercy, are woven into the law. **But, with solid evidence of**

recalcitrance and the severity of crimes performed, punishment must be carried out, including the death penalty.

2) **Every effort should be made to see that the law if fairly applied in individual cases and in all cases consistently**. This principle seems self-explanatory.

3) **Distinction between sins and crimes**. Passages like Matthew 5:38b and Romans 12:17-21 are instructions in personal relationships with believers and unbelievers, not the avoidance of self-defense or tolerance of repetitive crimes. Crimes within the framework of justice and mercy above, must be punished according to the law, as prescribed by Romans 13:1-5 and elsewhere. While Christians must be pacifists relative to personal revenge and tolerant to personal offenses, they cannot be tolerant to evil. God has ordained the "sword" of the civil government to this end.

While the church is limited to the power of spiritual judgment only, the power of the state may have to be appealed for intervention if the person who is disciplined becomes physically aggressive towards the church or any of its members. Likewise, the church may assist the state to carry out acts of mercy and love, even as the state exercises the power of the "sword" (physical punishment). So, each has its sphere, but the two should be mutually supportive to each other's mission.

You Can't Be Serious: The Old Testament Law Today?

I am so serious that I will go further. **The Old Testament Law is the only source of ethics and law that will deliver us from the modern culture of disease, debt, and death**. Am I then, a theonomist? Well, yes and no. I am a theonomist in the sense in which I just made that statement and the statements that follow here. I am not a theonomist by the caricature in which that term is usually applied. If you have come this far, come with me further. (And, for a reasoned view of theonomists, see Reconstruction under Worldview Areas.)

The Apostle Paul said, "You shall not muzzle an ox while it treads out the grain" (I Corinthians 9:9; I Timothy 5:18). Virtually every Christian, especially pastors, agree that this verse applies to the payment of support for ministers of the Word. Yet, look at the leap! From allowing an ox to graze while working in Old Testament times to the financial support of 21st Century ministers and missions is a huge leap! Christian, don't miss this leap. It is central to the concept of worldview and the solution of social and state concerns.

Or, "When you build a new house, then you shall make a parapet for your roof, that you may not bring guilt of bloodshed on your household if anyone falls from it" (Deuteronomy 22:8). A modern application would be to have a fence around one's swimming pool to prevent children and animals from falling in and drowning or on a balcony on a building. Again, from Old Testament homes with roofs on which people walked to modern swimming pools and balconies is a vast leap of time and culture.

I believe that diligent study would find great creativity in the application of these laws to modern society. But, if the study is not done, we will never benefit from God's gracious instructions.

If the choice that Moses gave to his people was to follow the law to life and prosperity or to disregard the law to their destruction and despair (see below), is our choice any different today? Is not our choice to follow God's law today the same as that proclaimed by our forefathers to the ends of "life, liberty, and the pursuit of happiness."[12]

But, This Importance of the Law Is Just "Old Hat"

We have forgotten our heritage. The Reformers (John Calvin, Martin Luther, John Knox, and others) knew this Old Testament link. I have quoted William Blackstone who probably applied more Biblical law to civil law than any other man in history. The English common law was sometimes called "The Law of Liberty of Moses." Its application to case law became so widely known that even today one definition of equity is that system of law.

And, there is the obvious heritage of the Ten Commandments. Our example of "muzzling the ox" as paying the preacher would be covered by the Eighth Commandment. Our example of fencing one's roof or swimming pool would be covered by the Sixth Commandment.

Perhaps, the greatest expression of the broad, but accurate, application of the Ten Commandments is the Larger Catechism of the Westminster Confession of Faith. In the discussion of this website title, "The", I have shown how Christians in the pro-life movement could have found balance in their views of capital punishment, just war, and self-defense from Q/A 136 in one phrase!

So, Christian, the Old Testament as the basis of law and culture is not new! As Blackstone said, it is as old as the Garden of Eden and man's musings in nature until Revelation. Explicitly, it is as old as the Word written itself. More recently, it is the fabric and foundation of the Protestant Reformation and the Great Awakening in America!

(Oh, by the way, if you agree that Paul was right, that is, God was right about "not muzzling the ox" and paying workers of the Word, then you are a true theonomist!)

Well, What About the New Testament?

If you want to throw out the Old Testament and avoid being a true theonomist, the New Testament will not let you off the hook. While the New Testament does not have the civil application of the law, as the Old Testament does, there is considerable evidence that the law continued to have the same high regard in the New Testament, as in the old.

There is also the question, "Where does any law come from?" **Law always and inevitably comes from someone's ethics, that is what one thinks is right or wrong or what one considers to be righteous or sinful**. As we will see in the next section, the sources for morality are quite limited, and their authority is quite suspect from the beginning (rule of a majority vote or individual power).

"But if our unrighteousness commend the righteousness of God, what shall we say? Is God unrighteous who taketh vengeance? (I speak as a man). God forbid: for then how shall God judge the world?" (Romans 3:5-6). My simple conclusion is that, if the law is God's criteria for judging the world, can there be criteria from any other source that is better?

> Let every soul be subject to the governing authorities. For there is no authority except from God, and the authorities that exist are appointed by God. Therefore whoever resists the authority resists the ordinance of God, and those who resist will bring judgment on themselves. For rulers are not a terror to good works, but to evil. Do you want to be unafraid of the

authority? Do what is good, and you will have praise from the same. For he is God's minister to you for good. But if you do evil, be afraid; for he does not bear the sword in vain; for he is God's minister, an avenger to execute wrath on him who practices evil. (Romans 13:1-4)

State authorities are to "minister to you for good" and "to execute wrath on him who practices evil." The full power of these simple phrases here can be easily missed. **How does a minister determine what is good and what is evil? If he cannot determine what is good and what is evil, then he cannot "minister."**

Now, as a Christian, where do you want him to get his concepts of good and evil? From the All Righteous God and His Word? Or, from totally sinful man and his creative ideas? Even, if you chose the latter, you must still have some standard by which to know what is good and evil from the thousands of ideas and proposals from history and modern times. **A standard of right and wrong is inescapable**. The only alternatives are back to an arbitrary majority or individual power. It follows that any magistrate who pervasively, persistently, and importantly avoids what is good and enjoins what is evil, is thereby no true civil magistrate, though he may retain considerable state power.

I simply propose that the New Testament and the Old Testament are the greatest source of moral good, and therefore, the greatest source for "good" civil law.

Nuances and More

I make no claim that the application of Old and New Testament law is either easy or straightforward. However, the first step for the Bible-believing Christian is to understand that God has provided this law for the benefit of mankind, both Christian and non-Christian.

There are really only two choices in law-making, as in ethics: man's ethics and law or God's ethics and law. And, under man's law, there are only two choices: rule of the majority (in legislative process, judicial decision [where more than one judge rules] or popular vote)

> (1) Rule of the majority in legislative process, judicial decision (where more than one judge presides) or popular vote.

(2) Dictatorship or judicial decision where one man presides

You might respond, "Even if the entire Bible is believed as law, the same two processes have to take place to enact law." Yes, I agree, **but in accepting the Bible as the source of law, all persons in the process of writing or positing law are limited to one body of knowledge and not the entire range of human opinion from all of man's history.**

And, **there is considerable historical precedent**, as recorded above. This history allows lawmakers to see how the peoples of those times, also distant from Biblical times and culture, applied law to themselves.

Sanction or Penalty for Crimes

Then, there is the problem of sanction, that is, what penalty is imposed for a crime? Without the Bible, where does one go for a punishment that fit's the crime? Perhaps, historically, this connection can be seen more clearly. With rex lex, the king is law, subjects could be executed for a petty crime against the state or against the king. And, not only the king, but any nobleman or high-ranking person could impose virtually any penalty on their serfs or slaves.

The institution of "an eye for an eye," by Moses, as directed by God, was actually a strict limitation on the culture of the times. When one man killed another, the family of the man killed would retaliate, not with a life for a life, but against anyone or several of the killer's family -- and, such back and forth killing could go on for generations. The Mosaic limit morally and legally limited such escalation of murders.

The concept of restitution, also limited such wanton allowance of "payment" for harm that was done through property damage. An Israelite could not just destroy the entire herd of someone who had stolen one of his sheep. He was due restitution "in kind," sometimes additional compensation applied for the hardship of doing without what was stolen or for other reasons, such as, the cost of catching the malefactor.

272

What Difference Does It Make? The Great Cost!!

"Trifles," you say. "We have a great system of law in American today!" I agree. We do have a great system of law. The best in the world. But, not the best in history, and a costly system even in its "greatness."

Dollars. Forgive me for not looking up the current number, but the cost of the War on Poverty since the mid-1960s is somewhere over $50 trillion. And, by the same standards by which this war was engaged, nothing has changed! $50 trillion! Any rational person would conclude that the plan was defective, but we continue to spend more and more.

Social security is bankrupt.

> The purchasing power of the dollar is about 1/10 of what it was in the mid-1950s. That means that it takes $1.00 to buy what you could buy for $0.10 in 1950. I remember going to the store for my mother to buy a loaf of bread for $0.14 (including one penny sales tax), which left me a penny for myself from $0.15.

> Over $1 trillion a year is now spent on medical care in the United States for a net negative effect on health of American citizens. That statement may be a jolt, but I have discussed this conclusion elsewhere. The Economics of Medicine

Deaths. Since *Roe v. Wade*, over 50 million unborn American children have lost their lives in abortion facilities.

> Infanticide has waxed and waned over the past several decades.

> Euthanasia is an ever-present threat.

> Civil laws facilitate IV drug abuse, illicit drugs, and sexual promiscuity.

Families and Children. Easy divorce has wreaked havoc with American families and its children. Fathers are able to leave their families with virtually no income and the courts make it difficult, if not impossible, for former wives to get support for her children.

> "Family" courts move "foster" children from one home to another, instead of placing them in a solid home permanently.

> "Family" courts go too far in allowing children to remain in homes of alcoholics, drug addicts, and other parents who have severely harmed their children by neglect.

> "Family" courts have taken children from parent who have given corporal punishment.

The cost of unbiblical laws is immeasurable in dollars, deaths, and the lives of families and children. It is no small consequence to ignore and defy the laws of God.

Related Terms

Just and righteousness. The relationship of justice and righteousness are evidenced by the fact that the same Greek word, dikaios, may be translated "just," as in "the just shall live by faith" (Romans 1:17), or "righteous," as in "the righteousness of God," (Romans 3:21). Often, these words are used the context of obedience to the law or the concept of justice or judgment.

Justice and judgment. "The words, 'justice' and 'judgment' are actually used interchangeably throughout the Bible. And for good reason. What is right and just and true contradicts and condemns what is evil and wicked and perverse." (George Grant, The Micah Mandate, page 89).

Synonyms of Biblical law. There are many synonyms of biblical law, especially in the Old Testament: precepts, commands, commandments, statute, principle, code, act, enactment, ordinance, decree, directive, edict, fiat, ruling, regulation, rule, prohibition, restriction, canon, testimonies, His ways, righteous judgments, Your Word, wonderful works, truth, and moral law. Many, if not most, of these are found in Psalm 119 alone!

Break Your Body and Break Up Your Life

The only difference between the law of gravity and God's laws for life is the freedom to choose in the latter. When a persons jumps off a building, the law of gravity takes over and his body will be broken on the ground below. When this law is broken, the choice is irreversible. But, what is often overlooked is that violation of God's laws for life are just as destructive, if not more so. Violation of God's laws of sexuality has resulted in the epidemic of sexually transmitted diseases that is present today. The violation of His laws for marriage has caused immeasurable heartache, economic expense, medical and psychological problems, and millions of children with the horror of divorce. The violation of laws of economics has caused runaway inflation. (See all the examples above.)

Freedom in Law

There is great freedom in God's law. When the laws of gravity and aerodynamics are obeyed, there is great freedom in flight via airplane, sail plane, kites, gliders, parachute, and sky-diving.

When God's laws for life are obeyed, there is great freedom and reward. Marriage gives security, mutual help, reduced expenses, time to pursue other interests, and the great reward of children. There are several studies that even show that sexual enjoyment (by self-assessment of the individuals themselves) in marriage exceeds that of singles.

Following God's laws of economic freedom in production and trade has produced the great prosperity of the West, and now East, even though that freedom is severely threatened today.

Too many people, perhaps even many Christians, think of God's laws as restrictive, but in reality they provide great freedom and peace for individuals, families, cities, states, and nations.

The Micah Mandate

The instruction of Micah 6:8 is a simple phrase, "to do justly, and to love mercy, and to walk humbly with thy God." It is quoted often by both liberal and conservative Christians. I trust, however, that you now realize that the first and second instructions of The Micah Mandate invoke the full application of the entirety of the Old and New Testament law at the level of individuals, families, and nations! This verse is no simplistic direction, but the same as The Cultural Mandate of Genesis 1 and The Great Commission of Matthew 28! George Grant has written a wonderful book by the same title as this section. (See Endnotes.)

Law Is Life -- Anti-Law Is Death

As Moses gave a choice to his people, we have the same choice today. "I call heaven and earth as witnesses today against you, that I have set before you life and death, blessing and cursing; therefore choose life, that both you and your descendants may live" (Deuteronomy 30:19).

Increasingly, the United States has chosen the opposite of God's law. Therefore, we are increasing the presence of real death.

The Golden Rule

John Calvin in his commentary on Matthew summarizes Christ's identity of The Golden Rule, "Therefore, whatever you want men to do to you, do also to them, for this is the Law and the Prophets" (Matthew 7:12).

> Our Lord does not intend to say, that this is the only point of doctrine laid down in the law and the prophets, but that all the precepts which they contain about charity, and all the laws and exhortations found in them about maintaining justice, have a reference to this object. The meaning is, that the second table of the law is fulfilled, when every man conducts himself in the same manner towards others, as he wishes them to conduct themselves towards him. There is no need, he tells us, of long and involved debates, if this simplicity is preserved, and if men do not, by inordinate self-love, efface the rectitude which is engraved on their hearts.

Summary Principles of Love, Law, Grace, Mercy, Justice, and Equity

For discussion of 1-2, please see Truth on this website. For the remainder, see the text of the discussion that follows these summary principles.

276

1. All Biblical ethics and worldview begins with the character or attributes of God. The most logically prior attribute of God is that He is absolute truth. He must be believed in everything about which He has spoken, else He has not more authority than a fallible man.

2. The 66 books of the Protestant Bible are inerrant and fully authoritative, as the very Word of God written. As special revelation, it has authority over conclusions about general revelation where the same subject matter is addressed.

3. After truth, God's righteousness (holiness) is His next logically prior attribute because all His other attributes are not as fully demonstrable without a comprehensive understanding of this one. God's righteousness may be described as being perfectly Holy and without sin or any tendency to sin ("no shadow of turning"). God is His own standard of Holiness; there is no standard above Him by which He can be judged.

4. Relative to man, God's Law, in all its fullness and particulars, is the written expression of His Holiness. God's Law (His will for obedience) is the standard to which man is called "on earth as it is in heaven." God's law is written throughout the entire Bible, Old and New Testaments.

5. God's entire creation is built upon law, from the inanimate heavenly bodies and plants to animals and man. These systems of inanimate objects and living things are most free and fully functional when they most closely correspond to His Law of original design. When a certain, unidentifiable point of transgression occurs, systems crash and destruction and death ensue.

6. Synonyms for God's Law include: precepts, commands, commandments, statutes, principles, codes, acts, enactments, ordinances, decrees, directives, edicts, fiats, rulings, regulations, rules, prohibitions, restrictions, canons, testimonies, His ways, righteous judgments, Your Words, wonderful works, moral Laws, and truth.

7. The cataclysmic consequences on both mankind and the universe, because of the Fall of Mankind in Adam and the Great Flood, demonstrates the ultimate value that God attaches to the observance of His Holiness, as reflected in His Law.

8. The fullness of man's salvation and the ultimate sacrifice of Jesus Christ in man's place cannot be understood most fully apart from an understanding of God's Law. In fact, the fulfillment of God's Law and the execution of punishment for transgression of God's law was (sic) the only means by which man could be saved.

9. God's Law together with His attributes of love, grace, mercy, and justice comprise the central message of the Bible in salvation and social justice among individuals, families, formal associations, and state governments.

10. Some theologians discuss the message of salvation as "Law and Grace," while others discuss it as "Law and Love", and still others as "Law and Gospel." Grace, mercy, and love are almost identical in their application to man.

11. There are more that 12 ways that the word "law" is used in the Bible. In this paper and on this website, "law" will be used to designate all laws (and their synonyms named above) of the Old and New Testaments except those that were explicitly ceremonial and those applicable only to Israel as a nation within the geographical boundaries prescribed by God.

12. Truly Biblical love (*agape* or *philos*) may never transgress any of God's laws. While the sacrifice and pursuit of Biblical love may exceed Biblical law, the latter gives explicit and practical direction to the former. For example, "husbands love your wives as Christ loved the Church." A husband may fulfill the bare minimum of the law or he may work to do all that he can to please her. (Link to discussion of *agape* and *philos*.)

13. God's perfect righteousness requires that His justice be perfectly executed. Thus, the slightest "transgression or want of conformity to God's law" demands death and banishment in Hell forever. Herein enters God's love, mercy, and grace.

14. While man is unable to keep God's law and is condemned by it, its perfect design for the human race is nevertheless to be implemented as fully and completely as possible by individuals, families, voluntary associations, the Church, and state governments. This implementation is first a duty to God, but secondly, the *summum bonum* of pragmatism

278

and has no association with the concept of legalism (the attempt to obtain merit or favor with God or forgiveness of sins by Him through obedience to the law.)

15. There are only two sources of civil law: the Bible or man's wisdom (fallen and fallible). There are only two possible choices for man in his execution of civil law: dictatorial (*rex lex* or the authority of one man in legislative or judicial decision) and the vote of the majority (in *vox populi*, "the voice of the people is the voice of God").

16. God's laws and principles are fixed and unchanging, but details of a situation determine which apply to that situation. For example, one may not bear false witness against his neighbor, but he may deceive a declared enemy in a just war. (Link to article in Truth.)

17. Biblical justice applies to the different areas of government: family, church, social groups, and state governments. Each sphere has its rewards and punishments. Only the state "bears the sword," that is, has the power for physical restraint and bodily punishment, including the death penalty.

18. The modern concept of social justice is severely skewed towards mercy without responsibility. While Biblical justice requires the application of mercy, God is most vengeful against the hardened heart and society should follow that example.

19. "Social justice" without the application of reasonable Biblical justice and mercy is chaotic and immeasurably costly in misery, money, and lives. The same choice faces people today that Moses presented to the Israelites: choose God's laws for health, prosperity, and life, or any other way of disease, debt, and death.

20. Christianity has a great heritage in the application of Old Testament law throughout Medieval Europe. Its greatest development was the common law of England, sometimes known as the Law of Liberty of Moses, which produced the Magna Charta and the foundation of law for the United States.

21. Civil law is always and only derived from ethics. Since there are extant only two kinds of ethics, Biblical and any other, civil law can only be derived from one or the other. There are great consequences of good from the Biblical system and great consequences of evil from the other, demonstrable in present times throughout the world and in history.

22. The consequences of breaking God's moral laws are as sure and certain as the law of gravity when one jumps off a building is smashed on the ground below. When one violates God's laws, sooner or later he will suffer the consequences of a broken heart, a broken heart, or a broken life.

23. The application of Biblical law requires great care to transfer it from the culture of Biblical times to modern day. But, such application is not only possible, but necessary. It is past time that Biblical scholars provide instruction to legislators in this process, before it is too late for the world.

24. Biblical laws give God-determined sanctions which are levels of punishment that are proportional to the crime committed. Throughout history and the modern world, capital punishment has been executed for petty offenses and crimes, whereas murderers are often set free and sometimes even honored for their crimes.

25. The Micah Mandate is often quoted as a simple lifestyle for Christians. However, a proper understanding of it contains all that has been discussed here, as representative of God's entire Biblical plan.

26. One summary of the Law is the Golden Rule (Matthew 7:12). As a summary of the Law, one must look to its explicit statements to know how to fulfill.

Endnotes

[1] In other words, in one sense the pre-Sinaitic period was one of "no law," for law had not yet "come ," In another sense, however, the law clearly was in the world, because sin is not imputed apart from law, and sin was clearly being imputed, as the fact of death demonstrates. Before Sinai, the law had already but not yet come, This is parallel to the gospel, which had already but not yet come during the Old Covenant; and parallel to the consummation, which has already but not yet come in the New Covenant era.

[2] On how I am using the terms 'Old Covenant' and 'New Covenant,' see Appendix A.

[3] Why did not Jacob have them put to death for blasphemy (misusing the covenant sign) and murder? Probably because he was not a magistrate, and as a father did not have the power to pass civil judgments. Jacob obviously feared reprisal from the near kinsmen of the Shechemites, who could properly act as avengers of blood. Perhaps we should see Jacob as functioning as a sanctuary for his sons, just as Abram had functioned as a sanctuary for Lot in Genesis 14.

[4] "You shall not add to the word which I am commanding you, nor take away from it, that you may keep the commandments of the LORD your God which I command you" (Deuteronomy 4:2).

[5] 613 Commandments of the Old Testament

[6] Robertson McQuilkin, *An Introduction to Biblical Ethics*, (Tyndale: 1989), pages 45-83, citing Robert C. McQuilkin, *God's Law and God's Grace*, (Eerdmans, 1958), pages 13-17).

[7] have substituted "worldview" for "ethic." They are synonyms. John Murray, *Principles of Conduct*, (Wm. B. Eerdmans, 1957).

[8] See Jay Adams, *Marriage, Divorce, and Remarriage.*

[9] See Jay Adams, *Handbook of Church Discipline.*

[10] There is a website devoted to The Law of Nature and of Nature and Of Nature's God, www.lonang.com. Just remember that Biblical law always trumps and is more explicit than "natural law." Quotes in text from Section 2.

[11] In my readings for this article, I frequently came across "beauty" relative to grace, mercy, and love. What greater beauty can there be than that of God's harmony in all things involving His universe and plan for mankind?

[12] I am told by a legal scholar that with the early influence of the Enlightenment, "life, liberty, and property" became "life, liberty, and happiness." If a man cannot own property, he cannot protect his "life" or have true "liberty." These concepts are mutually dependent.

14. Logic, Truth, and Epistemology

Unraveling the Concept of Logic*

The uses of the word, "logic." "There "are four senses (definitions) in which the word logic is used: (1) at the theoretical and symbolic level is a comprehensive term that refers to sets of axiomatic relationships, 'an analysis and evaluation of the ways of using evidence to derive correct (true) conclusions,' (2) in common speech at a nontechnical level is a synonym for words such as 'workable,' 'reasonable,' and the like a logical plan may be a workable plan, an illogical step may be a rash step; (3) (in) a formal presentation of an argument: that is, people engage in 'logical argument,' whether or not there are fallacies in the steps (that) they take; and (4) in common speech may refer to a set of propositions or even an outlook which may or may not be 'logical' in the first sense." (D. A. Carson, Exegetical Fallacies, Baker Academic Books, 2nd edition, pp. 87-88,)

Ed's Comments on These "Senses" of the Word, "Logic"

The reader should note that #1 represents logic in its formal sense. Many people are not familiar with this use. It entails propositions (statements of facts) from which conclusions are drawn. One should look at book on logic to see how these propositions may be stated and how conclusions are drawn from them. Certain arguments may be proven to be infallibility true, or to the contrary, may be proved erroneous.

A better name for #3 might be "rational" thinking, as it does not involve the formal steps of logic, but an attempt at clearly drawing one conclusion from other facts and statements. What is reasonable or rational is rarely formally "logical."

#2 and #4 may include almost any kind of reasoning in serious or casual conversations. It is doubtful that "logic" should be used for this process at all, as it hides the important use of formal logic.

It is most important that readers understand that there is a discipline of formal logic because it stands in stark contrast to all the other definitions. Formal logic can start with true statements (premises, axioms, presuppositions, etc.), and if the process of logic is applied correctly, then the conclusions are also true.

For example, The Trinity is common to all those who profess true Christianity, yet "trinity" does not appear in the Bible. The logical steps are these:

Only God is omniscient, omnipresent, and omnipotent.

The Father, Son, and Holy Spirit all have these attributes.

The Father, Son, and Holy Spirit are persons.

There is only one God.

Therefore, the Father, Son, and Holy Spirit are One God and Three Persons.

"Trinity" is an arbitrary choice of a word to apply to this conclusion. The word itself does not make its own concept true. The concept of Trinity is a logical conclusion from the premises which are absolutes. So, the conclusion argued logically is as true as its premises. All the steps, as a whole, is called a syllogism.

The reader may need to wrestle with this process. It cannot be done apart from reviewing at least the first few chapters of a book on formal logic. A failure to understand the use of formal logic will greatly hamper one's attempts at a Biblical worldview.

*See the "Role of Logic" in the following section

Truth: Concepts, Nuances, and the Scriptures

In this book, we try to condense discussions for the benefit of the reader. However, some subjects, such as truth and law, require that certain basics be covered, and those basics in themselves are somewhat length.

Brief overview of the following discussion: Coherence; meaning of words (philology and etymology); Biblical meaning; Jesus as Truth; subjective and objective truth; the "whole truth"; a Biblical study of truth; human and Biblical truth; playing God; the truth of Genesis 1-11; failure to study the Bible; telling the truth and not lying; the relevance of faith to truth; epistemology and truth; starting with assumptions (presuppositions); pragmatic value of functional truth; logic and truth; an enemy of God and His justice has no right to the truth.

A Lament and a Challenge

In general, I am greatly disappointed in theologians, preachers, and virtually all Christians who speak and write about epistemology and truth. By most standards relative to such things, I am a layman. As a layman, I wish to have things simplified. As a scholar, I wish to have things coherent. That is, I wish that all parts are consistent with the whole.

Coherency requires systematization. Coherency requires knowing and using precise definitions.

Now, certainly, I find great thoughts from the many Christian thinkers that I have read. For example, R. C. Sproul in his book, *Knowing Scripture*, states as a rule of interpretation of Scripture, "Determine carefully the meaning of words... with multiple meanings" (p. 79, 82). Wow! I marvel at the influence that Christianity might have in the culture of ideas on this one principle alone. Christians eschew definitions! Virtually all Christians: from the renowned Bible teachers and preachers to the professionals (physicians, Ph.D.s, lawyers, etc.) and the (formally) uneducated in the pew. (For more, see Hermeneutics.)

Amazing! Aggravating! Appalling! Jesus said, "I am the way, the truth, and the life." "In (Christ) are hidden all the treasures of wisdom and knowledge." Paul said, "The weapons of our warfare *are* not carnal but mighty in God for pulling down strongholds, casting down arguments and every high thing that exalts itself against the knowledge of God, bringing every thought into captivity to the obedience of Christ." And, these verses can be multiplied considerably.

Amazing! Aggravating! Appalling! Christians means "Christ-ones." Christ, as the truth. Christ, as the sum total of knowledge. Christ, as the omniscient One that He is. Surely, as Christ is all these things, His people ought to be diligent students of words and language, not intellectual first-graders!

> We have much to say about this, but it is hard to explain because you are slow to learn. In fact, though by this time you ought to be teachers, you need someone to teach you the elementary truths of God's word all over again. You need milk, not solid food! Anyone who lives on milk, being still an infant, is not acquainted with the teaching about righteousness. But solid food is for the mature, who by constant use have

trained themselves to distinguish good from evil (Hebrews 5:11-14, NKJV).

Oh, we know the Bible. Seminaries and libraries have thousands of volumes written by theologians from all ages from Augustine of Hippo to John Calvin to J. I. Packer. There is some great teaching there. Teaching from which I have benefited greatly.

But, in every age and among almost all theologians, there is a lack of definitions, especially precise and coherent definitions.

Do you know that there are at least four different uses of the word faith in the New Testament? Do you know that there are at least six different uses of the "will of God" in the Bible? Do you know that there are at least a dozen different uses of the word "law" in the Bible? Do you know that there are at least a dozen synonyms of the word "law" in the Bible? Do you know a Biblical definition of love? Do you know a Biblical definition of peace? For our purposes here, do you know both a biblical and secular definition of truth?

Christianity is in the ghetto in the United States, intellectually. If we do not rise to the occasion, Christians may be in the ghetto literally. And, that occasion, in my opinion, is one that requires a precise understanding of both philosophical and Biblical knowledge.

John 3:16 Is Enough for Me!

"Ah, you say. Don't bother me with complexity. I simply want John 3:16 for myself and to present it to the unsaved."

May I ask you to pause a moment. How does one understand John 3:16? "For God..." Who is God? How many gods are worshipped on this planet? For the true God, there are hundreds of names and characteristics of God throughout the Bible. "... so loved..." What is love? What is Biblical love? Do you know that you cannot know the love of God in its fullness, if you do not know the Law of God (Romans 13:8, 10; Galatians 5:14).

"... the world..." This word separates Christians of all times into those who believe in "free will" and those who believe in "election and predestination." "... that He gave...," a fairly simple verb. But, it does raise the question, "What is a gift?" Does something that is a "gift," have a contribution by the recipient? Is a gift that I help purchase or assist in its giving, truly a gift. If my son, Ben, gives me $5.00 to help buy his bicycle that costs $50.00, does he see the bicycle as a gift or something to which he contributed? With this example, we are back to the debate between "free will" and "predestination," for a person with truly free will contributes his $5.00 towards the purchase of his salvation.

"… His only Begotten Son…" Son denotes a Father. "Begotten" complicates the relationship. "Only" complicates it further. For several centuries after Christ, theologians debated the issues of the Trinity, resulting in the Apostle's, Nicene, Athanasian, Chalcedon, and other creeds crafted with thousands of hours of research and debate.

"…whoever…" "… believes…" "… not perish…" "… everlasting life…" I could pose similar complexities for these words, as well. John 3:16, simple? I think not.

I hear the argument coming, "One does not have to know everything about John 3:16 to believe it and be saved!" Well, I agree wholeheartedly, but will say three things about your proposal. 1) In spite of this long introduction, the issue before us is truth. Truth is the most important issue (below) that individual man or mankind itself faces. **If truth does not exist, nothing else matters**. If truth does not exist, anyone can do whatever they want and never be criticized by anyone else. If truth does not exist, it does not matter whether "God is love" and John 3:16, because one cannot know that they are true.

2) If one does not have to know everything about John 3:16 to be saved, exactly what does one have to know to be saved? I would have you make a list from 1-5 or 1-10 or 1-100 or however long your list is, but I challenge you to make a list. As you do so, you will find that it is not so simple after all. What did the thief on the cross know? For surely, he was with Christ that day in heaven.

3) Why will one person to whom you present John 3:16 accept it and another reject it? Why will the humanist vigorously deny it and work to persecute Christians? Perhaps, there is no way to make John 3:16 realistically simple. Perhaps, one might understand the Trinity and the cataclysmic destruction that resulted from sin with a little more contemplation of the words of John 3:16 from their fuller development throughout Scripture.

(I will not deny that hundreds of thousands have been saved through this simple verse and through a simple gospel. But, I will deny that any Christian can worship God with any fullness and reality [that is, according to Christ's directive, to worship God "in spirit and in truth"] without beginning to grasp

286

the immensity of the verse's meaning. And, that no Christian can understand John 3:16 without understanding many of the other verses that give a fuller meaning to the verse. And, finally, how can a Christian ever be satisfied with a stagnant knowledge of God and His salvation?)

"What Is Truth?"

On the issue of truth, many Christians and many non-Christians like to start with the question posed by Pilate to Jesus, "What is truth?" So, I might as well begin there. Some dilettantes deny that Jesus ever answered this question because He did not answer Pilate when he posed the question. However, Jesus answered it on many other occasions. I have cited one above. Another is, "If you abide in My word, you are My disciples indeed. And you shall know the truth, and the truth shall make you free" (John 8:31-32). "When He, the Spirit of truth, has come, He will guide you into all truth; for He will not speak on His own authority, but whatever He hears He will speak; and He will tell you things to come. He will glorify Me, for He will take of what is Mine and declare it to you (John 16:13-14). All true Christians believe that Jesus is the truth.

So, philosophically, how do we understand and apply Jesus or the Trinity as the truth? Just this, truth becomes a Person or Persons - the Trinity. They embody truth. They cannot lie. So, our first principle of truth is that truth is ultimately subjective -- that it is determined by a Person or Persons.

(The Trinity also answers another ethical dilemma, the problem of the one, the few, and the many. Righteousness for one requires righteousness for all. Or, what is right for one person is right for all people. Or, what is right for the individual is right for the family is right for a group is right for a city is right for a nation is right for the world.! But, that issue is for another time and place.)

Truth, then, is what God knows of an object or person. But, we are not God, so what can we know of His mind.

It is amazing to me that otherwise great teachers, usually Christians, in many ages have erred on this problem. The Pietists, like the Gnostics, have sought for a "deeper" life and deeper relationship with God. The Scholastics attempted to integrate Greek philosophy with Scripture. Quakers sought the "inner light." Many Scots held to "natural common sense." Thomas Jefferson and the modern Neo-orthodox tried to determine what is and is not God's Word in the Bible.

The only truth that we know of God is the 66 books of the Protestant Bible. For that reason, it is called Revelation. God revealing His mind to us. If God is truth, His Word is truth. And the only Word from God that we have is the Bible. The Bible, then, is the only truth that we can know.

"Ah," you challenge me, "I know from nature that God is infinitely creative to the extent that the best minds with the best technology that modern science can devise cannot comprehend, understand, or explain all its intricate details." Yes, but that only adds to your Biblical understanding that determined who the Creator is. So, Scripture always controls and directs our understanding of nature. And, that would be so of any other knowledge of God in nature.

And**, these 66 books of the Bible answer the greatest dilemma that searchers for truth encounter: objectivity**. As we will see later, truth on a human level is quite conditional to human frailties and intent to tell the truth. But, God has given us an extensive message that is totally external to ourselves to study, and He has prevented any addition to it. So, we have in its pages all that He intends to give us and our source of truth.

Truth, truth, and the "Whole Truth"

"Raise your right hand and tell the truth, the whole truth, and nothing but the truth." Everyone in the United States (with maybe the exception of a few atheists) who has ever testified in a court of law has said these words. But, can our testimony be truth?

Yes and no. And, herein, is the crux if the problem of truth, philosophically and practically, especially for the Bible-believing Christian.

Can man's truth be equated with God's truth? Obviously, not. Not only is man subject to lying, he is subject to unintended inaccuracy, illusion, mistake, and insufficient investigation. Yet, we are called to truth. "Therefore, putting away lying, '*Let each one of you speak truth with his neighbor*,' for we are members of one another" (Ephesians 4:25).

There seems to be a dilemma here. If man's truth cannot be equated with God's truth, then how can God call on man to tell the truth? How can our courts require of us "to tell the truth…?"

A friend of mine once wrote to me on this issue, using Truth and truth (upper and lower case t's), to designate man's truth and God's truth. He also used the qualifier, "empirical truth." Francis Schaeffer wrote about "truth" and "true truth." Many Christians who are psychologists and some others say that "All truth is God's truth."

Who do we get around or through this dilemma? Can the knowledge of man be called truth?

First, as we reviewed earlier, the same word can have different definitions and uses. There is the truth of God and the truth of man. God cannot lie and always tells the truth. Man may try with all his effort to "tell the truth," but will always be subject to considerable error, depending upon the situation, the strength of his senses, his intelligence, his memory, and other factors. No two people will tell the same "truth," as witnessed by thousands of court testimonies. If God were "in the dock," His testimony would always be the same. The testimony of the Father, Son, and Holy Spirit would always be the same.

Adding Complexity for Clarity: An Actual Study of "Truth" in the Bible

I am going to go out on a limb, defensible, I think. But, I will also make a demand to the minds of all thinking Christians, especially those in the role of pastors, teacher, and leaders.

My limb is a discussion of truth and falsehood as it is recorded in the Bible. You will need a concordance. This exercise can be done easily at a website where you can search the Bible in many different versions. (See Link under References below.) Find all the verses in the Bible that contain the word "truth."

The first thing to notice, consistent (coherent) with the Ninth Commandment, is that the large majority of commands to individuals (apart from communicating Scripture to others) is "not to lie" ("bear false witness," "deal falsely," "lying to his neighbor," "does not lie," "falsehood," "deceitful tongue," etc.), rather than to tell the truth.

At Biblegateway.com, a search of "truth" in the New King James Version showed 228 verses where the word occurred. A rough count reveals that only 20 referred to the truth of man (for example, Genesis 42:16, Proverbs 12:17, and Mark 5:33). Another 26 could be interpreted as referring to the truth of God (including His Word as Scripture) or the word of man (for example, Psalm 15:2, Proverbs 12:17, John 1:14, and Ephesians 4:25). Our exercise, then, leaves 182 that refer to the Word of God, as God actually speaking or His

Word recorded in Scripture, (for example, Psalm 25:5, Isaiah 65:16, Matthew 5:18, and Romans 15:8).

This study is not precise. Anyone who does it will likely come up with different numbers. Indeed, as I go back over the list another time, I can see where I might change my mind. But the precision of the study is not the issue. **The issue is the overwhelming emphasis that truth, as God discusses it, belongs primarily to Himself.**

I believe that God is illustrating man's truth over against His truth in the Bible. Now, I will yield to all the criticisms thrown at me hermeneutically, because only one verse is necessary to establish it as God's word to man. But, there is a philosophical issue that cannot be so easily avoided. **That issue is that by no standard conceivable is man's truth comparable to God's truth**.

Man's Truth and God's Truth

Let me answer one objection immediately. **Man can know truth**. Some have argued that man can only know truth analogically. But, I deny that statement. Man can know truth because he can understand what God says in the Bible. When Jesus says, "I am the way, the truth, and the life; no man comes to the Father but by me," I know that as the truth. I do not know the fullness of that statement as God does, but I can learn a great deal from the whole of Scripture about what it means. I can learn enough to rest in my salvation and expect the growth of my sanctification and eventual glorification.

But, apart from the Bible man does not know truth the way that God knows truth. Apart from Scripture, I do not know anything as God knows it. There is the story of the blind men who were brought to feel the elephant. One felt his trunk and thought that the elephant might be like a giant snake. One felt his hide and thought that he might be a large, living building. Another felt his ears and thought that he might have wings like a bird.

There are many, many other characteristics of the elephant. The trunk would have two holes at the end, it would taper, it would have different textures on the top and bottom, the tusks would be encountered at the junction to the head, etc., etc. The same variety would exist for all parts of the elephant. Then, beyond the senses of the blind men, there are the cells of all the different organs of the elephant. There are the sub-cellular elements, even genetic components of the cells themselves. On the macroscopic side, there is the elephant in relation to his habitat, in zoos, and how he might even influence the universe. What is the truth of the elephant?

The truth of the elephant and any object in the universe is everything of which it consists and its relationship to everything else in the universe. Anything else is "partial truth." Truth with a little "t." "Empirical truth." Not "true truth."

A simpler definition is that truth is **what is**. When Moses asked God whom should he tell the Egyptians that sent him, God said, tell them, "I am." God has no other referent other than himself. To tell all that He is can be told only by Himself. And, even if God were willing to tell all of Himself, man's finite mind could not contain the infinite mind of God. Man would have to be God to know all that He knows. Omniscience, omnipresence, and omnipotence cannot exist independently of each other.

But, I digress. Can we call any knowledge within man, apart from the Bible, to be "truth?" We need the Bible's proportion here. Overwhelmingly, truth exists in God and His Word. Overwhelmingly, that truth is important. Overwhelmingly, that truth must be known. Overwhelmingly, that truth must be applied into every area of knowledge. Overwhelmingly, that is the only infallible, at all times and in all ways, truth known to man.

"Playing God," "All truth is God's truth," and Genesis 1-11

I do not like the term, "playing God." It usually refers to man's use of technology. For example, genetic engineering in humans might one day be used to produce certain desired characteristics. Used in this way, man is not "playing God," because he cannot even conceive of what it would be to mimic God. This term misses the real issue, man violating God's commandments by setting his own ethical standards. The "playing God" is not the power of technology, but the thinking that I know better than God.

When someone, usually a psychologist, says "All truth is God's truth," they are truly "playing God." What these psychologists mean, and actually say, is that man's theoretical and empirical knowledge are on the same level as the word of God. They use the word, "integration." Integration means the merging of equal authorities. There is not authority equal to Scripture, as we have been reviewing.

(Other scientists use "all truth is God's truth" besides psychologists, but in my experience they do so far more commonly than anyone else.)

Now, I move from preaching to meddling. I am going to step on a lot of toes. **Preachers, theologians, and Christian leaders have subtly adopted "all truth is God's truth" when they allow the "science" of evolution to govern their theology.**

I contend that there is no other reason than evolution to posit "theistic evolution," "the gap theory," "a pre-Adamic race," "intelligent design," and other notions. There is no other reason than to attempt to gain intellectual credence with the *avante garde* and *intelligentsia*.

The major point is the authority and truth of Scripture as the very Word of God. "Hear, O Israel, the Lord our God is One." The unity of Scripture stands or falls as a unit. If the testimony of Scripture is not true on Creation and the Flood, how can it be defended as true on everything else?

I do not accept the argument that we did not know all that the Institute of Creation Research and other such scientists had developed until recently. First, there are still large numbers of supposed Bible-believers who still hedge on the Biblical account of creation. Second, from my reading of history, there has always been substantial scientific evidence to counter evolution, since Darwin coined the idea.

One example is archeology. In the 19th century and later, historians tried to use sources outside the Bible to disprove its historical dating and description of events. Some pastors and theologians hedged with "The Bible is true in all that it says regarding salvation and morals." Archeology has eventually, and virtually always, eventually cohered to the historicity of the Bible.

Another example is the discovery of the Dead Sea Scrolls. These documents demonstrated unequivocally that the Bible of today is the Bible that has always been. The minor differences in the prior texts of those found are inconsequential.

Praise God that He gives us such evidences! But, is not "Thus saith the Lord" sufficient? What is this continuing nonsense that "the Bible is true in all that it says regarding salvation and morals," but not history, science, or other areas.

If Christians deny the Word of God, why should we expect non-Christians to think it more than the collective writings of men?

(See References at the end here for more discussion of "all truth is God's truth.")

There Is More... and It Is Worse!

Christians deny the Word of God and its power by their actions. In seminary, theologians get a considerable education. From my perspective, with a few exceptions, it is quite adequate, if not thorough. Yet, it is rarely descends to the pew. And, with a global accusation that may not be entirely fair, I point the finger at these post-seminarians for not educating their pews. I am not sure why this situation exists. Certainly, the new preacher in a pulpit cannot being spouting Greek, Hebrew, and systematic theology. But, why cannot an education be built over time?

It is amazing to me that of all the organizations in the United States, **possibly the only group that does not expect or require a definitive education is the Church**. And, what is more amazing is that such an education is the most important of any other organization! At minimum, American children get twelve years of primary and secondary education. Maybe college. Maybe professional graduate school. By contrast, what do they get in church? Some Bible stories and some moralizing, and not much else.

There are at least three failures. 1) The fervent study of the Bible. In general, Christians learn is the jargon of their church or group. That will frequently be all that they learn. That is about all that they will hear in Sunday School or from the pulpit That is about all that they will read. That is about all of the Bible that they will study.

2) They will not read books that expand their biblical understanding, systematize Biblical knowledge, or expand their range of ethical application. The current movement of "worldview" is a hope that Christians are expanding their range of thinking. But, even here they must be careful that it is balanced and that is biblical.

3) There is an easy entrance into churches and an easy residence there. Little is expected in the way of getting a Biblical education. Again, why does God's own institution have no educational expectation of its members? This situation is severely deficient in an educated society and in the face of needed social and government direction today. The situation is literally damnable in its allegiance to God and His work for His people.

God's Word Needs to be God's Word

We are not to worship the Bible, but we should be consistent with in our practice with what it is. Why cannot the majority of Christians know some basic elements of systematic theology? Why cannot they know and apply Biblical ethics to their own profession, and to a lesser extent the professions of others? Why cannot they know how the Bible gives principles for civil government, the basics upon which the pinnacle of God-ordained civilization for a nation was established for the United States of America? Why should not every child by the time they graduate from college have a Biblical and theological education that has addressed every area at an appropriate lesser level that a seminary does for the pastor and theologian? Why not?

Is "Telling the Truth" and "Not Lying" the Same Thing?

The Ninth Commandment is "Thou shalt not bear false witness against thy neighbor." Let's do the easy thing first. Who is my neighbor? According to the Parable of the Good Samaritan, my neighbor is anyone with whom I come in contact who has need. According to the Great Commission, my neighbor is "all nations." So, I am not to bear false witness against anyone on earth and to present the truth of salvation in Jesus Christ to all peoples.

I contend that the command "not to lie" is both the same and different than the command "to tell the truth." The issue turns on a definition of the truth. I would define truth as "what is" or "everything that can be known about every object in the universe in relation to all other objects." "What is" exists regardless of our belief or interpretation of it. We could call this objective truth. With this definition, no man or woman can know truth. Yet, because God knows truth, we can know truth because He said it, and we can understand it because we are made in His image. (See prior discussion above… man can know truth.) So, the only truth that we can know or speak is that which is His own words. "The Lord is **great** and **greatly** to be praised." The only sure way to praise God is to praise Him with His own words or "by good and necessary consequence may be deduced from Scripture." (See Westminster Confession of Faith, Chapter 1, Section 6 at Link below.)

Truth is Personal, as we have already seen (above). For men and women, then, truth is an individual's best effort to tell as accurately and as detailed as the situation demands ("what is"). Notice the relativity here. It is limited to one person. His effort should be "best," not casual. "Be accurate", that is, tell in needed detail. The truth is dependent upon the situation. For example, giving directions to a person who is going somewhere in a car is not as significant as giving testimony in a court of law… but it might be…

I recall a person, either by directions given to them or devised on their own from reading a map, who ended on a dead end street in a gang infested neighborhood where he was shot and killed. Or, wrong directions could get someone going the wrong way on a one-way street and place their lives in danger or cause them to get a traffic ticket.

These situations bring me to ask, "Is there such a thing as casual testimony?" 1) Certainly not in the sense of the credibility of the person who gave it. If the person to whom information was given believes that they were deliberately deceived, then the giver-of-the-information has given evidence of his character. This conclusion will stick with the recipient of the information, even if his mistake was accidental or from incomplete information.

2) Most, if not all information given by one person to another, has serious consequences. We have looked at directions by automobile. What about simply answering a husband's question, "Where is my book that I was reading." Casually, his wife may say, "It is on the couch where you left it?" But, if she was wrong, and he spends 15 minutes looking for it in other places, bumps his head, or strains his back looking under it, their relationship is not enhanced by her causal remark. (There are many other possible results but examples should be kept simple!)

What if I give wrong instructions to my grandson about putting together a toy train? He may shock himself trying to put the electrical plug into the socket. He may pinch himself trying to put the track together. With enough mistakes, he may begin to think that granddaddy does not really now how to put a train together, and later, that he does not know anything at all that is worthwhile.

(Just in the writing of this section, I have come to appreciate greatly the consequences for both the giver and the receiver of requested information. It seems there is really no personal testimony or advice that is truly casual!)

Back to the Bible

But, back to our original question, whether "not lying" is the same as "telling the truth." There is a level at which we cannot we cannot equate our personal truth with the truth of God. The fact that we have to resort to "true truth" or truth with lower case "truth" instead of an upper case "Truth" gives evidence of this necessary distinction.

This issue may be the most important one for Bible-believing Christians today. That psychologists and others can claim "all truth is God's truth," and not be labeled as being heretical in the way that they mean it, indicates an environment in which the concept of truth is little understood. Worse, it indicates an environment in which the authoritative truth of the Bible is weakly understood and applied.

There should be greater efforts at every level of teaching, preaching, and writing to distinguish the truth that man can know on his own and the truth revealed by God in His Revelation.

The most remarkable characteristic of man's limited ability to know and communicate truth is its great pragmatic value. Most conversations between two or more people are clearly understood. I am to write this article and communicate some of my thoughts to you. But, this pragmatic value should not cloud the difference between man's communication and understanding of truth and God's communication and understanding of truth.

Indeed, one of the traditional tests of truth is its pragmatic value. Thus, revelational truth is the most pragmatic knowledge available. The Bible is not often talked about in terms of its pragmatic value. But, surely, as God's truth, it is the supreme example of pragmatism. To elevate an old proverb to its highest application, "Father knows best!" (See discussion of pragmatism and science below.)

So, I would contend that as far as truth is personal, "telling the truth" and "not lying" are the same. However, in the larger picture of objective truth that only God can know, these two directives are not the same. Our "truth" with the best intentions and the best skills that we can muster, falls woefully short of "what is." "Best" efforts and honest intentions can harm and even cause people's deaths.

"Not lying" is a command that I can clearly fulfill. I know when I cross the threshold of information that 1) is uncertain in my own mind or a 2) a deliberate fabrication of what I know.

In "telling the truth," I am limited to my own knowledge and capacities. What I can tell is a limited truth. I am not able to tell "the whole truth." One only has to hear two or more witnesses in a court of law or just in causal conversation, the description of "what happened" in a particular incident to see the error or anyone reporting "nothing but the truth." When I have worked in emergency rooms, the information that I have heard first hand from accident victims is barely recognizable in the paper the next day. Surely, whatever is reported is "subjective truth," but nothing about one's testimony totally and completely true.

And, is not man's limitation, by his fallibility and finitude, the underscore of the Biblical commands relative to one's testimony. 'By the mouth of two or three witnesses every word may be established" (Deuteronomy 17:6, 19:15; Matthew 18:16). Throughout the Law of Moses, witnesses are required. And, if a witness is found to lie, he is subject to the same sanction as the one who was accused would have been, had he been found guilty (Deuteronomy 17:19). And, if one has needed testimony and does not give it, he incurs guilt (Leviticus 5:1). Further, in capital punishment cases, the witnesses are to initiate the death penalty (Deuteronomy 17:7). Our witnessing is important!

The emphasis of this discussion is the infinite chasm between the truth that God knows and the truth that he has revealed and man's ability to know truth. My purpose is not to minimize the force of the command "not to bear false witness." Indeed, it should strengthen one's resolve for "honesty, and nothing but honesty," in any testimony. I would hope that the reader would sense the importance of his testimony in everything in life. A careless or thoughtless testimony can be the ruin or oneself or that of another.

Some Conclusions Thus Far

1) There needs to be more discussion of what is and is not truth at all levels of discourse among Christians; distinctions between truth as God sees it and how man sees it. The chasm that exists must be emphasized and explored. Such statements as "all truth is God's truth" must be condemned where necessary (and in my estimation, that is most of the time that it is used).

2) By corollary, the Protestant Scriptures must be held as the highest, purest, and most authoritative form of truth known to man. For the most part, I do not believe that at a practical level this declaration is active among "Bible-believers." Examples have already been given. We do not study it in our churches at this level. We have no real expectations that Christians learn the Bible at more than a superficial and conversant degree. We have allowed empirical and theoretical science to supersede the Bible as authority in a number of areas, particularly evolutionary science and psychology. We have failed even to understand, much less apply, the broad range of ethics and law that the Bible provides (as our American and Reformed fathers did).

Historically, when the word, "science," came to be limited to the natural and "precise" sciences only, a major step was taken away from the Scriptures as its own rightful authority as the Very Word of God. Theology was once called "The Queen of the Sciences." Few would understand that phrase today. So, that position of Scripture and theology must be regained and taught to all Christians. When properly understood, the "science" of today should have no more effect than BB guns on lions. No wonder the influence of Christians today is nil. They have no Word from God for the general culture and the legal system!

3) The Bible, sound theology, and the broad range of Biblical ethics must be taught in homes, churches, Christian schools, Bible colleges, and seminaries. Our college students should be able to defeat soundly any anti-Christian professor whom they encounter in a fair debate. (Granted, they are usually not fair. The professor assuming, and being given, an authority that is unmerited fairly or philosophically.) Such ethics are the essence of a Biblical worldview.

Definitions of Truth and Pragmatic Value

The question for Christians is, "Can we subject the Bible to the same tests of truth, as other forms of truth?" Well -- no. One reason is that there is no agreed upon definition of truth. And, even those that are given are inadequate. For example, here is one definition.

> "Truth is the faithful adherence of our judgments and ideas to the facts of experience or to the world as it is; but since we cannot always compare our judgments with the actual situations, we test them by their consistency with other judgments that we believe are valid and true, or we test them by their usefulness and practical consequences." (Titus, Smith, and Nolan, Living Issues in Philosophy, D. Nostran Company, New York, p. 209, 1979.)

This definition is full of subjective factors. How does one determine "faithful adherence?" Is there a more loaded term than "judgment?" What is a "fact of experience?" How does one determine "consistency?" What about: "world as it is," "we cannot always compare," "actual situation," "believe," "valid," "usefulness and practical consequences?" And, is not one rule of definitions that the world being defined is not used it the definition ("true" is used here)?

Surely, few would differ with the simple definition of truth as "reality" or "what is." The great problem is how to measure or understand "what is." For example, the leaves on a tree are green? I look at a tree and we all agree that it is green. However, with rose-colored glasses, it is not green any longer. For the color-blind or blind person, it is not green at all. So, the truth of green leaves has many variables. It is relative to certain conditions of the observer, yet the human race has always functioned quite well with green leaves and all the other color of objects.

Perhaps, the most deceptive aspect of an understanding of truth is a confusion of the pragmatic with what is indeed truth. The place of modern science is the best and most important illustration. Modern science has developed the internet, sent men to the moon and back, placed communication satellites in orbit, invented the plastic straw, placed electricity and other utilities in virtually all homes in the civilized world, etc., etc. Yet, science by definition never determines truth because its results are always limited to the parameters of its design. (See Science and Technology.)

For example, the speed of a falling object is determined by the formula, $S=1/2gt2$. Yet, if a person jumps out of an airplane, his body will not continually accelerate, but reach a terminal velocity at about 120 mph. Why does he not continually accelerate, as the formula suggest. Because the formula exists only under experimental conditions that include objects falling in a vacuum at sea level. The formula is quite useful (pragmatic), but its "truth" exists nowhere except in the laboratory.

This awareness should encourage great boldness among Christians. If no one can agree on how truth is determined, then at a minimum the Bible starts on a par with any other claims to truth. But, based upon our faith, the Bible becomes the greatest and only truth that we have. Instead of starting with man's truth, we start with God's truth and determine every other claim to truth by that standard.

Working Away from Little "t" Truth

Christians need to work towards a vocabulary that allows distinction from the truth of Scripture to other claims of truth. Words that I have come up with are: fact, functional knowledge, pragmatic value, and empirical or practical truth. Henry Stob has suggested "natural truths" vs. "supernatural truths."

I readily admit that I do not know what would be the best term. But, there is a serious need for discussions and papers on what is and is not truth, and how the Bible fits into those discussions. **The Bible is unique and supremely**

authoritative, and it must be given its rightful place in the area of truth. Theology should be re-established as the "queen of the sciences."

The Relevance of Faith

Central to the issue of truth is the concept of faith. Now, most Christians do not seem to understand that "faith" has an application that is far broader than the way that we use it in our Christian jargon. "Faith," in its generic sense, is involved in every decision from the moment that we "believe" that we are able to get out of bed, that our car will start, that we will be able to get to work safely, that we will have a job when we get there, that every appliance that we use will work, etc., etc. Faith is simply action based upon knowledge with an expected outcome. In the examples given, we act on prior knowledge towards an intended result.

But, that result is not guaranteed. Sometimes, with a back problem, we are not able to get out of bed; our cars don't start when we need them; we have an accident on our way to work, or we are fired when we get to work; and an appliance does not work when its on button is pushed. Yet, on a daily basis we act on our faith that those things will not happen, as they have in the past.

Faith in the realm of truth and religion is functions in the exact same manner, as generic faith. We act on knowledge towards an expected outcome. Reality (truth) determines whether that outcome indeed occurs. **Reality** determines whether our faith is true! (See Definitions of Truth, above.)

Among Christians, faith has too much of a mysterious, ethereal quality, when it is in reality quite concrete. One of the confusions is two phases of faith. There is "justifying faith," in which the Christian accepts that Jesus Christ died for his sins and expects all the hope and promises that that God gives with that status.

Subsequently, there is "sanctifying faith," in which the Christian lives his life, implementing more and more of his understanding of what God would have him to do. Now, obviously both these terms are included in "saving faith." Yet, the application of "saving faith" to conversion (initial confession and interest in the things of God), and its application to the life of faith (sanctification) are decidedly different. "Saving faith" alone is insufficient to be applied to both areas without better understanding than most Christians seem to have.

Those two kinds of faith are quite concrete and focus on specific knowledge in each segment which Christians are to act upon.

The confusion about what faith is, and is not, is another of the major reasons that Christians are so weak and irrelevant today. They think that somehow they have to conjure up some sort of energy to motivate them to learn and to do rightly. That is really magical thinking and has nothing to do with Christianity. Brothers and sisters, **you simply act upon what you know to do**. If you act, it is faith. If you don't act, then you only have knowledge, not faith. In saying "simply," I do not mean that it is easy. But, **you already know what to do**, so act on that knowledge and your faith will grow. (I have written a whole book on faith, which will eventually be placed online - Link.)

What About Epistemology?

Epistemology is also central to these discussions. Epistemology is simply, "how does one know what one knows." And, that simple definition assumes that one can know. If one can know, then one has some element of truth.

Rene Descartes said, "I think, therefore I am." For a simple phrase, it has profound assumptions. The thinker assumes that his own mind is trustworthy. He **assumes** that his senses (seeing, hearing, touching, etc.) give him reliable information. He is **assuming** his existence. When you are dreaming, do you think that it is real? Then, you wake up! How can you prove that you will not wake up from this "dream" of life?

It is not until you embrace the Bible that you know that your assumptions are true, or at least trustworthy. Albert Camus once said that the only logical conclusion in contemplation of any purpose of life is suicide. He was reasoning correctly from his presuppositions. Only when God says in His Book that what a person reads is true and understandable have your assumptions been proven, and you have arrived at truth. (See Summary Principles of Epistemology that follow here.)

Everyone Starts with Assumptions

Everyone starts with assumptions. Synonyms for assumptions include axioms, first principles, presuppositions, and premises. There are many words for such beginning principles, and the student new to this area, should see how many of these he can learn from the dictionary. Else, he will be hopelessly lost in trying to understand how one arrives at knowledge that is trustworthy and/or true.

Modern science, as we generally understand those words, starts with the assumption that the supernatural does not exist. Therefore, creation by God, the Flood, the Israelites crossing the Red Sea, the Virgin Birth, and other Biblical miracles are simply not "true" because of that assumption. There is no need for "proof," for proof itself is based upon assumptions. Therefore, it is fruitless to argue among people with different assumptions. Before they will accept your proof, you have to get them to accept your assumptions.

Again, the Christian should gain boldness when he realizes that everyone starts with assumptions. Then, from the beginning he is on equal footing with any other knowledge that differs from Biblical knowledge. When he includes all the empirical evidences for the Bible and for Christianity, then he is powerfully armed for his own faith in God and to take on all others who would challenge this knowledge.

The Role of Logic*

"Logic is the study of the methods by which the conclusion is proved beyond all doubt" (Gordon Clark, *Logic*, Jefferson, Maryland: The Trinity Foundation: 1985), p. 1).

"The whole counsel of God concerning all things necessary for his own glory, man's salvation, faith and life, is either expressly set down in Scripture, or by good and necessary consequence may be deduced from Scripture" (Westminster Confession of Faith, Chapter I:6).

This definition of logic and the statement of the Westminster fathers demonstrate how the Scriptures can be infallibly applied beyond its own words. For example, the word, "Trinity," nowhere appears in Scripture. Yet, there are numerous Biblical texts that "prove beyond all doubt" that God is a Trinity.

We are briefly surveying areas related to truth, so we cannot go into much detail about logic. But we can make some brief statements. 1) Logic starts with premises (assumptions, above). The process of logic has nothing to say about the truth of these premises. 2) If one's premises are true, and one reasons logically, then one's conclusions are always true, infallibly.

We are not discussing "rational thinking," which is a loose term to describe any number of processes by which conclusions may be drawn. ("Reasonable" is a synonym.) Logic refers to a formal system, which in many parts and process, is agreed upon by both believer and unbeliever.

302

It is important for us to review logic here because Scripture has principles that by logic extend "all things necessary" to areas not named by Scripture. For example, the Bible nowhere mentions the word "abortion" in an ethical sense. Yet, if the Bible states that the taking of all human life with the exceptions of self-defense, capital punishment, and just war, is murder; that human life begins at conception; then, abortion is murder.

If the premise from Scripture is true, and the conclusion is reasoned logically, then the conclusion is true, and therefore as authoritative as Scripture.

*Note: See the introduction of this chapter for related information on logic.

Exceptions to "Thou Shalt Not Bear False Witness"

I remember in the 1970s when the story of Corrie ten Boom became popular among Christians. On the one hand, there was great rejoicing from her testimony. On the other hand, her story caused great angst among Christians, including myself. The dilemma was this. "How does one not reveal that he is hiding Jews (on anyone else) when the Germans knock on your door and ask, 'Are you hiding any Jews?'"

But, if we had been Biblically knowledgeable, this situation poses no dilemma at all. The Hebrew midwives lied to Pharoah's inquirers about how their babies were able to be born alive (Exodus 1:19-20). Rahab was honored for her hiding of the Hebrew spies which necessitated lying to the King's officials so that they could report back to Joshua (Hebrews 11:31; James 2:25). God directed Joshua to deceive the men of Ai, in order to defeat them (Joshua 8). God directed Samuel to lie to Saul (I Samuel 16:2).

The principle that is derived from these examples where God directs lying to His people is that **the enemies of God and His justice have no right to the trut**h. Where life is threatened immorally and for unbiblical reasons, those who threatened have no right to the truth.

Now, one must be very careful how this exception is applied. For example, once an enemy is captured or his threat is otherwise completely and finally thwarted, he becomes "your neighbor," and he has every right to the truth that is due to him.

One does not always have to reveal everything to one's neighbor. That is, being truthful does not mean revealing everything that one is thinking or that one knows. If several dishes of a meal are just unpalatable, one can always compliment the hostess for the "delicious dessert" or whatever portion was good.

We cannot deal with all the nuances here, but again God's wisdom in our fallen state is revealed in "thou shall not bear false witness against they neighbor," instead of "thou must tell the truth and the whole truth to everyone."

Sola Scriptura Is Not Enough to Apply God's Truth

One of the five "sola's" of the Protestant Reformation was "sola Scriptura." I believe that in our day, that principle has been carried to an extreme that has actually reduced the authority of Scripture.

Now, before I explain, the reader should remember all that I have said above. The only truth that man can know is Biblical truth. That is sola Scriptura. The Bible is infallible, inerrant, authoritative as the very Word of God, and fully sufficient for everything that we need for salvation and righteousness. So, what to I mean, "Sola Scriptura is not enough?"

Just this, in studying and applying the Bible, Christians need to understand hermeneutics, logic vs. rational thinking, theories of truth, the empiricism of science, principles of epistemology, languages, and other areas of knowledge that bring out the breadth and depth of Scripture that will remain hidden without these areas.

Perhaps, the Reformers assumed these other applications to Scripture. Surely, Martin Luther, John Calvin, and others knew these areas with considerable competence. And, many seminaries train men for the pastorate and other vocations with many of them. Yet, there is a failure somewhere. **The Bible is just not being taught with the fullness that changes people, societies, and nations**.

I believe that sola scriptura, that the Bible is sufficient within itself, is the major problem with Christian influence today. **The Bible is more than adequate as instruction for any and all problems of mankind, but not without application of all the "extras" that allow for its fullest expression and application**.

Sola Scriptura rightly limits truth to God's Word only. But, sola Scriptura must be accompanied by methods and knowledge outside of itself for all of its wonderful message to be known and implemented for mankind.

The Pragmatic Test of Truth

Basically, the pragmatic test of truth is "what works." That is, whatever theory or practice has the best outcome is true.

But, "best outcome" is loaded with ethical (moral) value. Who determines that an outcome is "good?" Is the easy-divorce of today's permissible society and agreeing laws "good?" Or, is the Biblical design marriage "good?" Are easily and legally obtained abortions "good?" Or, is abortion some form of murder where the "good" is punishment by the state of those who practice it? Is imprisonment of criminals, regardless of the crime, a "good" thing? Or, should restitution, a clear Biblical principle, be applied in cases of theft?

A Biblical worldview is the most pragmatic system that can ever be devised. Moreover, it is the only system in which there is not conflict between the individual, the family, society, the church, the state (at all levels), the world, and God Himself, when rightly understood and applied! See Davis and Van Til below.

There is no question that modern science and technology have great usefulness. Yet, neither determines **what will be developed nor what will be applied in what situations**! See Science and Technology.

Summary Principles of Truth

The following are summaries of the discussion that follows. These statements involve nuances that are more fully discussed in the text. Please do not try to understand or draw conclusions from these positions, as "stand alones."

1. The concept of truth (and many Biblical concepts) is not well understood today because of a lack of **attention to definitions** that is found generally among pastors, teachers, and laymen alike.

Philosophers throughout all history have sought for an objective standard for truth. Getting away from subjectivity in truth has always been the great dilemma. But, **God has solved that problem for Christians: they have an objective source - the Protestant Bible!**

2. Every Bible verse, for example, John 3:16, is fully pregnant with meaning, if a more complete understanding of the words is known.

3. Truth is a Person or Persons (Trinity) who knows everything in the universe and its relationship to everything else.

Again, one of the great issues of truth throughout history has been the relationship of the subjective with the objective. In Christianity, we have that beautifully joined. God is fully objective (totally impartial in His understanding) while being a Person (subjective).

4. Truth is the 66 books of the Protestant Bible. Any claim that God has spoken truth to mankind in any other way or by additional content is heresy (Revelation 22:18-19).

5. "Telling the truth" by an individual person is fraught with difficulties that include unintentional mistakes, limited knowledge, finite senses (eyesight, hearing, etc.), and intentional deceit. No one can tell the whole truth except God.

6. The large emphasis of the Bible is on truth from God, spoken as "Thus saith the Lord" in historical context and written by the Old Testament prophets or otherwise recorded as God-breathed through the writers of Scripture.

7. Man can know the truth of the Bible. It is truth, not analogy.

8. All man's best efforts at truth are relative because he is finite.

9. "All truth is God's truth," as it is often used by psychologists, is heresy. "All truth is indeed God's truth, but any claim to truth must always survive the test of a thoroughgoing Biblical hermeneutic.

10. In every way that the Bible has been tested honestly and fairly, for example, archeology and evolutionary science, the Bible has been shown to be true.

11. Christians deny the Word of God and its power by their actions. While God promises that the Bible has everything for life and godliness in every area of knowledge, too many Christians virtually ignore its knowledge outside of personal salvation.

12. "Telling the truth" and "not lying" are the same from the subjective center of one person. They are the same for God.

13. Man's "truth" is always relative in that man's knowledge is limited to the factors listed in #5 (above).

14. Man's testimony, even in the "trivial" things of life, like giving directions to get to a certain destination, **is important to prevent harm to the other person**, as well as to preserve his own character and reputation. In matters of truth and Scripture, he must give even more diligence, since these matters involve issues of eternity.

15. Man's "truth," including the theories and empiricism of science, **has great pragmatic (functional) value**, in spite of its extreme limitations as truth. However, a Biblical worldview is the most pragmatic system possible for mankind. The Pragmatic Test of Truth

16. Virtually all Christians need to wrestle with the concept of truth, relative to the Bible and to a determination of truth outside the Bible. Certainly, the concept of truth should be discussed more in churches with practical application.

17. There needs to be a distinction between man's "truth" and God's truth. The words to use are subject to debate, but efforts at this nomenclature is imperative to giving the Bible the authority that Christians and the world needs.

18. A definition of truth is "what is" or "everything that is to be known about an object and its relationship to every other object in the universe." "What is" exists regardless of what we think of any part or whole in the universe. Thus, only God can know truth. But, man can know God's truth that He has revealed in His Word.

19. Faith has several definitions, and therefore, is misunderstood by most Christians. What an individual will accept as true is determined by his faith, not by "facts" or "proof."

20. Epistemology or "how I know what I know" is just another name for trying to arrive at truth.

21. A corollary of #19 is that **what one will accept as true is pre-determined by what one is willing to accept as true**. This is subjective or personal truth. The only objective truth is the Protestant Bible.

22. "Logic is the study of methods by which the conclusion is proved beyond all doubt." Logic, rightly applied, allows the extension of the truth of Scripture beyond its actual words.

Logic has nothing to say about the truth of the propositions that are reasoned from, only the process by which conclusions are reached. Conclusions reasoned logically from truth are truth, also. But, propositions of falsehood which follow logical reasoning are still falsehoods.

23. An enemy of God and His justice has not right to the truth from those who represent God and oppose this enemy.

24. The fullness of Biblical application and understanding requires methods that lie outside of "sola Scriptura."

Summary Principles of Epistemology

1. **Simple subject**. Epistemology for the Bible-believing Christian is **a simple subject**. He accepts the Bible as the very word of God written. If one claims to be a Christian and does not accept the Bible in this way, he is not a Christian. The Holy Spirit who regenerates cannot deny the Word that He wrote. Consistent with living a life in the Spirit, a Christian will be involved in a life-long, diligent study of the Bible (Hebrews 11:6).

Tests of this acceptance or defining issues in basic beliefs about the Bible include a) the Biblical account of Creation and rejection of evolution, including theistic evolution; b) acceptance of a worldwide Flood; c) special revelation as the final interpreter of general revelation, d) Biblical law as the interpreter of natural and any other source of law; e) Biblical truth having authority over all psychological theories and practice; f) the role of the church in individuals, families, society and state governments; g) the priority of worship as "the chief end of man"; h) identifying the two most important divisions of mankind: the saved and the unsaved; i) sexuality being permitted only in marriage between a man and a woman; and j) existence of supernatural beings, especially Satan, known as both the Prince of Darkness and The Angel of Light.

This is not an exhaustive list, but one that is sufficient to challenge those who might consider themselves Bible-believers. "The Lord our God is one," and His Word stands or falls as a whole. (See appropriate Worldview Areas for substantiation and discussion of these broad and basic concepts.)

2. **Objectivity and ultimate hope**. The Bible is, epistemologically, the ultimate hope of all serious and careful philosophers in history: an objective source of truth that governs and interprets all other claims of truth, never changes, and has a global acceptance as truth (as the gospel advances throughout the earth).

If truth is not objective, then truth does not exist because the only other means of epistemology is to accept one authority over all others or to let a majority vote (*vox populi*, bureaucracy, committee, legislative body, council of popes, etc.). Since individual authorities and votes change, truth by definition as never changing, cannot exist by this means.

3. **Truth, Knowledge, Valid Knowledge, and Non-contradiction**. The most valid knowledge of any object includes a serious Biblical knowledge of that object by a regenerate mind (person), as well as rational and empirical inquiry. When correctly understood, Biblical knowledge and any other knowledge never conflict or contradict the other. There is no separation into "sacred" and "secular" within a Biblical system. God, as a unity, created the entire universe as a unified whole.

Relevance of subject. Fullest consideration should be given to Biblical understanding of any subject, even those that seem objective, for example, mathematics, physics, and chemistry. The Bible's relevance in many areas of scholarly study is often easily dismissed or overlooked by many Christians. The direct relevance of the Bible progresses from (perhaps) minimal influence on the objective sciences to a necessary and controlling influence on the sciences that interpret what man is and what he does (for example, sociology and psychology). See Stob, *Theological Reflections*, pages 21-22.

Influence of time. Knowledge that seems valid or "true" at one time and place may be replaced by more careful and complete study. Only truth (see above) never changes. The attitude of modernists that truth is only found in modern times is blatantly false.

"Progression" of Biblical truth. While the content of the Bible never changes, Christians' understanding may change. Indeed, there is a sense of progressive revelation in which Christians build on the work of those who have gone before. For example, John Calvin greatly advanced Augustine's ideas and discussion of predestination. See The Mind of Christ.

Depth and breadth. With serious study and reflective thought, the depth and breath of any subject from a Biblical perspective can be considerable. For example, two of the authors of this website have developed a comprehensive worldview in medicine. See www.bmei.org.

Truth. The Bible is truth that both the regenerate and unregenerate can understand, as its words are read in the same way as any other book. It is truth, as reality, not an analogy of truth or correspondence to reality. However, the interest, understanding, and obedience of the regenerate mind should immeasurably exceed that of the unregenerate mind. The themes and definitions of particular words must be interpreted by Scripture itself. See **Regeneration** above. (See Stob, *Theological Reflections*, page 236.)

4) **The Unregenerate**. Unregenerate man cannot know truth, except as he willing and able to understand clear statements of Scripture. For example, he may understand "Trinity," that God is three Persons in One, as that simple statement (proposition) conveys a truth. He may not know as much fullness of that meaning as a regenerate person and embrace its personal significance, but the statement (proposition) is true whether understood by a Christian or a non-Christian.

The first chapter of Romans is clear that even the unregenerate have an inexcusable knowledge of God and his moral law. Precisely what is that knowledge is debated. Yet, Christians should interact with the unregenerate on the basis that he has a responsible understanding of these concepts.

Unregenerate man can know a great deal of facts (functional or valid knowledge) about various subjects to the extent that he can achieve great accomplishments from a human perspective.

5) **Regeneration**. Regeneration imparts no knowledge, not even knowledge from the Bible. Regeneration is of the heart, not the mind. See Regeneration. Therefore, a Christian is called to a lifetime of serious Bible study "that he may be transformed by the renewing of his mind" (Romans 12:2). That is, that his mind may fully inform the heart what God requires of him. (See Stob, *Theological Reflections*, page 236.)

This "transformation" of the mind does not mean that man can know truth in the way that God knows truth. Even when we no longer "see through a glass darkly," we will not have omniscience, knowing everything or anything exhaustively, as God does. This difference is both quantitative and qualitative, yet this difference does not diminish the reality that man can know truth, as truth, not an analogy of truth.

6. Non-contradiction. Knowledge (within general or special revelation) that seems **contradictory** is wrongly understood. Serious and systematic study in both areas, particularly special revelation can often resolve these apparent contradictions.

7. Hermeneutics. Knowledge of the Bible must conform to certain basic rules of interpretation. I strongly believe, along with many other pastors and theologians, that many disagreements among Christians and churches could be resolved by following these rules consistently. See

Danger of "agreeing to disagree." "Agreeing to disagree" is a most serious and divisive step for Christians. The Mind of Christ is one mind. Within the constraints of other responsibilities, Christians should work harder to resolve these differences.

8. Full-orbed Christian life. A full life of faith and practice in all the areas (family, church, vocation, etc.) to which God has called His people enables a depth and breadth of knowledge that can be developed in no other way. That "practice" includes serious Bible study with theological helps (commentaries, lexicons, concordances, etc.).

9. Influence of age and culture. Even the best theologian and Biblical scholar cannot escape the influence of the general thinking of his age and culture. The challenge is to apply the Biblical worldview to each generation.

10. **Only two worldviews**. Ultimately, there are only two philosophies or worldviews: Biblical Christianity and all others. Or, the two categories could be: Biblical Christianity and individualism, as the content of the Bible is fixed, while all other religions and philosophies are subject to the choosing of the individual. (See Clark, *A Christian View…* 3rd Edition, page 53.)

11. **Synonyms**. The quest for truth is not as complex as secular philosophy seems to make it. Words that denote a quest for ultimate truth and are virtually synonymous in concept are: religion, worldview, ethic, reality, ultimate reality, value, fact, ontology, metaphysics, cosmology, epistemology, faith, knowledge or valid knowledge, facts, being, critical philosophy, essence, existence, monism, speculative philosophy, substance, and ground of meaning. Again,

there are "ultimately" only two: Biblical Christianity (in all the fullness of sound theology and worldview [ethics]) and all others.

12. **Unexamined worldviews**. The large majority of worldviews, held by individuals including Christians, are unexamined. Principles and "facts" are simply accumulated over one's lifetime, randomly existing in one's mind, and applied situationally with inconsistency and according to personal desires.

13. **Presuppositions**. All worldviews, religions, and philosophies are based upon "givens," also know as presuppositions, premises, axioms of life, first principles, etc.

14. **Person**. Ultimately, truth is both objective and subjective, a Person, Jesus Christ. "I am the way, the truth, and the life..."

15. **Science**. Science (in its modern sense) is always (A) a construct of axioms, theories, premises, and other assumptions and (B) strict limitations of experiment. As such, science is never a source of truth, while it may achieve great functional value.

Further Study

For a full discussion of truth, Scripture, and epistemology, see The Bible and Truth: Comprehensive Review

Clark, Gordon. *God's Hammer: The Bible and Its Critics*. Chapter 2. An excellent review of the Bible as truth, based upon epistemological considerations.

Further Reading and References

Word searches are easy at Bible Gateway.

Westminster Confession of Faith

See John Frame on "Biblicism" at www.frame-poythress.org

Order Gordon Clark's book, Logic. You can order all his books there and read some of his shorter works from the Trinity Review, as well.

For the process of formal logic, see
http://www.philosophypages.com/lg/index.htm

"All truth is God's truth." In *Psychology and Christianity: 4 Views* (edited by Eric Johnson and Stanton L. Jones, published by InterVarsity Press), Gary Collins has the chapter on "integration" (the application of "all truth is God's truth), but he never defines the principles to know what is and is not "truth" in psychology, and therefore, never defines the method by which integration can take place. When one deals with truth and God's Word, all things in play must be carefully and seriously defined and delineated!

Arthur F. Holmes has a great little book entitled, ***All Truth Is God's Truth*** (InterVarsity Press) in which he discusses what in involved in the issues of truth. My only reservation about this book is that Holmes seems to fall short of a traditional understanding of the Bible as infallible, inerrant, and divinely authoritative.

Davis, John Jefferson. *Evangelical Ethics: Issues Facing the Church Today*. (Presbyterian and Reformed Publishing Company, 1993, pages 5-9. See Our Bookstore.

Stob, Henry. *Theological Reflections*, (Eerdmans, 1981), page 39.

Van Til, Cornelius. *In Defense of the Faith: Christian Theistic Ethics*. (Presbyterian and Reformed, 1980), page 58.

15. Saving Faith

Regeneration: Born-Again, Born from Above

"Regeneration is a mighty and powerful change wrought in the soul by the efficacious working of the Holy Spirit, wherein a vital principle, a new habit, ... and a divine nature are put into and framed in the heart, enabling it to act holily and pleasingly to God... a certain spiritual and supernatural principle... infused by God... an habitual holy principle wrought in us by God... what is changed is the Spirit of the mind, the dominant tendency... the mind itself is not changed in essence or in substance, but its bias, the prevailing character is changed... a new spiritual sense and new dispositions... giving a person ability and disposition... not a new faculty of understanding... but a new kind of exercise for the same faculty of understanding... lies deeper than consciousness... (a giving of) stability and perseverance." These words are a summary of Stephen Charnock, John Owen, Jonathan Edwards, and Charles Hodge in John Laidlaw, *The Biblical Doctrine of Man*, pp. 257-260 (Klock and Klock, 1983 Reprint of 1895).

My definition of regeneration is the change wrought by the Holy Spirit in the soul or spirit(1) of a person that changes trust (belief or faith) in oneself, as the source of truth about life and how to live it, to trust in the Bible, as God offers forgiveness in Jesus Christ and tells us who we are and what our responsibilities are. Regeneration is initiation of sanctification. Other terms in the Bible for regeneration are "born-again" and "born from above."

What happens at regeneration is commonly misunderstood among Christians and leads to wrong priorities. The common focus is on salvation (2), forgiveness in Jesus Christ, the (seemingly) simple statement of John 3:16. This focus is not to be minimized, but neither is the source of that information, The Holy Bible.

One of the best summary definitions is found in Noah Webster's Dictionary of 1828 (See reference below). "The new birth (is) by the grace of God; that change by which the will and natural enmity of man to God and his law are subdued, and a principle of supreme love to God and his law, or holy affections, are implanted in the heart."

The Bible is much more than the simple message of salvation. If that were its only focus, it could have been much shorter. There is the larger Old Testament and the large part of the New Testament that orders a way of life. To focus on Christ, as important and necessary as that is, is to miss the greater instruction of the Bible.

Ask yourself this question, "How much of the Bible from Genesis to Revelation do I really know?" Would God have written useless words? The full application of **the entire Bible** is what regeneration and its subsequent process, sanctification, is directed towards. The Cultural or Creation Mandate preceded the Fall in Genesis 1:26-28, and was reinforced in the Great Commission to "make disciples of all nations." Making disciples involves much more than just "saved" and waiting to die and go to heaven.

No Knowledge Is Imparted in Regeneration

Once, when I was reading Abraham Kuyper's Principles of *Sacred Theology*, a simple statement exploded on my mind and I believe, is one of the major keys to understanding salvation and the Christian life. That phrase is, **"Regeneration by itself is no enlightening**." That is, as powerful and life-changing as this work of the Holy Spirit is, **regeneration conveys no knowledge**. Regeneration is a change in one's disposition or attitude and the object of one's belief (faith). (Read again the introduction above.) But, the knowledge of what has happened and an understanding of the finished work of Jesus Christ is not conveyed by regeneration. That knowledge is conveyed by the Scriptures, spoken or read, and is included in God's working faith and salvation in the individual. But, that know is not conveyed by regeneration per se. The change is in the heart, not in the mind. (See Reference, Stob... below.) The mind is not the "head," as in "heart vs. head" that many Christians portray as some important contrast. (See Chapter 11, "Heart and Head.")

This lack of conveyed knowledge is the reason for the Scriptures. Through a diligent study of it, we learn what God has done for our salvation and what he requires of us. That knowledge is not conveyed by regeneration, but by faith in action in studying the Bible. God's plan is for "transformation" (*metamorphosis*, the same word for "transfiguration" in Matthew 17:12) by the "renewing" of the regenerated person's mind (Romans 12:2). The heart is regenerated so that the mind can be renewed to the transformation of the one regenerated.

316

Acceptance of the Bible as the very Word of God written and governing principle of one's life is exactly what faith is. While the focus of faith is in Jesus Christ for salvation, what does one know of Jesus Christ other than what is taught in the Bible? "If anyone preaches any other gospel to you than what you have received, let him be accursed" (Galatians 1:9). There is no knowledge of Jesus Christ outside of the Bible.

If knowledge were imparted with regeneration, then God would be giving new special revelation. That is, He would be adding to the Scriptures. The canon (all the books of the Bible and their content) are fixed now and until the end of time (Revelation 22:18-19).

Translation into the Kingdom of God

Regeneration establishes a person as a member of the Kingdom of God and a citizen of heaven (John 3:5). So that to be "born again" is to be a member of Christ's Kingdom and His Church (Matthew 16:18).

Because regeneration is a permanent change in the soul, **a Christian cannot help doing good works**. Our souls have been altered so that we cannot live other than to follow the instructions of God's Word. "Can the Ethiopian change his skin or the leopard its spots?" (Jeremiah 13:23). Of course, one must have instruction from God's Word in what those good works are. (Link to Law and Grace.)

Regeneration may occur from any moment after conception to just prior to death. It may be a sudden, intense experience or a more subtle quiet event. It may occur before consciousness early in one's life, even before birth. Children, born and raised to Christian parents, may never have a born again experience but their speech and behavior gives clear evidence that they "trust and obey" the Savior and His Word. That does not mean that such a person will not have a profound sense of sin and the necessity of repentance. Indeed, this is that evidence of regeneration.

This variation in timing and differences in experience are not often taught or preached. Thus, Christians often get confused whether they themselves are saved or others are saved. But, dear brothers and sisters, the Bible and practical experience answer this dilemma. The evidence of salvation is not based upon an experience of change, but evidence of salvation. (See Assurance of Salvation: Simply Considered.)

One evidence is specific knowledge. "If you confess with your mouth the Lord Jesus and believe in your heart that God has raised Him from the dead, you will be saved" (Romans 10:9). The second is works. "Faith without works is dead" (James 2:26). The answer does not lie in an experience at a moment of time or even "feeling saved," but in speech with specific content and the works (fruit) of one's life.

More on Regeneration

The following quote is from *The New International Commentary on the New Testament* by John Murray. While its subject is not identified as regeneration, Murray's discussion of the characteristics of "the flesh" and "the Spirit" actually describe the characteristics of the unregenerate ("the flesh") and the regenerate ("the Spirit"). "The flesh" and "the Spirit" are categories that are separated by a chasm (Luke 16:26) that is cannot be crossed by anything that man can do. Only God can regenerate the soul from "flesh" to "Spirit."

> The two expressions "after the flesh" (vss. 4, 5) and "in the flesh" (vss. 8, 9) have the same effect, with this difference that in the former the flesh is viewed as the determining pattern and in the latter as the conditioning sphere –**the persons concerned are conditioned by and patterned after the flesh**. "The flesh" is human nature as corrupted, directed, and controlled by sin. "After the Spirit" (vss. 4-5) and "in the Spirit" (vs. 9) are also to the same effect, with a similar distinction as to the angle from which the relationship to the Holy Spirit is viewed. **Those concerned are conditioned by and patterned after the Holy Spirit**.
>
> To "mind the things of the flesh" (vs. 5) is to have the things of the flesh as **the absorbing objects of thought, interest, affection, and purpose**. And "the mind of the flesh" (vs. 6) is **the dispositional complex**, including not simply the activities of reason, but also those of feeling and will, patterned after and controlled by the flesh. In like manner, to mind "the things of the Spirit" (vs. 5) is to have the things of the Holy Spirit as the absorbing objects of thought, interest, affection, and purpose, and the "mind of the Spirit" is **the dispositional complex**, including the exercises of reason, feeling, and will, patterned after and controlled by the Holy Spirit.

The expressions, "after the flesh" ("in the flesh"), "mind the things of the flesh" ("the mind of the flesh"), "walk after the flesh" stand in causal relationship to one another and are also, most probably, to be understood as causally related in the order stated. The **first** defines the basic moral condition, the **second**, the inward frame of heart and mind resulting from that condition, and the **third**, the practice emanating from both, but more particularly from the first through the second. The same principles in the opposite direction hold with reference to "after the Spirit" ("in the Spirit"), to mind "the things of the Spirit" ("the mind of the Spirit"), and walk "after the Spirit."

The mind of the flesh is death" (vs. 6) does not mean that the mind of the flesh causes or leads to (physical) death. There is an equation, and the predicate specifies that in which the mind of the flesh consists. **The principle of death is separation**, and here the most accentuated expression of that principle is in view, namely, separation from God (cf. Isaiah 59:2). This separation is thought of in terms of our estrangement form God whereby we are dead in trespasses and sins (cf. Ephesians 2:1). The mind of the flesh is therefore that kind of death.

The mind of the Spirit is life and peace" (vs. 6). The same kind of identification appears here. "Life" is contrasted with "death" and in its highest expression, which must be in view here, it means the knowledge and fellowship of God (cf. John 17:3; I John 1:3), the communion which is the apex of true religion. "Peace" can readily be seen to be the correlate of life. In this case, it is no doubt the subjective effect of peace with God (5:1) that is contemplated, the sense of being at one with God and the tranquility of heart and mind which the sense of reconciliation evokes (cf. Philippians 4:7). Peace is antithesis of the alienation and misery which sin creates.

Summary Principles of Regeneration

1. Regeneration takes place in the heart, one designation of man's immaterial self. It is a work of God the Holy Spirit in which God actively changes a person. As a person does not assist with his own physical birth, neither does he have any part in regeneration which is entirely an act of God the Holy

Spirit. The person is passive in the process, but its effect initiates and perseveres in faith, repentance, and sanctification.

2. Regeneration begins sanctification which is in itself a life-long process. Regeneration is a permanent change that can never be lost or reversed. This change initiates the ordo salutis which ends in glorification (the fulfillment and final stage of The Kingdom of God). A person who is truly saved (regenerate) can never become unregenerate, although he may "fall into grievous sins and for a time continue therein (Westminster Confession of Faith, Chapter 17, Section 3—see website link below).

3. Regeneration translates a person into the Church and the Kingdom of God. Regeneration is the **only** means by which a person becomes a member of the Kingdom of God or a member of the universal (catholic) church. Unfortunately, some "conversion" experiences mimic regeneration.

4. Regeneration allows infants and children to enter the Kingdom of Heaven upon their untimely death before their ability consciously to confess and repent or what some call "the age of accountability." (See the Westminster Confession of Faith, Chapter 10, Section 3)

5. Regeneration, as a change in the soul, does not convey any knowledge. It causes belief (faith) in the Scriptures as the Word of God and the message of salvation in God's Son. Thus, one evidence of a regenerated person is his love of the reading and study of the Word of God.

6. Since regeneration does not convey knowledge (see #5), all that we learn is by our study and others' teaching of the Bible (Ephesians 4:7-16). Direct verbal teaching from God (revelation) is no longer given, as God's speaking directly to men and women has ended (Revelation 22:18-19).

7. Since regeneration is an act of the Holy Spirit, He will never give direction that is contrary to the Bible. A perceived leading of the Spirit that does not agree with the Bible cannot be of the Holy Spirit, as He cannot contradict Himself.

8. Regeneration may occur early in life, or even before birth. Thus, all Christians with solid evidence of a life of faith will not have had a conversion experience. However, all who are regenerate (true Christians) will have ample evidence of faith, repentance, and progress in sanctification. Officers must keep these differences in mind when interviewing candidates for acceptance into the church.

9. Regeneration of a person always results in good works (James 2:17) and progress in sanctification.

10. Regeneration always precedes saving faith and repentance, although many persons may have many years, even decades, living the Christian life before God regenerates them (as the author himself experienced). The "second-birth" that many experience and claim as such is actually the true experience of being "born-again" (regenerated). They fail to understand the ordo salutis (see this website link above), and thus distort it.

Notes

1) I believe that a person is bipartite. Heart, soul, mind, will, and spirit are different views of the same immaterial substance of a person.. As colors are diffused through the various facets of a diamond, the immaterial dimensions of a person are described according to their function. While, indeed, man is a unity of body (material) and soul (immaterial), it is important to recognize that he has a substance that is non-physical.

2) Salvation, also, has a greater concept that is commonly realized. (Link - under construction)

3) The Church, as being used here, is the "holy catholic (universal) church," not a local body or denomination.

Book References

***The best summary of all the aspects of regeneration: *Practical discourses on regeneration* by Philip Dodderidge, University of Michigan Reprint Series, reprinted from the original, of 1855. Available from Amazon.com.

On regeneration before birth and early in life, see Abraham Kuyper, *The Work of the Holy Spirit*, Chapter 21 and Kuyper's *Principles of Sacred Theology*, p. 389.

On regeneration not infusing knowledge, see Abraham Kuyper, *Principles of Sacred Theology*, p. 580. Also, note the absence of the mention of knowledge in the introduction to this section above.

One of the best summaries, yet, again does not contain all the above is Louis Berkof, *Systematic Theology*, "Regeneration and Effectual Calling," pp. 465-479.

On regeneration of the heart and not the mind, see Henry Stob, *Theological Reflections*, pages 235-236.

Salvation: Its Phases and Wonderful Fullness: Often Considered Too Narrowly

You will note from what follows that salvation is commonly thought of too narrowly by Christians. We usually think in terms of regeneration, sanctification, and glorification (heaven). But, the fullness of what God the Father, God the Son, and God the Holy Spirit have given us is much greater. This information is a beginning work.

As you will note, this article is in outline form only. I hope to develop it into a full article sometime soon. If you have comments, either in not understanding these short phrases or in developing it further, please let me know.

Salvation consists of three (3) phases:

... we have been saved (justification) "Believe on the Lord Jesus Christ and you shall be saved."

... we are bring saved (sanctification) "Work out your salvation with fear and trembling."

... we will be saved (glorification) "For now we see in a mirror, dimly, but then face to face."

Saved from what?

1. **Ourselves**

A. Headlong rush towards self-destruction, dissipation in excess

B. Misery in this life; no sense of why "bad" things happen

C. No meaningful purpose in life

D. Self-determination of what is good or bad for me, that is, we have no reference outside of ourselves to determine what is right and wrong.

E. Wrong attitudes

F. Works of the flesh, see Galatians 5:19-20 below

H. Conflicts with others: see "F" above

I. False worship and misplaced love: idols of intellect, money, prestige, power, pride, family, achievement.

Galatians 5:19-20: deeds of the flesh: sexual immorality, impurity and debauchery; idolatry and witchcraft; hatred, discord, jealousy, fits of rage, selfish ambition, dissensions, factions and envy; drunkenness, orgies, and the like. (Galatians 5:19-20)

J. Crippling, life-controlling guilt; nothing in mankind's history (including all the works of psychology) has the answer to man's real guilt, and through an understanding of forgiveness, to resolve guilt feelings. (See Guilt and Guilt Feelings.)

2. From the control of outside circumstances and people

A. Danger from other people: random (car accident), purposeful (identity theft, burglary, murder, etc.)

B. Circumstances beyond our control: stock market crash

3. **Christless eternity**: Hell, weeping, wailing, and gnashing of teeth; Lake of Fire; loneliness beyond any despair known on earth; eternal screaming in anger; and unassuaged pain, torment, and fear.

4. **The wrath and curse of God**; "all men are without excuse"

5. **A harsh, capricious, and brutal universe**. There are meteors that might end life on earth, as we know it; nuclear war; earthquakes, floods, hurricanes, and all earthly disasters. Since God is Sovereign, there are no "random" events in His universe.

Saved to what?

1. **Physical health**: the fruit of the spirit, morality of the Law, peace of the Spirit, and rest in God's Providence produce the maximum health that can be experienced on earth. While some Christians have severe acute and chronic illness as believers, the health that they experience within these conditions is maximized for them as individuals within these same parameters. One of the words that is used for "salvation" in the Greek is the root of the word that is "hygiene" in English.

2. **Peace of mind, heart, and soul**. See what we are saved from above!!

Peace in the Bible almost always refers to being at peace with God, not with circumstances, other people, a decision made, or anything else. Peace in the Bible is a synonym of salvation.

3. **To make a better family, society, nation, and world (love)**: evangelism and missions to give others the blessings of salvation, ministries of mercy, obedience to the state, restitution and reconciliation of sins and crimes, providing a basis of law for civil government, etc.

4. **Hope**! Hope that all that is in this section will be realized and, then, heaven!

5. **Absolute control of a harsh, capricious, and brutal universe**. One of the concepts of salvation in the Bible is to be "saved" from a disaster, for example, a ship-wreck. In Christ, we are "safe" from all storms. While we may still experience the ravages of life, "underneath are the everlasting arms."

6. **A local and universal family (the Church)** and all its provisions of physical and spiritual nurture.

7. **All the resources of God's greatness (Providence) available to us for His purposes.** God will give us as little or as much as we need

(and so many of our wants) for ourselves, our families, and our ministries. If we lack, it is because our desires are inconsistent with His own.

For a textual discussion of salvation as being saved from certain problems to certain safety, see Henry Stob, *Sin, Salvation, and Service*, Board of Publications of the Christian Reformed Church, 1983.

Assurance of Salvation: Simply Considered

The most important question for anyone is, "How can I be assured that I am saved?" The answer is really quite simple, ""Believe on the Lord Jesus Christ, and you will be saved" (Acts 16:31).

You wanted more? Well, let us unpack that simple phrase. What does it mean to "believe?" Belief means to accept, as true, a statement as it is presented. The Biblical statement about Christ is that He is God (John 10:3) and that He provided the ultimate sacrifice for individual sin (I John 2:2). Do you accept that two-part statement as true? If so, you are saved! (For more on the concept of faith, see Faith: What It Is and What It Is Not."

"That's all?," you ask. "There has to be more." Well, not really. Inherent in that statement is that you believe that the Bible is true. Inherent is that statement is that a statement believed is a statement acted upon.

That is, if you believe that two-part statement, then you will act like a Christ-one. (Christian is what "believers" in Christ are called.)

Well, then, what do Christians do? Christians read and study their Bibles. They pray. They are baptized and participate in The Lord's Supper. They are members of a church where others believe this two-part statement to the extent that the Bible is taught and preached, the two sacraments just named are practiced, and erring members are disciplined. They evangelize. They raise their children "in the nurture and admonition" of the Lord. They experience the fruit of the Spirit (Galatians 5:22-23). They do not regularly and flagrantly practice the evils of the flesh (Galatians 5:19-21). They "love their wives (husbands) as Christ loved the church." And, they practice all the other "good works" that the Bible calls them to practice.

Indeed, herein is the failure of most of those who want assurance, and those who counsel them how to find that assurance: the consistent and fervent practice of good works is the evidence of one's belief. And, being

active in good works, Christians "strengthen their assurance" (WCF: Chapter16, Section 2). The reference verse of this assurance is, "Now by this we know that we know Him, if we keep His commandments. He who says, "I know Him," and does not keep His commandments, is a liar, and the truth is not in him. But whoever keeps His word, truly the love of God is perfected in him. By this we know that we are in Him (I John 2:3-5, NKJV).

So, the Christian who wants assurance and who is not active in a full life of good works, is avoiding perhaps the most crucial area that can give him assurance! In fact, he will decrease his assurance, because he is living a sinful life. Sin, without active confession and active obedience (applied practically in putting on right behavior), actually increases one's true guilt and feelings of guilt, driving the person further from assurance!

The error of those who want assurance, and those who counsel them, is to focus on "feeling" saved.

Feelings are transient. God and His Word are "the same yesterday, today, and forever" (Hebrews 13:8).

I feel good one moment, discouraged the next. I crawl out of bed some mornings ready to attack the day. Other mornings, I literally crawl out of bed. When I get sick, I feel bad. When I get well, I feel good. Someone imposes on me, I get angry. I barely avoid a serious auto accident and find myself trembling with fear. I worry about the safety and welfare of my children. Dear readers, feelings come and go, moment by moment, hundreds of times each day. Do we want to trust in those frail moments?

Or, do we want to trust in God and His Word which never change? Who always speaks true? Yes, the choice is that simple: feelings or God and truth (the Bible). God is perfectly just. He is completely trustworthy. Surely, we can rest our eternal salvation in His hands, not our own feelings.

Still, you may ask, "But I don't know if I really believe." **You cannot escape that way**. I have already said that if you believe, your life is characterized by all the activities above. There is evidence of belief or there is not evidence.

You may persist, "But I don't do many of those things. I believe that I should, but I don't!"

Ah! Pay dirt! Gotcha! Nailed! The crux of the matter. If you don't practice those things in some consistent and compete way, you don't truly

believe! This notion that you can believe and not practice consistent with that belief is the problem of doubt of modern Christians that they do not "feel saved." The Bible's use of faith (**the noun form of "believe"**) is always succeeded by action. When Peter doubted, he began to sink. He did not say, "Lord, I believe, but I am sinking!" The father of the demon-possessed child cried out, "Lord, I believe, help my unbelief" (Mark 9:24). He did not cry, "Lord, I believe, but not enough to help my son." If fact, in the previous sentence, Jesus said, "All things are possible to him who believes" (Mark 9:23).

"For as (a man) thinks in his heart, so is he," Proverbs 23:7. What a person truly is (believes) in his innermost being (heart), that he cannot avoid practicing. "For out of the abundance of the heart (belief), the mouth speaks" (Matthew 12:34).

Reader, you may have work to do!

1) If you do not believe that "belief without action is a lie," then you must prove me wrong **from Scripture**, for the Bible has definitions that often differ from secular ones. You can do a word search on "faith," "believe," and "belief" here. 2) If you believe that you are a Christian and are not practicing the many activities of the Christian's life (above), then you must implement those in your life. If you need practical help, read The Christian Counselor's Manual, these homework manuals, and other books by Jay Adams and Wayne Mack. They will give you clear and practical directions. 3) If you consistently practice these activities, then read on, and praise God!

I want to add one qualifier. **No one practices everything that God requires perfectly. At issue here are the overall activities and direction of the life. If you do not want to practice the activities of the Christian life in a full and meaningful way, you are not a Christian, pure and simple. If the large majority of your activities and conversation is what God requires, then you are a Christian and are saved, pure and simple**. The fact that you falter in these activities only means that you are not yet made perfect. That state is reserved for heaven.

The power of individual Christians and that of churches is being neutralized by church people who spend too much time worrying about whether they are Christians or not, instead of attacking the Gates of Hell. God is fully trustworthy in everything that He said. If you believe it, you will live it, fully but not perfectly, pure and simple. "Trust and obey, for these is no other way, to be happy in Jesus, but to trust and obey."

Get on with the life of a Christian. Stop wanting something more (feelings, an audible voice from heaven) than God gives. "Believe (and act) on the Lord Jesus Christ, and you will be (are) saved."

1. Understand that "faith" is the noun equivalent of "believe" and a synonym of "faith." . Do a word search for "faith" on this website. See the Section The Relevance of Faith in Truth: Concepts...

2. Do a word search for "emotion" on this website or read all the articles in the Worldview Area of Psychology, Counseling and Emotions

3. Do word searches in the Bible and read all verses that contain them on these words: heart, belief, believe, and faith. http://www.biblegateway.com/keyword/

16. Crime and Punishment

Summary Principles of Crime and Punishment

The following is a brief summary of crime and punishment. It is largely taken from Poythress, *The Shadow of Christ...* with some comments of my own. (All quotes from Poythress are used with permission of the publisher.)

Perhaps, no area of ethics or worldview has been so neglected by modern Christians that the area of crime and punishment except perhaps by theonomists The book cited here by Vern Poythress is by far the most extensive of which I am aware. Robertson McQuilkin, in his comprehensive book on Biblical ethics, also addresses the issues of Crime and Punishment (pages 352-369).

A definition from Webster's 1828 dictionary is a starting point.

> Crime. An act which violates a law, divine or human; an act which violates a rule of moral duty; an offense against the laws of right, prescribed by God or man, or against any rule of duty plainly implied in those laws. A crime may consist in omission or neglect, as well as in commission, or positive transgression. The commander of a fortress who suffers the enemy to take possession by neglect, is as really criminal, as one who voluntarily opens the gates without resistance.

> But in a more common and restricted sense, a crime denotes an offense, or violation of public law, of a deeper and more atrocious nature; a public wrong; or a violation of the commands of God, and the offenses against the laws made to preserve the public rights; as treason, murder, robbery, theft, arson, etc. The minor wrongs committed against individuals or private rights, are denominated trespasses, and the minor wrongs against public rights are called misdemeanors. Crimes and misdemeanors are punishable by indictment, information or public prosecution; trespasses or private injuries, at the suit of the individuals injured. But in many cases an act is

considered both as a public offense and a trespass, and is punishable both by the public and the individual injured.

Carl F. H. Henry weighs in similarly.

> There is ... a serious danger in trying to bypass the Bible's concrete expression of God's justice. However, there is also a danger in the opposite direction. We could try to ignore questions of principle entirely, and without reflection apply the Mosaic law in a slavish, wooden way." (Poythress, page 225) By far, the more serious neglect of our times is the neglect of the study and equitable application of all Biblical law.

> "While historically it was emphasized that offenders are penalized to vindicate the righteousness of God, it became popular to assert that punishment exists for the good of society or the correction of the offender. (*Aspects of Christian Social Ethics*, page 162)

1. Crimes defined by the state are not always sinful acts (Exodus 1:15-19; Acts 5:29). Currently, abortion in the United States is legal, but forbidden by God (Exodus 20:13)

2. "Any sin is an injury against God and will be repaid by Him at the Last Judgment (I Corinthians 3:17 and page 156). Thus, any crime, if a sinful act (see #1 above), is also a sin against God. Just punishment for crimes must reflect the ultimate example of love, mercy, and punishment that God demonstrated in the sacrificial death of Jesus Christ. No sin will go unpunished by God Himself except for those forgiven in Jesus Christ. Love and punishment are not inconsistent with each other but are part of the same process according to God's laws and the laws of the state. For example, God's love of His own does not preclude the consequences of sin (and crime) in this earthly life. A convicted murder who is sentenced to capital punishment who is, or has become, a Christian is still subject to that sentence of death.

There is also punishment at a personal level, perhaps better called "chastening." God chastens his own (Hebrews 12:6). Parents chasten their children. Employers chasten employees.

3. "All actions of the state ought to conform to God's standards of justice revealed in Christ." (Poythress, page 156) Also, see #1 above.

4. "The modern state derives its authority from God and from Christ" (Romans 13:1-7 and page 156). All governments of the past also derive their authority from God. Jesus Christ is the King of Kings and Lord of Lords. The government is on His shoulders. He will eventually put all enemies under His feet.

5. "Christians can properly serve as officers of the state" (page 157).

6. "The same Christian who as a judge pronounces judgment may as a Christian pray for the criminal, exhort him to repent, and perhaps even give him some gift to bring happiness into his life" (page 158).

7. "The state deals with injuries against other human beings, not injuries against God" (page 159). Great errors and harm have been caused by the Church using civil power to achieve its ends, or the state being involved with ecclesiastical disputes of doctrine.

(Ed's note: In this context, we are discussing events that are labeled "crimes." What is said here does not necessarily preclude "blue laws" or oaths of office that have to do with the first table of the Ten Commandments.)

8. In fulfilling its responsibilities, the state must not insist on attaining divine perfection.... (For example), Moses indicates that two witnesses are necessary for conviction (Numbers 35:30; Deuteronomy 17:6; 19:15)" (page 160).

> The common argument by many Christians, relative to capital punishment, is that we can never be certain of a person's guilt. Yet, God has instructed that 2-3 witnesses in the due process of law is sufficient for capital punishment. If God trusts man to execute capital punishment, then Christians who argue against capital punishment because of the possibility that the accused may be innocent, even though he was convicted by due process, are arguing against God Himself.

9. "The state is obliged to act only when disputes and injuries are not settled privately" (page 161). Today, in many cases of personal injury, the state is the prosecutor, having taken a prerogative that it does not have. Of course, here we are speaking of civil offenses, and not those of which God clearly requires the state to prosecute, for example, rape and murder.

10. "The earthly character of the state and the imperfect, shadowy character of its of its justice resemble the situation of Israel in many ways. There is something to be learned from Israelite law about ways in which God's justice can be concretely embodied and practiced by imperfect agents in an imperfect world" (page 161).

11. Biblical justice includes the "twin features of restoration (retribution) and punishment... In some cases, fit punishment may also achieve subsidiary results in terms of deterrence and rehabilitation.... The thief who learns honest work in the process of being forced to pay may learn the value of honest work.... (But) according to modern humanism, retribution is barbarous.... "Despite its plausibility, basing punishment exclusively on deterrence and rehabilitation is ultimately inhumane... (converting) the offender into an object to be manipulated rather than being responsible for wrongdoing.... In reality, rehabilitation becomes a code-word for unlimited bondage" (page 162).

There follows three chapters to the above (briefly presented) ideas:

Chapter 12: Just Penalties for Many Crimes

Chapter 13: Just Penalties for Sexual Crimes

Chapter 14: Deterrence and Rehabilitation

These are excellent chapters, but I would like to focus on the concept of modern penology, which contrasts so vividly with the Biblical idea of restitution and punishment.

Prison does not fit Biblical criteria of just punishment. This subject is sorely neglected, by virtually all Christian teachers, from professors of ethics to Christians in prison ministry who fail to see the unbiblical and "cruel and unusual punishment" that prison life is for inmates.

"Most modern societies use imprisonment as the primary form of punishment for crime.... The deliberate use of prison for the punishment of offenders ... is a disaster. (page 235) I recall studies that recidivism is about 80 percent. A disaster, indeed! And, the victim gets nothing.

1. **"A proper response to crime (civil justice) involves four elements**: restoration, punishment, deterrence, and rehabilitation. Restoration and punishment must be our primary concern. But deterrence and rehabilitation can

be significant secondary indicators of whether a proposed solution makes contact with the reality of the human condition." (page 236) See note below.

2. "We should distinguish carefully between using prison for punishment and using it as a means of custody before trial. The use of some form of custody until the time of trial is attested in the Bible itself (Leviticus 24:12; Acts 21:34; 23:35).... To prevent this practice from becoming an unacknowledged or unintentional form of punishment, state authorities have an obligation to work for practices that promote speedy trial." (page 235)

3. "Prison in itself obviously restores nothing. Moreover, in cases where restoration involves the use of money, prison (as it now functions -- Ed) works against restoration by destroying the offender's capacity to work in order to obtain money to pay his victim." (page 236)

4. "No plausible means exists for determining a just quantity of (time for) punishment. If (in other types of) punishment, it matches the crime... its quantity is automatically determined at least in a rough way... (But) how much time in prison corresponds to the amount of a theft? We cannot say, because time and money do not directly match. How much time corresponds to murder? ... to adultery?" (page 237)

5. "Criminals have a greater chance to reform if they are in contact with normal society.... The abnormalities of prison life can never become a viable environment for training in righteousness. In fact, prison frequently produces results in the opposite direction because the morality of a subculture of criminals reverses the morality of normal society." (page 239)

6. "Because doing time does not effectively match the nature of the criminal's crime, it does not effectively take away his motive for committing crime again" (page 238).

7. Prison is an opportunity for prisoners to perpetrate crimes on other prisoners. The "bad attitudes" and evil behaviors of some inmates hinder any rehabilitation that might take place among prisoners who are motivated in that direction.

8. "Prisoners have the most hope of for rehabilitation if they feel that the justice of their punishment" (page 239). Many with the exception of psychopaths and others with hardened consciences have an innate sense of justice. They are willing to accept punishment if it seems appropriate to their crime. And, if they restore some or much of the damage (restitution) that they caused, then, they have a sense of restoring themselves.

9. Prisons actually increase the cost of punishment. I recall more than 20 years ago that the cost of maintaining one prisoner for one year was over $30,000. With inflation, that cost must now be around $50,000. On this basis alone, a criminal who has finished his sentence has not "paid his debt to society." He has increased it, but while he may be responsible for his crime, he is not responsible for that incurred debt that the state has foisted upon him.

Quotes are from Vern S. Poythress' *The Shadow of Christ in the Law of Moses* (Philipsburg: Presbyterian and Reformed Publishing Company, 1991), which devotes 100 of its 422 pages to Biblical justice. I have cited selective texts here as an introduction to this subject. Selections are used with permission of the publisher.

Note: Robertson McQuilkin (*An Introduction to Biblical Ethics*, Wheaton, Illinois: Tyndale House Publishers, Inc., 1989) lists four purposes of civil justice in response to crime, also (pages 357-360). He names three of the same as Poythress: rehabilitation, deterrence, and punishment (punitive). However, McQuilkin does not list retribution. Instead, he names "protection of the innocent."

Robertson McQuilkin has written this great book that I fully endorse. It is far more comprehensive than most books of the subject of Biblical ethics. However, I do not agree with "protection of the innocent" as a purpose of Biblical justice for crimes. While this "protection" does occur in the case of imprisonment and capital punishment, McQuilkin himself agrees that imprisonment has "utterly failed" (page 362).

Actually, restoration (which McQuilkin does not mention) likely will place the criminal in close proximity to the victim in several ways: monetary or equivalent payment to the victim or actually working for or under the victim.

A fifth purpose (beyond McQuilkin) of Biblical punishment is that the offender knows that he has been justified. While this result is a by-product and not a goal of the process, nevertheless it has a restorative effect. The offender knows when inappropriate punishment, as imprisonment, has been carried out, or whether justice has been done. While he may balk or even resist the process, justice will restore in his soul the wrong that was caused by his offense.

Additional Resources

http://www.americanvision.org/articlearchive/07-01-05.asp. On capital punishment in the New Testament, the woman caught in adultery, "an eye for an eye and a tooth for a tooth," personal vengeance, turning the other cheek, Pharisaic traditions vs. Mosaic law, etc.

17. Theology and Eschatology

In Defense of Systematic Theology and Biblical Systematics in General

What is systematic theology?

The Bible is no more a system of theology, than nature is a system of chemistry or physics. We find in nature the facts which the chemist and physicist has to examine, and from them to ascertain the laws by which they are determined. So the Bible contains the truths which the theologian has to collect, authenticate, arrange, and exhibit in their internal relation to each other. This constitutes the difference between biblical and systematic theology. The office of the former is to ascertain and state the facts of Scripture. The office of the latter is to take those facts, determine their relation to each other and to other cognate truths, as well as vindicate them and show their harmony and consistency. This is not an easy task, or one of slight importance.

Why is systematic theology necessary?

It may be naturally asked, why not take the truths as God has seen fit to reveal them, and thus save ourselves the trouble of showing their relation and harmony?

The answer to this question is, in the first place, that it cannot be done. Such is the constitution of the human mind that it cannot help endeavoring to systematize and reconcile the facts which it admits to be true. In no department of knowledge have men been satisfied with the possession of a mass of undigested facts. And the students of the Bible can as little be expected to be thus satisfied. There is a necessity, therefore, for the construction of systems of theology. Of this the history of the Church affords abundant proof. In all ages and among all denominations, such systems have been produced.

Second, a much higher kind of knowledge is thus obtained, than by the mere accumulation of isolated facts. It is one thing, for example, to know that oceans, continents, islands, mountains, and rivers exist on the face of the earth; but it is a much higher thing to know the causes which have determined the distribution of the land and water on the surface of the globe; the configuration of the earth; the effects of that configuration upon climate, on the races of plants and animals, on commerce, civilization, and the destiny of nations. It is by determining these causes that geography has been raised from a collection of facts to a highly important and elevated science. What is true of other sciences is true of theology. We cannot know what God has revealed in his Word unless we understand, at least in some good measure, the relation in which the separate truths therein contained stand to each other. It cost the Church centuries of study and controversy to solve the problem concerning the person of Christ; that is, to adjust and bring into harmonious arrangement all the facts which the Bible teaches on that subject.

Third, We have no choice in the matter. If we would discharge our duty as teachers and defenders of the truth, we must Endeavour to bring all the facts of revelation into systematic order and mutual relation. It is only thus that we can satisfactorily exhibit their truth, vindicate them from objections, or bring them to bear in their full force on the mind of men.

Fourth, Such is evidently the will of God. He does not teach men astronomy or chemistry, but He gives them the facts out of which those sciences are constructed. Neither does He teach us systematic theology, but He gives us in the Bible the truths which, properly understood and arranged, constitute the science of theology. As the facts of nature are all related and determined by physical laws, so the facts of the Bible are all related and determined by the nature of God and of his creatures. And as He wills that men and women should study his works and discover their wonderful organic relation and harmonious combination, so it is his will that we should study his Word, and learn that, like the stars, its truths are not isolated points, but systems, cycles, and epicycles, in unending harmony and grandeur.

Besides all this, although the Scriptures do not contain a system of theology as a whole, we have in the Epistles of the New Testament, portions of that system wrought out to our hands. These are our authority and guide.

The above were selected from Charles Hodge, *Systematic Theology*, Volume I, Part 1, pages 1-3.

See also:

Gordon H. Clark, *In Defense of Theology*, Trinity Foundation, 1984.

Rousas J. Rushdoony, "The Necessity of Systematic Theology," in *Systematic Theology*, Volume I, Chalcedon Press, pages 1-58.

The *Ordo Salutis*

Ordo salutis simply means "order of salvation."

It can be viewed from (1) God's viewpoint from eternity past, in time, to eternity future, or (2) simply in space, time, and history

It is both objective and subjective. Objective is what happens outside the person, that is, God's actions. Subjective is the effect on the person, that is, his response to what God has done. All these steps are completed in every person whom God has chosen. None occur without all the others happening sequentially and certainly.

Eternity past (objective)

> Covenant of Redemption (Trinity agrees on their plan of salvation)
>
> Foreknowledge = "fore-love"-- God loves His own
>
> Predestination and Election: God determines specific plans to save His own

In space, time, and history (both objective and subjective)

> Effectual calling (subjective)
>
> Regeneration ("born from above," "born-again," and conversion; subjective)
>
> Faith and repentance = conversion[1] (subjective)
>
> Justification (forensic; objective)
>
> Adoption (forensic; objective)
>
> Sanctification (subjective)

Perseverance (objective)

Eternity Future

Glorification and Union with Christ (heaven; subjective)

Principles of Hermeneutics

The first ten principles listed here are taken from *Knowing Scripture*, by R. C. Sproul (© 2009 by R.C. Sproul). It is a remarkably condensed, but thorough, review of hermeneutics for both the layman and the theologian. (Used by permission of InterVarsity Press, P. Box 1400, Downers Grove, IL 60515-1426. www.ivpress.com)

I have quoted Dr. Sproul briefly for you to get an idea of what each principle means, but there are several more pages of explanation on each that I have omitted. These ten principles comprise only one chapter of the book, so he has much more in the way of hermeneutics for you!

I (and Dr. Sproul, as well -- see below) are convinced that if these principles were followed diligently, we would have far fewer churches, denominations, and disagreements among Christians.

Following the ten principles of Dr. Sproul, I have listed some other simple principles that I have found helpful.

1. **"The Bible is to be read like any other book."**

> "The Bible is uniquely inspired and infallible, and this puts it in a class by itself. But, for matters of interpretation, the Bible does not take on some special magic that changes basic literary patterns of interpretation." (63)

> "But if the Bible is to be interpreted like any other book, what about prayer? Shouldn't we seek assistance of God the Holy Spirit in interpreting the Book? Isn't divine illumination promised to this book in a way that differs from other books?" (Dr. Sproul goes on to answer those questions.) (64)

2. "The Bible should be read existentially."

"I do not mean that we should use the modern 'existential' method of interpreting Scripture whereby the word of Scripture are taken out of their historical context for subjective meaning (for example, as Rudolf Bultmann does)." (65)

"What I mean is that as we read the Bible, we ought to get passionately and personally involved in what we read. I advocate this not only for the purpose of personal application of the text but for understanding as well." (66)

3. "Historical narratives are to be interpreted by the didactic."

"Didactic literature is literature that means to teach or to instruct. Much of Paul's writing is didactic in character… (for example) the Gospels record what Jesus did and the Epistles interpret the significance of what He did. Such a description is an oversimplification in that the Gospels often teach and interpret as they are giving narration. But, it is true that the emphasis in the gospels is found in the record of events, while the Epistles are more concerned with interpreting the significance of those events in terms of doctrine, exhortation, and application." (68)

4. "The implicit is to be interpreted by the explicit."

"In the business of language, we make distinctions between that which is implicit and that which is explicit. Often, the difference is a matter of degree and the distinction can be muddled. But, usually we can determine the difference between what is actually said and what is left unsaid, though implied. I am convinced that if this one rule were consistently followed by Christian communities, the vast majority of doctrinal differences that divide us would be resolved." (page, 75, Ed's emphasis)

5. "Determine carefully the meaning of words."

"Whatever else the bible is, it is a book which communicates information verbally. That means that it is filled with words.

Thoughts are expressed through the relationship of those words. Each individual word contributes something to the whole of the content expressed. The better we understand the individual words used in biblical statement, the better we will be able to understand the total message of Scripture." (page 79)

"**Words with multiple meanings**. There are scores of words in the bible that have multiple meanings. Only the context can determine the particular meaning of a word. For example, the Bible speaks frequently of the will of God There are at least six different ways that this word is used" (examples follow). (page 82)

For more discussion on this important issue, see *Knowing Scripture* at the end of this article.

6. "Note the presence of parallelisms in the Bible."

"One of the fascinating characteristics of Hebrew literature is its use of parallelism. Parallelism in ancient Near Eastern languages is common and relatively easy to recognize. The ability to recognize it when it occurs will greatly aid the reader in understanding the text." (85)

"There are three basic types of parallelism: synonymous, antithetic, and synthetic." (85)

7. "Note the difference between Proverb and Law."

"A common mistake in Biblical interpretation and application is to give a proverbial saying the weight or force of a moral absolute. Proverbs are catchy little couplets designed to express practical truisms. They reflect principles of wisdom for godly living. They do not reflect moral laws that are to be applied absolutely to every conceivable life situation." (89)

8. "Observe the difference between the Spirit and the Letter of the Law."

"We all know the reputation of the Pharisees in the New testament who were quite scrupulous about keeping the letter of the law while violating the spirit constantly." (90)

"There were a variety of types of legalist in the New Testament. The first and most famous was the type that legislated rules and regulations beyond what God had commanded. Jesus rebuked the Pharisees for making the tradition of the rabbis as authoritative as the Law of Moses…. Another way the law is distorted is by trying to obey the spirit of the law but ignoring the letter. Letter and spirit are inseparably related. The legalists destroy the spirit and the antinomian destroys the letter." (91)

9. "Be careful with Parables"

"People usually enjoy sermons that are based on parables… Yet from the viewpoint of the New testament scholar, the parables present unique difficulties in interpretation." (94)

"(One problem) is the original intent of the parable… whether (Jesus) used parables to elucidate His teaching or to obscure it." (91)

10. "Be careful with predictive prophecy."

"Handling predictive prophecy from the New Testament and the Old is one of the most abused forms of biblical interpretation. Interpretations range from the skeptical, naturalistic method which virtually eliminates predictive prophecy to the wild, bizarre method that sees in every contemporary event a 'clear' fulfillment of a biblical prophecy." (97)

"If we examine how the New Testament treats Old Testament prophecy (an example of Scripture interpreting Scripture), we discover that in some cases an appeal is made to fulfillment of the letter (such as the birth of the Messiah in Bethlehem) and

342

fulfillment in a broader scope (such as the fulfillment of Malachi's prophecy of the return of Elijah." (97)

While I do not have the qualifications of Dr. Sproul, and do not want to equate my work with his, I have found the following principles to be helpful.

11. **Orthodox beliefs and systematic theologies are a one good test of one's interpretation**.

"There is nothing new under the sun," wrote the Preacher of Ecclesiastes. "Ortho" means "straight, right, true." "Doxa" is simply doctrine or teaching.

So, orthodox means "true teaching." In this case, it is true teaching that has occurred throughout church history. Whenever you hear some teaching that "does not quite sound right," that is, consistent with what one has heard in the church, red flags should go up in your mind. You should ask yourself or the person giving such teaching, "What has the church taught consistently and specifically throughout history" on this subject?

Of course, this method is fraught with inconsistencies. There is the Roman Catholic tradition of papal infallibility vs. the Reformers sola scriptura. There is the predestination of the Reformed tradition and the free will of the Arminians. There are the three forms of millennialism.

However, the comparison of present teaching with that of the past is useful. 1) All Christians of all ages form the mind of Christ (Link on website). 2) The study of the history of the Church, particularly her doctrines, is a good exercise for us independent-minded moderns. 3) There is a consistency in historical orthodoxy that might be surprising to some Christians, when they study the central teachings of the Church by her best theologians who are consistent over the centuries.

For example, there are The Apostles' Creed and the Nicene Creed. And, while the Westminster Confession with its Larger and Shorter Catechisms are not adopted by the majority of churches today, it grew out one of the most scholarly and transforming periods of the Church's history.

12. **"Is" ("are") is not an equals sign**.

A common verse quoted among Christians is, "God is love" (I John 4:8, 16). While God is certainly the highest and best meaning of love, His attributes and His Person are far greater than one word. He is omniscient, omnipresent, omnipotent, just, merciful, jealous, unchanging, truth, Mighty God, Everlasting Father, etc. (just to name a few characteristics and names of God found in the Bible).

Of course, this is a specific application of Dr. Sproul's first principle (above). "Is" and "are" may be followed by a noun or an adjective. Rarely, is what follows these verbs equivalent to the subject of the sentence.

13. **A text without a context is a pretext, that is, the meaning of a text is determined by its context. The context may be the entire Bible**.

A) To understand what a verse means, it must be read and examined in the context of the passage in which it appears. For example, "For God so loved the world that He gave His only begotten son, that whoever believes in Him should not perish, but have everlasting life" (John 3:16). The context is clearly about a person's being regenerated ("born again" or "born-from-above) and being translated into the Kingdom of God. It is also clear that "The wind blows wherever it pleases," meaning that the Spirit of God chooses those that become regenerated.

Another example is that of "where two or three are gathered together in My name, I am there in the midst of them" (Matthew 18:20). That passage is in the context of church discipline, not the special presence of God among more than one believer gathered for prayer. Indeed, if this passage were about community prayer, what would one do with "The effective, fervent prayer of a righteous man avails much" (James 5:16).

B) Ultimately, the context of any verse is the entire Bible. The context of book, chapter, and verse is not always sufficient to determine the meaning of a verse. This application requires a considerable knowledge of the Bible or a comprehensive cross-reference text. But, then, if every Christian read through the Bible periodically, would not an association of verses be more likely to be recognized? This application also requires a systematic theology, so that all statements can be fitted into the whole. This hermeneutic would also be one meaning of "Scripture is the best interpreter of Scripture."

14. The Bible has the answer to every problem that I face in life (or sometimes called, "the sufficiency of Scripture").

Essentially, this is re-statement of several verses in the Bible, such as II Timothy 3:16-17 and II Peter 1:3-4.

When faced with problems, the tendency is to look everywhere or talk to anyone except **God's instruction manual for human beings created by Him**. Answers are often sought in psychology, Far Eastern religions, the occult, etc., etc. Only the Bible is truth, as it is written by God Himself.

It is also comprehensive. Consider whom you should marry. While it may not tell you the name of the person, it will tell you what kind of person that you should marry. You are free to choose a mate within those parameters. Or, what career should you choose? The Bible may not tell you the particular profession, but it will tell you those that are righteous and those that are not.

15. The Bible -- for many words -- has its own definitions that would not be found in dictionaries written by non-Christians (and too often those written by Christians).

A good illustration of this hermeneutic is "love." Biblical love includes such statements, as "If you love me, keep my commandments" (John 14:15), "love is the fulfillment of the law" (Romans 13:10), and "For all the law is fulfilled in one word, even in this: "You shall love your neighbor as yourself" (Galatians 5:14). A definition of love must include those instructions.

A short definition that might be helpful is, "Love is an action that is aimed at the highest Biblical good of the one loved." (Link for discussion of love)

16. **Read all the words of every passage in context**.

This principle is a corollary of #13. Not only should the context be examined, the whole context of the passage must be examined. This context may be a paragraph, a chapter, or even a whole book.

An example is the Book of John, Chapter 3. There is a lot about Nicodemus in the first few verses: he is a Pharisee (probably a high ranking one), he "came by night," and he called Jesus a "Rabbi" and "a teacher come from God." All that information applies to the subjects that Jesus discusses, such as being "born again," "the kingdom of God," and Jesus being God's "begotten" son. Who and what Nicodemus is influences Jesus' answer and must be understood in that religious context.

Perhaps, it is even more important to read all the context in Old Testament passages because it involves so much narrative and a culture that is very unfamiliar to us.

17. **Believers must KNOW the Bible in order to interpret it**.

The greater their knowledge of books, chapters, major themes, and individual verses, the greater will be Christians' understanding. Those who wrote the Westminster Confession of Faith, for example, knew the well-know verses and the obscure verses that helped them shape the statements for the Confession.

In light of this principle and the importance of the Bible, all Christians should have a plan to read through the entire Bible periodically, every 1-3 years.

18. The Bible must be read with a consciousness of who and what God is... His attributes.

"Our wisdom, in so far as it ought to be deemed true and solid Wisdom, consists almost entirely of two parts: the knowledge of God and of ourselves." This is the first sentence of John Calvin's *Institutes of the Christian Religion*. Too many Christians do not really know God.

In #12 above, we briefly examined, "God is love" (I John 4:8). One cannot understand the love of God without understanding the God of the Law (commandments, precepts, statutes, etc. of Psalm 119), for Christ's sacrificial death was efficacious because He had fulfilled the law, in every detail. Further, an understanding of the depth and breadth of His sacrifice is greatly lessened without an understanding of God's requirement that His law be fulfilled.

God is knowledge, wisdom, power, omnipresent, omniscient, omnipotent (neither can exist without the other), Wonderful Counselor, Might God, Everlasting Father, Prince of Peace, King of Kings, Lord of Lords, creator of a universe governed by laws, sustainer, Word, law-giver, etc., etc.

19. As one reads the Bible, he must develop some systematic approach that fits the whole together.

This principle is a corollary that Scripture must interpret Scripture. An example is the *ordo salutis* or order of salvation in this sequence: effectual calling, regeneration, faith and repentance, adoption, justification, sanctification, perseverance, and glorification.

Of course, such a systematic approach challenges the concept of "no creed but the Bible" or "no creed but Christ." But, these statements are creeds in themselves, as they are statements about Scripture and Christ which are not quotes of Scripture. Indeed concerning Christ, there are many claims to whom

Christ is. (This website -- highlighted -- demonstrates the necessity of having a creed about Christ.)

20. **The Bible is not to be read magically**.

This principle primarily has to do with those who "lucky-dip." That is, they look for an answer to a problem by opening the Bible blindly, run their finger down a page, and then look to see what it says to apply to their lives. This approach is not different that the person who claims that "God" or the "Holy Spirit" told me to do such and such. This claim is the same as adding to the Scriptures which is clearly condemned (Revelation 22:18-19).

Endnote

[1] "Repentance is the twin sister of faith - we cannot think of the one without the other, and so repentance would be conjoined with faith. Conversion is simply another name for repentance and faith conjoined and would therefore be enclosed in repentance and faith." John Murray, *Redemption Accomplished and Applied* (Grand Rapids: Eerdmans, 1955), page 87.

18. The Church and the Kingdom of God

The Mind of Christ: Abraham Kuyper, John Calvin, and Biblical Theology

> But he who is spiritual judges all things, yet he himself is rightly judged by no one. For *"who has known the mind of the LORD that he may instruct Him?"* But we have the mind of Christ (II Corinthians 2:15-16).

> *"For who has known the mind of the LORD? Or who has become His counselor?"* (Romans 11:34)

Abraham Kuyper has described The Mind of Christ more fully than any theologian that I have read. Thus, I am going to let him speak for himself, quoting at length from his book, *Principles of Sacred Theology.*

By way of brief introduction, Kuyper discusses an encyclopedia of knowledge that is "mined" from the gold of Scripture in all ages according to the challenges that are presented to it. In the early centuries, Christians encountered Ariansim, Arminianism, Gnosticism, and many other errors and heresies. Later, Biblical truth experienced syncretism with pagan culture, as the Gospel spread around the world. Biblical truth even had to overcome its own dominant church (Roman Catholicism) which had distorted the Gospel for individuals and churches. In modern times, we face all the "-isms" that include secular (humanism, socialism, communism, etc.) and the religious (Mohammedism, Hinduism, Judaism, etc.).

The Word of God is more than sufficient for these challenges. Indeed, these allow the Bible to be developed more fully than in the past. Initially, Christians and the church may be overwhelmed by these challenges, even experiencing martyrdom. But, little by little, the Word and the Spirit have overcome on the individual, social, cultural, and national levels. This progress has always been impure and stuttering, but nevertheless advancing in the knowledge of the truth.

The reader must keep is mind that Kuyper has dogmatically stated a "two-fold starting point": the Bible as the very Word of God written and *palingenesis* (being born-again or regeneration). While every thought even in the believer is tainted by sin, Kuyper is excluding unbelievers entirely from contributing to this organic growth of the mind of Christ in believers. Neither would he include the imposter theologians who deny the infallibility and inerrancy of the Scriptures and that the 66 books of the Protestant Bible are all fully and completely God's Word written.

Kuyper describes the process for us.

> "The revelation of God is not an act of a single moment, but a *continuous process*, which extends itself across the ages… according to the nature of its successive content… this revelation must not be interpreted as an atomistical self-communication of God to *the several individuals*, but must be taken as a revelation to man in his generations, that is, to the organic unity of (regenerated) humanity, and only in this organic unity to the single man." (257-258)

> Only in the combination of the whole race of man does this revelation reach its creaturely completeness . . . The knowledge of God is a common possession, all the riches of which can only be enjoyed in the communion of our race . . . but because humanity is adapted to reveal God, and from that revelation to attain unto His knowledge, does not individual complement another, and only by the organic unity and by the individual in communion with that unity, can the knowledge of God be obtained in a clear and completer sense. (272)

> "(Not) every believer is able to think out in a clear way, the entire content of revelation. This is only done by all believers together." (289)

> One who, himself of a sound mind, should have to live on some isolated island among insane people, would run a great risk of becoming himself insane; and in such a condition, a very strong mind could only maintain the reality of its consciousness. Just because we do not exist atomically, also in our consciousness, in order to remain firm our own sense cannot afford to lose the support of a similar sense of others." (389)

It is the Holy Spirit who, by illumination, enables the human consciousness to ever richer insights into (Scripture's) content.... A believer of the 19th century knows much more than a believer of the tenth or third century could know, but that additional knowledge is ever dug from the selfsame gold mine... This, of course, does not imply that the former generations fell short in knowledge of God, but simply, that the development of the human consciousness in those times did not make such demands on the knowledge of God. A child can be as rich in his God as the full grown man, but because the consciousness of the adult is more richly unfolded, the holds the knowledge of God likewise in a more richly folded form... But however far this increase of knowledge may proceed in the future, it will never be able to draw its material from any other source than from the Holy Scripture.... the substance of the knowledge of God which comes to us ... *is identical with the Holy Scriptures* (402).

"It lies entirely in the organic character of revelation, that it passes through two periods, the first of which brings it to its complete measure (the closing of the canon - Ed) and the second of which allows its, having reached its full measure, to perform its work. And this is what we face in the difference between inspiration and illumination. (419)

John Calvin

John Calvin did not develop the idea of a community of mind of all Christians of all ages, as Kuyper did. However, he did occasionally note that reality.

For even Paul himself, in another place, after testifying that all the mysteries of God far exceed the capacity of our understanding, does nevertheless immediately add, that believers are in possession of the Lord's mind, because they have received not the spirit of this world, but that which has been given them by God, whereby they are instructed as to his otherwise incomprehensible goodness. See the footnote to Calvin's Commentary on the two verses above.

Biblical Theology

Biblical Theology has some dimension of this mind of Christ. While this theology has a diverse nature and application, I mention it here with this definition.

> Biblical theology is principally concerned with the overall theological message of the whole Bible. It seeks to understand the parts in relation to the whole and, to achieve this, it must work with the mutual interaction of the literary, historical, and theological dimensions of the various corpora, and with the inter-relationships of these within the whole canon of Scripture.

In this more narrow focus, biblical theology strives to more fully develop and understand the Bible and corresponds to our thoughts here.

However, in no way would I condone any theologians of this method who do not fully subscribe to inerrancy and infallibility. Biblical theology has within it a number of neo-orthodox and others who would hedge on some of the Bible's clear messages or on the truthfulness of some books and passages.

Summary Principles of the Mind of Christ

1. The mind of Christ only exists in regenerated (born-from-above) minds that are totally committed to the inerrancy and infallibility of Scripture. While the Holy Spirit is a teacher in this process, He never gives anything that might be considered new revelation in addition to the current 66 books of the Protestant Bible.

2. The mind of Christ is often advanced by the tremendous intellect of one mind, but in its truest sense is always corporate through the mind of two or more believers, the local Session, the local congregation, assemblies of churches, and the universal ("catholic") church of all ages.

3. The mind of Christ builds on the work of others. Individuals who work "atomistically, ignoring the great work of others both present and past, are renegades to the corporate nature of Christianity and a danger to the understanding of revealed truth.

4. The mind of Christ is sufficient for all Christians in their time of history.

352

5. Biblical theology is a method to increasing the knowledge of the mind of Christ, but is not identical with it.

6. The mind of Christ is identical to a fully developed, Biblical worldview.

The Kingdom of God: Scripture Notes

The following notes are really raw! But, I present them here as a beginning to get readers to begin an "every verse study" of all the references to The Kingdom of God and The Kingdom of Heaven in the Bible, primarily the New Testament, and primarily the words of Jesus in His Parables!

Jesus presented the Kingdom as though His hearers would understand that to which he was speaking!! For example, the disciples asked who would be greatest in the Kingdom.

The King is Jesus Christ. Citizens are the regenerate.

Characteristics of citizens of the Kingdom: (must be regenerated)

Kingdom of "Heaven" is more prominent than Kingdom of God

    Time of occurrence:

        "at hand" (certainly implies that it was not present before);

        the least in the Kingdom is greater than John the Baptist who was the greatest of the Prophets (different era, dispensation, manifestation of God, etc.);

        Abraham, Isaac, and Jacob are in the Kingdom (Matthew 8:11 - healing of the Centurion's servant);

        "the law and the prophets were until John," Luke 16:16;

        God's Kingdom has always existed in heaven, Psalm 103:10

        Daniel 2:44 "a kingdom that will never be destroyed"

        God has always ruled the kingdoms of the world

All Beatitudes would apply, because the context is the Kingdom of heaven;

Matthew 13: whole chapter

"the poor in spirit" "theirs is the Kingdom of heaven" (v. 3)

"those persecuted for righteousness' sake"

Levels in Kingdom: "breaking commandments" and "teaching others to do so" are least…(punished by having a millstone tied around his neck and cast in to the sea (but not into outer darkness) while whoever "does and teaches the commandments" are **greatest**…;

Membership:

righteousness that exceeds that of the scribes and Pharisees";

regeneration (John 3); those who do the will of my Father in heaven (7:21); Matthew 13:18;

confession of Christ before men; **greater than John the Baptist** (?) - "the least in the Kingdom (Matthew 11)

warfare: a certain zeal (violence) for the things of God (Matthew 11:12); **the gates of Hell** will not prevail against the assault of the Church;

the mysteries of the Kingdom have been revealed to us (Matthew 13:11) ® the Kingdom is no longer a mystery? Luke 8:10

preparation of the heart (Matthew 13:18ff), i.e., regeneration;

worth great sacrifice (Matthew 13: parables of hidden treasure and pearl of great price)

keys of the kingdom: giving Peter (the Church) the keys to the kingdom (Matthew 16; 18:18) - whatever you bind will be bound in heaven;

casting out of demons, Luke 11:20

Satan falling "as lightning," Luke 18

Non-membership:

those who call me, "Lord, Lord," and do not do "the will of my Father in heaven";

denial of Christ before men;

tares: those who have every appearance of being in the Kingdom (Matthew 13)

cannot visualize or realize ("see") the Kingdom; many places: Matthew 13 - mysteries; "he who has ears, let him hear";

Characteristics:

great growth (mustard seed, parable of leven, Matthew 13)

things that are new and old, good and bad (Matthew 13, parable of dragnet)

personal humility and servanthood; "the greatest and the least are reversed" (Matthew 18, 20);

forgiveness that is infinite (Matthew 18 - how many times to forgive), proportionate to that of our debt to Christ (parable of unforgiving servant - Matthew 18)

all ethics (righteousness) of New Testament - synonymous: do Word Search on this file, Romans 14:14-23); "What If Jesus Had Never Been Born?" --> all the "right" changes made on earth

little children (identification with), Matthew 18 and 19; "like" and "faith of"; humility as a little child;

eternal life (Kingdom of heaven), "Master, what shall I do to inherit eternal life?" -- Matthew 19

riches are a severe, but not impossible, hindrance, Matthew 19

rewards are at the whim of the King, Matthew 20

concerns **all humanity**; judgment of all peoples, all nations called and converted;

eunuchs have been made so for the Kingdom! (Matthew 19:12)

link with salvation, Matthew 19:23, "who then can be saved?"

link with heaven, Matthew 19:28, "the new heavens and the new earth" = regeneration of all things

Jesus miracles, signs of the Kingdom of God

link with righteousness, Matthew 19:28ff

Israel had been promised the Kingdom, but they failed to embrace it (Jesus), Matthew 21:43

many are invited, but few are chosen, and they have to have the right "wedding garment", Matthew 22:2ff

Matthew 23:13, Pharisees shut out people from the Kingdom

be prepared and watch, Parable of the bridesmaids, Matthew 25

invest "talents" wisely, parable of talents, Matthew 25

Kingdom of works, you who clothed, fed, visited, thirsty, etc., selection of sheep and goats, Matthew 25

predestined, "prepared before the foundation of the world", Matthew 25:34

"The law and the prophets were until John. Since that time the kingdom of God has been preached, and everyone is pressing into it. And it is easier for heaven and earth to pass away than for one tittle of the law to fail," Luke 16:17

flesh and blood cannot inherit the Kingdom, I Corinthians 15:50

unity of heaven and earth, spiritually: we can enter the Holy of Holies, God has come to earth, God's spirit is on earth, we invite "heaven on earth" in Lord's prayer, "invisible church" (all saints on earth and heaven), saints rule in heaven even now, veil has been rent and we may enter the Holy of Holies, etc.

link of freedom of the soul to freedoms on earth

death of the Old World order: Jesus preached the end of the world, but is did not occur physically, instead spiritually

foretaste of heaven

Definition: the fulfillment of God's will on earth as it is in heaven (Lord's Prayer); the Kingdom of God and the Kingdom of heaven are identical; the **gospel** is the Kingdom (Matthew 24:13, Acts 8:12, 20:25)

Judgment:

angels will separate the wicked from the righteous (Matthew 13)

Questions and mysteries:

Contiguity of Kingdom on earth with new heavens and earth? Matthew 19:28

Contiguity with Creation Mandate; Noahic, Abrahamic, and Mosaic Covenants

These were "shadows" (e.g., Poythress' book)

(Above) Mystery has been revealed

Does the Kingdom replace the rule of Adam and Eve (mankind?). That on a physical level, now spiritual?

The Church: Summary Principles

Introduction: With the possible exception of Eschatology, perhaps no other area of worldview is more divisive of the body of Christ than concepts of the Church. Obviously, what follows here reflects my own conviction from a Presbyterian point of view. As with all other principles, I am trying to be as Biblical as possible. I trust that readers of other persuasions will read with that goal in mind. There may even be some surprises in store for you: things that you would not expect a Presbyterian to say or some things of which you had not thought as a non-Presbyterian!

(Again, the summary principles that follow are not in order of priority.)

1. **A definition of the Church for worldview purposes**. Biblically, the Church is all true believers, both those alive on earth and those already in heaven. However, worldview has to do with this world, so for this purpose the Church will be limited to all those who are regenerate ("born-again") and alive on earth. These individuals are variously called in the Bible" Christians. sheep, wheat, believers, the regenerate, and "born-again." As a group, they are call the Church, the body of Christ, the Bride of Christ, the family of God., a royal priesthood, a holy nation, a fellowship (Greek, koinonia), and other names. By contrast, those who are not members of the Church are non-Christians, tares, unbelievers, the unregenerate, and the reprobate. Their identity is being "non-Church" or sons of Adam and daughters of Eve; otherwise they have no common identity.

The true Church on earth is not identical with the "visible" Church or all professing Christians. Many Biblical passages reveal that the unregenerate exist among professing Christians, especially the parable of the wheat and the tares. Jesus' warned us about attempts to separate the wheat from the tares.

Nevertheless, this precaution is not intended to allow any idea to be expressed within the Church. **The primary identifying mark of a Christian should be his or her attitude towards the Bible**. In general, the regenerate will embrace the Bible in such terms, as truth,

358

infallible, inerrant, special revelation, Word of God, and fully authoritative. He will love to read and study it. **The same Holy Spirit who regenerates** (John 3) **also wrote the Bible** (Acts 28:25; I Corinthians 2:13; Ephesians 6:17; II Timothy 3:16-17). It is illogical (and inconceivable) that the Holy Spirit who regenerates would deny His very own Word! (See Bible preaching/teaching as one criterion of the visible Church below.)

3. **Jesus Christ is head of the Church** (Ephesians 5:23). No serious Bible student should disagree with that statement. Yet, is that just some lofty spiritual idea that has not practical application?

The elders represent the headship of Christ in the visible Church. In a few paragraphs, I cannot argue the centuries of wars of church structure. But, I can present the Biblical picture of who heads the Church. The primary passages of criteria for church leadership are Acts 15, I Timothy 3, and Titus 1. While "deacon" is used in I Timothy 3, "elder" (Greek, *presbyteros*) is by far the most common word for church leader. And, "elder" is consistent with the name of the leaders of Israel in the Old Testament. (Although "elders" sitting in the gate, the place of government, are sometimes identified only with civil authority, that focus is just too narrow. By necessity, legal rulings are based in ethics, and therefore had a spiritual focus, as well.)

Elders are gifted by God and recognized by the congregation. Notice that the passages cited above have criteria that **the man is already demonstrating in his home and social life**! A man is **not** given this office with the hope that he will fulfill it or because he "shows promise" of being a good elder. He must be demonstrating the spiritual presence of Jesus Christ in his life by his righteousness, leadership in the home and community, and knowledge of the Word of God. In the New Testament times, these men were primarily appointed by Apostles. However, there are no apostles today. Tradition, however, has established that the governing officers of local churches are elected by the congregations in Protestant churches. But, the most important dimension for church government is **the proven spirituality of the men elected. These officers are the mind of Christ in the local church, as they deliberate about Biblical conclusions**. Christ, as head of the Church, is not some ethereal statement with no basis in practical experience, but the voices of the elders of the local church (and regions, as in Acts 15) in unity.

Even so, the decisions of the elders are not infallible. As the Westminster Confession of Faith says that "All synods or councils, since the Apostles' times, whether general or particular, may err; and many have erred." The Bible always remains the "canon" by which all decisions are measured. One wonders how confessions and creeds could be written for the Church at large today with all her diversity.

Women should not be elders. The passages above and others that describe the role of women are clear that the spiritual leaders of the church should be men.

4. **Jesus Christ is the Bridegroom and the Church is His bride (Ephesians 5:22-33)**.

5. **The relationship of the Church to the Kingdom of God**. (A) **"The Kingdom of God creates the church**. The redemptive role of God brings into being a new people who receive the blessings of the divine reign." (George Eldon Ladd, Baker's Dictionary of Theology, 1960, page 313).

(B) "In so far as **the visible Church is instrumental in the establishment and extension of the Kingdom, it is of course subordinate to this as a means to an end**. The Kingdom may be said to be a broader concept than the Church, because it aims at nothing less than the complete control of all the manifestations of life. It represents the dominion of God in every sphere of human endeavor" (Louis Berkhof, Systematic Theology, 11th printing, 1969, page 570).

(C) **Any person who is regenerated is also a "member" of the Kingdom of God** (John 3:5). "The Church is the living, burning center of the Kingdom, a witness to its presence and power, and a harbinger of its final coming" (The Kingdom of God: Henry Stob).

This relationship may be summed up in this way.

> "In relation to the Kingdom, the Church may be defined as the totality of those who at any time have been delivered by the power of God's reign in Christ from the toils of sin and death and have been reconciled to God. As such the Church is the living, burning center of the Kingdom, a witness to its presence and power, a harbinger of its final coming. It is not the Kingdom, it is narrower than the Kingdom, but it is its

central component." (Henry Stob, *Ethical Reflections*, 1978, page 69)

This statement is made with the understanding discussed above that the Church contains both wheat and tares, that is, those regenerate and those unregenerate. See the Summary Principles of the Kingdom of God.

The Church provides the power to Christians to advance the Kingdom. The Christian is instructed by the Lord Jesus Christ to be "in the world, but not of it." Wow! Anyone who does not grasp the difficulty of that command has not wrestled with the light and darkness of each realm either intellectually or practically! God has given Satan a certain freedom of control and power "in the world." So, we "wrestle not with (just) flesh and blood, but principalities and powers of the air." Then, we have the ever present "flesh" and "old man" of Romans 7. These are powerful adversaries,

But, the Church is (1) a teaching institution and (2) a "hospital." As a teaching institution, it is to provide the teaching necessary to become agents of the Kingdom of God. In fact, it is **only** within local and universal Church that the **Christian is able to mature** (Ephesians 4:11-16). And, as Francis Schaeffer forcefully stated another of Christ's commands, Christians are to have "demonstrable" love towards one another, in the fullness of what New Testament love is all about, self-sacrifice and putting others first. Members of the church have a priority to their own to meet their true needs, in fellowship, and in community (Galatians 6:10).

There is a misconception on the part of some who identify themselves as Christians that they can worship God or live spiritually without the organized church. However, this position is difficult, if not impossible, to defend from Scripture. "Forsake not the assembling of ourselves together" (Hebrews 10:25). The sacraments of Baptism and Communion takes place in the meeting of the visible church. The organized Church is to admit and discipline members. Etc. In fact, the opposite position that anyone who does not participate in the corporate life of a local church is not regenerate is far stronger, if not definitive.

What a powerfully balanced program of the Holy Spirit this is! Christians travel back and forth between the Church and the world. **They need both instruction and demonstrable love and strength**

for their continuing advancement of the Kingdom and warfare in the world. God has provided all the Christian needs within the Church.

6. **The necessity of Church discipline**. Every local church and denomination must answer this question, "What constitutes a local church (denomination)?" In the Presbyterian and Reformed tradition, there are three criteria: preaching of the Bible, administration of the Sacraments of baptism (mode not specified), and church discipline. The last has a positive and "negative" component. Positively, discipline includes all forms of teaching: preaching, formal instruction (Sunday School, Bible school, seminary, etc.), and one-on-one (discipling).

But, there is a "negative" side, the confrontation of church members who have publicly known sin in their lives. Essentially, it is the application of Matthew 5:23-24, Matthew 18:15-29, I Corinthians 5:1-13, especially verse 5). The public peace and purity of the church demands this "negative" side of church discipline. **If, then, such discipline is one of the criteria that defines a church, how many churches in the world (and especially in the United States are true churches**? Perhaps, this neglect is one of the reasons that the Church is so impotent in the world today. The failure of those churches who exercise this discipline not to challenge the non-disciplining churches is their own failure to discipline. Indeed, the argument can be made that the disciplining churches should name those other churches and declare them non-churches.

The failure of discipline by any church is, in itself corporate sin, and multiplies the problems for congregants and other churches. How many innocent spouses must either leave their own churches or participate with their offending spouses in their home church? If a church does not discipline, then they allow departing members with serious and public sins to be received into the fellowship of other churches who are unaware of this sin that has not been disciplined.

The "negative" aspect of church discipline. I have use "negative" in contrast to the "positive" side of discipline above. However, **the goal in discipline is always with hope for a positive outcome, repentance of the erring brother or sister**. The manner in which this discipline is carried out is one of compassion and recognition of one's own tendency to sin (Galatians 6:1). But, even excommunication has

362

positive effects. It purifies the church and shows the erring sinner the gravity of his unrepentance, that his very soul is in jeopardy of eternal damnation (Matthew 18:18). And, while he is in this life, he is subject to the "destruction of his flesh" by Satan Himself (I Corinthians 5:5).

Are all "churches" true churches? If the above criteria are the true Biblical criteria of the church, then by definition all those who fail in these ways are not churches!

7. Spiritual gifts are for the building up of the Church in numbers and edification to maturity. It is exciting that Jesus Christ's spiritual gifts to His Church are identified with His ascension, "When He ascended on high, He led captivity captive, and gave gifts to men" (Ephesians 4:8). To re-iterate from above, it is only within local and universal Church that the **Christian is able to mature**.

Spiritual gifts can generally be divided into four categories: teaching/preaching, helps (mercy), administration, and evangelism (Romans 12; I Corinthians 12, and Ephesians 4). Evangelism increases the church's numbers. Teaching/preaching educates. Works of mercy provides for needs. And, administration makes everything work smoothly.

Spiritual gifts only apply to the Church, not to activities outside the Church. While Christians may have great talent for work outside the Church (music, education administration, public service, etc.) that is part of God's Kingdom, spiritual gifts are for the building up of the church. While these special abilities may be manifested outside the church, their effect is different. Spiritual gifts bring about a unity and maturity of a body (a special group of people), whereas talents outside the church are a temporal blessing to those who receive them and have no special unifying effect. While the same gift, for example, a musical gift, may be a blessing by common grace outside the church, the effect and use by God is entirely different.

8. The Church is one of the spheres of government instituted by God. Government begins with the conscience of self-government (Romans 14:23). Based upon a serious study of God's Word, the conscience may challenge organized bodies within the church, as Martin Luther did. The power of physical restraint and punishment, "the power of the sword," resides with the state. The family has its sphere of government in the running of the family and the education of its children.

The Church holds the "keys" of the spiritual realm, that is, the right teaching and preaching of the Word of God, the giving of the Sacraments, and church discipline. **The power of excommunication is infinitely greater to be feared than capital punishment**. Capital punishment ends a life, but one still has the chance of eternal life. The one excommunicated faces the possibility of eternity in Hell where the judgment of elders is true.

Para-church organizations have a doubtful place in God's Kingdom except possibly on a temporary basis. In God's economy, para-church organizations have no standing. While God has certainly used them in the furtherance of the Gospel and even the Church, that mechanism is not His plan. His work on earth is formally and officially through the Church. Only to the Church has He given the keys to the Kingdom and is the Bride of Christ. A para-church organization has no means of church discipline when it errs. Over a period of time, all para-church organizations could be brought under a local church. churches or denomination. The dependence of para-church organizations on the Church is demonstrated in that most of them could not exist without the donations of local churches! Support of para-churches also takes away money from ministries that the local church should be about. See reference below.

9. **Only male heads of households should vote on issues within the Church**. While limiting eldership to men solves most of this error, certain governing issues still reside with the congregation, such as, electing of officers. Again, passages that define headship within the home and limitation of responsibilities in the church show clearly that leadership resides with men. If the family cannot agree on a church vote, how can it rule the church? If it does agree, only one vote per household is needed.

Problem of voting by children and minors in the church. In many churches, there is a conflict between "communion" membership and "voting" membership with children. That is, children may make a clear profession of faith and thereby ought to be admitted to The Lord's Supper. Yet, they clearly lack the wisdom to discern most voting issues of congregations. Opening the church to membership based clearly upon profession of faith, yet limiting voting to men, solves this dilemma. This solution is one of many that are resolved by a Biblical understanding in which there is never a conflict of authorities were roles are clearly understood.

(In times past, voting on civil issues was not only limited to men, but to property owners.)

10. **There is a real spiritual unity of all Bible-believing churches**. "There is one body and one Spirit, just as you were called in one hope of your calling; one Lord, one faith, one baptism; one God and Father of all, who is above all, and through all, and in you all" (Ephesians 4:4-5). While denominations separate on doctrinal and other issues, all true churches have major identities in common, best expressed by these verses.

There is a real unity of Old Testament peoples with the New Testament churches. First, was Adam and Eve. Next, was Adam and his family of eight. Next was Abraham and his descendents as the nation of Israel. The Geneva Bible of 1599, for example, virtually equates Old Testament Israel with the church.

For more on church unity, extant and proposed, see the Frame-Poythress reference below.

11. **Acts 15 warrants the gathering of elders of the churches to settle controversial doctrine**. The importance of these councils is demonstrated most clearly in the early church with the agreement on the Canon of Scripture, the trinity of the Nicene Creed, the two natures of Christ at Chalcedon, the denunciations of Pelagianism and Arminianism, and the formulation of Reformed doctrine in the Westminster Assembly. While not well known, The Biblical Council on Inerrancy, The Biblical Council on Hermeneutics, and the Coalition on Revival are modern examples of ecclesiastical councils. Churches who differ with the pronouncements of all these councils of history are on thin ice, theologically and truthfully.

12. **The church in Sabbath assembly is the primary means of the worship of God, the preaching of the Word, the administration of the Sacraments, and the sealing of church discipline**. While individual Christians are to worship God on their own, there is an importance of corporate gathering on Sundays that supersedes that personal time. The one who believes that he can worship God on his

own, apart from the Sabbath assembly is woefully in error. He who believes that he can get everything of Biblical instruction without preaching is also mistaken. Finally, the gathering of the saints, as God has prescribed, establishes a unity and agreement of the body of Christ that is strong to prevent schisms.

13. Government of the local church. A pastor should not be the center of the local church. (A) I see nothing in the New Testament of pastors determining what a church is and what it does in the manner of modern churches in the following ways. The pastor heads the church board; he leads worship services, especially giving the pastoral prayer and sermon; he is recognized in the congregation, as someone special who gives a certain spiritual presence that no one else can give; he is essentially the only one who can determine directions and activities for the church, and in most situations, he is the only one called on to teach or to pray. By contrast and in consistency with Scripture, the pastor should be recognized for his preaching and pastoral work, but seen only as one elder of the many who govern and shepherd.

(B) I have been a part of three congregations, and have observed another, who were temporarily without pastors. I have been amazed at the way that certain laymen have risen to the task of providing what pastors normally do. As soon as the new pastor comes, they fall back into their (mostly) passive roles.

I do not necessarily want to place blame. It may lie with laymen themselves, not rising to a level of education and experience that equals that of the pastor. It may lie with the pride, that is within all of us, of pastors to be the center of everything. Is may simply lie with church tradition.

But, I believe that pastors must call and disciple their elders to be more central in the life of the church, and laymen must respond or initiate this more active role themselves. Over my lifetime, there have been various emphases on "power in the pew." But, these movements have not grasped the training and experience necessary for that "power." There should be years of serious training and study of the Bible and theology, as well as experience with discipling and service.

Some elders should be made full-time and salaried. Those elders who show special gifts and power of office should consider full-time work in their church and be salaried by their boards. Anyone who has been involved with employing others, knows that the advantages of promoting an employee who has a proven track record locally, vs. one who is virtually unknown. Since "elder" has a specific characteristic of age, "full-time" work in the church should be a consideration of specially gifted elders.

(C) **Pastors come and go, but the tenure of elders is much longer**. Having less concentration of power in a pastor would make for an easier transition from one pastor to another. And, better trained and educated elders would have more discernment for the recruiting of the next pastor.

Pastors should consider longer tenures at churches. Pastorates in smaller churches have become mere stepping stones to larger and more prestigious churches. This movement is seriously destructive to the continuity and development of those smaller churches.

Women's organizations within the church should be moved under the authority of the deacons and elders. The New Testament is clear that the government of the Church is by the rule of men, not women. Modern women's organizations have grown to the extent that they have their own meetings, teachers, retreats, and government. These activities take them away from their husbands and from the government of elders and deacons. While women have gifts to offer ministries of the church, they should not be independent. Historically, "circles" were time for women to be involved in ministries of mercy. Now, they too often become groups centered on themselves.

Additional Reading

http://www.9marks.org/

Nine Marks of a Health Church by Mark Dever

http://www.frame-poythress.org/frame_books/Evangelical_Reunion/Chapter1.html.

Online book on the unity of the church vs. denominations by John Frame.

367

http://www.biblicalworldview21.org/Worldview_Areas/Coalition_on_Revival.asp

Coalition on Revival Document on Church Unity

http://www.ccel.org/contrib/exec_outlines/cjb/cjb_14.htm

A Biblical consideration of para-church organizations.

Clowney, Edmund P. Contours of Christian *Theology: The Church*. InterVarsity Press, 1998, 336 pages.

Summary Principles of the Kingdom of God

As I have researched and written on these Worldview Areas, two studies have been the most rewarding for me. First was God's Holiness, Law, Love, Grace, Mercy, Justice, and Equity and now, the Kingdom of God.

In only a few hours, the reader-student can research this subject himself or herself. There are over 400 verses in the Old and New Testaments that refer to the "kingdom of God," "the Kingdom of heaven," and "kingdom" in the Bible, mostly in the New Testament and mostly in the Gospels. And, if you only look at the verses in Matthew alone, you will have most of the understanding of this concept. Perhaps, while the idea of the Kingdom may be foreign to many Christians, in Scripture its descriptions are quite detailed and comprehensive. This study could/should change your concept of God and His plan for your life! See Bible Search below. (Go to www.biblegateway.com, and look for Keyword Search." You have options for entry of more than one word.)

The Kingdom of God is Biblical worldview or Biblical ethics, comprehensively applied!

(Methodology: Here and throughout this website, I do not try to give exhaustive references of Scripture. For most concepts, there are numerous correlative texts that are not cited. There are actually numerous verses on my of the following concepts. I have listed and briefly discussed more of these verses on the Kingdom elsewhere.

1. **The Kingdom of God and the Kingdom of heaven are one and the same concept**. The two names are used interchangeably by Jesus Christ and the writers of the New Testament ((Matthew 25:31-46, 26:26-30; Luke 22:14-23). The Lord's Prayer itself makes this link. "Thy Kingdom come, Thy will be done, on earth, as it is in Heaven."

The Kingdom of God is one and the same as The Great Commission, the "gospel of the Kingdom" (Matthew 24:14). Thus, the work of the Church extends far beyond the simple presentation of personal salvation in Jesus Christ. It is the "discipling of the nations." It is the implementation of justice and mercy at every level: individuals, families, churches, voluntary organizations, and states. See "Missionary endeavors… below.

Definitions. I have constructed three definitions which are intended to have the same meaning. This concept is so rich that several definitions help to bring it out. I will use the "Kingdom of God" or just the "Kingdom" here and throughout this website.

(A) The Kingdom of God is the progressive implementation of God's rule "on earth, as it is in heaven," to be completed when He judges mankind finally into Heaven or Hell, with temporal blessings and cursings that extend to both Christians and pagans.

(B) The rule of the Holy Spirit as Christ's representative on earth and the rule of the Father in heaven, primarily manifested on earth in the regenerate and the Church among all nations, who bring a portion of heaven (peace and joy) to earth by their rule of righteousness (ethics or worldview) under Biblical authority in conscience, family, voluntary organizations, and civil government, to be consummated with the new heavens and the new earth.

(C) Peace and righteousness (ethics and worldview) that is effected by the Holy Spirit in individuals, families, voluntary organizations, and civil government in all nations, as they govern these areas consistently with the Word of God, manifested primarily through the influence of the regenerate and the Church (Romans 14:17; Hebrews 7:2; Hebrews 12:11; James 13:18), to be consummated with the new heavens and new earth.

Definitions from other authors. See References below.

The Kingdom of God is the new world-order, in heaven and on earth, produced by the revolutionary changes brought about in Jesus' fulfillment of the Old Covenant in His life, death, resurrection, and ascension. (Peter Leithart)

The Kingdom of God is (a) the universal rule of Christ over all things, both redeemed and non-redeemed; (b) the special, saving rule of Christ over His people: (c) the life, wisdom, holiness, power, and authority that Christ grants to His people; or (d) the permeating influence of the Word and Spirit in the world. (Coalition on Revival, # 2 of Articles of Affirmation and Denial on the Kingdom of God)

2. **Membership in the Kingdom**. Membership in the Kingdom of God and the invisible Church have the same criterion: **regeneration**. In John 3:1-21, as one of the primary passages on regeneration, Jesus states "Most assuredly, I say to you, **unless one is born of water and the Spirit, he cannot enter the Kingdom of God**. That which is born of the flesh is flesh, and that which is born of the Spirit is spirit" (verse 5). And, in Titus 3:5, regeneration is inextricably linked to the work of the Holy Spirit: "But when the kindness and the love of God our Savior toward man appeared, not by works of righteousness which we have done, but according to His mercy He saved us, through the washing of regeneration and renewing of the Holy Spirit." This concept is not limited to these two verses, but they will suffice here. Regeneration has been discussed more fully elsewhere.

Faithful angels are members of the Kingdom. Fallen and rebellious angels (demons) are leaders of the spiritual world against the Kingdom.

3. **The effect of the Kingdom of God: blessings and cursings**. The Kingdom affects both the regenerate and the unregenerate through the behavior of both, as their thinking, speech, and behavior work is consistent (blessings) with God's instructions (laws) to mankind or they are inconsistent (cursings). The primary responsibility, however, for implementation of the Kingdom falls upon the regenerate, as individuals, families, and The Church.

Someone has said, "The only Hell that Christians (the regenerate) will ever experience is their life on earth, and the only Heaven that pagans (the unregenerate) will ever experience is their life on earth." These statements are full of the reality of the Kingdom of God and the Kingdom of Darkness (the world, the flesh, and Satan). They also mention the "goodness" of God's common grace and the overflow effects of His Kingdom.

4. The establishment of the Kingdom of God is by both the spiritual (supernatural) activity and the work of the regenerate. God's supernatural activity includes such acts as the crossing of the Red Sea, Daniel's interpretation of dreams, Christ's resurrection of the dead, the manifestations of Pentecost, regeneration of believers, establishment of national rulers, and historical events that have enhanced the spread of the Kingdom, such as, Greek, the universal language of the time of Acts; the printing press that preceded the Reformation; the English common law that was foundational to America as a nation; and the defeat of the Spanish.

While these events are momentous and awesome, the greater work of the Kingdom has been carried out in the regenerate, simply following His instructions and commands.

Works of the regenerate, God's miracles, and His Providence are different ways to effect the same Kingdom. With only a few exceptions, God advances His Kingdom through His people. These advances may be individual acts (Martin Luther's posting of his theses), movements of peoples (all those who implemented the Reformation), councils of the church (various), hospitals and hospices, and missionary endeavors. All the great achievements because of Biblical Christianity are staggering to consider from a moral perspective. See Great Social Reform Because Jesus Lived.

5. The Kingdom of God began with the ministry of Jesus Christ and later the "procession" of the Holy Spirit from the Father and the Son. John the Baptist and Jesus both said that the Kingdom of God was at hand" (Matthew 3:2, 4:17, 10:7). The ministry of John the Baptist is the end of the prior work of God among mankind. the Kingdom of God (Matthew 11:11).

The Kingdom of God is implemented, primarily, by its members: Christians as individuals and The Church, as a body. While the Holy Spirit works above and beyond the regenerate, His work is primarily through individual Christians, families, and the Church. Only these have the sustaining power and knowledge of God and His ways to implement His "will on earth as it is in heaven."

The Old Testament era involved shadows and types of the Kingdom of God. First was The Creation Mandate (Genesis 1:28), given to two people who failed in their Fall. Next, the mandate was stated after The Fall and The Flood to eight people (Genesis 9:1-17). Later, God chose Abraham and his descendents, the nation of Israel, to more fully and specifically to manifest one Kingdom on earth (Israel - Genesis 12:1-3). All these people failed to implement God's directives. God Himself, as the Trinity, has implemented the final Kingdom which will never fail nor end (Luke 1:33). (For more on the relationship of the events of the Old Testament to the Kingdom, see Henry Stob, Ethical Reflections, 1978, pages 62-71 ¾ to be posted on this website.)

These are not dispensations in the theological sense of what is commonly called "dispensationalism." While in a real sense these different periods may be called dispensations, they never present salvation by any other means than Jesus Christ's sacrificial death. Those saved before Jesus, actual time on earth are still saved in the same way, even though Jesus' time was future. The one exception was for Adam and Eve only: they could have been saved by "works," that is, keeping the one rule that God had given to them.

6. **God has already powerfully manifested His Kingdom on earth**. Regardless of a Christian's view of millennialism, the Kingdom of God has had undeniable, powerful effects on planet earth. These include the marked reduction of human sacrifice and slavery, orphanages for abandoned and unwanted children, universal education, hospitals and other caring institutions, global exploration, modern science, English common law, The United States of America, and many other reforms (simply because Jesus fulfilled His mission). While even these "goods" may be used to evil purposes, in general, they have been to the benefit of mankind.

The manifestations of the Kingdom are not found in the "greatest" of philosophers. Certainly, one manifestation of the Kingdom is the defense and loving care of the most defenseless in any society. There is virtually no other philosophy or religion, conceived by the "greatest philosophers" and religious teachers in history, that obligates mankind in this way.

Infanticide by abandonment and exposure were almost universal before cultures were exposed to Christianity. Consistently, "None of the great minds of the ancient world -- from Plato to Aristotle to Seneca and Quintilian, from Pythagoras and Aristophanes to Livy and Cicero, from Herodotus and Thucydides to Plutarch and Euripides -- disparaged child-killing in any way. In fact, most of them even recommended it.... They blindly tossed lives like dice." (George Grant, Third Time Around: A History of the Pro-Life Movement from the First Century to the Present, Wolgemuth and Hyatt, 1991, page 12.)

7. **The Church and the Kingdom are not identical**. This dimension of the Kingdom may be the most difficult to grasp. How can the Kingdom be more than the Church? In these ways. Christians perform good social works (feeding the hungry, clothing the poor, developing orphanages, etc.) that are direct, physical blessings to unbelievers. Christians enact Biblical laws which promote justice for all who are under that jurisdiction. Christians' behavior and their ethics and laws influence social behavior in general. So, while only the regenerate can be members of the Kingdom, its blessings extend far beyond its members.

The Kingdom is Biblical worldview in action. Comprehensive, Biblical worldview that is implemented by Christians and the Church is identical with the Kingdom of God.

8. **Christians err seriously when they limit their citizenship to heaven only**. Without doubt, Christians are pilgrims whose destiny is their Father's house with many mansions (John 14:2). But, the very Lord's Prayer itself, which every Christian prays, calls them to be effect God's will "on earth as it is in heaven." Regardless of one's millennial position, this petition is a strong call for Christians to implement his Regency on earth. Moreover, the argument can be made that Christ's Incarnation, as well as God's activity in history, legitimizes earthly pursuit of justice and righteousness in every sphere of human activity.

As we will see below, since the Kingdom is contiguous with Heaven, **heavenly citizenship begins now**! As we will see also, Christians will rule in heaven. We will not be passive. Should not we begin our training for heaven now?

Readers should not confuse the "social gospel" of liberal Christianity with this call for Christians and The Church to be agents of change on earth. Somewhere in the last 250 years, social change became identified with liberal Christians, even to the call for armed revolution where injustice reigns. During the same time period, "fundamental" Christians divorced personal pietism from social action.

Reader, note the context of my message here: regeneration of souls and Biblically guided action! I am as far from such a "social gospel" as one can be. The time has come for Bible-believing Christians to unite once again the full gospel message with The Great Commission of "making disciples of all nations" and implementing "God's will on earth as it is in heaven."

(Sometime soon, I plan to write an article on the argument for postmillennialism **apart from** passages of Biblical prophecy. I think that the arguments for millennial positions are misplaced. We ought, instead, to simply obey what God has called His people to do in all the descriptions of His Kingdom that are discussed here.)

9. **Undeniable truths concerning the Kingdom of God**. There are clear Biblical statements and positions that are virtually impossible to deny without being inconsistent and illogical. They are inescapable truths, regardless of one's eschatology. A simple review of all the verses that pertain to this subject is all that is necessary for these conclusions. I have named many of those verses, detailed the thoughts of many verses, and discussed these truths in this Summary. Perhaps, naming them briefly and concretely will help readers realize the clarity of what the Bible says about the Kingdom.

> A. The Kingdom of God, the Kingdom of heaven, The Great Commission, and the implementation of Biblical ethics and Biblical worldview are one and the same.

> B. The Kingdom began with Jesus Christ's ministry on earth and the procession of the Holy Spirit from the Father and the Son.

C. Only the regenerate can be members of the Kingdom. Evidence of their regeneration is their good works. (See Glossary definition of Good Work on this site.)

D. Jesus Christ is the King of the entire universe. He is The King of Kings and The Lord of Lords with the Government upon His shoulders.

E. The Lord's Prayer petitions that the Kingdom is "to come" and that God's will is "to be done as it is in heaven."

F. The Kingdom is growing (parable of the Mustard Seed), will never fail, and will be consummated in the reality of Heaven itself.

G. Jesus Christ will eventually place all His enemies under His feet.

10. **Perhaps, understanding the Kingdom should precede one's grappling with millennial issues**. My work on these Summary Principles on the Kingdom is my first real study of the Kingdom of God. What has most amazed me about this study is not only the number of references in the Bible on the subject, but the detail about what the Kingdom is.

I fear that we Bible-believing Christians so much in love with our favorite verses, proof texts, and systematic theology that we neglect to study the Bible itself. Faith (noun) and believe (verb) are another example. There are at least five meanings of the word faith in the New Testament. Do you know what they are? All you have to do is use a concordance and look up all the verses on faith and believe. Such a study is not difficult or complex, but it will take some hours. I would prefer that you do the study, but you can read my short book on faith for some insights.

But, **the point is simply to study what the Bible says on the Kingdom of God**. I have posted my raw notes, which are not complete, which can be a beginning for you. Such a study may have some bearing on your millennial position.

11. **Perhaps, God prefers that His people reign, rather than be persecuted**. The United States may be the battleground for whether

persecution of Christians takes place here and in other Western countries. Frankly, I prefer not to be persecuted! But, some Christians either by their millennial position or by their passivity for whatever reasons, are opening the gate very widely for their own persecution.

Where Christians have opportunity, I do not believe that God wants His people to be persecuted. Now, certainly I would never minimize the suffering of Christians past and present. I would rather almost anything happen to me, rather than to be seen in that light. However, the Scriptures seem clear to me that ultimately His saints are rulers, not subjects of martyrdom. We will judge angels (I Corinthians 6:3), sit on God's lesser thrones (Revelation 4:4), and were intended to "have dominion" over the earth from the beginning (Genesis 1:26).

Certainly, the Kingdom of God is about humility, "the least will be the greatest" and the "meek shall inherit the earth." However, the passages that I just cited and many others speak of dominion, ruling, and judging. An historical model is found in the Puritans who demonstrated humility and willingness to rule (albeit imperfectly, as will always be the case on earth). Perhaps, the modern equivalence of "winsome," as a model for Christians, should also be that of a solder for Christ. Why cannot vigorous leadership be dynamic and aggressive, as part of being "winsome?"

> The Puritan was made up of two different men; the one all self-abasement, penitence, gratitude, passion; the other proud, calm, inflexible, sagacious. He prostrated himself in the dust before his Maker, but he set his foot on the neck of his king." See my summary on the Puritans and the original work cited there.

There is no question in my mind that the United States is the pinnacle of God's Kingdom on earth through its basis in Mosaic law, as historically developed in English Common Law, John Calvin, William Blackstone, and others. However, **that greatness is seriously threatened today, not by all the leftists and liberals, but by the neglect of worldview application by God's people** in the comprehensive and conscious manner of our founding fathers (imperfect, and sometimes not even true believers, though they were).

The "personal peace and affluence" criticized by Francis Schaeffer, the "don't polish brass on a sinking ship" of the pre-millennialists, and

376

general worldview apathy and ignorance of most evangelicals are allowing the leftists and liberals to gradually take over this country. They have almost succeeded, but I do not believe that it is too late, if more Christians fall on their faces before God, seeking His forgiveness, and then repenting to understand the full Biblical application of His truth to every area of life. Perhaps, a Biblical study of the Kingdom of God could spark some interest in causing "God's will to be done on earth, as it is in Heaven."

But, patriotism and the identity of the United States as one manifestation of the Kingdom, should not be equated. We must not have the idea that we will support "my country, right or wrong." Indeed, currently, America strays far from her Biblical roots and in many quarters is hostile to Biblical faith and ethics. So, American Christians must be careful not to place patriotism over Christ's Lordship through Biblical truth.

12. **Jesus Christ will one day be established visibly to everyone on earth and in heaven, as the King of Earth and Heaven**. All millennial positions eventually establish His Kingdom. So, the disagreement is when and how that happens, not the reality itself.

The Kingdom of God is continuous and contiguous with Heaven itself. After the old heavens are destroyed by fire and the new heavens and earth are established, then will our time in heaven will begin (II Peter 3:7-13).

13. **One of the primary manifestations of the Kingdom is the basis of civil law in Biblical ethics and law**. I have reviewed how civil law changes the behavior of the citizens under it through their pattern of behavior and fear of punishment. Law is legislated morality.

Other manifestations include the same rule of Biblical ethics and law in government of self (conscience), the family, and voluntary social organizations. Individual Christians should be activists to establish this rule of ethics and law in their sphere of influence.

14. **Another primary manifestation of the Kingdom are works of mercy by individual Christians on their own and in their families, voluntary social organizations, and churches**. See Summary Principles of Social Justice.

Non-Christians may also do these works under the influence of the regenerate (as individuals and their institution) and under their own consciences that reflect the innate ethics and law of God. However, their depth and breadth of motivation can never match the power of the Holy Spirit working in His people.

Most of the scenes of judgment involve the reviews of social responsibilities of individuals (for example, Matthew 25:31-46).

15. **Vocation has its identity with the Kingdom of God**. Today, too many Christians see "working for the Lord" as being only in the context of The Church or being a missionary. A conscious concept of the Kingdom of God makes any ethical endeavor a "working for the Lord" ¾ to advance His Kingdom "on earth as it is in Heaven."

16. **Is there an opposing Kingdom**? Yes and no. There is no opposing Kingdom in the likeness of the Kingdom itself. The opposing forces to the Kingdom are "the world, the flesh, and the Devil." These forces do not have an organizing entity, as the Holy Spirit is the organizing and motivating force of the Kingdom.

Is Satan the ruler of the opposing Kingdom? Yes and no. While Satan's goal is certainly to thwart God at every turn and to overthrow Him, His power and influence is limited. He knows that the battleground lies in man and mankind. But, the very nature of evil in himself, in his demons, and within men themselves does not have an organized focus. Men's selfishness makes them enemies of each other. Each one wants his own rule, power, and influence. Each devil wants the same thing for himself. The Devil, and indeed, all godless beings, can only rule by deceit and fear of punishment. He cannot "draw all men unto Himself." He cannot woo men into following him blindly without deceit and intimidation.

In my opinion, all these that oppose the Kingdom of God will eventually triumph to their own ends. One of my concepts of Hell is its total individuality ¾ every man and demon for Himself. And, Satan will "rule" over this chaotic nightmare, as he will be the most powerful being there.

In a philosophical sense, Satan can never win in the way that he desires. The only organizing influence is the goodness of God. Evil by its very nature can only destroy. It cannot build anything that is

378

permanent, good in the ultimate sense, or worth the allegiance of men or angels in the long run. Evil beings, including Satan, only have influence to the degree that they stir the selfish desires of others.

17. **We win**! Every Christian acknowledges that Christ was victorious from the grave and will establish His Kingdom upon His Second Advent. Then, why do we not live like we are winners? As described above, there is really no contest. On one side is the omnipotent God and His work in space, time, and eternity, loving men unto His leadership. On the other is "every man (and demon) for himself."

18. **The Kingdom is continuous and intergenerational in time**. As we have seen, the Kingdom continually grows in time until it is translated into Heaven. As is developed in Summary Principles of the Family, God's primary mode of evangelism is through the family. This intergenerational movement fits with the development of the Kingdom whereby momentum and power is built from generation to generation.

19. **State welfare is not a manifestation of the Kingdom**. There is nothing right about state welfare. It steals from one group to give to others. It imposes a huge administrative cost. (I have seen estimates from 75-90 percent.) It promotes laziness among its recipients. It gives without regard to responsibility and true need, based upon some arbitrary category of persons. It dehumanizes its recipients, making them into helpless victims. It promotes class warfare, giving "rights" to recipients, as well as establishing groups of "haves" and "have nots." It trains recipient children in "the ways that they should (not) go." It promotes illegitimate marriages and weakens the role of husbands. And, more.

20. **The relationship of the Kingdom of God to the Church**. (A) **"The Kingdom of God creates the church**. The redemptive role of God brings into being a new people who receive the blessings of the divine reign." (George Eldon Ladd, Baker's Dictionary of Theology, 1960, page 313). (B) In so far as **the visible Church is instrumental in the establishment and extension of the Kingdom, it is of course subordinate to this as a means to an end**. The Kingdom may be said to be a broader concept than the Church, because it aims at nothing less than the complete control of all the manifestations of life. It represents the dominion of God in every sphere of human endeavor." (Louis Berkhof, *Systematic Theology*, 11th printing, 1969, page 570)

Perhaps, this relationship may be summed up in this way.

> In relation to the Kingdom, the Church may be defined as the totality of those who at any time have been delivered by the power of God's reign in Christ from the toils of sin and death and have been reconciled to God. As such the Church is the living, burning center of the Kingdom, a witness to its presence and power, a harbinger of its final coming. It is not the Kingdom, it is narrower than the Kingdom, but it is its central component. (Henry Stob, *Ethical Reflections*, 1978, page 69)

21. **Missionary endeavors must implement the idea of the Kingdom of God**. From all the above, missionary efforts throughout the world are too narrowly focused. They are focused on the salvation of individuals and their incorporation into local churches. However, the Church is an agency of the Kingdom of God. Therefore, the goal of missions must be the implementation of the Kingdom of God, as they understand it from a Biblical study.

I believe that the current teaching by most missionary agencies is setting the stage for national disasters because of this narrow focus. Even "saved" souls still have within them the "old man" (the flesh or the sin nature). Thus, judicial discipline is necessary in the local church, and civil law (based upon the Word of God) is necessary for godly rule of local, regional, and national governments in the civil realm.

Historically, the leaders of the Reformation knew this truth. Prior to them, European and English common laws (based upon the Mosaic Law) knew this truth. Now, in modern times, this foundation has largely been forgotten and neglected. Its omission from modern evangelism and missions is a major failure of those endeavors. **The Great Commission, as it is proclaimed today, is largely a Truncated Commission! And, the Church without judicial discipline is a Church with unnecessary impurity and corruption**.

References

Online Bible Keyword Search - Do your own study using the keyword search feature as a concordance: Kingdom of God, Kingdom of

Heaven, Kingdom (sort out those passages that refer to a kingdom under some human king and his earthly kingdom)

The Kingdom of God: Peter Leithart

Coalition on Revival: Affirmations and Denials

John Calvin on the Two Kingdoms

19. Art and the Arts

A Concordance Search of "Beauty" and "Beautiful" in the Bible

The following are objects named as "beauty" or "beautiful" in the Bible. These are a summary of 100 verses found on a concordance search of these two words in the NJKV. Virtually all are listed except for a limited list of "certain women," as far and away the most common usage in the Bible.

I am aware of the limitations of this exercise. Other words, such as, splendid, majestic, or elegant could have been searched. However, my limitation to "beauty" and "beautiful" seems to illustrate what is necessary for a consideration of "art" and "the arts" in the Bible.

Certain women: Genesis 6:2; 12:11; 24:16; 29:17; Esther 1:11; II Samuel 11:12

*****Words**: Genesis 49:21

*****Garments for the priest in the tabernacle**: Exodus 28:40

Certain trees: Leviticus 23:40

Certain cities: Deuteronomy 6:10, Isaiah 13:19 (Babylon); Ezekiel 27:3, 4, 11, 12, 17 (Tyre)

    Jerusalem: Psalm 48:2, 50:2; Isaiah 52:1; Lamentations 2:15

Certain houses: Deuteronomy 8:12, Isaiah 5:9

Other garments: Joshua 7:21;

*****David's praise of Saul and Jonathan**: II Samuel 1:19

*****Beauty of God's holiness**: I Chronicles 16:19; II Chronicles 20:21; Psalm 29:2, 96:9

Precious stones: II Chronicles 3:6; Luke 21:5

The make-up that women use: Esther 2: 3, 9;

*Of God (or praise of Him): Job 40:10; Psalm 27:4; Psalm 33:1, 90:17, 96:6, 147:1; Isaiah 28:5

> **In salvation**: Zechariah 9:17

> **Of His governance of Israel**: Zechariah 11:7, 10

*Of Christ: Isaiah 4:2, 33:17, 52:7

Lacking beauty: Isaiah 53:2

"Man": Psalm 39:11, 49:14

Adulterous woman: Proverbs 6:25

God's creation: Ecclesiastes 3:11

Ships: Isaiah 2:16

Flowers: Isaiah 28:4; James 1:11

An idol man in the image of a man's body: Isaiah 44:13

Contrasted with ashes: Isaiah 61:3

*Temple: Isaiah 64:11; Acts 3:2, 10 (gate in the Temple)

The nation Israel: Jeremiah 3:19, 13:20; Lamentations 2:1; Ezekiel 16:14, 15, 25; Hosea 14:6 (restored)

The people of Moab, symbolized by their "rod" of rule: Jeremiah 48:17

Physical riches that God gives: Ezekiel 16:7, 12, 17, 39; 23:26, 42

Of cedars in Lebanon (as a symbol of Egypt): Ezekiel 31:7, 8, 9; 32:19

*The Kingdom of God: Matthew 13:45 (likened to pearls)

Whitewashed tombs (outward beauty that covers inward corruption): Matthew 23:27

The feet of him who brings good news: Romans 10:15

Moses, as a child: Hebrews 11:23

*A gentle and quiet spirit: I Peter 3:4

Some Conclusions

1. **The Bible commonly uses "beautiful" and "beauty" in the same ways that virtually all peoples use them**. Illustrations include women (the most frequent use in the Bible, and perhaps commonly), ships, trees, world and universe, etc.

2. **The distinctive use of these two words in the Bible apply to God's being or praise (worship) of Himself (in the Persons of the Trinity) and in salvation**. Thus, "beauty" and "beautiful" are not limited to the of physical objects, but to the Creator of beautiful things, as a spiritual being and His salvation of those that He has called to Himself.

3. **A summary of "beauty" and "beautiful," then, might be the focus of God's being and His two great acts, Creation and Salvation**. All persons, at some time in their lives (before some of their hearts are hardened) esteem God's nature and the beauty of His Creation (Romans 1:18-23). Their failure is to exclude His third dimension of beauty, salvation, in which they become able to "worship Him in the beauty of His holiness" (above references).

* References to God, His worship, or spiritual concepts that are not physical in their being perceived by man's senses.

384

Art and the Arts

An Introduction

The history of art and the arts is primarily that of crafts that enhance beauty in everyday life and in worship. Perhaps, more than any other worldview area, art and the arts must be placed in the context of history to begin to grasp summary principles. We will begin with some definitions from Webster's 1828 Dictionary and the 2007 online version of Merriam-Webster.

Culture, 1828

1. The act of tilling and preparing the earth for crops; cultivation; the application of labor or other means of improvement.

2. The application of labor or other means to improve good qualities in, or growth; as the culture of the mind; the culture of virtue.

3. The application of labor or other means in producing; as the culture of corn, or grass.

4. Any labor or means employed for improvement, correction or growth.

Culture, 2007

1. The act of developing the intellectual and moral faculties especially by education.

2. Expert care and training.

3. Enlightenment and excellence of taste acquired by intellectual and aesthetic training. Acquaintance with and taste in fine arts, humanities, and broad aspects of science as distinguished from vocational and technical skills

4. The integrated pattern of human knowledge, belief, and behavior that depends upon the capacity for learning and transmitting knowledge to succeeding generations. The customary beliefs, social forms, and material traits of a racial,

religious, or social group. The characteristic features of everyday existence (as diversions or a way of life) shared by people in a place or time (popular culture, southern culture. The set of shared attitudes, values, goals, and practices that characterizes an institution or organization (a corporate culture focused on the bottom line). The set of values, conventions, or social practices associated with a particular field, activity, or societal characteristic (studying the effect of computers on print culture).

Art, 1828

1. The disposition or modification of things by human skill, to answer the purpose intended. In this sense, art stands opposed to nature.

2. A system of rules, serving to facilitate the performance of certain actions… as the art of building or engraving.

Arts are divided into useful or mechanic, and liberal or polite. The mechanic arts are those in which the hands and body are more concerned than the mind, as in making clothes, and utensils. These arts are called trades. The liberal or polite arts are those in which the mind or imagination is chiefly concerned, as poetry, music, and painting.

3. Skill, dexterity, or the power of performing certain actions, acquired by experience, study, or observation, as a man has the art of managing his business to advantage.

Art, 2007

1. A skill acquired by experience, study, or observation (the art of making friends).

2. A branch of learning: (1) one of the humanities or (2) plural, liberal arts (archaic: learning, scholarship).

3. An occupation requiring knowledge or skill (the art of organ building).

4. The conscious use of skill and creative imagination especially in the production of aesthetic objects. Also, works so produced (fine arts). One of the fine arts or a graphic art.

5. Archaic, a skillful plan. The quality or state of being artful.

6. Decorative or illustrative elements in printed matter.

Edmund Clowney, former President of Westminster Theological Seminary (Philadelphia), has made these observations:

> The political revolutions in America and France and the Industrial Revolution in England brought about not only a change in Western culture but also a new way of speaking of culture. **Before that change, painting was thought of as a craft**. The long corridors lined with portraits in the great house of Britain were not begun as museum galleries. The paintings were hung to remember ancestors, not to exhibit artists' works. As Andre Malraux has observed, the modern attitude to "art" has created a "museum without walls." Not only do we stack museums with historic "works of art" stripped of their original purpose, we have come to think of the ceiling of the Sistine Chapel or even the cathedral at Chartres as a "work of art." Art critics serenely ignore the religious motivation of museum paintings and display professional outrage at anyone who might dare to offer a moral objection to "artistic" pornography. Painting, sculpture, photography, music, poetry ¾ **that which we call "art" has become an end itself; indeed, it is given an absolute value that not only resembles religion but also demands religious commitment**. (Henry, *God and Culture*, pages 235-236 -- Ed's emphasis)

The reader should note that today's common use of "culture," as an identity with the customs of a particular group, does not even appear in the 1828 definition. "Culture" at that time, like "art," denoted "added value" to a work that had another purpose than just being an object to admire, as "art" is today.

The changes that have occurred in the words, "culture" and "art," illustrate, as Clowney discusses, the modern debates about "art" and "the arts." (Henceforward, I am going to use "art" to include "the arts" for simplicity of expression.) Until relative recently in history, **art was the energy and creativity that virtually all people used within whatever occupation that they found themselves**.

The Sistine Chapel has been mentioned. Now, I am sure that Michelangelo could have found a better canvas than the high ceiling to which he was commissioned! Also, one that was easier for him to do his work and easier on the necks of viewers! But, the purpose of that great mural was to enhance the beauty of the Chapel, as a place of worship (or perhaps for the fancy of the reigning Pope).

As Clowney also mentioned, museums started as galleries of portraits of relatives and great personages. The *Mona Lisa* was a **portrait** that has become a famous **painting**. It was not commissioned to be a great piece of art in a museum, but either to commemorate a person or enhance the beauty of one's mansion or castle. Its becoming "art," as we understand the term today, was somewhat accidental, not intended in its production.

The great cathedrals with their flying buttresses were not created as independent "works of art," but a greater way to demonstrate the grandeur and glory of God in a place of worship. (It is a great tragedy that these cathedrals with their physical beauty no longer reflect the beauty of a worshipping people.)

Thus, art had an identity within life itself to express beauty in whatever area of life in which it appeared. That area of life today we call "culture." But, that word, as seen in the definitions above, was almost identical to the meaning of art, that is, an enhancement of the activities of everyday life for enjoyment or beauty.

I believe that this review explains the confusion in art today. **Art only has an identity with the way of life of the artist and the "culture" to which he belongs. Art is an enhancement of one's beliefs and everyday life. Thus, art flows from the subjective values and ways of life of the peoples who produce it¾ the definition of "culture," as we use it today**. Its fullest application flows from the skill (craft) of the one who creates in whatever mode of expression in which he is involved.

But, the attempt has been made to separate art into a category that is divorced from its subjective nature. Thus, the "art wars" that we have today. The Renaissance and the Enlightenment have achieved more consistency with their subjective message, that of divorcing man's existence from a necessary reference to the God of the Bible. In their earlier stages, they could not separate themselves entirely from their Christian worldview which dominated their era. **However, now that "God is dead" ¾ by their proclamation ¾ neither harmony of design nor skill is required in their concept of "art."** As we will see, God is a Person of order and beauty. Modern humanists cannot acknowledge order and beauty in art any more than they can acknowledge (worship) a God of beauty and order.

Pornography is another example. As "art" developed in the West, the human form, was a primary focus of "art." Michelangelo's "David" glorified the magnificent body of a young man. Today, male (and female) pornography is defended as "art," consistent with the humanist worldview of "freedom" of sexual expression. But, art in this sense, shows the degradation that occurs as thought and expression moves away from the grandeur of God.

But, many, if not most, have tried to make art something that is objective. Even Christians have made this mistake. Francis Schaeffer stated in his section on "The Art Work as a Art Work," that "the first (principle) is the most important: A *work of art* has a value in itself" (page 50 - emphasis his). Gene Edward Vieth, Jr. talks about "**objective merit**" (page 40 - emphasis Ed's). Later, he states, "The fine art of the museums must also be judged by **aesthetic standards** (page 50, emphasis Ed's). He writes as though these standards exist apart from some group-culture. They to not. Standards are derived by agreement for a group from each individual's subjective [personal] values.)

Let me give an example. Take the Mona Lisa into one the many refugee camps in Africa. An individual or family there would likely use it as part of a wall or roof. Take it one of the primitive tribes that still exist in the world. If they don't worship it as a god, they would likely use it as a decoration among their customary baubles. If a family owned the Mona Lisa, they would sell it far short of its current value, if it were the difference in their family being fed in a famine. Even one of the most famous paintings in the world is not universally valued! In one photo of a primitive people, viewers see light bulbs on their necklaces.

The lack of objective value can be seem in an historical example. During World War II, museums, churches, and other valuable buildings and landmarks were destroyed for the higher value of the war efforts. While these destructions may not have been often intended, they were expected "collateral damage" to the war effort.

The idea of any kind of value being objective is a common misconception of both Christians and non-Christians. Gold and silver come very close to being objective standards because they are almost universally valued. But, again, the primitive tribes think of gold and silver only as pretty baubles, not the value given to it by worldwide markets. See Summary Principles of Economics.

George Grant in his Gileskirk series on "Modernism" states that nationalism was a development of the late 19th Century in Europe. Perhaps, this attempt to coalesce many cultures under the broad umbrella of nationalism contributed to the modern concept of "art." As we have seen, art was primarily an inherent element of the customs of a group of people and a way of life, but with nationalism there came the attempt to find value that was common to all peoples in one nation. Of course, the movement of nationalism and art to a more widespread value were part and parcel of the philosophical movements that were shaping the world in recent centuries. As there is now a movement to an artificial unity of all nations, there is an attempt to make art "universal." It will not happen … until Jesus Christ personally rules the entire earth.

The United States is an example where there have been a myriad of cultures and their religions (beliefs and lifestyle), for example, the industrial North, the Old South, the Indians (quite distinct among themselves), African blacks, and Mexican immigrants. **The founding fathers understood this diversity, forming a "united states," not the nationalistic entity that the United States has become today**.

All these concepts and identities must be recognized in any discussion of art. Any attempt to objectify art is doomed to failure because "beauty is always in the eyes of the beholder." Tom Wolfe has estimated that the "art world¾ that is, the network of patrons, curators, and museums¾ consists of 10,000 people" (not including artists themselves). **In a world of billions of peoples and thousands of cultures, how is it this small body of people thinks that it can determine what is and is not art**? Such intent is the pinnacle of hubris! There are times that we should just laugh at their paint spatters and piles of junk, rather than engage in serious debate which only cedes most of their argument to their way of thinking.

And, thus exists the current dilemmas in the arts. By any traditional standard of art, much that is called "art" today is not. Art grew out of skill and craft with the imagination of beauty from within the mind of its creator. **That art requires skill, craft, and diligence is about as close to an objective standard that I can conclude**. The simple composites of paint, common items of everyday use, and virtually no effort of many modern and "abstract" art just do not qualify as art in this way.

Within all these mixes of subjective values, the most important is one's religious beliefs (first principles, life philosophy, worldview, cosmology, etc.). **Value is always primarily determined by one's religious views. Thus, art by its very nature is religious**.

A concrete example is the work of Robert Mapplethorpe. His "art" is simply the more consistent application of humanism that began with the Enlightenment and the Renaissance. These "great" movements were the beginning expressions of man's conscious divorce from the God who was worshipped in the Middle Ages and produced the Reformation. Robert Mapplethorpe is consciously anti-God. Most modern art is consciously anti-God and Biblical Christianity. Everything else can be tolerated except that philosophy.

Art vs. skill. Dr. Clowney touches on this issue in his quote above. The artist may have great technique¾ line of brushstrokes, mixing of colors, and mastery of dimension.

and not produce what art connoisseurs would call good or great art. Thus, there is a quality to the whole that supersedes the "craft" of the work.

But, the reverse is much more difficult. An artist would have great difficulty producing what many might call good or great art **without** some level of competence in his craft.

To confuse the issue even further, we commonly speak of "lines" of beauty in architecture. Thus, there is an esthetic appeal to symmetry, lines that please the eye, shapes that blend and enhance the whole, and other such geometry. These lines and shapes are craft, mostly, if not entirely. They are far less complex than the great classical paintings, yet many call these "art." Are they?

In literature, there are various forms: prose, poetry, white papers, scientific papers, and many more "kinds." Each has a certain "beauty," according to its subject matter, style, syntax, and use of language. Again, there is a blurring of craft, appeal, and beauty. Then, with this wide array of craft and sense appeal, what is art?

Group-culture. For our purposes here, I am going to create a term, "group-culture." While culture normally refers to tribes or groups within local geographic areas, as those studied by *National Geographic*, there exists groups of people today who define art as what they themselves like. (See reference above.)

But, there seem to be groups even apart from this *avante garde* group who have similar tastes, but who do not form a culture in the usual and traditional sense. That is why I choose "group-culture" and not just culture as my reference for those who determine what "art" is (to themselves).

Art is really about group-cultures, not individuals. While certainly any individual may define for himself what is and is not art, the usual discussions of art involves group-cultures. They speak of "art appreciation," "art critics," "value" (especially in monetary terms), and fitting artwork into come established classification. Also, I cannot imagine any person on planet earth being able to create a "work of art" that no one else would not also value, from the sublime to the ridiculous. Also, to speak of art as anything individual, is to make this whole discussion too complex even to begin to have some coherency.

The author's dilemma. The worldview area of art and the arts is the most difficult that I have yet tackled for several reasons. I am not inclined towards the arts. Indeed, virtually everyone who knows me well thinks me quite analytical. If a simplistic view of personality can be used, then I would be on the extreme away from those who are inclined towards "art appreciation," its value, and perhaps even more so, those who produce art. At the same time, however, I may be just the person for to analyze this area since I may be more objective, having no vested interest and little subjective bias.

Summary Principles of Art and The Arts

1. **In its essence, art is a work whose beauty is subjectively valued by a group-culture that identifies with it**. As we discuss lines, shapes, and composites vs. a detailed painting and forms of literature, their appeal and value is as broad as the number of groups who identify with parts or the whole of a work.

Let me use abstract "modern" art, as an example. Its appeal is to a limited audience. To many, abstract art is just a confusion of lines, shapes, and colors. Much of it is simple and easily assembled or painted, not requiring the intricate craft of classical art. Yet, there is an audience to whom abstract art has deep and serious appeal, even to payment of large sums to acquire it. To some of these people, classical art has no appeal or value, yet this art has a much longer history, and I suspect, much larger audience.

In this subjectivity, the slippery concept of value rules. In reality, this value can almost always be denominated in dollars (or some other form of currency). What a person or group is willing to pay reflects the extent to which they value an object. **Value comes from worldview, that is, one's most basic philosophy, religion, or worldview. Or, to use another word, value is what one worships (First Commandment)**.

Art, then, in the classical and modern sense cannot be separated from the worldview of the group who labels anything as "art" or beauty is in their eye minds. This link explains what is commonly accepted as "classical" art, the great paintings of such men as Michelangelo and Leonardo da Vinci with their Christian motifs but sometimes with a blend of the Renaissance, as man begins to break free of a Biblical worldview.

2**. One could argue for art being at least the product of a learned skill that is diligently applied and a portrayal of a particular order, even if limited to that group-culture**. What skill or effort is required to throw paint against a wall? Or, to collect a pile of junk? Or, to place a crucifix in a jar of urine? Or, to paint one's body with chocolate? Yes, we must allow the group-culture to determine its art, but they have a great difficulty in getting much of the rest of the world to accept it as art without acquired skill and diligence.

Abstract art. Some abstract is diligently pursued that could be claimed as a skill. However, what does even the *avante garde* patron have to consider with a piece of abstract art? He has to imagine how it speaks to him or what it portrays to him. What has been done, then? **The abstract form of art has been given definition, form, or context in the viewers mind**! Even the group-culture that argues for abstract art must give it **form and orderliness** for it to be valuable to themselves. Now, I would not be so naïve to think that that some would not agree with this conclusion. However, I simply ask, "What does a person do when confronted with a piece of abstract are?" He begins to try to see meaning in it. Virtually everyone does this.¾ my argument is confirmed. His meaning, however, is not in the art. Dare one to say that such "meaning" is a sort of Rorschach test?

3**. Because of its link to a group, art should be funded by that group, not by a larger mass of people who do not "appreciate" that type of art**. The current conflict about funding of the "arts" ultimately derives from several other errors in understanding worldview: (a) that government expenses are limited to those purposes that God has designed, primarily promoting justice and peace (see Worldview on Government, etc.) and (b) that "nations" can set policy for those group-cultures under its authority (see comments from George Grant above).

4. **Television, movies, and novels with some striking exceptions are not art except in a limited extent**. There is a difference between entertainment and art. These media are primarily about entertainment, not art. Certainly, there have been some productions in these media that some (most?) could sanction as "art." These **might** include "Gone With the Wind" (movie) and *Crime and Punishment* (novel). At the moment, any program produced exclusively for television that would qualify as "art" does not come to mind. Perhaps, some live coverage or "fair and balanced" documentary. However, the craft of special effects, virtually since the beginning of "moving" pictures, is to be applauded.

(I suppose in fairness and balanced, many novels would indeed be considered art, yet the modern mill of paper back trade novels makes up the large majority of sales. And, some movies, such as "The Lord of the Rings" trilogy is startling in its creativity. Yet, movies in general are just mass-produced.)

Certainly, group-cultures identify with certain programs, as Star Trekkies come to mind. But, even within these groups, it is obvious that what they are concerned with is entertainment, not what we would today call "art." I know of no avant-garde group that has claimed any Star Trek series, as "art." (They have claimed worse, however!)

Christians need seriously to evaluate the place of television (primarily), movies, and novels relative to their "redeeming the time" (Ephesians 5:16, Colossians 4:5). **One wonders what reformation of American culture might occur, if the time that Christians spent watching television and reading novels were spent in serious study of their Bibles, theology, ethics, and worldview.**

What does it say about our homes that the television is in the geographically central place in our homes. I daresay that the television has become an altar! And, many Christians would defend their watching television with a "religious" vigor that they do not display when they defend their faith in God. For some, novels (cheap or classical) might fit into that category of a serious use of time.

394

5. **Art, then, is as diverse as the number of cultures on the face of the earth and the common values within those groups**. One of the errors of modernity is to think narrowly and superficially of other groups. For example, "Greek thought" is often referred to as though there were one way of thinking to all Greeks of that ancient civilization. The various tribes of American Indians were strikingly different in their hunting, houses, and habits, yet they are frequently referred to as though they were similar, if not identical.

6. **If a group wants to call something "art," they may make that claim. But, they should not expect other group-cultures necessarily to agree with them**. Perhaps, art is like happiness, one does not achieve happiness by trying to be happy. Happiness is a by-product of right behavior and trusting (resting) in the Providence of God. Art should simply be allowed to be whatever a particular group-culture wants it to be. We should not be concerned about the arts; we should just let artists create and their audiences appreciate.

7. **Christians, however, must consider what God calls "beautiful."** Biblical worldview is governed by what the Bible says. Interestingly, the Bible to a large extent reflects what most people would call beautiful: women, ships, trees, garments, and cities. See Beauty and Beautiful in the Bible.

But, God is Himself is not physical, He is a Spirit (John 4:24). As the great and ultimate being that He is, He and His attributes would have to be the most beautiful things to any believer's mind.

If some churches choose to be plain, simple buildings, that is their choice and understanding of Scripture. If some churches want elaborate stained-glass windows, then they certainly have a model for them in the Tabernacle in the wilderness and the Temple that Solomon built. Some churches want contemporary music for their services, even including dance. Others want the formality of traditional and staid worship.

I would contend, however, **that beauty of the architecture or church buildings should be a reflection of the beauties of God**. While I understand the simplicity of buildings as an attempt to emphasize the spiritual nature of our salvation and to avoid the sin of the Second Commandment. Yet, God's universe is not simplicity of design. It is a wonderful array of physical objects and an almost limitless myriad of plant and animal life. Beautiful objects, as skill and orderliness with imagination, are a reflection both of God's creation and His holiness. Whether stained glass windows are allowed or not is beyond our discussion here, but I believe that the arguments of some Reformers that pictures are allowed, even encouraged by the Scriptures, as long as they are not central to worship and are not worshipped themselves.

Now, I will move from "preaching" to "meddling," relative to the "worship wars." I do not believe that the cacophony of some "contemporary worship" has **form** and **orderliness**. Some contemporary worship does, so I am not condemning all expressions. However, even where some speak in tongues, Paul calls for orderliness and form in worship (I Corinthians 14). John Frame has discussed these issues eloquently in his book, *Contemporary Worship Music: A Biblical Defense* (Presbyterian and Reformed, 1997).

8. **"Art appreciation" classes should be renamed "A Review of Kinds of Art," "An Education In Kinds of Art," or some similar title**. A student should not be expected to "appreciate" any "art" form that does not please him or her. As a broadening of an understanding of different culture-groups, such study can be worthwhile, but art is defined by the individual and his group-culture, not by any person or group for the entirety of humankind.

9. **Christians and the imagination**. It seems to me that Christians have adopted the world's concept of the imagination. In secular education, there is a "free-thinking" philosophy that is to allow children to be creative. But, **what seems to have been lost in this approach is that a broad and studied background is needed to be creative**. Creativity does not come from a blank mind, but one that is filled with forms and thoughts from others who have studied and labored. At one's time of study, these studies may be considered fixed, even stagnant. Yet, creativity is built on what others have created.

God created from an infinite store of knowledge. He is our model of creativity. While there seem to be amazingly talented people who can create from childhood, these are the exception rather than the norm. Great mathematicians started with, and built upon, rote multiplication and division tables, not an empty mind. Creative artists must also build their complexity upon these simple foundations.

Value is a concept that needs much wider discussion within Biblical Christianity. At the most basic level, value is what determines everything that anyone does. Christians have the only truly unique source of determining value, God Himself as revealed in His word. **Thus, nothing except God Himself and His Word has any intrinsic or objective value**. True value can only be found as it identifies with the Person of God and His works.

Beauty should enhance everything that Christians do. As God defines beauty, His people should be beautiful. Our homes, schools, and churches (above) should be made beautiful within the constraints of economic stewardship. The reader will note from previous comments that this enhancement of all things is the historical meaning of art. As God's people, we need to incorporate His beauty into our lives.

10. **Any "communication" of art is restricted to its group-culture**. Leland Ryken reports an account of a person who first knew that Jesus rose from the grave at the blast of trumpets at an Easter Service. Now, the blast of a the same trumpet sounds in rural Africa is going to convince no one that Jesus rose from the dead! While the emotional appeal may cause one to focus more concretely on the startling and majestic act of Jesus' Resurrection, the knowledge of the Resurrection and the context in which it occurred had to be present in that person's mind to relate a trumpet blast to that event. Again, if you take a painting of the Last Supper into the jungles of Africa, all they will see is some men eating together in a strange custom. The significance of that event will only come through knowledge of the truth that it represents. **Communication that occurs from art only does so in the context of its group-culture which must be understood in the form of propositions to be understood**.

In this sense, propositional truth is prior to beauty. This phrase is simply another way to say that art flows out of a worldview.

Also, any truth that an art form can communicate is dependent upon the worldview in the minds of those who believe in that worldview.

13. **One could make the case that certain scenes in nature are the most universally accepted forms of beauty**. Virtually every group-culture on earth has some appreciation of various scenes in nature as "beautiful." While these scenes are not creations by man, their value as beauty does reside in the depths of man's heart. According to God's Revelation, this beauty is sufficient to prove to every person the beauties of the Person of God (Romans 1:18ff). These scenes find their way into virtually every historical culture on planet earth.

14. **The wonderful variety of art forms throughout history and modern times is only a small reflection of the creativity of God**. Whatever man's thoughts and whatever his portrayals of art, God has already thought of them in eternity. And, his creativity is itself eternal as the only wise God. We may marvel at all the great works of art that man has created, and we should, but all should be "for the glory of God."

The antithesis of art, relative to God, is that art always glorifies some thing or some body. Again, see comments on worldview above.

15. **The gifts of individuals span the entire spectrum of God-given talents**. On one end of the spectrum are those who highly talented in some art form along with those who may not have the talent, but deeply and pervasively appreciate the arts. On the other end of the spectrum are those who are highly analytical and have little to do with art appreciation. **It is difficult for persons from one group to communicate with the other**. They have different points of reference and value. But, as stated above, communication by words and sentences is what always gives specific interpretation of art. Communication by art is always limited by its group-culture.

As a general rule, women in everyday life are more concerned about art than men are. But, to make that general application without great attention to exceptions to this rule is a major error in thinking about human groups. Women decorate their homes while many men could care less. Women are more often involved in crafts and art classes. But, men have these interests and talents, as well.

Far too much has been made of the right vs. left brain theory. Supposedly, science has determined that the right side of the brain is more concerned with feelings and art appreciation, while the lift side is more concerned with "facts." But, as one can easily see throughout our worldview applications, **every idea and object has both a subjective and objective component**. To try to separate these entirely is wrong-headed and ignorant. And, when one considers all the evidence on right-left brain, such distinctions are not so concrete as some would like to conclude.

References

Introductory definitions from www.etymonline.com , www.m-w.com , and http://1828.mshaffer.com/

Clowney, Edmund P. "Living Art: Christian Experience in the Arts," in *God and Culture: Essays in Honor of Carl F. H. Henry*, edited by D. A. Carson and John D. Woodridge (Eerdmans, 1993), pages 235-253.

Ryken, Leland. *The Christian Imagination: Essays on Literature and the Arts.* (Baker Book House, 1981).

Ryken, Philip Graham Ryken. *Art for God's Sake*. (Presbyterian and Reformed, 2006).

Sayers, Dorothy. "Toward a Christian Esthetic," in *The Whimsical Christian: Reflections on God and Man*, (Collier Books, 1987), pages 73-91). Thoughts on "Christian esthetics," the Church and the arts, and art vs. entertainment.

Schaeffer, Francis A. *Art and the Bible*. (InterVarsity Press, 1973).

Vieth, Gene Edward, Jr. *State of the Arts: From Bezalel to Mapplethorpe* (Crossway Books, 1991. A worthwhile, comprehensive review.

20. Ethics

Summary Principles of Biblical Ethics

(Ed's note: The following is an article that I wrote more than twenty years ago, as a basis for ethics. I present it here as a defense of my position that ethics and worldview principles are one and the same. Thus, all work in Biblical ethics is directly transferable to those Worldview Areas in which they correspond. Those interested in learning and developing worldview principles should use those excellent works that have been done in Biblical ethics, but do not have "worldview" in their title.)

Among Christians a new consciousness in ethics has been raised by abortion, infanticide and euthanasia. The horror of these practices is often called "sound medical practice." This situation brings into question all the ethics of a worldview that allowed such practices to become routine. Many ethicists have observed that Protestants have lagged behind in their development of ethics. **As evangelicals, we must be concerned that our approach to ethics is thoroughly and distinctively Biblical.** The work that has been done in ethics by most evangelicals, however, does not meet this qualification.

The statement of this failure is not meant to impugn the intentions of those who have tried. They may not have known what is required. The task is not a simple one, but neither is it impossible. We will define an approach for those who desire to be truly evangelical, that is, Biblical.

First, let me clarify the word "evangelical." An evangelical is a Christian who believes the inerrancy of the Bible (some distinguish between inerrancy and infallibility, but I do not), the existence of God in three persons (the Trinity), central truths about Jesus Christ (His deity, virgin birth, sinless life, substitutionary atonement, true miracles, bodily resurrection, ascension, and personal return), the necessity of regeneration, the indwelling Holy Spirit in the believer, the eternal conscious existence of believers in heaven and unbelievers in hell, and the spiritual unity of all believers. These seven "fundamentals" appear in the National Association of Evangelicals' Statement of Faith. Organizations and churches may make slight modifications, but these convey the basic position.

These fundamentals are not arbitrary. They have been hammered out over the twenty centuries that the church has existed. A correct synonym for evangelical would be "orthodox," but it is less desirable because of its association with certain denominations and Neo-orthodoxy. The watershed issue, however, has been stated by Dr. Francis Schaeffer in his last book.(1) Formerly, inerrancy and/or infallibility meant that the Bible was without error in the whole or in its parts. Lately, however, some evangelicals have begun to limit these terms.

> This may come from the theological side in saying that not all the Bible is revelational. Or it may come from the scientific side in saying that the Bible teaches little or nothing when it speaks of the cosmos. Or it may come from the cultural side in saying that the moral teachings of the Bible were merely expressions of the culturally determined and relative situation in which the Bible was written and therefore not authoritative today.

The person who speaks or writes must be identified with his position concerning Scripture. Without this identity it is dangerously deceptive to accept the teaching of anyone who claims to be an evangelical. There are wolves among the sheep (John 10:1-18). With some discernment they can be identified, and we will cover some means by which this discernment can be made. On the foundation that Scripture is inerrant and infallible, what principles enhance our ability to develop Biblical ethics? My observation is that among evangelicals, the development of these principles is much more the problem than agreement in theory. Arbitrarily, I am dividing these principles into two categories: three basics and twelve directives.

The Three Basics

The first basic is the sufficiency of the Bible to provide principles that govern all problems that we encounter, even in the complexity of modern science (1I Timothy 3:16-17; II Peter 1:3). In many instances, principles that apply are one or more steps removed from the explicit statements of Scripture. Logic, systematization, and harmonization, however, can give a certainty and finality about many ethical problems that may not be explicitly found in Scripture.

The second basic is the Bible as the starting-point for these principles. Too often, Christians start with the positions that other Christians take rather than what the Bible says. Although their ethical principles may be Biblical, they still must be proved by Scripture and identified with specific texts. "Christian" ethics is not necessarily "Biblical ethics." Christians ethics too often are what some Christians propose or what they do. Such ethics may have nothing to do with Biblical truth.

What must be examined is the thoroughness of the ethicist's work and his commitment to Biblical truth as the authority of God. A major error today is that a principle is based upon one or two verses that do not take into account many others that deal with the same topic (that is, systematics is not applied). An example is the concept of medical practice. I am unaware of any work that reviews all words and concepts relative to the practice of medicine in the New Testament other than in two sections of my book.(2)

The third basic is the authority given to Scripture. In other words, how seriously is what the Bible says taken into account? For example, it is clear that the Bible both forbids murder and states that life begins at conception. Compromise of that authority begins when the deformity of the child, the rape or incest of the mother, or the mental illness of the mother is used to justify induced abortion. To say that the Bible is the authority does not mean that other sources are not valuable or that they do not help us to understand Scripture. As the final authority, however, Biblical principles must be given functional control (a term coined by Dr. Robertson McQuilkin). The "edge" must always be given to the Bible if there is any doubt or conflict with another opinion. It is crucial to hold the position that no condition or idea can overrule Biblical principle or statement. Christian psychologists and psychiatrists often make this error. I have detailed arguments to illustrate some of their errors in my book.(3)

Twelve Directives to Biblical Ethics

1. Biblical ethics are distinctive. The Christian is engaged in "a gigantic battle that splits the universe."(4) Our Biblical ethic by its nature must contrast with the particular ethic of any worldview area. The Bible describes this contrast in various ways: a lack of unity, light and darkness, righteousness and lawlessness, disagreement, no fellowship, the temple of God and the temple of idols (11 Corinthians 6:14-16); the foolishness of the world and God's wisdom (I Corinthians 1:18 31); and a lack of conformity (Romans 12:2). This contrast does not mean that we will differ at every point because all men have some knowledge of right and wrong (Romans 2:15) and of God's presence in the universe (Romans 1:19ff).

2. Biblical ethics build on the work of other Biblical scholars. I have encountered more than one Christian who has stated that he is going to develop a Christian approach to his profession without recourse to the work of others. The intent is right; the means is totally unbiblical. Such an attitude reflects the epitome of modernism and individualism. First, all believers are dependent on other believers (I Corinthians 12; Ephesians 4:11-16). Second, no one person in an entire lifetime can learn Greek and Hebrew, develop his own systematic theology, write commentaries on all the books of the Bible, and in essence develop a library on the Bible that is necessary to assure oneself and others that one's work is consistent with all that the Bible teaches.

Who or what do we build upon? Primarily, we build upon the extensive knowledge already available in the church. Creeds, confessions, commentaries, textbooks on systematic theology, and other such works have been painstakingly written over the centuries to mine the depths of the Word of God. Obviously, all these cannot be read or studied, but one can select those that are faithful to the Bible, as the revealed will of God,, and that will give concrete identification to the Biblical truth that is relevant to the area in which one is studying. This position is not to say that these words are without error, but one can know the basic truths of our faith with sufficient certainty to distinguish truth and error. The necessary comprehensiveness of this approach brings us to the next principle.

3. Biblical ethics includes all Christian minds. Since all believers make up the body of Christ, the Christian mind consists of the minds of all Christians. No one can be left out. This inclusion means that every Christian potentially has some thought to contribute. I say potentially because his contribution must be consistent with a comprehensive and systematic Biblical ethic and because every Christian does not necessarily have a new thought. The teachable mind receives ideas from unlikely sources, but a journal can be an effective vehicle to develop this Christian mind. A journal provides a wide exposure of Christian minds to each other; the authors express their thoughts and the readers can respond with additions and disagreements. Thus, the Christian mind becomes a more comprehensive process.

4. Biblical ethics are scientific. Prior to modern times "science" applied to any area of knowledge that was approached systematically. For example, theology was called the "Queen of the Sciences" (a reflection of what we have called "functional control" above). Today, science is narrowly confined to the natural sciences. Here, we are using science according to its former meaning. Biblical ethics must be systematic. Until any knowledge is systematic its inconsistencies and errors can remain obscure. Each principle must be

403

compared and contrasted with others to see if and where it fits into the whole. Unfortunately, logic and philosophy are no longer generally taught in both secular and Christian schools. These disciplines can provide the methodology for systematization. Further, any systematization of Biblical ethics must be consistent with some established systematic theology as the foundation to Biblical ethics.(5)

5. Biblical ethics become more fully developed through experience. Experience challenges our ethics: Are they comprehensive to cover all contingencies? Are they defined with enough clarity to be readily applied? Are they consistent from one situation to another? Should our principles be modified because of the situation? The last question seems more of an existential, than a Biblical, philosophy. But, reality may at times require a certain modification, sometimes to a broader principle and sometimes to a more restricted principle. For example, we would like to say that a baby should never be delivered so prematurely that it has no chance to live. Real situations, albeit rare, do require that a choice be made between the continuing presence of the baby in the mother's womb and the mother's life. Of course, extreme care must be taken that situations are always governed by principle, and not vice versa, but until principles are tested in the reality of situations, some openness to modification must be maintained. This interaction of principle and practice is thoroughly and clearly presented elsewhere.(6)

6. Biblical ethics requires an understanding of hermeneutics. Sound theology is not haphazard. Standard principles of interpretation have been developed and these are ignored with the certain result that serious error will occur. Biblical ethics require that Scripture be interpreted; such interpretation must be careful and complete. It cannot be done without some understanding and application of hermeneutics. Fortunately, Dr. R.C. Sproul has written a concise book that contains much of what we need.(7) See Bookstore to order.

7. Biblical ethics requires precise definitions. Theologians say that some words are "univocal," that is, words that have only one meaning. The modern existentialists have obscured such precision of definition and evangelicals have been unduly influenced. Precise definitions are rarely a part of evangelical writing, frequently with the excuse that they make reading too "dry." For such lack of definition and precision evangelicals are losing their distinctiveness. Biblical ethics defines the way of "the way, the truth and the life" (John 14:6) and "the narrow way" (Matthew 7:14). Can it accomplish its purpose with imprecision?

8. Biblical ethics requires certain spiritual gifts. With the popularity of teaching about spiritual gifts, the willingness of Christians to follow almost anyone is a striking failure to discern those who have teaching gifts. I have been painting a very laborious task for Biblical ethics. Few will be willing or have the desire to pursue such a course except those whom God has gifted for that work. The many who are not called to this task will not have such a desire, but they are lacking in their spiritual duty when they ignore these Biblical requirements for their teachers. Spiritual gifts necessary to develop Biblical ethics are teaching, wisdom, knowledge, discernment and prophecy (as forthtelling, not foretelling).

9. Biblical ethics must consider the situation. In our reaction to situational ethics (re: Joseph Fletcher), evangelicals have often overlooked the place of the situation in Biblical ethics. The principle is this: The situation determines which Biblical principles apply to that situation. The key concept is that the situation does not determine the principles. The situation is set within the Biblical worldview and governed by it. Traditional situational ethics essentially have no principles and certainly none that are absolute and specific, as the Ten Commandments are. An example of this principle is a teenager who receives a prescription for birth control pills from her physician. His act would be immoral if she wanted the pills for contraception. His act would be moral if she needed the pills to control heavy menstrual bleeding (a common problem). The act is the same; the situation determines which principles apply. For more on this subject, see Standard, Goal, and Attitude as Perspectives on Ethics.

10. Biblical ethics must be a concern of the local church. The local church exists to nurture believers in their spiritual development. Since complete casuistry is impossible in in any approach to ethics, many believers will need or ought to seek counsel for ethical decisions that are not clear. The pastor and elders of their church are God's chosen men to provide the particular application needed. Although a church may refer its members to a Christian leader of another church for such counsel, most churches should be able to develop their own resources through the teaching of those who have the spiritual gifts for such counsel.

11. Biblical ethics must have appropriate review before they are made public. The susceptibility of Christians to erroneous teaching is clear in Scripture (I Timothy 1:3-11, 4:1-5; II Peter 2:1-22). Likely, our modern approach to publishing Christian materials violates these warnings. As we have listed those spiritual gifts that are required to develop Biblical ethics, those same gifts should be possessed by Christian editors. Many Christians believe that any publication by an "evangelical" organization or company is trustworthy. That assumption is seriously erroneous. The role of guardian of the truth is assigned to church leaders, specifically pastors and elders or their equivalents (I Timothy 4:6). Freedom of the press is necessary in a free society, but the freedom of the evangelical press is limited to Biblical truth guarded in a Biblical manner. These church leaders should be much more active to discern what their members read.

12. Biblical ethics finally rests within the conscience (self-government) of individuals. Theory becomes practice in the situation where individuals live. It is perilous for Christians to ignore the teaching and counsel of others. We have discussed the impossibility that one Christian can even begin to accomplish all that is required to know Biblical principles. Preferably, individuals are taught and should seek this teaching in their local church. In turn this expectation requires church leaders to have been taught by others through books, lectures, preaching, tapes and other means. Thus we see the universal church and the particular (local) church in their respective, God-ordained roles.

A Serious Approach Is Needed

Will this diligent course of action guarantee Biblical ethics? Obviously, it will not. My concern, however, is the superficial manner in which such ethics are frequently undertaken. This superficiality is common throughout evangelicalism.

A call to serious and careful study is needed everywhere. With an application of these principles, we are more likely to arrive at agreement on many issues and have some certainty of our results. Most Christians are not called to make this effort, but all are called to discern to whom they should listen and to contribute in some way (no matter how small) when they have an insight or they have a Biblical reason to disagree with what has been said. The Christian mind needs to be developed to its fullest capacity for our times. The process, however, must follow certain prescribed principles or its result is likely not to be Biblical and honor our Lord and Savior Jesus Christ.

Our goal is articulately stated by Dr. Abraham Kuyper:

> Only in the combination of the whole race of man does this revelation reach its creaturely completeness . . . The knowledge of God is a common possession, all the riches of which can only be enjoyed in the communion of our race . . . but because humanity is adapted to reveal God, and from that revelation to attain unto His knowledge, does not individual

complement another, and only by the organic unity and by the individual in communion with that unity, can the knowledge of God be obtained in a clear and completer sense.(8)

Endnotes

1. Schaeffer, F.A., *The Great Evangelical Disaster*, Westchester, Illinois; Crossway Books, 1984, p.50

2. Payne, F.E., *Biblical/Medical Ethics*, Milford, Michigan; Mott Media, 1985, pp. 101-107.

3. Ibid., pp. 155-180

4. Blamires, H., *The Christian Mind*, Reprint. London: SP.C.K., 1963, Ann Arbor, Michigan: Servant Books, 1978, p.70.

5. Stob, H., *Ethical Reflections*, Grand Rapids: Eerdmans Publishing Company, 1978, pp. 31-49.

6. Ibid.

7. Sproul, R.C., *Knowing Scripture*, Wheaton, Illinois: Intervarsity Press, 1977.

8. Kuyper, A., *Principles of Sacred Theology*. Trans. by J. Hendrik de Vries,. Reprint. Encyclopedia of Sacred Theology: Its Principles. Charles Scribner's Sons, 1898. Grand Rapids: Baker Book House, 1980, p.

Glossary of Biblical Definitions for Worldview

This glossary of Biblical definitions focuses on words that are important to the concept of a Biblical and Christian worldview and to personal salvation. 1) The latter focus is not comprehensive, but we have chosen those words that Christians commonly misuse and thereby limit their experience to honor God, His blessing in their lives, and affect the world for change. We strongly believe that neither fullness in worldview nor fullness in the Christian life can be achieved without focused attention on definitions. After all, salvation and obedience are foundational to a sound Biblical and Christian worldview! Of special importance are these words: **emotions**, **ethic**, **ethics**, **evangelical, heart**, **law**, **justice**, **philosophy** (and all its synonyms), **regeneration**, **righteousness**, **salvation**, and **truth**. 2) The glossary is a mini-overview of a Biblical and Christian worldview. To know these definitions and many of their nuances is to have a basic understanding of worldview! 3) This glossary is concerned with establishing definitions that are consistent throughout this website. 3) My research has shown that The Creation (Cultural) Mandate, The Kingdom of God, Biblical Worldview, Biblical Ethics, The Gospel, and The Great Commission are one and the same.

Multiple definitions. Readers should keep in mind that almost every word has **more than one definition**. We usually only list the one here that is most relevant to worldview and salvation. See more about biblical definitions.

Sources of definitions. Many of the definitions are my own, with priority given to Biblical uses. Some are direct quotes of references cited. Some are compilations of several sources. All are designed to give the reader the best definition within all the considerations of a Biblical worldview.

Absolutes: statements that are true anywhere at any time, for example, the Law of Non-Contradiction.

Addiction: a term used by professionals (physicians, psychologists, psychiatrists, etc.) and laymen to refer to problems of a repetitive nature that dominate a person's life, usually in a severely destructive way. The term is used so loosely as to be of little value. Its modern denotation began with addiction to heroin, and as such, included a physical dependence on a drug, as well as its severely habitual nature. However, it is now commonly used for such things as "sexual addiction" and "gambling addiction" that clearly have no drug dependence inherent to the problem. Apart from the drug dependence, addictions are better labeled as "besetting sins." Also, see Additional Comments.

Agapeo (verb), **Agapé** (noun): to love and love, respectively. See subsection of Love.

Angel of Light: This description of Satan is given in II Corinthians 11:14. The danger of Satan and his fallen angels is not in their evil, grotesque appearance, but when they come masquerading with kind and good ideas. Satan's first words in the Bible are "has not God said," distorting God's Word to Eve and seducing her. This disguise has great implication for those trying to understand a Biblical worldview: principles may come quite close to being God's Word, but be the actual word of Satan. So, we must be diligent in our study of God's Word systematically that our theology, ethics, and worldview are clearly and soundly Biblical.

Anthropology: the study of the origins, nature, and destiny of man. Any study of man must begin with the study of God (the Bible) or it will be incomplete, erroneous, or falsely understood. This science must be controlled, directed, and filtered through Scripture. Psychology is a major division of anthropology. In fact, by our definition here, psychology is anthropology, separated (mostly) from the history (origins) and future (destiny) of man. Thus, theology (the study of God) and psychology (the study of the mind of man) are central to anthropology. This identity is the reason that Psychology comprises a large section of our Worldview Areas. Men and women's relationships to each other is Sociology. The Christian will, then, connect God, man, and his social life with The Two Great Commandments, "You shall love the Lord your God with all your heart, with all your soul, and with all your mind," and "You shall love your neighbor as yourself" (Matthew 22:37, 39). (Note the "psychological" terms of **heart**, **soul**, **mind**, and

Luke adds, "strength.") As these Two Commandments are a summary of the Ten Commandments, and indeed, all the commandments of Scripture, Anthropology, Psychology, and Sociology are central themes of God's Word to man. See our Areas of Psychology and Sociology.

Anthropomorphism: human characteristics that are ascribed to God. "God is spirit" (John 4:24). Thus, any description of God having body parts (eyes, hands, head, etc.) is an anthropomorphism. It is correct to identify characteristics of the human mind, where man corresponds to the image of God. A common error is to ascribe emotions to God. Very simply, God is immutable or unchangeable, "the same yesterday, today, and forever." Emotions are a precondition to change (past, present, or future) and, often, particular thoughts, speech, or behavior occur because of the effect of these emotions. For a short discussion, see Feelings in Body and Soul. For a more complete discussion, see A Definition of Emotions.

Apocrypha: etymologically, "hidden or obscure." Protestants use this word to refer to the books that the Roman Catholic Church believes is Spirit-inspired, but we do not. Roman Catholics, then, would not refer to these books as Apocrypha, since to them they are indeed the Word of God. Thus, the proper designation of the Canon is "the 66 books of the Protestant Bible."

Apologetics: the development of any worldview area that gives evidence (defense) of Biblical truth: archeology, creation science, philosophical consistency (coherence, correspondence, epistemology, etc.), agreement of over 40 Biblical authors, positive changes in history (individuals, groups, and nations) because of the life of Christ and His effect on people, etc. Apologetics are exceedingly beneficial to Christians themselves, to complete their faith and to see a complete Biblical worldview. Apologetics conferences are wrongly named because they inevitably involve instruction to Christians and are, thus, not a defense of the faith to unbelievers.

Belief: synonym of faith. See Faith below.

Believe: verb form of faith. See Faith below.

Bible-believer, or Bible-believing Christian: synonym of Evangelical (below).

Biblical counseling: See **Nouthetic counseling**. The two terms are equivalent.

Biblical ethics: See **Ethic** and **Ethics**.

Biblical psychology: see **Psychology** below.

Biblical theology: Study that is principally concerned with the overall theological message of the whole Bible. It seeks to understand the parts in relation to the whole and, to achieve this, it must work with the mutual interaction of the literary, historical, and theological dimensions of the various corpora, and with the inter-relationships of these within the whole canon of Scripture. Biblical Theology

Biblicism: simply, the belief that the Bible is man's only source of truth and that the Bible governs and defines all areas of knowledge. Biblicism is often used, derogatorily and falsely, to those who believe and work from this premise, that they are narrow-minded and do not value other sources of knowledge (especially, natural revelation) and that they do not use other sources of theology. True Biblicism uses all sources of knowledge, but always allows Scripture to be the controlling authority. For a more complete discussion of this word, see Biblicism Applied to the Study of History.

Born-again, Born from above: See **Regeneration**.

Canon: "canon" is derived from the Hebrew word "qaneh" which means a reed used as a measuring stick. It was the term used by the early church fathers to denote which books were true Scripture, inspired by God. Believers in the early centuries had to decide which manuscripts were Spirit-inspired and those that were not. Protestants and Roman Catholics differ on what is the true **Canon**.

Career: a modern word meaning the Work or Vocation in which one is engaged to produce income. Career is not a proper concept for Christians because it divorces this area of work from Vocation, the "calling" of God.

(The) Catholic Church: the universal church, as in The Apostle's Creed, "I believe in the holy catholic church." This term is not to be confused with the Roman Catholic Church. See **The Church**.

Charity: voluntary giving to a specific need, wisely, within Biblical parameters (for example, "if a person will not work, neither shall he eat," II Thessalonians 3:10), to anyone that has true needs. For more see principles of charity and do a Search of "charity" on this website. **Charity**, as a Biblical concept. never includes any form of government welfare.

Christian: one who believes in the Scriptures as Truth and the very Word of God, trusts in His Son Jesus Christ for salvation, and is obedient to the commandments of both the Old and New Testaments.

(The) Church: consists of both the visible and the invisible church. The visible church are those true Christians who are alive on earth at any one time and profess the basic truths of the Gospel. The invisible church are those who are true believers and those who have died and are already in heaven. In The Apostle's Creed, "holy catholic church" refers to this concept of The Church, not the Roman Catholic Church. The invisible, not the visible, **Church** will be the Bride of Christ (Ephesians 5:25-33), as the visible Church includes tares among the wheat.

(The Local) Church: a local body of **The Church**, founded upon some form of agreement among its members.

Civil Government: see **(The State)**.

Civilization: "the sum total of a society's spiritual, intellectual, ethical, and institutional values, which in varying degrees will permit those living in it to develop as completely and harmoniously as possible." See What Is Civilization? (page 15) A concept which must be re-thought within a Biblical worldview. Great architecture, substantive writing, structured government, and other entities, the commonly accepted criteria of "civilization," along with the presence of human sacrifice and child abandonment (as was present in "the grandeur that was Greece and the glory that was Rome") does not qualify as being "civilized." A civilization must have some consistent application of Biblical justice.

Coherence Theory of Truth: the test of truth that all statements (judgments, propositions) must be consistent or harmonize with other statements that are known to be true. (Also known as the test of consistency of truth.) The great problem is what each individual or group is willing to accept as "true." The Bible provides the only such system for mankind. "Hear, O Israel, the Lord our God is One!" "In Him are hidden all the treasures of wisdom and knowledge."

Common Grace: God's benefits to mankind for both the regenerate and the unregenerate. These benefits are far greater than might be recognized at first glance. Not only does He send the rain, sunshine, and harvest, He has structured the universe with fixed properties that are discoverable by man's mind and investigation and that are always predictable for man to construct his life and design his inventions for his own benefit.

Conciliarism: the concept that doctrine of the Roman Catholic Church resided more in official church councils, than in the interpretation of the Pope. This difference in doctrine was a major conflict in the Roman Catholic Church during the 15th and 16th centuries.

Conscience: that faculty of the mind that makes judgments about whether a thought, spoken work, or action is right or wrong. Because of man's being finite and sinful, as well as having imperfect Biblical understanding, the conscience may be in error on specific judgments. As Christians mature and become more knowledgeable in the Word, they have "their senses trained to discern good and evil" (Hebrews 5:14), that is, their consciences are more consistently aligned with the Scriptures. The violation of the conscience is always wrong, even when the judgment of the conscience is wrong (Romans 14:5, 23; James 4:17)!

Councils, Church: see the name of the council, for example, Trent, Council of.

Counseling: See **Nouthetic counseling**.

Covenant: a contract made between a higher authority with a lesser one that sanctions benefits for obedience and penalties for disobedience.

Generally, in theology there is the Covenant of Works that God had with Adam and the Covenant of Grace that God has with His people because of the merits of Jesus Christ. The Covenant of Grace began with the promise to Adam and Eve that her seed would "bruise the head" of Satan, as Christ presented Himself as the perfect atonement. Thus, all believers of the Old Testament were under the Covenant of Grace, not a Covenant of Works. See WCF, Chapter 7.

Creation: "it pleased God the Father, Son, and Holy Ghost, for the manifestation of the glory of his eternal power, wisdom, and goodness, in the beginning, to create, or make of nothing, the world, and all things therein whether visible or invisible, in the space of six days; and all very good." (Westminster Confession of Faith, IV:1).

(The) Creation Mandate: the sum of God's decrees given to mankind before his Fall. These are (1) "the procreation of offspring, (2) the replenishing of the earth, (3) subduing the same, (4) dominion of the creatures, (5) labor, (6) the weekly Sabbath, and (7) marriage" (John Murray, Principles of Conduct, page 27). The **Creation Mandates** should be linked to The Great Commission which includes "make disciples of all the nations" and "teaching them to observe all things that I have commanded you... "under all authority in heaven and earth" (Matthew 28:19-20). They can also be linked to The Lord's Prayer in "Thy Kingdom come, Thy will be done, on earth as it is in heaven" (Matthew 6:10). See **Cultural Mandate**. In essence, **The Creation Mandate, The Great Commission, The Kingdom of God, and The Two Great Commandments** are one and the same. See discussions on this website for the equivalence of these concepts.

Creed: for the Christian, a creed is any statement that represents Biblical knowledge other than the original Hebrew and Greek texts. That is, any statement other than the original text is a representation of it. Translations, in particular, involve detailed choices of words and nuances to represent what was said. While "creed" is usually associated with creedal statements, such as, The Apostles' Creed, any translation of the Bible is also a creed. The Christian who claims "No creed but Christ" or "No creed but the Bible" has not understood how language communicates from one person to another, one generation to another, and one culture to another. See No Creed But Christ.

414

(The) Cultural Mandate: another designation of **The Creation Mandate**. This phrase has more emphasis on all the cultures of the earth being brought under the dominion of Christ. That is, the culture is "transformed by the renewing of minds" through application of a Biblical worldview. This **Mandate** is repeated in **The Great Commission** to "go and disciple **all** nations."

Death: the Biblical definition of death is separation from a former state of existence. There are four types of death. 1) Separation from self, other people, and God because of the sin of Adam and Eve (Genesis 2:17, 3:7, 9-11, 23) and one's own sins. 2) Separation from this sinful way of life (the "flesh" or "old man") upon regeneration, profession of faith, and repentance. 3) Physical death, when our soul/spirit is separated from the physical body. 4) The Second Death, the most terrible punishment of being separated from God and the fellowship of any other living person forever (Revelation 20:14, 21:8). Man's greatest fear is the fear of death (I Corinthians 15:26; Hebrews 2:15). "The last enemy that will be destroyed is death" (I Corinthians 15:26). Thus, in heaven there will be no separation from our true selves, others, and God Himself.

Deduction: the process of **Logic** (see definition below).

Deism: "... the belief or system of religious opinions of those who acknowledge the existence of one God, but deny revelation: or deism is the belief in natural religion only, or those truths, in doctrine and practice, which man is to discover by the light of reason, independent and exclusive of any revelation from God. Hence deism implies infidelity or a disbelief in the divine origin of the scriptures." (From Webster's 1828 Dictionary, below) Deism is sometimes described as God created the universe, but then let it continue to exist on its own without His intervention, as a clock is started by a clock-maker. Miracles are not allowed in this system because they require supernatural intervention into those "self-continuing" motions.

Determinism: "the view that human choice is entirely controlled by previous conditions. The realm of nature, including man, is an unbroken chain of cause and effect." Titus, Living Issues..., page 429. See Predestination.

Dialectic: "process of thinking by means of dialogue, discussion, debate, or argument. In ancient Greece, the term was used literally... Dialectic is questioning and conversation for Socrates... but Plato regarded it as a systematic method for studying ... suprasensible reality... German philosophers of the modern era applied the term "dialectic" only to more narrowly-defined patterns of thinking ... for Hegel, (dialectic is) the fundamental process of development—in both thought and reality—from thesis to antithesis to synthesis." See "dialectic" in Philosophical Dictionary... below.

Dialectical Materialism: "Philosophical doctrine expounded by Engels and Marx. By emphasizing the independent reality of matter and the primary value of the natural world, they rejected the idealism of Hegel. But they fully accepted his notion of dialectic as an inexorable process of development in thought, nature, and history." See "dialectical materialism" in Philosophical Dictionary... below. "(Dialectical materialism) "holds science in high esteem and claims that the sense perceptions of science provide our only real knowledge, (but) is an approach from the point of view of politics and history, rather than from that of the natural sciences... and (on) a view of historical development in which matter in the form of the economic organization of society is regarded as basic. (Synonyms are) "historical materialism and economic determinism." Titus, Living Issues..., page 257.

Dichotomy: the belief that a person consists of two parts, the material and immaterial. The material component is the physical body. The immaterial is variously called the spirit, soul, heart, and mind, depending upon the context in which it is used in Scripture and the particular function which is being discussed.

Divine Right of Kings: the same as **Rex Lex**.

Dualism: the philosophy, religion, or cosmology that forces of both good and evil exist in the universe. In some ideologies, one is more powerful than the other. In some, they are equal. In at least one, they collaborate. The victory or one or the other may be certain or uncertain, being in doubt until the end of time.

Emotion(s): "the momentary (acute) and ongoing (chronic, continuous) disturbance within the mind (soul, spirit) caused by the discrepancy

416

between perceived reality and one's desires." (From A Definition of Emotions.)

Empiricism: "reliance on experience as the (only) source of ideas and knowledge. More specifically, empiricism is the epistemological theory that genuine information about the world must be acquired by a posteriori means, so that nothing can be thought without first being sensed." (From online dictionary of terms below.) Contrast with Rationalism.

Empirical method: the process of drawing conclusions from various observations. It differs from the scientific methods in that it is a more casual and not well-defined process. See Scientific Method.

Epistemology: simply, how does one know what one knows? Profoundly, how can one know with sufficiency to answer the most serious questions of life. How can one know truth? It is the great dilemma of all the great philosophers of history. It is also the essence of faith and belief: on what basis can I be certain of what I am to do in this life and what I can hope for after death? Christians who think about the basic questions of epistemology will strengthen their faith immeasurably. See **Philosophy** below.

Equity: 1) a synonym of justice (see below). 2) Fairness. 3) Most importantly, a body of legal doctrines and rules, developed to enlarge, supplement, or override a narrow, rigid system of law, as in the history of English common law which had a settled and formal body of legal and procedural rules and doctrine to protect rights and enforce duties that had been fixed by substantive law. Equity provided remedies in situations in which precedent or statutory law might not apply or be fair. In this sense, all laws and commandments of the Bible are to be applied to governments at all levels (self-government and all duly bodies (guilds, cities, counties, states, nations, and world).

Ethic: 1) When used to describe one's foundational views, that is, "My ethic is..", this word is equivalent to "worldview." 2) It may also refer to one ethical principle, for example, "Abortion is the killing of an innocent child before birth." As such, ethic is equivalent to a worldview principle. See **Ethics, Godliness, Law, Justice, Righteousness**. All these terms are intimately related to the other. "Morality is not a mere

417

aggregate of separate virtues. Only in the context of the whole do single virtues (ethics) acquire meaning." (Henry Stob, *Ethical Reflections*, page 184.)

Ethics: the application and study of right and wrong to all activities of life. It may also be used consistent with "ethic," 1) above, as in "Biblical ethics" or the "Biblical worldview." Both of these would then be the same as the Biblical concept of "righteousness" or "godliness." **Ethic** may be thought of as a synonym of a general concept of worldview, while **ethics** are more particular in their application. See **Ethic** above.

Evangelical: one who believes that the Bible is the infallible, inerrant, and fully authoritative Word of God in every area of personal life and worldview. Evangelical is a synonym of "Christian" or "Bible-believer," when these words are used correctly. The doctrinal statement of the Evangelical Theological Society is, "The Bible alone, and the Bible in its entirety, is the Word of God written and is therefore inerrant in the autographs."* God is a Trinity, Father, Son, and Holy Spirit, each an uncreated person, one in essence, equal in power and glory" (Evangelical Theological Society). Christians commonly wrongly interchange "evangelical" with "evangelistic." See "evangelistic" below.

*The autographs are the original texts as they were written by the Apostles. None are extant today, but examinations of thousands of manuscripts, including the Dead Sea Scrolls, affirms that Christians today actually have "the very Word of God written," as the Holy Spirit has preserved the inspired text for His people from the time of its first being written.

Evangelistic: traditionally, the preaching or sharing of the Gospel of Jesus Christ. Today, it may be used for attempts to spread the teachings of any belief.

Evolution: the theory that "the process that all natural reality (organic and inorganic) develops irreversibly in a direction of increasing complexity and order by inherent physico-chemical processes" (John R. Reed, *Plain Talk about Genesis*, Word Ministries, Inc. and Deo Volente Publishing, 2000).

Existentialism: "the only truth is ... the dictates of one's own being as expressed without the influence of God, man, society, morals and mores, or anything external to the biological impulses of the man" (Rushdoony, *Systematic Theology*, page 15). This approach is the only one, even if the process itself is meaningless.

Expert: a person with advanced training and education in some area. The great problem with experts is that their "advanced training and education" is "foolish," if not governed by the laws of Scripture. This foolishness can have seriously negative consequences. For example, God says that children are to be punished corporally, in contrast to the American Academy of Pediatrics which stands opposed to the that directive. "You shall beat him with a rod, And deliver his soul from hell" (Proverbs 23:14).

Fact or Facts: 1) a synonym for truth, "what is" or reality itself. For a fact to be true, it must be placed within the Biblical framework that defines its existence. A "fact" does not exist apart from a philosophical or religious system. See Sir Fred Hoyle's quote under scientific method. 2) Knowledge of a situation, object, or person that is sufficiently and commonly known among enough people to be acted upon with considerable reliance and a relatively predictable outcome, but it is not necessarily true. For example, the sun will rise tomorrow is a fact. It is not true because sometime in the future, the sun will not rise. By virtually all philosophies and worldviews, time and the universe will not continue, as we know it, forever—whether one's belief system is Bible-based or naturalism.

Faith: action taken, based upon one's knowledge (by reflex, experience, study, advice from others, etc.), with a specific outcome expected (hope). Reality (God's laws of design and His Sovereignty) determine whether that expectation occurs. See The Relevance of Faith and my book Without Faith It Is Impossible to Please God.

Generic Faith: faith applied to matters not directly applied to matters of salvation. In the most strict sense, nothing is outside "salvation," but the term, "generic faith," helps to show that faith is commonly and unavoidably necessary to all activities of life. The mechanism of application to "salvation" is no different than in everyday life.

Saving Faith: faith applied in matters of salvation for Christians whether in conversion and justification or sanctification. See The Relevance of Faith above.

Faith and Truth: Faith does not determine truth, but an individual's faith determines what he is willing to accept as true.

First principles: like axioms in geometry, these are the unproven presuppositions that form the basis for anyone's worldview. Synonyms are religion, philosophy, worldview, ethic, reality, ultimate reality, value, fact, ontology, metaphysics, cosmology, epistemology, faith, knowledge, being, critical philosophy, essence, existence, monism, speculative philosophy, substance, and ground of meaning (not all of which are listed in this Glossary).

(The) Flood: a worldwide covering of the earth with water, as God's judgment on the earth. Not only was there a deluge of rain, the "deeps" and the "heavens" were opened, as part of this event. There were definitive changes in the earth's geology and likely other changes in the processes of nature, as well. See Uniformitarianism.

Fool, Foolish: these English words carry from Scripture the idea of atheism and humanism. "The fool has said in his heart that there is no God." So, when the Scripture uses "fool" or any of its forms, God is speaking of a conviction that a man or mankind is God, and not God Himself. This position is that of the unregenerate.

Free Will or Freedom of the Will: 1) philosophical sense: the mistaken notion, thought to be necessary to moral responsibility, prevalent among philosophers and many Christians, that man is "free" to make any choice that he desires. The error in this thinking is that some form of predestination is unavoidable. No man make decisions without being pre-conditioned by his physical capacities and his accumulated knowledge over which he had no control in his early years. See Predestination. 2) The Biblical concept is that man is not forced to make any particular choice. His "freedom" is to choose consistent with what he is and what he desires without external compulsion. See Responsibility. Also, see Chapter IX of the Westminster Confession of Faith.

Freedom: the fullest implementation of God's laws that allows an object or person to function at their highest level. The total absence of law in the natural world is nothingness, as even atoms, the most basic unit of matter are subject to strict laws that allow them to function, as they were designed. The universe functions, as it does, in all its glory, according to its laws of design. The absence of law in a society is total chaos with nothing or no one safe from destruction. Thus, the choice of no law is never an option for anything or anyone to function at any level. The application of God's law to all physical and spiritual (individual, family, social organizations, and the State) spheres allows the highest level of function of all His created objects. Thereby, freedom of these objects is achieved.

Functional Knowledge or Functional Value: a synonym of 2nd definition of Fact.

Gifts: see **Talents** and **Spiritual Gifts**.

Godliness: see **ethic, ethics, law, love, righteousness**.

Good Work(s): any action by a regenerate person that is prescribed by God's Word. While the same "work" by an unregenerate may have a "good" effect on himself and on society, God cannot accept it as good because it comes from a sinful heart with selfish motives. See Chapter 16 of the Westminster Confession of Faith.

(The) Gospel: the full Gospel includes individual salvation (past, present, and future), discipline (preaching, teaching, sacraments, and investigation of overt sin—process of Matthew 18:15-19), and a Biblically complete worldview and ethics. Most churches leave out the fullness of what salvation is, the process of dealing with overt sin, and worldview and ethics. The Gospel is the same as The Great Commission (see below).

Government: the exercise of authority and rule over a person or group. **Government starts with self-government**. If fact, if self-government in all people was perfect, then there would be no need of the other governments: family, church, voluntary associations, and the levels of state government (city, county, state, and nation). Jesus Christ governs all these areas and has given specific laws for their governance in Scripture. Unfortunately, "government" today is equated with civil government, distorting and wrongly directing actions that are needed to correct societal wrongs and injustice.

Grace: an act of benevolence from one being to another that is freely given and which is without any merit or claim by the recipient. The greatest example of grace is his gift of salvation and all the great blessings (faith, hope, spiritual fruit and gifts, adoption, etc.) that come with it. There are many similarities of grace to Love. See Common Grace.

Special Grace: those excellent gifts to the Regenerate which include special revelation (The Bible), saving faith, fruits of the Spirit, spiritual gifts, the church (local and universal), and much more.

(The) Great Commission: "teaching them to obey everything I have commanded you" (Matthew 28:20). The Great Commission is the same as The Gospel, The Creation Mandate, The Kingdom of God, Biblical Ethics, and Biblical Worldview.

Health: (1) Adam and Eve in the Garden of Eden (the first Paradise) before the Fall. (2) The regenerate in heaven (the last Paradise). (3) The fullest implementation of God's instructions (commandments) to an individual's or group's lives. All three of these definitions include both **physical** and **spiritual** health, as they cannot be divorced from one another. An unregenerate person cannot be "healthy" in the Biblical sense, although he may achieve some level of health of mind and body by some humanistic standard. See Physician and Pastor as Co-laborers, Part I and Part II.

Heart: one of the spiritual (non-material or non-physical) aspects of a person (others are soul, spirit, mind, will, and conscience); the life that we live within ourselves, unknown to anyone except God; the thought-life of a person; the source of all motives and desires. Thinking and understanding, rather than emotions, is the predominant activity of the heart.

Hermeneutics: the rules by which Scripture is interpreted.

Historical method: that which comprises the techniques and guidelines that historians use as primary sources and other evidence to research and then to write history. (Slightly altered from Wikipedia, referenced below.)

History: the highly selective study of people of the past and the events in which they were involved, according to some philosophy of life or worldview. For the Christian, God's hand or His Providence must be seen as the controlling force, working all things according to His own purposes ("according to His good pleasure which He purposed in Himself," Ephesians 1:9). In particular, the interpretation of events is highly dependent on one's motives in studying the past at all. Much, if not most of history written during and after the 20th Century, is extremely biased against its portrayal of Biblical Christianity as having any significant role anywhere at any time.

Historiography: the critical evaluation of how history is written, including method, bias of philosophy, accuracy with other sources, and theory of human behavior used (to name only a few).

Humanism: a word with a complex history and application which rejects any positive contribution from a supernatural source (most frequently the Bible) as solutions to the problems of mankind. Today, humanism usually means **Secular humanism**. In essence, there are only two religions (philosophies or cosmologies): Biblical Christianity and humanism. It has been so since Satan asked the question to Eve, "Has God not said..." Since then, the greatest issue for any human decision has been either "what God has said" or "what man has said." For more on the history and complexity of this word, see "humanism" at the Wikipedia reference below.

Religious humanism: "the branch of humanism that considers itself religious (based on a functional definition of religion), or embraces some form of theism, deism, or supernaturalism, without necessarily being allied with organized religion, frequently associated with artists, liberal Christians, and scholars in the liberal arts. (They may be) subscribers to a religion who do not hold supernatural assertions as a necessary source for their moral values may be religious humanists" (from "Religious humanism" at Wikipedia--reference below).

Image of God, Imago Dei: the mind of man created to "think God's thoughts after Him." The ability to storage knowledge and process it through the intellect and the will. See The Image of God.

Induction: a method of reasoning in which "the truth of the premises merely makes it **probable** that the conclusion is true." (See Dictionary of Philosophical Terms... referenced below.) Induction proceeds from observations to conclusions about "probable" consistency and coherence in those observations. Deduction within the laws of logic render true conclusions is the premises are true. **Induction** does not render true conclusions, only "probable" ones.

Inescapable concept: a conclusion that is logically necessary. An inescapable concept simplifies and narrows debate within and among worldviews and opinions. For example. Predestination is an inescapable concept. Synonyms would include unavoidable or inevitable concept.

Integration: the attempt to merge the "truth" of nature with the truth of Scripture, that is, natural revelation and special revelation. This approach should raise considerable alarm to those who adhere to Biblical Christianity. However, this process is impossible procedurally, because some authority other than Scripture must be chosen to decide how this integration is to take place. That authority is usually the person who attempts the integration and who does not have either the training or the education for this process. Almost always "integration" is used in association with "All truth is God's truth," another phase that should raise warning flags when a Christian uses it.

"Judge not, that you be not judged" (Matthew 7:1): One of the most misinterpreted verses in the Bible. Its explanation follows in the context, "For with what judgment you judge, you will be judged; and with the measure you use, it will be measured back to you" (verse 2). Verse 1 does not say that we are not to judge, for judgment is unavoidable in human interactions. We are to judge others, as we are to judge ourselves, according to the "canon, the measuring stick of Scripture." Therefore, we are to judge with grace and truth, justice and mercy, and the spirit and the letter of the law to ourselves, families, social groups and culture, and in politics and government. The Apostle Paul explains judging further in I Corinthians 6:1-11.

424

Jurisprudence: the study or science of legal theory and philosophy. "The study of jurisprudence, next to that of theology, is the most important and useful to men." (Quote is from Webster's 1828 Dictionary.) The modern concept and practice of law is amorphous, virtually whatever judges and jurists want it to be. See Summary Principles of Government, Law, etc.

Justice: the application of Biblical law in the appropriate situation or each person getting his just due, both reward and punishment, by the same criteria. Why designate the appropriate situation? God's justice has the range of application from the individual's conscience in society (social justice), to the laws of church government that require correction (discipline) of its members, and to the taking of a life in capital punishment after due process of state law. Properly applied, justice is always merciful, even to its ultimate application on earth in capital punishment. Final and perfect justice will be executed in the Last Judgment.

Keynesian economics, Keynesianism, and Keynesian Theory: an economic theory based upon the ideas of twentieth-century British economist John Maynard Keynes. It promotes a mixed economy in which where both the state and the private sector have important roles. It is virtually the opposite of Misian economics. (Adapted from Wikipedia.)

(The) Kingdom of God: "a community of persons animated by ... the Spirit of God... set down in an environment completely serviceable to righteousness, peace, truth (justice and mercy), and every other value" that began with the giving of the Holy Spirit and that will be fully established in the future. A work separate from the Church, although She is the living, burning center of the Kingdom, a witness to its presence and power, and a harbinger of its final coming." Augustine's City of God. **The Kingdom of God** is The Great Commission, Biblical ethics, and biblical worldview. See The Kingdom of God. Quotes from Henry Stob, *Ethical Reflections*, pages 67-69.

(The) Kingdom of Heaven: equivalent to **The Kingdom of God** (above) and **The Great Commission** (above).

Laissez-faire economics: economics theory which advocates that markets and the private sector operate best without state intervention. This approach is consistent with Misian economics and a Biblical approach to economics. It is the opposite of Keynesian economics.

Law: a decree by some authority that when obeyed will bring some benefit or when disobeyed will bring some penalty. God is first truth, and then law. These attributes lay the foundation of His justice for the application of His love, mercy, and grace. He has established laws* for nature (animate and inanimate) and for mankind. Relative to the latter, God's law is representative of His righteousness and holiness. Rightly understood, there is no conflict in His laws of self-government, the family, the church, social organizations, and state governments (local, state, and national). The greatest Freedom that any object or being can experience is to function within the laws of God — whether in nature or organizations of men. When God's laws are broken, destruction, disease, injury, and death inevitably result. See Love below. "Law" is used at least 12 different ways in Scripture, see What Is Biblical Law? Synonyms for law in the Bible include commandment, statute, precept, instruction, judgments, righteous judgments, word, testimonies, His (God's) ways, a lamp unto our feet, and a light unto our path. (See Psalm 119.)

Law of Absolutes: The Law of Non-Contradiction necessitates of the statement, "There are no absolutes," that there exists at least one absolute. By this simple methodology, God has necessitated Absolutes in His Universe, Himself being the First Principle of Absolutes.

Law of Contradiction or Law of Non-Contradiction: the belief and axiom of logic that a proposition and its opposite statement cannot both be true. Associated with this law is the Law of Absolutes.

Law, natural: derivation of law without using supernatural revelation (The Bible).

Legalism: (1) the attempt by man to obtain merit or favor (that is, be justified, especially for one's sins) with God through confession or obedience in themselves, whether he is obeying Biblical law or principles derived from Biblical law or any other set of rules or religious practices. The **unregenerate** can do nothing to please God (Romans

8:8) and the **regenerate** have already been completely forgiven in Christ to which he can add nothing (Romans 8:1). Justification (complete, total, and final) is one of the most important concepts for a Christian to understand in the concept of salvation. The Christian who understands justification is never concerned with legalism.

Legalism for the regenerate can be subtle. We can begin to think that we must live perfectly in order to please God. God does not require perfection in our living, especially when we have repetitive ("besetting") sins. He does require confession of all of our sins. And, on this basis, we need to keep short accounts with God. But, we never have to "earn" His favor. In fact, we cannot earn His favor. Christ has given us (imputed) His perfection.

The full and complete application of the law in a Christian's life is not legalism. It is simply obedience to God's instructions (commandments). The law, then, gives the Christian instruction for loving God and loving others, the Two Great Commandments. As a newborn baby needs instruction on the laws of human conduct, the regenerate Christian needs instruction on how to live before God and others (I Peter 2:2). Biblical law is that instruction. Law and love are intimately woven together. See Love.

Placing obligations on God: There is also a sense in which legalism places obligation or debt upon God. If we can earn his favor, He "owes" us. If we can perform steps A, B, and C and expect a particular action from God for us or in us, we have obligated His service to us. God is conditional to our requests or actions. This He cannot do. His purposes forever and always are His own (Ephesians 1:5, 9).

(2) a set of rules, frequently that are extra-biblical (as the Pharisees had) or selectively Biblical that is used to determine whether another person or group is sufficiently "spiritual" to be acceptable to the person or group holding those rules. Modern issues involving legalism include young-earth vs. old-earth creationists, theonomy, charismatic gifts, observance of the Sabbath, eschatology, and a variety of dietary and health practices. These rules violate the oneness of Ephesians 4:1-5 for all the regenerate.

Leisure: a humanistic notion that is often substituted for the Biblical concept of rest. The Bible knows nothing of leisure: only Work and Rest, both of which are instructed in the 4th Commandment and the New Testament concept of Good Works, especially Matthew 11:28-30. Leisure has the idea of being free from work and doing what one wants to do. Biblically, one is never free from God's commandments. Getting sufficient Rest is one of God's commandments, cited in this definition. One may counter, "Leisure may be used for Bible study or mercy ministry." I would answer, "These are Good Works, not leisure!"

Lex Rex: literally, "the law is king." Also the title of Samuel Rutherford's book, published in 1644, early in the deliberations of the Westminster Assembly that produced the Westminster Confession of Faith. Apart from the influence of the Bible, virtually all cultures had the standard, rex lex, "the king is law." Whatever the king said was law--no man had any rights above what the king said. Under Biblical law, a man has the right to appeal to the law as written in his country.

Licensure: standards that are set by the state which have to be met for individuals in a particular profession to practice their trade. De facto, the state has thus create a monopoly that limits creativity and new developments in that profession. See Licensure of Medical Practice.

Logic: "the study of the methods by which the conclusion is proved beyond all doubt," or to the contrary, by which the conclusion is proved to be erroneous. The process of Logic, however, says nothing about the truth of the premises. The truth or falsity of the premises in not part of the logical process. See The Role of Logic (in truth) and Unraveling the Concept of Logic.

Logos: "word" in New Testament Greek. However, when used in reference to Jesus Christ, as "In the beginning was the Word, and the Word was with God..." (John 1:1), it has a greater depth and breadth of meaning than may not be realized. John Calvin translates it as "Speech." Some other possible translations are: computation, accounts, measure, esteem, consideration, value, ratio, proportion, pretext, purpose, theory, argument, proposition, principle, law, rule, thesis, hypothesis, reason, formula, debate, narrative, fable, speech—to name a few. For more on logos, click here.

Love: sacrificial acts (speech and behavior) within Biblical or Godly parameters (law, precepts, principles, etc.) for the greatest good of the one loved (God, spouse, child, neighbor, and even enemies). Biblical parameters (law) limit "anything goes," as acts of love. For example, a man cannot divorce his wife because the "loves" another woman. Sacrifice on the part of the one who loves illustrates its supreme value. Obviously, love is one of the richest of Biblical concepts. It is commonly misunderstood by many Christians, even concerning the greatest act of love in history, God's sacrifice of His Own Son for the greatest good of those whom He loved. See Law, Justice, Love, Law, etc.

Love - *Agapeo* and *Phileo*: From the conversation between Peter and Jesus, these words are often contrasted. Biblically, however, they have the same meaning! (1) Jesus and Peter would have spoken Aramaic in which there are no corresponding words for *agapeo* and *phileo*, that is, to designate "brotherly" love from the "agapé" of the New Testament. (2) John often introduces "slight variations in all sorts of places without real difference of meaning," e.g., John 3:5. (3) Peter answers, "Yes, Lord." "Why would he say 'Yes,' if he means 'No?' ... He is accepting Jesus' word, not declining it." (4) Elsewhere in the New Testament, *phileo* is used where it cannot possibly be "brotherly" love, mandating at the very least it sometimes means the same as *agapeo*. Examples are found in John 5:20 ("as the Father loves the son"), John 16:27 (of the Father's love for His own), I Corinthians 16:22 (love for Jesus Christ), and Revelation 3:19 (the Father only rebukes those whom He loves). I would contend, along with Gordon Clark, that *agapeo* and *phileo* throughout the New Testament are synonyms. (The quotes and other notes herein are from *Leon Morris' International Commentary on the New Testament: John* [1977 Edition], pages 870-873.)

Materialism: 1) the belief that only matter is real, in contrast to **Rationalism** or **Idealism** that considers only thought or mind as real. Under materialism, "mind" is an "epiphenomenon." 2) The Biblical, moral concept whereby "things" are over-emphasized in one's life, even to the extent that "things" are worshipped. "You cannot serve God and mammon" (Matthew 6:24). Synonym of **Naturalism** and **Positivism**.

Mathematics: "The science of quantity; the science which treats of magnitude and number, or of whatever can be measured or numbered.

This science is divided into pure or speculative, which considers quantity abstractly, without relation to matter; and mixed, which treats of magnitude as subsisting in material bodies, and is consequently interwoven with physical considerations." (From Webster's 1828 Dictionary, reference below.)

Mechanism, Mechanistic Materialism: the philosophy of naturalism that nature can be described in terms of mechanical laws. For example, "mind and its activities are forms of behavior. Psychology, then, becomes a study of behavior, and mind or consciousness are interpreted as muscular, neural, or glandular behavior. These processes may then be explained by physics and chemistry. Values and ideals become merely subjective labels for physical situations and relations." Titus et al, Living Issues..., page 251. See **Dialectical Materialism**.

Mental Illness: a term that is so generally used and misused, as to be of virtually no use. The term is an attempt to equate physical illness with aberrant emotions and behaviors. Based upon a philosophy of materialism, this attempt is understandable. However, man is both Body and Soul (Spirit, Heart, Mind). The problem is that there is no "normal," as a standard. Because of the Fall of mankind in Adam, this lack of a standard can be understood. As the New Adam, Jesus Christ is our normative standard within the limits of our being human and He being God.

Metaphysics: one of the four branches of philosophy (along with ethics, logic, and epistemology). It "is concerned with the nature and structures of being or ultimate reality... (with) such issues as the nature of existence, properties, and events; the relation between particulars and universals, individuals and classes; the nature of change and causation; and the nature of mind, matter, space, and time." (John Jefferson Davis, *Theology Primer: Resources for the Theological Student*, Baker Book House, 1981, page 30).

Mind (of man): see Image of God.

Mind of Christ: see article Mind of Christ this website.

Mind-body problem: "The difficulty of explaining how the mental activities of human beings relate to their living physical organisms"

430

(from the philosophical dictionary below). From a Biblical perspective, this problem does not exist, as man has an immaterial mind, as well as a material brain, portrayed in Scripture. See Image of God, Mind, Soul, and Spirit.

Misian Economics: the economic approach of Ludwig von Mises which is essentially the same as Laissez-faire economics.

Modern medicine: all medical theory and practices are based upon evolution and naturalism, even **Mechanistic Materialism**.

Modernism, modernist, modernity: the attitude (arrogance) that modern knowledge is virtually all that could be valid or true. It exists in both Christians and non-Christians. Many modern Christians see no need to study the writings and teachings of past Christians. Yet, he who does not or will not learn from history is condemned to repeat the same mistakes of the past. Modernism is also simply a continuation of the Enlightenment's attempt to find meaning apart from God and within man himself.

Moral responsibility: synonym of **Free Will**.

Morals, morality: See **Ethic** and **Ethics** which are synonyms. Sometimes, morals or mores are defined by what a society or group of people does without regard to Biblical standards.

Natural law: See **Law, natural.**

Naturalism or Scientific Naturalism: "the belief that all objects, events, and values can be wholly explained in terms of factual and/or causal claims about the world, without reference to supernatural powers or authority" (from Dictionary of Philosophical Terms... below). For Christians this "supernatural powers or authority is the Bible. Synonym of **Materialism** and **Positivism** (1).

Neighbor: Anyone with whom a person may come in contact, as close as one's spouse or more distant as one's enemies in warfare to missions around the world that provide physical help, as illustrated in the parable of the Good Samaritan (Luke 10:25-37) or that evangelize the unreached. Obviously, one's responsibilities increase, as the proximity of the neighbor increases. The closest neighbor is your spouse or other member of your family, if not married.

Nouthetic Counseling: equivalent to Biblical counseling. "Nouthetic" was coined by Jay Adams from the N.T. Greek Word, *noutheteo*. It "is motivated by love and deep concern, in which (Christians) are counseled (according to the Bible) and corrected by verbal means for their good, ultimately of course, that God may be glorified," for example, see Romans 15:14. (*Competent to Counsel*, p. 50)

Ontology: thought that is concerned with the nature of ultimate reality. Synonym for **Truth**, **Ethic**, **Metaphysics**, and **Worldview**. While there may be shades of differences between these words, each is concerned with what is the most basic foundation for reliable thought.

Pagan: an unregenerate, one who has not been "born-again," by the process of **Regeneration**. All people are separated into two groups, Pagan and Regenerate. No Worldview that does not take this division into deliberate account cannot be considered to be a Biblical Worldview. Remember, a Pagan is a person both worships other gods, shakes his fist in the face of God as His enemy, and "does whatever he wants," regardless of what God says is right and wrong.

Peace: primarily used in the Bible as designating the relationship between a believer and God. Unless one realizes the degree of enmity and hatred that God has for sin and unbelieving sinners, one cannot appreciate the breadth and depth of Biblical "peace."

Phileo (verb): to love. See **Love**.

Philosophy: (from philo- "loving" + sophia "knowledge, wisdom," literally "one who loves knowledge of wisdom".) 1) at a personal level, one's worldview or ethic, whether examined or unexamined, coherent or inconsistent, informal or formal (as an established system agreed to by many persons, as in humanism or Roman Catholicism), and including or excluding a supernatural (metaphysical) dimension, founded upon some set of first principles (axioms, presuppositions, assumptions, postulates, propositions, etc.) accepted by faith as true. 2) Formally, "a persistent attempt to acquire an understanding and appreciation of the cosmos as a whole; a passionate endeavor to see the world of men and things as they truly are; the untiring effort to disclose the structure and pattern of the world, to discern and apprehend the interrelation of things, to see how part is linked to part, and how all things join to constitute a single and intelligible whole" (Henry Stob, *Theological Reflections*, Eerdmans: 1981). Sum: a diligent attempt to know truth (see **Truth** below). Ultimately, there are only two philosophies (religions or cosmologies): that which is consistently and coherently Biblical, and all others. **Philosophy** and **Religion** are synonyms. See **Religion** and the Synonyms listed under First Principles.

Pietism: the dominant measurement of one's Christian experience since the mid-19th century. Essentially, it is believing and living the Christian life, based primarily upon one's emotions. To some extent, all Christians measure their lives in this way. To some extent, sanctification is an emotional experience. But, pietism has come to dominate Christians' understanding and experience. Some examples include basing decisions on finding "peace," "the Lord told me to ____ " (do a certain thing), I "feel" that this verse means _____, and "I felt good about the worship service today." For more on this subject, see

Politics: from the Greek, *polis* or state. "The science of government; that part of ethics which consists in the regulation and government of a nation or state, for the preservation of its safety, peace and prosperity; comprehending the defense of its existence and rights against foreign control or conquest, the augmentation of its strength and resources, and the protection of its citizens in their rights, with the preservation and improvement of their morals. Politics, as a science or an art, is a subject of vast extent and importance." (Webster's 1828 Dictionary)

Positivism: "the belief that natural science, based on observation, comprises the whole of human knowledge... reject(ing) as meaningless, the claims of theology and metaphysics. The most influential twentieth-century version is logical positivism" (from A Dictionary of Philosophical Terms... below). Synonym of **Materialism** and **Naturalism**.

Postmodernism: "Most generally, abandonment of Enlightenment confidence in the achievement of objective human knowledge through reliance upon reason in pursuit of foundationalism, essentialism, and realism. In philosophy, postmodernists typically express grave doubt about the possibility of universal objective truth, reject artificially sharp dichotomies, and delight in the inherent irony and particularity of language and life." (From the philosophical dictionary in references below.) One consistently prevalent and dominating tenet of both Modernism and Post-modernism is the exclusion of Biblical Christianity and its God from any meaning related to man's existence. Post-modernism at its core is simply irrational; there is no meaning anywhere. This position simply contradicts men and women's everyday pursuits of knowledge, purpose, and relationships.

Pragmatism or Pragmatic Theory of Truth: one of the classic tests of truth. The Word of God is the most practical book ever written.
Pragmatic Knowledge or Pragmatic Value: a synonym of 2nd definition of **Fact**.

Predestination: 1) philosophical or cosmological sense: any theory of the causes and effects that determine what an individual is and does. Some theory of predestination is unavoidable (inescapable) because no person chooses his genetic and spiritual condition, nor the early teachings of his parents and others. All decisions after the age of "accountability" are absolutely determined by these prior factors. Also, on this basis no one is "free" from predestination to be able to make "free" choices. 2) God's ordering of all events from eternity past to the present to eternity future "who works all things according to the counsel of His will" (Ephesians 1:11). See **Free Will**.

Proof: the evidence which is acceptable to a person concerning some statement about reality. Absolute proof of God, materialism, or any other philosophical or religious system does not exist. When the atheist asks for "proof," he has already decided what he will or will not accept to support or deny his position. Proof is always relative to the philosophy, religion, and beliefs of any person.

Psychiatry: the practice of psychology by practitioners who are licensed to practice medicine. The only difference between psychologists and psychiatrists is that the latter are able to prescribe medications and procedures that are considered "medical" by the state licensing authority. All evaluations and references to "psychology" on this website apply equally to psychiatrists and psychiatry. Most

Christians who are psychiatrists practice secular psychology. (See **Psychology**, below.)

Psychology (true or Biblical): is the study of an individual person's thoughts, speech, and behavior relative to himself, his neighbor, and God, as governed and defined by specific Biblical criteria. Secular psychologists and Christian psychologists who try to "integrate" psychology with Biblical principles would deny this Biblical criterion. See **Anthropology**.

Psychology, Secular: All psychology that does not have the Bible as its governing truth in all areas of theory and practice. Even the psychology that is taught and practiced by most Christians is secular psychology.

Psychotherapy: the sophisticated name given by psychologists to simply talking with people who need advice about some problem in life with themselves or others. While it may involve listening, asking questions, and giving advice or directions, it is still just conversation. The preferred term is *Counseling* which can be done by anyone with some training and/or experience, especially those who know and can apply the Word of God. Studies have shown that the effectiveness of a person giving "psychotherapy" has no correlation with their level of education.

Puritans: the word was first applied to Christians in England at the time of the Reformation who believed that all Roman Catholic worship should be "purified" according to Biblical standards of worship. As with most labels, there were a variety of beliefs within the ranks of the Puritans, both in England, America, and elsewhere. In general, the Puritans were known for their strong Calvinism and their vigorous practice of a Biblical mindset. They are a model to be emulated in their Biblical humility and rock-solid stance for righteousness, even to challenge kings and other government authorities.

Quakers: a sect founded by George Fox about 1660 whose beliefs include each individual being directly responsible to God (they have no priests or pastors and no religious ceremonies and do not call themselves a church), and being guided by an "inner light" that comes directly from "God within." Since they accept this "inner light" as equivalent or superior to God's Revelation in the Bible, they could not be labeled "Christian," in the Evangelical sense (above). They are also called the Religious Society of Friends (RSOF).

Rational thinking: the informal process of moving through an argument in a "reasonable" or "consistent" manner. This process has little relevance to formal logic which (applied correctly) is quite precise and may draw conclusions that are just as true as its premises.

Rationalism: "the belief that human reason alone can discover the basic principles of the universe... the mind has the power to know some truths that are logically prior to experience, and yet not analytic (that is can be broken down into smaller parts). Titus, Living Issues..., pages 17, 435.

Realism: "the belief that the objects of our senses exist independently of their being known or related to mind." Titus, *Living Issues* ..., page 435.

Reality: the presence of the Sovereign God through His laws for the physical universe, living organisms, man, and the spiritual world. Negatively, no living thing is free from these laws without severe consequences. Positively, everything in the universe functions at its best according to these laws -- see Freedom. For example, the laws of the universe keep planets in their orbits. The laws of biochemistry sustain the cells of living creatures. Spiritual laws must govern one's behavior towards God and others or quarrels, fights, and wars result. This Reality prevents any creature from being independent of either God or everything else in the universe.

Reconstruction: a synonym of **Theonomy**.

Reformation: a movement of the Holy Spirit that causes an increasing rate of the number of persons who are regenerated, and they apply Biblical truth to the mores of a culture and the legislation of its laws. **Jesus Christ** has caused the greatest reforms in history generally and vastly underrated by Christians and non-Christians alike. Contrast with **Revolution**. True reformation has a broad and lasting influence on individuals, **The Church** and churches, and cultures, contrasted with **Revival** which usually has only a temporary effect, primarily restricted to individuals and local churches.

(The) Reformation: the great historical events that began with Martin Luther's nailing his 95 theses to the door of the church in Wittenberg and an entire reconsideration of **The Church** and all its teachings strictly according to Biblical interpretation.

Regenerate: the person who has been acted upon by God's Spirit to be "born-again" or "born from above." See **Pagan** and **Regeneration**. The whole of the human race is divided into these two categories called sheep and goats, believers and unbelievers, wheat and tares, etc.

Regeneration: The change wrought by the Holy Spirit in the soul or spirit of a person that changes trust (belief or faith) in oneself, as the source of truth about life and how to live it, to trust in the Bible, as God offers forgiveness in Jesus Christ and tells us who we are and what our responsibilities are. Regeneration is initiation of sanctification. Other terms in the Bible for regeneration are "born-again" and "born from above."

The new birth is by the grace of God; that change by which the will and natural enmity of man to God and his law are subdued, and a principle of supreme love to God and his law, or holy affections, are implanted in the heart. *Webster's 1828 Dictionary*

Regenerate man, with the assistance of the Holy Spirit , has a more valid understanding of the Bible than unregenerate man.

Religion: on a practical and functional level, a synonym of **Philosophy** and **Worldview**, that is, the most basic rules (usually unexamined) by which a person governs his life. However, commonly and traditionally, it is erroneously limited to established religions, usually ones with supernatural beliefs. (For more on this common use of "religion," see its reference at Wikipedia.com-- below.) At the most basic level, there are only two religions: Biblical Christianity and all others. See the Synonyms listed under First Principles.

Responsibility: man is responsible for his thoughts and actions because God says that he is, not because he is morally "free." Man is free to choose consistent with all his predetermined conditions. See **Free Will** and **Predestination**.

Rest: those activities that allow a person to become strengthened to Work and do Good Works, and not become "weary in well-doing." These activities include the instructions in the 4th Commandment for the Sabbath and sleep, primarily. Some activities of a quiet nature, such as light reading, walking, and quiet conversation may be included here.

Retirement: a modern concept that at the end of one's primary means of producing income, a person does whatever he wants, usually what he has always wanted to do, but never had the time. It is an unbiblical notion because one never "retires" from God's Work or Good Works. However, such "retirement" can be a great opportunity for one to be more fully engaged in Good Works to advance the cause of The Kingdom of God.

Revival: changes in individuals and local churches in response to special times and manners of preaching which is usually temporary in effect. Contrast with **Reformation**.

Revolution: "the radical change of social patterns in their essential constitution, through violence and compulsion." (Henry, C.F.H. *Aspects of Christian Social Ethics*, page 17) Contrast with Reformation.

Rex lex: literally, "the king is law." Also known as the **Divine Right of Kings**. See **Lex rex**.

Right, Rights: rights are ethical or legal claims of duties or freedoms that are given to those people under a higher authority. The only legitimate rights are those given by God in His Word. The Declaration of Independence declares that all peoples have "inalienable rights, that among these are life, liberty, and the pursuit of happiness." Since God is the highest authority, there is not court of appeal higher than Himself.

Righteousness: all that God requires of men and women, as defined by the Bible. There are the Two Great Commandments of loving God and neighbor, the Ten Commandments, the "new commandment" of Christ, and all the other commandments, precepts, and principles of the Holy Scriptures. Within Biblical definitions, righteousness is a synonym of Biblical ethics and Biblical worldview.

Salvation: simply, "to be rescued from something." Thus, to understand any form of salvation, one must know from what he has been saved. Salvation in the Bible is no different. But, few Christians seem to understand the full extent of the terrible and severe circumstances from which they have been rescued, and the great opportunities to which they have been given in their earthly life, not just heaven. The Kingdom of Heaven begins now!

Science: a pivotal word for worldview concepts. Beginning with the Scholastics about 1200, theology was called "The Queen of the Sciences." "Science," then, referred to any area of systematic study. Webster's Dictionary of 1828 (see References below), in his 2nd definition states, "In philosophy, a collection of the general principles or leading truths relating to any subject. Pure science ... is built on self-evident truths; but the term science is also applied to other subjects founded on generally acknowledged truths...." In modern times, "science" refers to the physical and natural sciences. The great problem is that the more precise sciences of physics, chemistry, and mathematics connote the same precision to such areas as biology, psychology (of man), and medicine, that these latter areas do not have.

Scientific Naturalism: See Naturalism.

Scientific method: a system of steps by which theories about the physical universe may be tested and "proved." This proof is limited to the design of the experiment. It is not proof in the philosophical sense of finding truth. Many people are deceived by the use of proof in this way. The scientific method, by design, is limited to proofs in the physical world. It can say nothing about the supernatural world because the method excludes any supernatural interference by design. See Proof.

"Writers on scientific method usually tell us that scientific discoveries made "inferentially," that is to say, from putting together many facts. But this is far from being correct. The facts by themselves are never sufficient to lead unequivocally to the really profound discoveries. Facts are always analyzed in terms of the prejudices of the investigator. The prejudices are of a deep kind, relating to our view on how the Universe "must" be constructed." Sir Fred Hoyle, Highlights in

Astronomy (San Francisco: W. H. Freeman and Company, 1977), page 35-36.

Scientism: the philosophy that only through the natural sciences may truth or knowledge be obtained. Biblically and philosophically, however, such science cannot quality as a source of truth.

Secular Humanism: humanism based upon secularism.

Secularism: a modern term that certain practices or institutions (public or private) should exist separately from **Religion** (as erroneously and narrowly defined-- see **Religion**). "In the extreme, it is an ideology that holds that religion has no place in public life" (from Wikipedia below).

Social justice: the comprehensive application of Biblical law, love, and mercy to all levels of government: self, family, voluntary groups, churches, and state (local, state, and national). Great errors in the modern application of social justice is, first, neglect of Biblical law, but more specifically, the omission of responsibility, opportunity for retribution, and egalitarianism. Jesus Christ has caused the greatest changes towards social justice by both civil law and compassion generated by the love of Christ.

Socialism: "a political and economic theory that advocates the public ownership and management of the principal means of production, distribution, and exchange." (Titus..., *Living Issues*..., page 437) "The political application of the belief that man's salvation lies in the application of intelligence to man's problems." (Rushdoony, *Salvation and Godly Rule*, page 115)

Sociology: "the systematic study of the development, structure, interaction, and collective behavior of organized groups of human beings." (2) See **Anthropology**, as this area must be Biblically defined to be acceptable to a Biblical worldview. **Social justice** is a better name for this area.

Solas, The Five of the Reformation: sola Scriptura, soli Deo gloria, solo Christo, sola gratia, and sola fide. In the same order, the only and ultimate authority are the 66 books of the Protestant Bible, only glory to God, only by Christ is a person saved and has any merit with the Father, only by grace without any human works is one saved, and only by faith and not by works is one saved. See Trent, Council of.

Soul (of man): the immaterial component of man that thinks and feels. See **Mind** and **Spirit**. (Human) spirit is virtually synonymous with soul. Heart, soul, mind, and spirit are all facets of the immaterial component of man. See **The Image of God**.

Spirit (of man): the immaterial component of man that thinks and feels. See Mind and Soul. See The Image of God.

Spiritual Gifts: those special abilities given by Christ, as he ascended into heaven, to individual Christians for the building up of the visible and invisible **Church**, numerically by evangelism, spiritually by teaching and preaching, and physically by works of mercy (Ephesians 4:7-16).

(The) State: as noun or adjective, any legally constituted government: city, state, county, or nation. Christians need to re-institute the concept that "government" includes self-government, that of the family, church, and other formally organized bodies, not just legal institutions. The more that non-state government is exercised, the less the need for the state. A synonym is Civil Government.

Syllogism: the arrangement of all the steps of formal logic. See **Logic**.

Talents: abilities, given by God, to believers and unbelievers, for the enrichment of mankind. These may be technical, for example, in engineering or architecture, or artistic, in music or painting. Contrast with **Spiritual Gifts**.

Theistic evolution: the synthesis of some theory of evolution that is directed by God over long periods of time. Neither the Biblical account nor the evidences of evolution necessitate this conclusion.

Theonomy: literally, "the law (nomos-) of God (theos-); the application of all the laws (statutes, commandments, precepts, etc.) of the Old and New Testaments to the individual, family, social groups, church, and nations—with the exception of those sacrificial, ceremonial, and dietary laws that Jesus Christ fulfilled in His sacrificial life, death, resurrection, and ascension. For a discussion of the strengths and weaknesses of theonomy, see Reconstruction and Theonomy: Reviews.

Tradition: doctrines or practices within churches or Christian groups that has become customary from one generation to the next. Tradition is perhaps the most dangerous threat to Biblical truth. The Roman Catholic Church never had a chance to be corrected by the Reformation at the Council of Trent because their tradition was held on the same level of authority, as Scripture. Today, Protestant churches often unwittingly allow tradition to supplant Biblical truth.

Transformed by the renewing of your mind (Romans 12:2): the word "transformed" comes from the Greek word, metamorpho, which is only used in two other situations in the New Testament, of Christ's transfiguration (Matthew 17, Mark 9, and Luke 9) and the transformation that occurs to believers in heaven (II Corinthians 3:18). This word is a powerful statement of what will happen to his being when he is diligent to "renew his mind." Most Christians never even approach this diligence and therefore never experience that "transformation."

Trent, Council of: met three times over a period of 18 years: 1545-1547; 1551-1552; and 1562-1563, as an official response to the standards of the Reformers and Conciliarism. This council could be considered a watershed for the Roman Catholic Church. The central cry of the Reformation was sola scriptura, that Biblical authority exceeded any other form of authority (truth). From this central tenet, the Reformers gained important understandings of justification by faith without humans works of any kind (Ephesians 2:8-9). But, the Council of Trent chose to continue with their other "authorities": the councils of the church, church tradition, and the *magisterium*. Thus, they never worked from Scripture alone and continued their distortion of Biblical truth, salvation, and Christ's sufficient work upon the cross.

Trichotomy: the belief that the person consists of three parts: body, soul, and spirit. It is the belief of this author that this position is unbiblical, as only two states exist within God's order: the material (physical—what can be touched, felt, smelled, tasted, and seen or that which is composed of atoms and molecules) and the immaterial (spiritual—God, angels, Satan, fallen and fallen angels) which for man

442

is variously called his soul, mind, heart, and spirit. Trichotomy is usually a method for psychologists to claim that there is a realm for their expertise, the spirit, while the physician takes care of the body and the pastor takes care of the soul. See **Heart** and **Mind**.

Truth: 1) objectively, reality or "what is"; the universe as it really is; how every part of the universe is related to every other part. 2) The 66 books of the Protestant Bible. 3) Subjectively, Jesus Christ, "I am the way, the truth, and the life" (John 14:6). See **Faith** for the relationship of faith and truth.

"All truth is God's truth." A true phrase that is quite complex in its application. It is mostly used (erroneously) by psychologists and scientists who are Christians in an attempt to integrate natural revelation (nature) and special revelation (the Bible). Virtually every attempt at integration minimizes, if not denigrates, the proper authority of the Bible and the nature of its truth. See "All truth is God's truth,"

Truism: synonym of **Fact**.

Ultimate reality: synonym for **Truth**, **Ethic**, **Metaphysics**, **Religion** and **Worldview** -- see those words in this Glossary.

Unconscious: see Subconscious mind.

Uniformitarianism, Uniformity of Nature: the position of modern science that all processes and laws in nature have always functioned, and will function in the future, as they do in the present. The Biblical position differs, first, in that God created everything. Second, the Fall of Adam and Eve caused cataclysmic changes in the universe, such that it groans for regeneration (Matthew 19:28; Romans 8:19-22). Third, the Flood caused changes in nature that had not happened before and have not happened since. Fourth, God will one day destroy the present universe and create a new one (II Peter 3:10-13).

University: schools which developed out of the monasteries of the Middle Ages which sought to "uni-fy" all sources of knowledge from an understanding of both God's Word and World (natural science). The authority given to natural revelation (nature) and special revelation (Bible) has varied among thinkers from the beginning of this attempt.

Because both man and nature have experienced the effects of the Fall, however, this pursuit should properly given the authority to The Bible.

Unregenerate: all persons before the Holy Spirit has changed them through the process of **Regeneration**. The entire population of mankind from The Beginning are either regenerate or unregenerate (sheep and goats, saved and unsaved, Christian and pagan, etc.).

Utopia: a word invented by Thomas More (1478-1535) as the title of his book that described a fictional island with perfect harmony of legal, social, and political systems. *Utopia* was derived from Greek, *ou-topos*, meaning "no place," and *eu-topos*, meaning "good place." Since that time, it has been applied to any situation with hoped-for characteristics of *Utopia*, a place that from a Biblical perspective will never exist until Jesus Christ establishes His final Kingdom.

Valid Knowledge: a synonym of 2nd definition of **Fact** (above).

Value: the degree to which a person will be motivated to obtain an object or a goal; value is totally subjective -- no object determines its own worth, only the person who desires it. For example, one ounce of gold in one situation (prosperity) may buy a month's worth of groceries, while in another situation (famine), it may buy only one loaf of bread. Ultimately, God (as a Person) determines what something is worth which He has revealed in His Word.

Vocation: *vocatio*, Latin for "calling." (1) In the narrow sense, the career or primary focus of one's working energy. It may or may not be one's primary source of income. For example, many women are "called" to be mothers. (2) In the fullest sense, vocation includes all "good works," that is, all the tasks to which God calls His people, including Bible and theological study, worship, raising families, works of mercy, and evangelism. Some of these are incumbent upon every Christian; others are special callings with God's provision of natural talents or spiritual gifts.

Welfare: "financial assistance paid by taxpayers (and administered by state agencies) to people who are unable to support themselves" (Wikipedia definition, modified by Ed). Under Biblical principles and law, there is no justification for this concept of Welfare.

Westminster Confession of Faith: the doctrine produced at the request and funding of the English Parliament with representatives from most of the Reformed bodies in England, Scotland, and Ireland, written between 1643-1648. It consists of the confession itself and the Larger and Shorter Catechisms. See WCF.

(The) Will: that faculty of the mind by which we determine either to act or not to act in a particular direction, or the faculty which is exercised in deciding, among two or more objects, which we shall embrace or pursue. The will is directed or influenced by the judgment and the **Conscience**. The mind's understanding or reason compares different views; the judgment determines which is preferable, and the will decides which course of action to pursue. In other words, we reason with respect to the value or importance of a decision; we then judge which is to be preferred; and we will act to achieve what we consider the most valuable. These are but different operations of the mind, soul, or intellectual part of man. (From Webster's 1928 Dictionary below).

Worldview: See "Worldview" in that section on the Homepage and its links to more discussion. See **Ultimate Reality** and Synonyms under First Principles.

Work: any continuous application of energy toward an end. (From Funk and Wagnalls Encyclopedia, edition unknown, cited by Rushdoony in Salvation and Godly Rule, 1983, page 399.) This definition centers on the Biblical concept of Good Works where the "end" is the Glory of God and the good of men or mankind. Vocation is a better term that "work" for one's Career or primary means of producing income, as it has the sense of being "called" by God as an "end."

Zoroastrianism: This religion dates back to the 6th century B.C., started by Zoroaster (Zarathushtra) and was once the dominant religion of Greater Iran. It is a cohort of the ancient Vedic Hinduism, considered by some to have influenced Judaism and Christianity (although such a position would deny verbal inspiration of the Bible). It proclaims one God, Ahuramazda or Wise Lord, who is a friend of mankind, a junior partner with God in the goal of defeating and removing all evil from the material world by the end of time when everything will be made perfect.

Evil is considered as the absence of good, but does not have an independent existence. This religion is still practiced by 200,000-300,000 people today. Followers are also called Zarthushtis. For further information, see various texts and online sources for Zoroastrianism. Information and quotes here come largely from Maneck Bhujwala.

References

1. I frequently go to *Webster's 1828 Dictionary*, as a reference for words, because it precedes 1) the watering down of language, 2) the infiltration of liberal thought on words and culture, and 3) the influence of pietism, mysticism, and emotional thinking on Christians that began in the mid-19th century.

2. *Merriam-Webster Online Search*

3. *A Dictionary of Philosophical Terms and Names* @ http://www.philosophypages.com/dy/index.htm. This is an excellent resource for managing the complexity and confusion of these terms.

4 . Harold H. Titus, et al, *Living Issues in Philosophy*, 7th Edition, D. Van Norstrand Company, 1979.

5. *A Glossary of Medieval and Reformation History*: http://www.wscal.edu/clark/glossary.php.

6. *Etymology online*, www.etymonline.com.

7. *Online dictionary of philosophical terms*, http://www.philosophypages.com/dy/

8. *Wikipedia*: http://en.wikipedia.org/wiki/Main_Page